SOYA STRAIT

W9-DEJ-405

HOKKAIDO

Abashiri

Sapporo

Hakodate

TSUGARU STRAIT

Aomori
AOMORI

Akita
AKITA

IWATE

YAMAGATA

Yamagata   MIYAGI

Niigata   Sendai

FUKUSHIMA

TOCHIGI

IBARAKI

YO
Tokyo

CHIBA

nds

PACIFIC OCEAN

ABBREVIATIONS

KAG.   KAGAWA
KAN.   KANAGAWA
KUM.   KUMAMOTO
TOK.   TOKUSHIMA
YAM.   YAMANASHI

0   100   200   300

Scale in kilometers

Prehistory of Japan

This is a volume in

Studies in Archaeology

A complete list of titles in this series appears at the end of this volume.

Prehistory of Japan

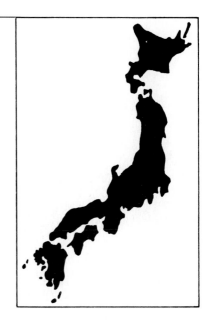

C. Melvin Aikens
Department of Anthropology
University of Oregon
Eugene, Oregon

Takayasu Higuchi
Department of Archaeology
Kyoto University
Kyoto, Japan

ACADEMIC PRESS

A Subsidiary of Harcourt Brace Jovanovich, Publishers

New York   London   Toronto   Sydney   San Francisco

ACADEMIC PRESS, INC.
111 Fifth Avenue, New York, New York 10003

United Kingdom Edition published by
ACADEMIC PRESS, INC. (LONDON) LTD.
24/28 Oval Road, London NW1 7DX

Library of Congress Cataloging in Publication Data

Aikens, C. Melvin.
 Prehistory of Japan.

 (Studies in archaeology)
 Bibliography: p.
 1. Man, Prehistoric—Japan. 2. Japan—
Antiquities. I. Higuchi, Takayasu. II. Title.
III. Series
GN855.J2A36   952'.01   81-12850
ISBN 0-12-045280-4   AACR2

PRINTED IN THE UNITED STATES OF AMERICA

82 83 84 85   9 8 7 6 5 4 3 2 1

Contents

Preface

Japan lies off the coast of East Asia, bearing essentially the same relation to that continent as the British Isles do to the European mainland. In terms of latitude, general vegetation patterns, and the meteorological dominance of its outward shore by a warm current originating in the southern oceans, the eastern edge of North America also compares well with Japan. (There are also similarities with the west coast of North America, though the overall "fit" is less good.) In each of these areas—Japan, parts of North America, and Europe—there appeared in early postglacial times rich hunting–gathering cultures that flourished in temperate woodland environments of great abundance and variety. The economic and occupation patterns that evolved exhibit striking parallels, displaying the great power of the environment in shaping human cultural forms. Late in prehistory, Japan was affected by relationships it developed with the distant Chinese civilization, just as the native culture of eastern North America was affected by the example of Mexico, and northwestern Europe was affected by its intercourse with Mediterranean civilization. Again, there are significant parallels, especially in the realms of growing societal complexity, the emergence of food production, and the expansion of the political sector (see Aikens 1981).

For a comparative perspective on the process of cultural evolution, these environmental and developmental parallels are of the greatest importance. The Japanese case is of particular concern in this frame of reference because, although it has been richly detailed by a century of archaeological investigation, it has not received the attention it merits in a worldwide context. Simply put, most of the information is available only in the Japanese language, which most of the international scholarly community does not read.

Prehistory of Japan describes the most important archaeological evidence of human activity in the Japanese islands from Paleolithic times down to the emergence of the historic Yamato state at about A.D. 700. Dominant themes are the continuity of Japanese cultural tradition, the changing economic and societal adaptations of the prehistoric Japanese to their rich and varied natural environment, and the development over time of increasingly higher levels of sociocultural complexity. Illumination of the important transformations that took place during the evolution of Japanese culture is sought through consideration of environmental, economic, and social factors. The relative importance of continental influences on the growth of Japanese culture, much overstressed in most discussions on the subject, is put into more realistic perspective by viewing the Japanese way of life as an indigenously evolving adaptive system, having ancient roots in the native landscape and being responsive primarily to its own natural setting and to its own internal workings. Impetus for growth and change came from within the native system; continental elements were drawn in, selectively and deliberately, to serve Japanese purposes.

Chapter 1 sketches the environmental setting and outlines the implications of Japanese–Korean and other linguistic relationships for Japanese prehistory. Chapters on the Paleolithic, Jomon, Yayoi, and Kofun periods follow. Archaeological data are presented through detailed summaries of selected, particularly informative, sites. These vignettes are so arranged as to provide chronological and regional perspectives on the culture of the country as a whole during each major period of its prehistory. Descriptions of artifacts and cultural features stress broad functional categories, with treatment of typological minutae reserved for situations where the formal nuances are directly relevant to specific problems under immediate discussion. In the final chapter the main themes of the book are summarized to characterize the long-term evolution of Japanese culture and to suggest the basic factors that shaped its development.

The immediate objective of this book is to publicize, in English as a language of international communication, some of the more salient aspects of Japan's long and fascinating prehistory. It is not the first such attempt by any means, but 15 years have passed since the last book-length synthesis was published in English, and much new information has accumulated since then. More specialized treatments of certain limited areas of Japanese prehistory have also appeared occasionally in North American, Asian, and European scholarly journals, but it is time for a new summary overview of the whole topic, and that is what this book purports to be. The authors offer it in the hope of bringing the richly provocative record of prehistoric Japan more fully into the awareness, and into the thinking, of those interested in a broad anthropological perspective on human cultural adaptation and development.

Acknowledgments

I

Work on this book may be said to have begun in 1970, when, intrigued by what I then knew of prehistoric Japanese culture, and wishing to add a new dimension to my archaeological experience—then confined to western North America—I began the study of the Japanese language. In the decade between that beginning and the completion of this book, many people and several institutions have contributed to my education. I can name only a few of them here, though all have my gratitude: Yoko McClain, my first teacher of Japanese at the University of Oregon; J. Edward Kidder, professor at International Christian University, Tokyo, whose pupil I became during one of his sojourns as visiting professor at the University of Oregon; the U.S. National Science Foundation, which in 1971–1972 provided me a Science Faculty Fellowship for a year's study of Japanese prehistory; Takayasu Higuchi, professor at the Institute of Archaeology, Kyoto University, who graciously sponsored me on two visits to Japan, guided my studies, and, happily, became coauthor of this book; Kyoto University, which welcomed me in 1971–1972 and again in 1977–1978 as a guest scholar; the excellent teachers of the Kyoto Japanese Language School who tutored me through many months of alternately pleasurable and painful study in 1971–1972 and 1977–1978, and gave me the linguistic facility needed to pursue the study of Japanese archaeology in earnest; Professors Sosuke Sugihara of Meiji University, Chosuke Serizawa of Tohoku University, Tatsuo Sato of Tokyo University, Fumio Miki of the National Museum in Tokyo,

Kiyotari Higuchi of Kokugakuin University, Masakazu Yoshizaki of Hokkaido University, Taketsugu Dejima of the Tokyo University Hokkaido Research Station at Tokoro, Kyoichi Arimitsu of Kyoto University, Yoshiro Kondo of Okayama University, Tetsushi Kawagoe of Hiroshima University, Takashi Okazaki of Kyushu University, and Mitsuo Kagawa of Beppu University, who extended special kindnesses during my visits to their institutions; Mochitaka Tsuiki, whose hospitality and generosity with type specimens was much appreciated; Mitsuzane Okauchi, Seigo Wada, and Mahito Uehara, of the Kyoto University Museum of Archaeology, whose kind assistance in assembling needed library resources and museum specimens is keenly remembered; the Japan Foundation, which provided a generous and indispensable fellowship to support a year of study in Kyoto during 1977–1978; the University of Oregon, which gave me leave of absence in 1971–1972 and sabbatical leave in 1977–1978, and at all times a supportive and congenial setting within which to pursue my research; and my traveling companions Alice, Barton, and Quinn Aikens, whose interest and good company added pleasure to the quest.

C. Melvin Aikens

II

Some special debts have been incurred in the preparation of the book itself. Professors Roy Andrew Miller, of the University of Washington, and Samuel E. Martin, of Yale University, generously gave permission to quote extensively from their work on Japanese historical linguistics, and offered most helpful and constructive comment on the linguistic issues. All their advice was appreciated, and most was heeded, but they are not of course responsible for any excesses or errors that may remain in the discussion on linguistic prehistory.

Many Japanese scholars and publishers gave permission to photograph specimens or to reproduce previously published illustrations. Their generosity is acknowledged individually in the figure captions throughout the text. The archaeological site names referred to in the book were systematically checked by Seigo Wada, Yoshinobu Fujiwara, and some of their colleagues at Kyoto University, a major task that can only be adequately appreciated by one familiar with the vagaries of the Japanese writing system and place-name usage. We are most grateful for their help.

The maps in the text were prepared by students of William G. Loy of the University of Oregon. To the students, who were careful and diligent, and to Loy, who with characteristic generosity and enthusiasm offered to take on and direct the effort, we owe a special debt of gratitude. Other line illustrations were prepared by Elizabeth Suwijn, who drew Figures 1.3, 1.4, 2.2, 2.30, 3.2, 4.2, and 5.38; and Houghton Caywood Knight, who drew Figures 2.9, 2.23, 3.31, 3.65, 3.66, 4.17, 4.31, 4.32, 4.33, 5.2, and 5.3. Working with Suwijn and Knight was a great pleasure. Portions of the manuscript were typed at various times by Alice Endo Aikens, Thelma Aman, and Margaret Olson. Their skill and patience are much appreciated.

C. Melvin Aikens
Takayasu Higuchi

Prehistory of Japan

1 : Introduction

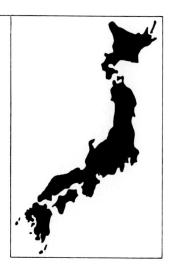

Japan lies in the Pacific Ocean off northern China, Korea, and Manchuria. Its four principal islands—Kyushu, Shikoku, Honshu, and Hokkaido—describe a long, narrow arc from southwest to northeast (Figure 1.1). The main archipelago, about 2000 km in length, spans nearly 1500 km of north–south latitude from the twenty-fourth parallel in southern Kyushu to the forty-fifth parallel in northern Hokkaido. Correspondingly, the climate and vegetation of Kyushu verge on the semitropical, whereas Hokkaido occupies the northern extreme of the north temperate zone. Further climatic and environmental variation is induced by the tropical Japanese Current, which flows along the Pacific shore in a northeasterly direction. This current warms the Pacific side of Japan all year; the continental side, subject to weather systems originating in the Siberian interior, has a cooler and seasonally more extreme climate, with deep winter snows.

The land is almost everywhere mountainous. In central Honshu the so-called Japanese Alps reach about 3000 m in elevation. Most of the country's mountains are much lower, but they are rugged and steep, drained by short, swift rivers. Open country is limited; the most important expanses are the coastal plains, the sites of such modern cities as Fukuoka, in Kyushu; Hiroshima, Okayama, Osaka, Nara, Nagoya, Tokyo, and Sendai, in Honshu; and Sapporo, in Hokkaido.

The islands are heavily wooded, covered by broad-leaved evergreen forests in the south and mixed coniferous–deciduous forests in the north. The biotic diversity and richness of these woods are great. In

1

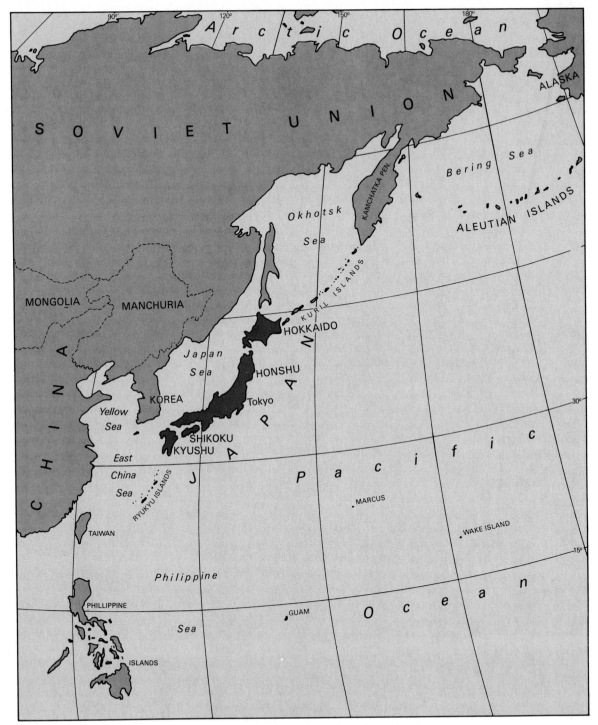

Figure 1.1 Map of Japan showing its relationship to East Asia.

central and northern Japan especially, they yield, in addition to lumber and other building materials, many kinds of edible roots, greens, seeds, nuts, and small game. These are sought even now as occasional delicacies by rural folk, and in earlier times they formed a major part of the aboriginal diet.

In southwestern Japan, the shallow Inland Sea and related straits separate the islands of Kyushu and Shikoku from southern Honshu. This waterway, 10–70 km wide and nearly 450 km long, has a highly indented coastline and is said to contain around 3000 islands, most of them tiny. The outer coastlines of Japan are equally rugged, and tens of thousands of kilometers of bays and inlets make the country extremely rich in marine and littoral resources.

In the context of this landscape the Japanese tradition has flourished and grown over thousands—perhaps tens of thousands—of years. Evidence from physical anthropology and historical linguistics gives warrant for believing that the direct physical and linguistic ancestors of Japan's modern occupants—both Japanese and Ainu—have dwelt in their home islands for many thousands of years. Archaeology shows the culture history of Japan to have been a development of remarkable continuity and integrity, in which both stability and change were accommodated without stagnation or rupture. The following pages address the evidence from human biology and language, after which the archaeological data are treated in a series of separate chapters.

The Japanese People

The Japanese and their continental neighbors share the straight black hair, brown eyes with epicanthic fold, and yellowish brown skin characteristic of the Mongoloid race. There are no equally simple and obvious somatic features that set the Japanese themselves off as a distinctive group, but minor variations in the shape of the skull and in stature have been adduced in an attempt to establish the position of the Japanese relative to their neighbors.

An influential study of cranial indices derived from length–breadth measurements on a series of Japanese and other skulls, as well as similar measurements made on the crania of living people, was made by Imamura (1968). He first undertook this study in the late 1930s, and his more recent report is a restatement of those findings. New evidence has accumulated in the intervening years, which he feels supports rather than alters his original conclusions.

The specimens studied represent four large geographical regions. The first and largest series included skulls from various districts of Japan, Korea, Taiwan, and China. The second major grouping comprised specimens from Southeast Asia: the Philippines, Burma, Java, and Borneo. The third series, comprising a Greater Indian grouping, was from Nepal, India, and Tibet to the west, and the fourth included skulls of Mongol, Burzat, Kalmuck, Aleut, and other Northeast Asian peoples. When plotted on a graph of cranial dimensions, Japanese and Chinese measurements fell together as a single group. This group occupied a central position on the graph and was encircled by Southeast Asian, Greater Indian, and Northeast Asian groups. In short, the dispersion of specimens according to their cranial indices on the graph corresponded in a rough way to the geographical dispersion of their sources.

A similar pattern of distribution was obtained from a somewhat larger modern sample of measurements made on living people. When data on stature were graphed along with the cranial indices, a still similar, though more dispersed, pattern resulted. Here, the Japanese specimens drew away from both Chinese and Korean ones, though there was some overlap.

A detailed study of the physical characteristics of modern people from different regions of Japan and South Korea, reported by Kohama (1968), has served as a basis for the discussion of Japanese–Korean as well as Japanese–Ainu relationships. On the basis of his synthesis, Kohama speaks of two major physical types among the Japanese proper. In Hokkaido, in northeastern Honshu, along the narrow continental side of western Honshu, and in central Kyushu, live people who are set off by a number of minor variations from those who dwell along the coasts of the Inland Sea and beyond, as far northeast as the Tokyo area. In terms of the characteristics studied, the people of the Inland Sea region tend to resemble the South Koreans, whereas those of northern Japan are closer to the Ainu of northern Honshu and Hokkaido.

The somatic observations considered in Kohama's study included various cranial dimensions; stature; relative proportions of limbs and torso; nose, eyelid, and earlobe form; and the ability or inability to taste the chemical phenylthiocarbamide (PTC). A geographical division appears clearly in Kohama's map of cranial indices, which shows that people of the Inland Sea region and South Korea tend toward roundheadedness or brachycephaly, whereas those of northeastern Japan are more longheaded, though still within the medium, or mesocephalic, range (Figure 1.2).

Similar progressive changes from north to south, involving pure Ainu, mixed Ainu, northeastern Japanese, southwestern Japanese of the Kyoto region, and South Koreans, appear in other dimensions (Figure 1.3). Measurements of cranial diameter decrease from an aver-

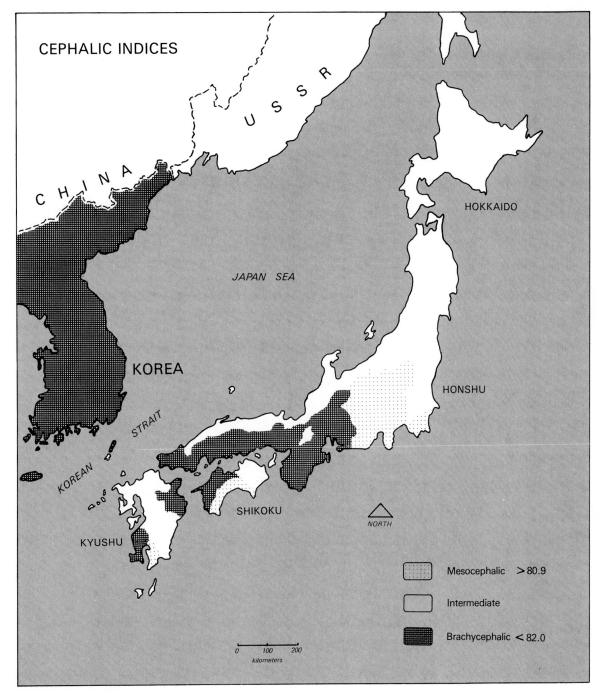

Figure 1.2 Geographical variation in cranial indices within Japan and South Korea. (After Kohama 1968: Figure 4.)

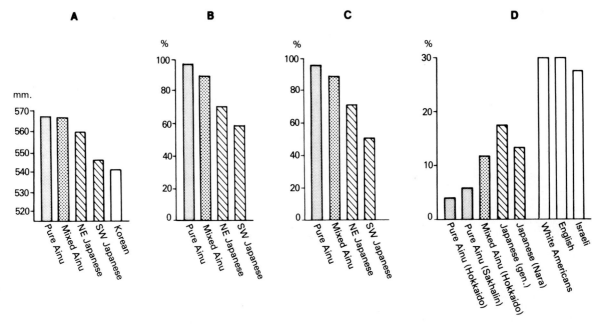

Figure 1.3 Ainu and Japanese regional variation: A, average cranial diameter; B, frequency of the double-fold eyelid; C, frequency of the detached earlobe; D, frequency of PTC taste-sensitivity (Caucasian data for comparison). (Based on Kohama 1968: Figures 5, 12, 13, 14.)

age of 567 mm for the pure Ainu of northeastern Japan to an average of 541 mm for the South Koreans. Stature, conversely, increases slightly from north to south. At the same time, interestingly enough, the two major components of stature, length of legs and length of torso, vary inversely from one another; length of legs decreases from north to south, whereas length of torso increases.

Nonmetric, discrete physical characteristics show patterns of north–south variation similar to those of the continuous measurements. The eyelid with double fold reaches nearly 100% frequency among the Ainu, and drops below 60% among the Japanese of the Kyoto region. The frequency of occurrence of the detached earlobe follows a nearly identical pattern. Conversely, the ability to taste the chemical PTC is low among the pure Ainu of the far north, and becomes significantly higher among Japanese living farther south. For these points there are unfortunately no comparative data from Korea.

Ohno (1970) summarizes other evidence from several sources, showing that fingerprint variations and the ABO blood groups also exhibit this north–south pattern of distribution within Japan. The proportion of whorls to arches and loops in fingerprint patterns is low among the Ainu, as indicated by their fingerprint index of only 51. For the eastern Japanese the index is 89; for the western Japanese, 97; and for the South Koreans, 99. Blood group B is relatively more common and A relatively less common in the northeast, whereas to the southwest the proportions are reversed. This trend follows that of all the other evidence for Japan itself, but, disconcertingly, in South Korea the proportions are the opposite of what might be expected. There, type B is relatively common and A is relatively uncommon, just as in northeastern Japan. This inconsistency in what is otherwise an impressive series of rather good clinal distributions between northern Japan and southern Korea is a puzzle for which no simple explanation presents itself.

These accumulated observations identify the Japanese as a people closely related in physique to their Korean and Chinese neighbors, yet distinguishable from them. They further show that a good deal of physical variability exists within the population of Japan itself. This generally takes the form of clinal shifts from north to south, in metric dimensions such as stature and bodily proportions, and in the frequency of occurrence of certain discrete physical characteristics. Much of this variability is subsumed under the concept of separate northeastern and southwestern physical types.

An older interpretation of these basic facts, no longer seriously defended, held that the original population of Japan was entirely Ainu, who were putatively of Caucasoid physical type, and that the present-day Japanese are the product of massive miscegenation between native Ainu and immigrant Koreans of Mongoloid stock. The most popular current interpretation is that these trait distributions reflect mixture between the Ainu of the north and a more southerly indigenous Japanese population, compounded by an infusion of Korean blood into this indigenous Japanese population from the opposite direction.

It is also possible, however, to view these somatic variations in less typological terms, as a reflection of normal gene flow within a large geographical area where distribution patterns have been influenced more strongly by environmental factors than by migrational ones. Worthy of serious attention in this regard is the remarkable congruence of certain variations in the human population with variations in the climatically and geographically controlled natural vegetation zones of Japan.

Another major body of information on the history of the Japanese people is provided by the discipline of historical linguistics. When a

The Japanese Language

human group speaking a common language becomes spread over a wide area, and especially when it becomes divided by geographical barriers or split by the intrusion of other people of different speech, the normal everyday processes of linguistic change ensure that over time the original linguistic unity will break up into increasingly divergent languages. Detailed and systematic similarities between now-existing languages, especially in the vocabulary and sound systems, but in word order and grammar as well, indicate that these languages are divergent forms of a common linguistic unity that existed at some time in the past. With sufficient research, the comparative method allows the mapping of stocks of related languages, and the construction of family trees outlining the branching system of relationships between the ancestral protolanguages and descendant languages of each stock.

Historical linguists have not yet achieved a consensus about the origin and relationships of the Japanese language, but the possibilities are narrowly limited. The major linguistic stocks of the eastern end of the world include the Altaic languages, spoken over much of central and northern Eurasia; the Sinitic languages, spoken within the Chinese culture sphere of eastern Asia; and the Malayo-Polynesian languages, spoken by island peoples around half the globe, from Madagascar in the western Indian Ocean to Easter Island in the eastern Pacific. Of these it has long been established that Japanese is not in origin a Sinitic language, even though it is now written in part with Chinese characters and has absorbed an enormous number of Chinese loanwords. The Japanese themselves have always been quite clear on this question, from their earliest contacts with Chinese culture and language. Discussion has instead centered around the similarities of Japanese to the Altaic languages of the adjacent Asian coast, and to the Malayo-Polynesian languages of Taiwan and the Philippines.

A principal focus of study has been the relationship of Japanese to Korean, and through Korean to the Tungus-Manchu, Mongolian, and Turkic languages of the Altaic stock. The concept of a Japanese–Korean linguistic relationship dates at least to the eighteenth century among Japanese scholars, and was first proposed by a European philologist in the early nineteenth century (Lewin 1976). Despite this long history of investigation, the question of common origins is still not considered to be adequately resolved by some linguists. It must be recognized in this connection, however, that absolute proof is never available in any branch of science. Judged by the usual standards of independent and interlocking evidence, and considering the lack of an alternative interpretation that is even remotely as defensible, the thesis that the two languages are indeed derived from a common ancestor seems impressively well documented.

The word order and grammar of Korean and Japanese are remarkably close. Lewin compared, line by line, translations of Japanese texts into Korean, and translations of Korean texts into Japanese. Direct word-for-word translation from one language to the other produced fully comprehensible renderings, and showed complete agreement between the Korean and Japanese sentence structures. In the following example, which makes the nature of this sort of analysis clear, /.../ indicates a subject or theme clause, [...] indicates a modifying, attributive clause, (...) indicates a modifying sentence attribute, and + indicates a relationship to the predicate. The quotation is from Ryunosuke Akutagawa's *Rashomon*. The Korean text is shown below the Japanese text; an English translation follows.

/ [*Shibaraku*	*shinda-yō-ni*	*taorete-ita*]	*rōba-ga* +
/ [*Hanch' am-dongan chusun-dusi*		*najappajo-itton*]	*nop'a-ga* +
(*shigai-no*) *naka-kara* +	((*sono*)	*hadaka-no*)	*karada-wo* +
(*songjang-*) *sog-eso* +	((*ku*)	*ppalgasung-ui*)	*mom-ul* +
okoshita-no-wa / +	(*sore-kara mamonaku-no*)		*koto-de-aru*.
iruk'in-gos-un / +	(*kurigo*	*olma-andoen*)	*ttae-yotta*.

It was not long before the old woman, who had lain for a space like one dead, raised her naked body up from among the corpses [Lewin 1976:399].

Such striking parallels cannot have resulted from chance, and require a historical explanation.

Another feature common to both Japanese and Korean is a system of honorific forms of address, which includes "partner-related honorifics," "statement-related honorifics," and further distinctions based on whether the person being honored is acting or is the object of the action. Many languages use honorific forms of address, or have involved systems for acknowledging differences in social level between speakers, but the similarities found in Korean and Japanese set these two languages apart. The two systems closely resemble one another in many points of specific, and arbitrary, linguistic detail, which implies a historical connection.

There is thus no doubt that structural similarities indicate a historical relationship of some kind between the Korean and Japanese languages. By themselves, however, these similarities are insufficient to resolve the question of whether this past relationship was one of culture contact and borrowing, or one of mutual descent from a common ancestral language. A fuller corpus of shared features, extending to matters of minute detail, is required for a convincing demonstration that the relationship is more than superficial, and is indeed a deep-going ancestral or "genetic" one. Such evidence, long lacking, has

TABLE 1.1
Lexical Evidence Relating the Korean and Japanese Languages[a]

Meaning	Korean	Japanese	Proto-Korean-Japanese
Accompany	teli-	tur(e)-	*tɔry-
Although	..to	..do	*..do
Arrive	"tah-	túk-	*tɔx-
Bamboo	tä	take	*taxye
Bear	"kom	kumá	*kuma
Bee	"pël	pati	*pal(y)i
Blow	pul-	púk-	*pɔlğ
Boat	pä	púne	*pɔnye
Body	mom	mi	*myom
Breasts	cëc	tití	*cyic(yi)
Brink	"ka	kisí	*kyɔtsyi
Brush	pus	pude	*pudye
Brushwood	sëph	siba	*syibxa
Bunch	tapal	taba	*tabal
Cage	uli	ori	*ori/eri
Carry	nalï-	nos(e)-	*nɔš
Chicken	talk	tori	*tɔrkyi
Clan	ul	údi	*uldxyi
Claw	thop	tume	*txumpye
Close it	tat-	tód(i)-	*tɔ́d-
Cold	chu w/p-	samu-	*tsxwampu-
Correct	mac-	masa	*mats(a)-
Crab	ke	kani	*kani
Crowd	muli	muré	*mur(ye)
Cut off	calï-	tát-	*cál-
Desire	pala-	por-	*pɔr(a)-
Dry up	kamïl-	kawák-	*kabák-
Empty	kophu-	kará	*kwɔr(?x)(a)-
Enjoy	cïlkë w/p-	yorokób-	*jɔ́rókeb-
Enter	tïl-	yir-	*dyar-
Fertile	këlïm	koyé	*keř-
Field	path	patake	*pataxye
Filter it	këli-	kos-	*keš
Fire	pul	pí	*pyal
Flesh	sal	sisi	*syɔš
Foot	pal	así	*vašyi
Give	"tal-	yar-	*dar-
Hang	tal-	tur-	*tɔr
Hang	"kel-	kák(e)	*kalg
Hard	kut-	kata-	*kwat(a)-
Heap	"tam-	tum-	*tɔm
Hemp	sam	asa	*(a-)sam
Hold	tïl-	tór-	*tɔ́r-
Hoop	the	tagá	*tağya
House	cip	yipé	*jïpye
Island	"sëm	sima	*sYyima
Liked	"coh-	súk-	*tsux
Line	cul	sudi	*tsuldyi
Liquor	sul	sake	*swalğye
Look for	chac-	sagas-	*tsáğáts-

(continued)

TABLE 1.1 (*continued*)

Meaning	Korean	Japanese	Proto-Korean-Japanese
Marsh	nïph	numá	*nɔmpxa
Measure	mal	masú	*mašu
Meet	mac-	mát-	*mac-
Melon	oy	úri	*uri
Mildew	"kom(phangi)	kabi	*kwɔmbyi
Morning	achim	ása	*atsxám
Mother	ëmë-(nim)	omo	*eme
Mountain	me	mine	*myonyex
Mountain	me	mori	*morix
Needle	panïl	pári	*paryɔl
New	sä	sára	*sarya
Oak	kal	kási	*kašyi
Oyster	kul	kaki	*kwalǧyi
Paste it	palï-	par-	*pár-
Pick it	"cu w/p-	tum-	*cump
Piggyback	ëp-	op-	*ep-
Pigweed	pilïm	píyu	*piřɔm
Place	'thë	toko	*txexe
Plain	pël	pára	*par(a)
Red	pulk-	aka-	*válk(a)-
Scratch	kïlk-	kák-	*kalk-
Sea	palɔl	wata	*balál
Sea bream	tomi	tápi	*twɔmbi
Sell	phal-	(w)ur-	*bxɔr-
Side	yëph	sóba	*sYebxa
Skewer	koc	kusí	*kutsyi
Spade	sap	sapi	*salpyi
Spittle	chim	tubá	*cxumba
Split open	palï-	war-	*bár(y)-
Spread it	"pali-	par-	*pár(y)-
Star	"pyël	posi	*pYešyi
Stinking	k o/u li-	kusá-	*kušya-
Stomach	pä	pará	*párya
Stone	"tol	yisí	*dyoš
String	cul	turú	*cur(u)
Stupid	ëli-(sëk)-	oró-ka	*ery(o)-
Suffice	cala-	tar(i)-	*cár(a)-
Summer	yëlïm	natú	*nYolɔm
Swell	"pu l/t-?	púy(e)-	*pɔr-
Swellfish	pok	púgu	*pug(u)
Tail	choli	sirí	*tsxyori
Thing	kës	kotó	*kes
Tie up	"mä-	mak-	*máx(y)
Time	cëk	tokí	*cekyi
Tread	palp-	pum-	*pɔlmp-
Valley	kol(-ccak)	kura	*kura
Vanish	sïl-/sal-	sár-	*sár-
Waist	hëli	kosi	*xeši
Warm	nuk-	núku-	*nuk(u)-
Water	mul	midu	*myaldu

a From Martin 1966.
Note: Asterisks signify reconstructed forms.

been supplied by a series of rigorous comparisons of over 300 selected pairs or sets of Korean and Japanese words that show numerous systematic congruencies in form and meaning (Martin 1966). Additional work (Martin 1975), though cautious in tone, supports the case for a common ancestry.

Some of the lexical items presented by Martin as evidence of a genetic relationship between Korean and Japanese are reproduced in Table 1.1. These words, items of equivalent meaning that exhibit regular sound correspondences, constitute the core of the analysis. Such correspondences allow an inferential reconstruction of the common ancestral word forms; even more important, the total set of interlocking correspondences thus established shows certain systematic interrelationships that are too complex to have resulted from borrowing alone, and hence must be due to direct descent from a common ancestor.

A brief digression may facilitate the appreciation of this list, since a reader unfamiliar with the principles of comparative linguistics might well feel some skepticism about an approach that claims significant similarity for words spelled as differently as, for example, Korean *teli-* and Japanese *tur(e)-* (Table 1.1). In weighing such evidence it is essential to remember, first, that *sounds* in the language being studied, not the alphabetic symbols used in romanizing the language, are the real objects of comparison. Second, it must be kept in mind that what is important to establish is a regular pattern of systematic correspondence, one sound in one language regularly equivalent to another sound in another language. The two words *teli-* and *tur(e)-* do, in fact, present identical sequences of phonetically similar sounds. The initial consonant of each word is clearly the same. In both words vowels follow the initial consonant, and both these vowels are produced in the same area of the mouth, with very little difference between them. In both words another consonant follows. In romanizing the Korean word this consonant is written as *l,* showing that the sound is formed by touching the tongue to the roof of the mouth, immediately behind the teeth. In the Japanese word, the sound in question is romanized as *r,* but in fact when spoken it is formed with the tongue placed in a virtually identical position (unlike English *r,* which is formed quite differently). Finally, both words end in another vowel, and again the vowels are phonetically close to one another. This is an example of the simplest kind. Other correspondences—as, for example, where Japanese *s* and Korean *l* regularly occur in the same position in certain related words—are more complex, but for that reason even more convincing as evidence. Table 1.1 gives evidence of these and other such systematic correspondences. Miller's (1976) discussion of the comparative linguistic method as applied to Japanese studies is required reading for those interested in pursuing methodological matters further.

Since Martin's major lexical study was published, yet more evidence supporting the conclusion that Japanese and Korean are genetically related descendants of a common ancestral language has appeared. A striking correspondence between Korean and Japanese verb morphology, which is exhibited in a number of words of varying meanings and therefore almost certainly not due to borrowing or chance resemblance, is presented by Miller (1967:65–66). In both Korean and Japanese, transitive and intransitive verbs often occur in paired sets distinguished by the formant *-i, as shown in the following examples.

Korean

In some words, addition of the formant *-i forms transitive verbs from intransitive ones:

Intransitive	Transitive
mek-'eat'	mek-i-'feed'
cuk-'die'	cuk-i-'kill'
kkulh-'be boiling'	kkulh-i-'boil it'

The same formant is used with other words in reverse fashion, to form intransitive verbs from transitive ones:

Transitive	Intransitive
nanu-'divide'	nanui-'be divided'
mo(i)-'bring together'	mo-i-'come together'
til-'hear'	til(l)-i-'be heard'

Japanese

The same uses of the *-i formant are seen in Japanese verbs. Here juxtaposition of the *-i form with the final -a of the Japanese words altered the phonetic shape of the ending at an earlier stage in the history of the language, resulting in -e in the actual forms found in the language. This does not affect the validity of the comparison; in fact it makes it more convincing, since it shows that the Japanese forms could not have been borrowed, or imitated, from Korean.

Intransitive	Transitive
tat-a- 'stand'	tat-a- + i = tate- 'erect (something)'
sirizok-a- 'retreat'	sirizok-a- + i = sirizoke- 'expel (something, someone)'
ir-a- 'enter'	ir-a- + i = ire- 'insert (something)'
ak-a- '(something) opens'	ak-a- + i = ake- 'open (something)'

Transitive	**Intransitive**
tok-a- 'untie, melt down (something)'	*tok-a- + i = toke-* (something) melts, comes undone'
kudak-a- 'smash (something)'	*kudak-a- + i = kudake-* 'be smashed, broken'
kira-a- 'cut (something)'	*kir-a- + i = kire-* 'be cut, severed'

That Korean is genetically related to the Tungus-Manchu, Mongolian, and Turkic languages of Northeast Asia's Altaic stock has been convincingly demonstrated (Poppe 1950, 1960; Ramstedt 1949).

TABLE 1.2
Lexical Evidence Relating Japanese and the Other Altaic Languages[a]

Abbreviations: pA, proto-Altaic; pT, proto-Tungus; Mo, Mongolian; MMo, Middle Mongolian; Osm, Osmanli; Ev, Evenki; OT, Old Turkish; MTk, Middle Turkish; Tk, Turkish; Chu, Chuvash; Chag, Chagash; Lam, Lamut; Ma, Manchu; Go, Goldi; K, Korean; MK, Middle Korean; pKJ, proto-Korean-Japanese; J, Japanese; OJ, Old Japanese; Oi, Oirat; Tat, Tatar. An asterisk signifies a reconstructed form.

Rule of Correspondence: pA or pT, *$^*d$ or *$^*\check{z}$ before original **-*u*- :: OJ, *tu*- (*$^*du$, *$\check{z}u = tu$)

1. 'warm'   pA, *$^*dul\bar{\imath}g\bar{a}n$; Mo, *dulayan*; Ev, *dul-*; MTk, *jil\"iy*; J, *(a)tu-*; pKJ, *$^*(a-)t\partial$-; MK, *t\partial s(c-)*
2. 'pair'   pA, *$^*\check{z}ur$; Ev, *$\check{z}\bar{u}r$; Ma, *$\check{z}uru$, $\check{z}uwe$*; OJ, *ture*
3. 'ten'   pT, *$^*\check{z}uwan$; Ev, *$z\bar{a}n$; Ma, *$\check{z}uwan$; OJ, *t\"owo*
4. 'summer'   Mo, *$\check{z}un$; Ev, *$\check{z}uga\~n\bar{\imath}$; Lam, *$\check{z}uga\~n\bar{\imath}$, $\check{z}uwu\~ni$*; Ma, *$\check{z}uwari$; OJ, *tuFari*
5. 'dative form'   pT, *$^*du$; OJ, *tu*

Rule of Correspondence: pA or pT, *$^*d$ or *$^*\check{z}$ before original **-*o*- :: OJ, *to*- (*$^*do$, *$\check{z}o = to$)

1. 'steal, take'   pT, *$^*\check{z}or$-; Ev, *$\check{z}orom\bar{\imath}$-; Lam, *$\check{z}orm\bar{\imath}$-; OJ, *tor-*, *t\"or-*; pKJ, *$^*tw\partial r$, *$^*t\partial r$; K, *t\~il-*
2. 'wave, pool'   pA, *$^*dolkin$; Mo, *dolgijan*; Ma, *dol\check{c}in*; J, *toro*

Rule of Correspondence: pA or pT, *$^*d$ or *$^*\check{z}$ before original **-*\"u*- :: OJ, *yu*- (*$^*d\"u$, *$\check{z}\"u = yu$)

1. 'transport, carry'   pA, *$^*\check{z}\"ug$-; Mo, *$\check{z}\"uge$*; Ev, *$\check{z}ug\bar{u}$, $\check{z}ug\bar{u}w\bar{u}n$*; Lam, *$\check{z}ug\bar{u}t$-; OT, *j\"uk*; OJ, *yuki*, *yugi*, *yuge*
2. 'form, appearance'   pA, *$^*d\"ur_2i$; Mo, *d\"uri*; Ma, *durun*; OT, *j\"uz*; OJ, *$^*yur\"o$ > *yir\"o* > *ir\"o*
3. 'insert'   pA, *$^*d\"ur_2$-; Mo, *d\"ur\"u-* < *$^*d\"ure$*; Ev, *dur\bar{e}ki*; Chu, *j\u{a}rana* < *$^*j\"ur_2ani$; OJ, *$^*yir$- > *ire-*; pKJ, *$^*dyar$-; MK, *t\~il*
4. 'soft'   pT, *$^*\check{z}\"ulb$-; Mo, *$\check{z}\"ugelen$* (< *$^*\check{z}\"ulegen$ < *$^*\check{z}\"ulewen$ < *$^*\check{z}\"uleb\`en$); Lam, *$\check{z}ulber$, $\check{z}olbexr\bar{\imath}$*; OJ, *yuruF-*
5. 'warm, hot'   pT, *$^*d\"uli$-; Ev, *dul'i-*; OJ, *yu*
6. 'from'   pT, *$^*dul\bar{\imath}$; OJ, *yuri*, *yori*

Rule of Correspondence: pA or pT, *$^*d$ or *$^*\check{z}$ before original **-*\"o* :: OJ, *y\"o*- (*$^*d\"o$, *$\check{z}\"o = y\"o$-)

1. 'four'   pA, *$^*d\"o$-; Mo, *d\"orben*; Ma, *duin* < *$^*d\"ugin$ < *$^*d\"o-g\"un$; Ev, *digin*; pT, *$^*d\"ug\"un$; OJ, *y\"o*

Rule of Correspondence: pA or pT, *$^*d$ or *$^*\check{z}$ before original **-*a*-, **-*\"a*-, or **-*\"e*-, immediately preceding an original stop (-*p*, -*b*, -*g*) :: OJ, *ta*. The same, originally preceding an original continuant (*w*, *l*, or zero) :: OJ, *ya*- (*$^*da$, *$\check{z}a = ta$; *$^*da$, *$\check{z}a = ya$, for example)

1. 'boot, foot covering'   pA, *$^*z\"ab$-; Mo, *\check{z}abi*; Ma, *\check{z}aja* < *$^*\check{z}awi$; Ev, *\check{z}aw*; J, *tabi*
2. 'bend, twist, uncombed wool'   pA, *$^*dap$-; Mo, *dayaki* < *$^*dap\`ak\"i$; Osm, *japaq\"i*; J, *tawam*

(continued)

The genetic relationship of Japanese to the Altaic linguistic unity, implied by the Japanese–Korean connection just discussed, has been directly demonstrated by Miller (1971). A brief resume of selected evidence extracted from his corpus of comparisons will illustrate the far-reaching common features shared by Japanese and the other Altaic languages. These features go well beyond what could be attributed to historical contact and borrowing alone.

Patterns of regular sound change in items of equivalent meaning, which extend across a spectrum of different Altaic languages including Japanese and Korean, are evident in Table 1.2. Such corre-

TABLE 1.2 (*continued*)

3. 'fool (around)' pA, *dap-; Mo, dāgan < *dapàkan; Osm, japaq; J, tawak-
4. 'together' pA, *dag-; Mo, dagā-; Ev, daga; OT, jaqïn; J, tagaí(ni)
5. 'eight' pT, *žapkun; Ma, žakûn; Ev, žapkun; J, tako
6. 'mountain' pT, *daw-; Mo, daba-; Ma, daban; Ev, dawakit; J, yama
7. 'secret' pA, *dal₂-; Mo, dalda; Ma, dali-; OJ, yasirö
8. 'lick continuously, gobble up' pA, *dalu-; Mo, doluya; Lam, dal-; Osm, jala-; J, yarak-a-s
9. 'burn' pT, *žäg-; Ma, deiži-; Go, žəgdə-; Ev, žəgdə; J, tak-; pKJ, *táx-; MK, thɔ-
10. 'arrow' pA, *žë; Ev, zeje; Lam, žej; Mo, žebe; MMo, žer; J, ya; pKJ, *ja(k); K, cak-
11. 'eat' pA, *žëp; pT, *žäp-; Ev, žep Lam, žeb-; Ma, že; J, tab-; pKJ, *cab-; MK, ca(ɔps)-
12. 'carrion, refuse heap' pA, *žëm-; Mo, žeme; Ev, žemū; J, yabu
13. 'night' pKJ, *je; K, cë-; pT, *dolba; OJ, yo-, yorö, yora, ya; J, yoru
14. 'give' pA, *dal-; Mo, dolig; OT, juluy; J, yar-; K, tal-; pKJ, *dar-
15. 'generation' pA, *žal-; Ma, žalan; MMo, žalga-; OJ, yö

Rule of Correspondence: pA, primary *č before original *-ï- :: OJ, tu- (*čï = tu)

1. 'rod' pA, *čïbïk; Tk, Oi, Tat, cïbïq; OJ, tuwe
2. 'wet' pA, *čig; Tat, čiq; Oi, Tat, čī; Tk, čig; Mo, cigig; K, cëc-; J, tuk-e
3. 'furuncle' pA, *čïp; Tk, čïban; Mo, čigiqan; J, tubu; cf. J, tubaki
4. 'sin' pA, *čïpï; Mo, čibil; Oi, čibil; J, tumi
5. 'roll up, accumulate' pA, *čïmr-; Tk, čïmrïn; Tat, čïrma-; Mo, čïma-; J, tum ᵃ/₀r-
6. 'fly, wing' pA, *čïbïn; Oi, čïmin; Chag, čibin; J, tubasa, tubame
7. 'pinch' pA, *čïm-; Oi, čïmcï; Tk, čïmdik; J, tum-, tumam-; K, cuʷ/ₚ-; pKJ, *cump-
8. 'come out' pA, *čïka-; OT, čiq-; Oi, Tk, Tat, čïq-; OJ, (i)-du-r-

Rule of Correspondence: pA, primary *č before original *-a- :: OJ, tᵒ/ₐ- (*ča = tᵒ/ₐ)

1. 'time' pA, *čak; MMo, Mo, čaq; OT, čaq; MK, cëk; K, cok; pKJ, *cekyi, *cokyi; OJ, töki
2. 'burn (something)' pA, čak-; MMo, čaqï-; OT, Chag, Osm, čaq-; Jak, sax-; J, tak-

Rule of Correspondence: pA, *t before *-i- :: OJ, ti- -du- (*ti = ti, -du-)

1. 'strength' pA, *tïgïrak; Mo, čigiriaq; OT, tïyraq; J, tikara
2. 'study' pA, *tatig; Mo, tačija-; Ma, tači-; Ma, tačixijan; J, tadun-

Rule of Correspondence: pA, *d before *-ï- :: OJ, yö- (*dï = yö)

1. 'happy' pA, *dïrg-; Mo, žïrya; Chag, jïraw; Kaz, žïr; OJ, yörökö-b-; K, cïlkëʷ/ₚ-; pKJ, *jɔrɔkeb-

ᵃ After Miller 1971: 84–86, 98–99.

spondences, occurring in languages spread across so vast an area, must be ancient indeed, going back to the time when all the Altaic languages were one. This table will repay careful study, with special attention to the rules of correspondence that define the patterns of linguistic change.

Another striking piece of evidence for genetic relationship is the correspondence in verb morphology demonstrated by a comparison of the Old Japanese and Old Turkish forms for "suffice." In the modern Japanese language there are a small number of important verbs in which the distinction between transitive and intransitive forms is indicated not by the addition of suffixes (a common enough morphological device elsewhere in the language), but by variation of the final consonant of the root itself. Examples of this morphological process are *tar-* 'suffice', *tas-* 'make (something) sufficient'; *kar-* 'borrow', *kas-* 'lend'; *nor-* 'ride', *nos-* 'transport (someone, something)'. In just this way, the Old Turkish verb for "suffice" follows the same pattern as its Old Japanese counterpart:

Old Japanese	*tar-* 'suffice'	*tas-* 'make (something) sufficient'
Old Turkish	*tol-* 'suffice'	*tos-* 'make (something) sufficient'

This morphological parallel is in itself significant, and its strength as evidence is magnified by the fact that the correspondence of Turkic *l* and *s* to Japanese *r* and *s* in comparable phonetic environments is well established by other, independent data. We know from many other correspondences in other kinds of words that when Turkic *l* corresponds to Japanese *r*, we have evidence for an earlier *l*-like sound in the original linguistic ancestor; when Turkic *š* corresponds to Japanese *s*, we have evidence for another similar (but distinct) sound.

The way in which the ancestral proto-Altaic language broke up into the modern Altaic tongues still spoken today is diagrammed in Figure 1.4. The intermediate languages shown in the diagram, such as proto-Eastern Altaic and proto-Northern and Peninsular Altaic, represent speech communities that existed at intermediate levels of time, ultimately breaking up and diverging further to give rise to the descendant languages shown. That the modern languages are derived from such intervening tongues, rather than each having descended in a straight line from the original proto-Altaic linguistic unity, is inferred from the degree of similarity that the modern languages bear to each other. Korean, Japanese, and Ryukyu, for example, share more crucial features with each other than any of them does with any of the group that includes Manchu, Goldi, and other languages. This implies that the two sets of modern tongues mentioned are each descended from

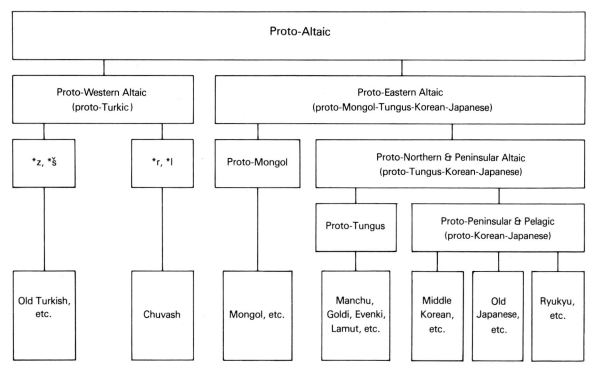

Figure 1.4 Genetic relationships of the Altaic languages. (Redrawn from *Japanese and the Other Altaic Languages*, 1971, by Roy Andrew Miller. By permission of the author and the University of Chicago Press.)

two different ancestral languages that had themselves, as shown in the diagram, diverged from a common source at a yet earlier period.

This process of branching may be followed back until we reach the original, and extremely ancient, proto-Altaic speech community. A similar process reaching even further back in time probably lies behind the existence of the proto-Altaic language itself. There is some linguistic evidence to suggest that the Altaic languages are distantly related to another whole series of tongues, including Hungarian, Finnish, Samoyed, and others, which are now usually grouped as the Uralic languages. These are spoken across a broad area of northwestern Eurasia, from the Ural Mountains to the Baltic Sea. If the Uralic and Altaic languages do in fact go back to a common ancestral speech community, it was one that existed at a very remote time indeed, perhaps close to that of the initial peopling, in late glacial times, of the northernmost parts of the world.

Attempts have been made to date some of the linguistic splits within the Altaic stock, using the technique of glottochronology.

Given the nature and limitations of the method, the results are far from conclusive, but they are too intriguing to ignore entirely. One analysis of a standard 200-word comparative checklist of basic vocabulary items showed that Japanese and Korean shared about 15% of these words (Miller 1967:82–83). This implies that Japanese and Korean split apart about 4600 years ago, according to the method's fundamental assumption that when one language splits into two, the number of basic vocabulary items from the 200-word list that are shared by the two daughter languages will decrease by about 20% in each successive 1000-year period. Calculations by Hattori (1959) placed the time of divergence at about 4700 years ago, and a comparable date for the Korean–Japanese split can be calculated from the results of Martin's (1966) lexical study. Martin identified 20 cognates in a standard comparative checklist of 100 basic vocabulary items. Since the 100-item list is believed to have a loss rate of 14% per 1000 years, the finding of 20 Japanese–Korean cognates implies that the two languages split apart a little less than 5000 years ago.

Japanese and Manchu share about 7% of the 200 basic words compared by Hattori (Miller 1967:82–83). This implies, according to the glottochronological method, that the initial breakup of the speech community that gave rise to Japanese, Korean, and Manchu (the "proto-Peninsular and Pelagic" unity of Figure 1.4) occurred between about 5500 and 6200 years ago.

It seems likely that all these calculations (indeed glottochronological calculations in general) seriously underestimate the actual time depth of the linguistic divergences in question. On the one hand, recently borrowed loanwords may have swollen the total of cognates. Such inflation of the cognate percentages would suggest a shorter period from time of divergence to the present than was actually the case. On the other hand, it is remarkable but true that the glottochronological method actually underestimates by about 100% the historically known age of divergence between many of the very languages that figured so prominently in the development of the method itself!

The period during which French, Italian, Spanish, and other Romance languages diverged from their common Latin ancestor is fairly well dated by written historical records. The breakup apparently began about 2200 years ago, and was well under way by the beginning of the Christian era. Yet estimates based on the glottochronological method suggest that the earliest splits occurred little over 1000 years ago, with the most recent divergences (Spanish–Portuguese and Italian–French) occurring less than 400 years ago. This discrepancy in the method apparently went unremarked in the pilot study that developed the glottochronological approach, because there the individual Romance languages were only compared to the common ancestral Latin, and not to each other (Rea 1958). The reader interested in a detailed general discussion of the glottochronological method should consult Hymes (1960). For present purposes, this one example is sufficient to emphasize that glottochronological dates seem inherently likely to be underestimates rather than overestimates, and that the splits between Japanese, Korean, and Manchu discussed earlier probably took place a good deal earlier than the glottochronological dates for them suggest.

The relationship of Japanese to the languages of Northeast Asia now seems securely established, but Oceanic connections have also been proposed. Some scholars have argued that Japanese has not merely Altaic origins, but is a true mixed language, resulting from the "Altaicization" of a Malayo-Polynesian language. According to one view (Ohno 1970), the original language of Japan was a Malayo-Polynesian tongue. This language was later overwhelmingly influenced by the intrusion of an Altaic language, giving rise to a linguistic hybrid that combined the vocabulary and sound system of Malayo-Polynesian with the grammar and morphology of Altaic. Another view makes Altaic the original language and Malayo-Polynesian the intrusive element, with the same linguistic consequence (Murayama 1976).

An incisive review of Ohno's book setting out the Malayo-Polynesian thesis has stressed the weakness and superficiality of the evidence adduced in favor of the theory (Miller 1971). Murayama and Obayashi (1973) have since independently published a number of proposed etymologies linking Japanese and Malayo-Polynesian words, but a fellow specialist's review of this work characterized many of these etymologies as "tortuous" and showed that, in some cases at least, a far less complicated (and therefore scientifically preferable) etymological analysis could derive the words in question from Altaic rather than Malayo-Polynesian forerunners (Miller 1974).

In any event it is generally held by most historical linguists that true mixed languages, in the sense of the term proposed for the Japanese case, do not in fact exist. No convincing example has ever been documented, even where linguistic contact is known to have been intense and long continued. English absorbed a great many French words as an aftermath of the Norman invasion of England in the eleventh century. The Japanese language has absorbed an overwhelming number of Chinese words since about the eighth century, during a thousand years as a medium for the absorption of Chinese elements into Japanese culture. English and Japanese were of course significantly expanded and altered by these intrusive linguistic elements, but in neither case did there occur the sort of phonological and grammatical blending implied by the theory of Japanese as a mixed language. Finally, the Spanish conquest of Mexico and much of South America introduced the language of a conquering elite under circumstances very like those imagined to have brought about the Altaicization of a native Malayo-Polynesian language in Japan. Yet, even in this case, no mixed language was developed. Spanish simply replaced the native languages, absorbing in the process many loanwords, but undergoing no structural blending even remotely like that envisioned by the thesis of Japanese as a mixed Altaic and Malayo-Polynesian language.

How, then, may the observed similarities between Japanese and the Malayo-Polynesian languages be accounted for? It simplifies the problem greatly to point out that most historical linguists do not consider gross typological and phonological similarities of the sort observed between Japanese and Malayo-Polynesian to be substantial evidence of linguistic relationship. This is simply because similarities of this kind and degree are known to exist between other languages so remote from one another as to leave no doubt at all of their historical independence. It is quite possible, therefore, that the general typological and phonological similarity of Japanese and Malayo-Polynesian is merely accidental.

If it seems to stretch the limits of coincidence that two languages that simply chance to share such similarities also simply chance to be neighbors, it is instructive to consider that the Malayo-Polynesian tongues, distributed across a range of some 20,000 km, have many linguistic neighbors, of which Japanese is only one. In such a circumstance, there are multiple opportunities for chance resemblances to appear between Malayo-Polynesian and neighboring languages, and inevitably some will share more similarities with it than others.

Nevertheless, it is unnecessary, even unreasonable, to attribute every similarity between Japanese and Malayo-Polynesian vocabulary items to chance alone. During the period of the Yayoi culture (very roughly 300 B.C.–A.D. 300), rice, metal, and other exotic elements flooded into Japan. In particular, the wet-field system of rice cultivation is certainly of southern origin, and its occurrence in Japan indicates at least indirect cultural contact with a region of Southeast Asia where Malayo-Polynesian speakers were undeniably present. Ohno (1970) and Murayama (1976) have pointed out that several Japanese words that they believe to be of Malayo-Polynesian origin also have counterparts in the language of South Korea. This would be expected if, as archaeological evidence suggests, rice growing and other cultural traits were introduced into both Japan and South Korea at about the same time, from the same outside source. That a number of new people arrived at the same time whose speech, if not Malayo-Polynesian, at least included loanwords of Malayo-Polynesian origin, is a distinct possibility.

In the Japanese islands themselves existed another native language whose relationship to Japanese has long been discussed, although so far it has not been made the object of rigorous comparative study. Ainu-speaking hunters and gatherers occupied all of Hokkaido and parts of northeastern Honshu in early historic times, but their number was subsequently much reduced by the northward expansion of Japanese settlers, and the Ainu now exist only as a few small remnant groups in Hokkaido. The Japanese and Ainu languages bear a general structural similarity to each other in word order, the use of distinctive grammatical particles, and some other features. Japanese and Ainu also share a number of words, though it appears that many of these are loanwords, and it has not been rigorously established to what extent, if any, the remaining cognates might represent the historical residue of an ancestral vocabulary reflecting common origins.

A tentative glottochronological calculation based on the *assumption* that Ainu and Japanese are genetically related suggests that they split apart between 5000 and 8000 years ago. If in fact it were convincingly established that Ainu and Japanese are descended from a common ancestor, and keeping in mind that glottochronological ages inherently tend to be underestimates, this would suggest a great age for their divergence from one another. Since the posited genetic relationship is not conclusively established, however, strictly speaking the calculation shows only that the number of words shared by the two languages (be they loanwords or residual ancient vocabulary) is rather small.

When all the linguistic evidence for common ancestry has been considered, however, and found insufficient to meet the rigorous demands of the historical–comparative method, it nevertheless remains true that Ainu resembles Japanese more closely than it does any other language. And after Japanese, its most obvious affinities are with the other Altaic languages, spoken across all of Northeast Asia in aboriginal times. Ainu is clearly an ancient tongue in Northeast Asia, whether it is a complete isolate or a very distant relative of Japanese and the other Altaic languages, and undoubtedly it has been spoken there for at least as long as has Japanese itself.

Dialect variation in modern Japanese is also of historical interest, for variant speech patterns are divided along lines that reflect a major cultural division between northeastern and southwestern Japan, going back to ancient times. As Figure 1.5 shows, a series of boundary lines,

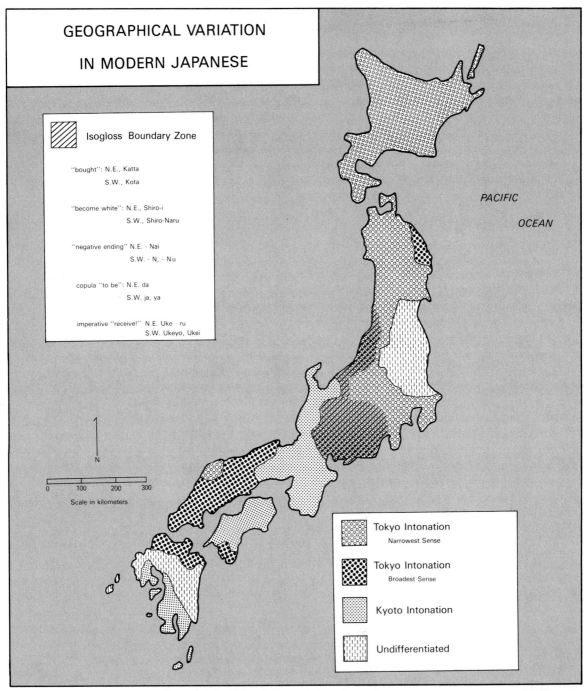

Figure 1.5 Dialect isoglosses and regional variation in intonation patterns in modern Japanese. (Redrawn after Figures 3 and 5, in *The Japanese Language*, 1967, by Roy Andrew Miller. By permission of the author and the University of Chicago Press.)

close together and often coinciding, mark speech variations that divide northeastern and southwestern Japan. For example, 'bought' is *katta* in the northeast, *kŏta* in the southwest; 'become white' is *shiro-i* in the northeast, *shirō naru* in the southwest; negative ending is -*nai* in the northeast, -*n* or -*nu* in the southwest; the copula form 'to be' is *da* in the northeast, *ja* or *ya* in the southwest; and the imperative 'receive!' is *uke-ru* in the northeast, *ukeyo* or *ukei* in the southwest. Other items as well conform to this division (Miller 1967).

In addition to this major northeast–southwest dialect isogloss division, there persist even now several regional dialects sufficiently distinctive as to be unintelligible to a listener whose native dialect is the standard speech of the Tokyo area. In Aomori Prefecture, northern Honshu, and in Kagoshima Prefecture, southeastern Kyushu, such variant speech systems coexist with the Tokyo speech that has been promulgated as Standard Japanese by the national educational establishment since the Meiji Restoration of 1868. Other regional differences in language are lesser, but in all a half-dozen or so loosely defined dialect subareas may be distinguished within the four main islands of Japan, defined by contrasts in pronunciation, morphology, and pitch contrast or intonation (Figure 1.5).

This linguistic diversity indicates the maintenance of subcultural divisions over a long period of time. Major dialect differences between "civilized" southwestern Japan and three different subregions of "frontier" northeastern Japan were well recognized by poets and writers of the early imperial court at Nara. The evidence for these divisions survives today in the *Man'yōshū*, a collection of early poems compiled in the eighth century, which includes a number of "frontier guardsmen's verses" in the "quaint" eastern dialects. It seems that the division between southwestern and northeastern Japan was already old and well established during the Nara period. And the fact that a similar division may also be perceived in archaeological maps treating of much earlier periods suggests that the people of northeastern and southwestern Japan have maintained distinctive identities for a long time.

Conclusion

The evidence reviewed in this chapter indicates that the Japanese and Ainu have long occupied the islands where they now reside. The Japanese language is spoken nowhere else in the world, except by very recent emigrants from the home islands. Its nearest linguistic relative is Korean, which by all accounts is nevertheless sufficiently dissimilar to imply a long period of separation. Glottochronological estimates suggest that Japanese and Korean diverged from a common ancestral

language about 5000 years ago, and given the vagaries of the method
this is almost certainly a marked underestimate.

The Ainu language has not been adequately studied, but available
information shows that it is more similar to Japanese and the other
Altaic languages of Northeast Asia than to any other tongues.
Whether these similarities indicate mutual divergence from a common
ancestor or borrowing of features between neighboring languages, they
nevertheless imply an ancient relationship of some kind between
Japanese and Ainu.

Regional dialect differences within modern Japanese, and dialect
differences documented in written form as early as the eighth century,
imply subcultural differences long maintained in a country long settled. A major north–south speech boundary running across central
Honshu coincides with a division based on somatic characteristics of
the human population, and, as will be seen, with a division recognizable on the basis of prehistoric artifact type distributions as well. These
boundaries in turn all coincide roughly with a major natural vegetation boundary, between the broad-leaved evergreen forests of southwestern Japan and the temperate coniferous–deciduous forests of the
northeast.

In sum, the somatic, linguistic, and environmental evidence co-
heres to suggest that the present-day occupants of Japan have deep
roots in the land. The archaeological record, reviewed in the chapters
ahead, suggests a corresponding cultural continuity over many millennia.

2 : The Paleolithic Period

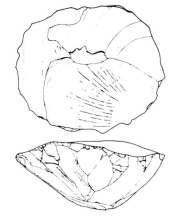

Human beings might have entered what are now the islands of Japan over dry land during long intervals of the Pleistocene epoch. The existence of land bridges is indicated by fossil finds from all over Japan, and by certain floral and geological data that also give some insight into the environmental conditions then prevailing. A brief discussion of some of the most important evidence will provide a background against which the early peopling of Japan during the Paleolithic period may be considered. This account depends heavily on a monumental synthesis by Minato and others (1965), which should be understood as the source of the information to follow, except where other references are specifically cited.

The islands of Japan form a curving arc about 2000 km in length, which lies along the northeastern edge of the continent of Asia. Between the tip of the Korean peninsula and the island of Kyushu, the Korea–Tsushima Strait separates Japan from the continent by a distance of about 200 km. From Cape Soya at the northernmost tip of Hokkaido, across the northern Japan Sea to the adjacent mainland, is a distance of about 300 km. Elsewhere as much as thrice that distance intervenes between the main island of Honshu and the continent. To the north, Hokkaido is separated from the long, slender Soviet-held island of Sakhalin by the 40-km-wide Soya Strait; Sakhalin itself is cut off from the continent only by the relatively minor Tatar Strait, which at its narrowest point is less than 10 km across.

The floor of the Korea–Tsushima Strait is a broad, flat plain generally about 100–130 m below sea level, but it is interrupted by a narrow north–south channel about 200 m deep between the island of Tsushima and the tip of the Korean peninsula. The Tsugaru Strait, which separates Hokkaido and Honshu, is about 130 m deep near its shallow western end; by contrast, the shallowest parts of the Soya and Tatar straits are only 50 and 10 m deep, respectively. The land connections implied by Middle and Late Pleistocene fossil distributions probably resulted from the exposure of these shallow reaches of the ocean floor brought about by the worldwide lowering of sea level during Pleistocene glacial maxima. Japan is such a tectonically active region, however, that the possibility of minor shifts in the earth's crust having also been involved cannot be ruled out. Some Early Pleistocene fossil distributions definitely indicate that major tectonic shifts were involved in producing the land bridge phenomena of that period.

That a land connection between the southern end of the Japanese arc and the adjacent mainland existed during Early Pleistocene times is shown by the fossilized bones of such early elephants as *Archidiskon*, *Stegodon*, and *Parastegodon*, and by two kinds of deer, *Muntiacus* and *Cervus*, which are found in deposits of Early Pleistocene age in southern Japan and in the Ryukyu island chain. These species all belong to the so-called Siva-Malayan and Sino-Malayan faunas, of southerly origin, and they must have entered Japan from that direction. The Ryukyus stretch away from Kyushu to the south and west, in the direction of Taiwan and south China. The seafloor in that region now lies far too deep for land to have been exposed by even the most extreme lowering of sea level during the Pleistocene glaciations. It is clear that the ancient land connection implied by the faunal remains must have been long ago obliterated by subsidence of the earth's crust, probably along the line of the present Ryukyu island chain.

Floral evidence from beds of Early Pleistocene age in central Japan suggests that a land connection was also present at the latitude of the Korea–Tsushima Strait, during cooler phases of that period. This is indicated by fossil remains of the subalpine and mountain conifers *Pinus koraiensis* and *Picea maximowiczii*, and the north temperate *Menyanthes trifoliata* and *Phellodendron amurensis*. These are endemic to Korea and Manchuria, though they are now long since established in the mountains of Honshu, where they have persisted since their introduction from the continent.

The presence of Naumann's elephant (*Palaeoloxodon*) throughout the islands of Japan in deposits of Middle Pleistocene age indicates that land connections with the continent, and between the four main islands of Japan, continued into that time. Fossil hominids of Middle

Pleistocene age are well attested in the famous site of Choukoutien, China, near Peking, about 2000 km west of Tokyo, and it would have been geographically quite possible for such early humans to have entered Japan and spread throughout the islands during this period.

The Late Pleistocene fossil fauna of northern Honshu and Hokkaido gives evidence of another major influx from the continent, this time of species that suggest the existence of land connections via both the Korea–Tsushima Strait region and the island of Sakhalin to the north. The Giant deer (*Megacervus*), horse, and bison are cool-temperate forms, and probably entered Japan via a connection with Korea. The mammoth (*Mammuthus primigenius*), known only from Hokkaido, is a northern form that must have entered from the continent via Sakhalin, on land bridges across the present Tatar and Soya straits. Boreal lemmings, wolves, and brown bears, known as fossils from very late Pleistocene cave deposits on Honshu, indicate that a land connection between Hokkaido and Honshu, across the Tsugaru Strait, also existed during at least part of the latest Pleistocene. This was probably at the time of the final glacial maximum, when sea levels were at their lowest.

Many details of the geological history of Japan's land bridge phase remain uncertain, but evidence already in hand makes it clear that the country's completely insular condition is a relatively recent phenomenon (Figure 2.1). For much of its Pleistocene history, Japan was an appendage of the Asian continent, enclosing the Japan Sea as a vast bay, connected to the Pacific only through narrow straits. Though the final swamping of land connections to the continent is not yet locally dated with precision, the faunal evidence and dating of worldwide sea-level fluctuations suggest that rising water would have finally made Japan the fully insular land it now is between about 18,000 and 12,000 years ago (Kotani 1969).

The Japanese islands themselves took on much of the topographic and stratigraphic detail of interest to the archaeologist during the same period as saw the rise and fall of the land bridges. During the Early Pleistocene, the subsidence of the earth's crust that had begun in Late Pliocene times maintained the existence of the Inland Sea in southern Japan; at the same time, the high mountains of central Honshu were further uplifted. Uplifted ancient plains, such as the Kunoe Terrace of northeast Honshu, and the Omine Plain of Kyushu, now lying at elevations of 100–600 m, further reflect the widespread tectonic movements of this and subsequent periods.

During the early Middle Pleistocene, a eustatic rise in sea level correlated with the Mindel/Riss interglacial stage drowned much of the Tokyo region. This is shown by the marine sediments of the

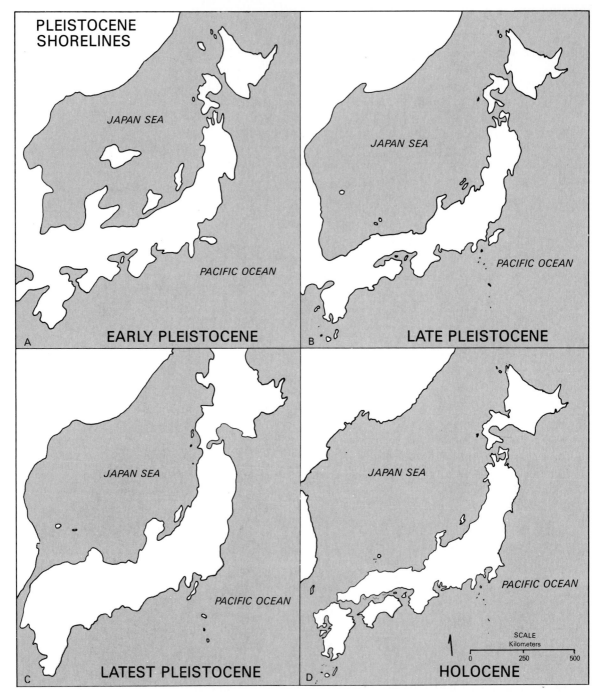

Figure 2.1 Progressive stages in the separation of Japan from the Asiatic mainland during the Pleistocene period. (After Minato *et al.* 1965: Figures 30.27–30.30.)

Byobugaura Formation, which overlie wave-cut shoreline features in that area and fill drowned valleys that had formed earlier, when the shore lay farther seaward. As the sea receded during the later Middle Pleistocene Riss glacial stage, a thick deposit of airborne volcanic ash, the Tama Loam, was laid down over the Byobugaura Formation. This ash, widespread in central Honshu, was ejected by volcanoes immediately west of the Tokyo region, which became extremely active at this time. In the Inland Sea area an upwarping known as the Rokko Movement reached a climax, resulting in extensive retreat of the sea and expansion of the coastal plains.

During the Late Pleistocene, another major rise in sea level at the time of the Riss/Würm interglacial stage created erosional and depositional features all around the coasts of Japan. The Tokyo region was again flooded, and Paleo–Tokyo Bay was greatly enlarged, by this so-called Shimosueyoshi Transgression. The marine deposits laid down by this event are known in the Tokyo region as the Shimosueyoshi Formation, and time-stratigraphic equivalents are known from Hokkaido to Kyushu. The island of Hokkaido was at this time virtually divided in two by a channel running through the Ishikari lowland in which the capital city of Sapporo is located. In Kyushu, gravel deposits are known whose depositional surface now lies more than 50 m above sea level, indicating a stage of remarkable marine transgression there too.

The Late Pleistocene sequence of the Tokyo region, beginning with the laying down of the Shimosueyoshi Formation, comprises the main geological reference series for the dating of early human occupation in Japan (Figure 2.2). Many if not most of the earliest sites now known occur within this stratigraphic series, or within others that can be correlated with it. The sequence from this point on is generally treated in terms of three successive subdivisions, the Shimosueyoshi, Musashino, and Tachikawa stages. The volcanic ash deposits associated with these stages collectively make up the famous Kanto Loam, which blankets the entire Tokyo region.

The earlier part of the Shimosueyoshi Stage is, as just noted, represented by the marine deposits of the Shimosueyoshi Formation. These mark the extent of Paleo–Tokyo Bay, a vast area underlying the modern megalopolis of Tokyo–Yokohama. These deposits, 10–13 m in thickness, form the basis of a plain or terrace whose surface lies about 40 m above present-day sea level. After the waters of Paleo–Tokyo Bay had receded, exposing this Shimosueyoshi Terrace, it was subsequently covered by airborne volcanic ash deposits up to 7 m thick. This is the Shimosueyoshi Loam, for which there are now a series of fission-track dates ranging from about 130,000 to 66,000 B.P. The

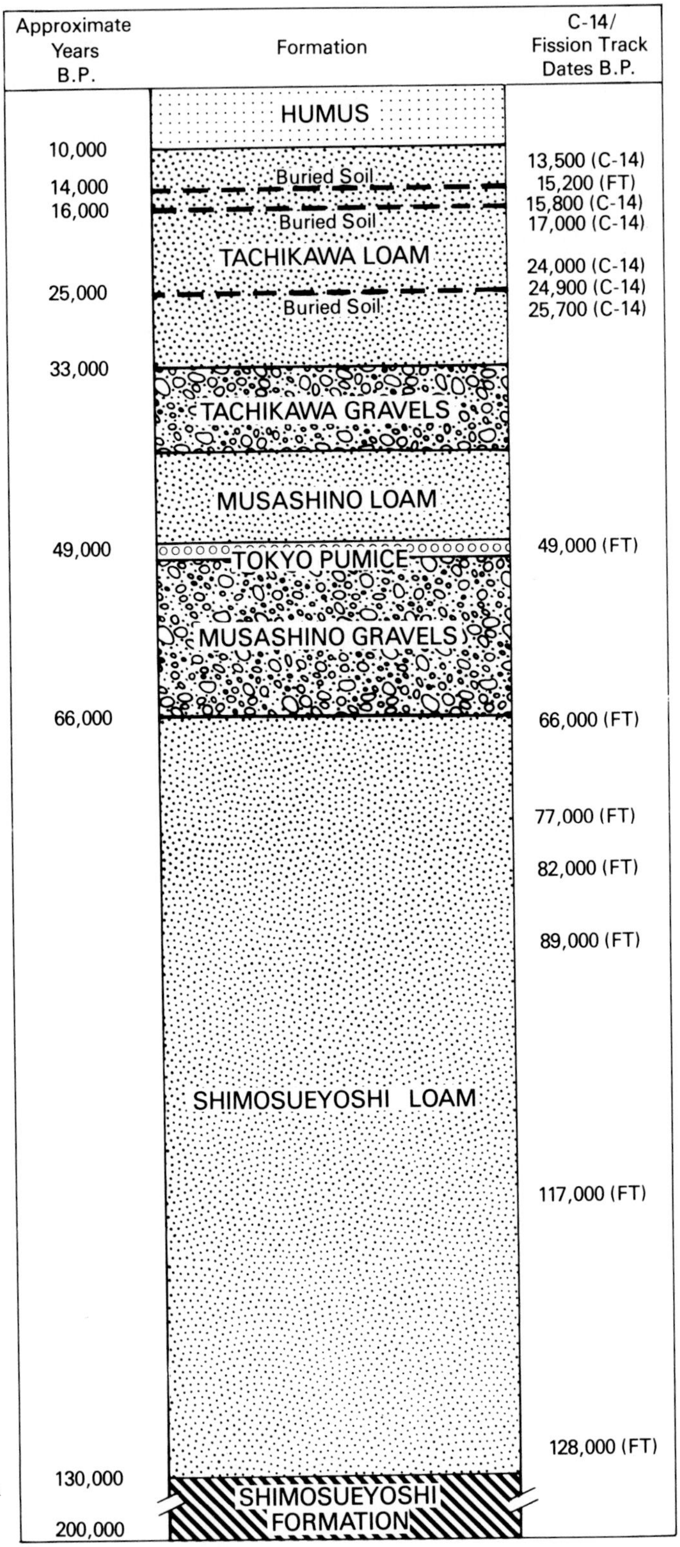

Approximate Years B.P.	Formation	C-14/Fission Track Dates B.P.
	HUMUS	
10,000		13,500 (C-14)
14,000	Buried Soil	15,200 (FT)
16,000	Buried Soil	15,800 (C-14) / 17,000 (C-14)
	TACHIKAWA LOAM	24,000 (C-14)
25,000	Buried Soil	24,900 (C-14) / 25,700 (C-14)
33,000	TACHIKAWA GRAVELS	
	MUSASHINO LOAM	
49,000	TOKYO PUMICE	49,000 (FT)
	MUSASHINO GRAVELS	
66,000		66,000 (FT)
		77,000 (FT)
		82,000 (FT)
		89,000 (FT)
	SHIMOSUEYOSHI LOAM	
		117,000 (FT)
		128,000 (FT)
130,000	SHIMOSUEYOSHI FORMATION	
200,000		

Figure 2.2 Late Pleistocene stratigraphy in the Tokyo area. (Based on Serizawa 1974: 167 and Watanabe 1977: 58–65.)

Shimosueyoshi Terrace itself probably dates about 200,000 B.P. (Serizawa 1974).

The Musashino Stage is attested by gravels laid down along the course of the Tama River, and by the Musashino Loam, a volcanic ash that fell immediately after the gravels were deposited. The gravels, which form the Musashino upland or the so-called Musashino Terrace, directly overlie Shimosueyoshi sediments at certain localities, and elsewhere fill valleys that had been eroded into the Shimosueyoshi Formation. The Musashino Loam is a brown volcanic ash, from 3 to 4 m thick, which fell throughout the southern Tokyo region. Its lower portion contains a distinctive orange bed about 10 cm thick termed the Tokyo Pumice. This pumice, believed to be ejecta from the central group of volcanoes at Hakone, is an important time-stratigraphic marker horizon for which a fission-track date of about 49,000 B.P. has been obtained. In the northern part of the Tokyo region, another comparable marker bed, the Hassaki Pumice from the Akagi volcanoes, has been ^{14}C dated to about 40,000 B.P. (Serizawa 1974).

The Tachikawa Stage brings the Late Pleistocene to a close. It is represented by the Tachikawa Gravels, which form a terrace along the Tama River stratigraphically postdating the Musashino Gravels, and by the air-deposited Tachikawa Loam, which lies conformably upon the Tachikawa Gravels. The Tachikawa Loam, which occurs widely throughout the southern Tokyo region, is a deeper brown than the Musashino Loam, and is believed to have been ejected by the Paleo-Fuji volcanoes.

One fix on its approximate age is established by a ^{14}C date of 24,000 B.P. for volcanic mudflows in the region of Mount Fuji. These mudflows are believed to be related to the volcanic activity that produced the Tachikawa Loam. The lower strata of the Egota peat bed, which are embedded within the Tachikawa Loam, have produced ^{14}C dates ranging from 29,000 B.P. to 11,000–12,000 B.P., which provide a reasonable estimate of the time spanned by the loam deposits.

In the Tokyo area the Tachikawa Loam usually varies between 2 and 4 m in thickness, and is subdivided by buried soils that formed during intervals between major ash falls. These soils are indicated by black bands of carbonaceous and nitrogenous earth, of which three are known to occur widely. The lowermost band is ^{14}C dated between roughly 24,000 and 26,000 B.P., the middle one between about 16,000 and 17,000 B.P., and the uppermost one at approximately 13,000 or 14,000 B.P. (Watanabe 1977). Many archaeological sites have been found within the Tachikawa Loam and its local time-stratigraphic equivalents elsewhere in Japan, and this association, including the stratigraphic position of sites relative to the buried soils, has been crucial in establishing their approximate ages.

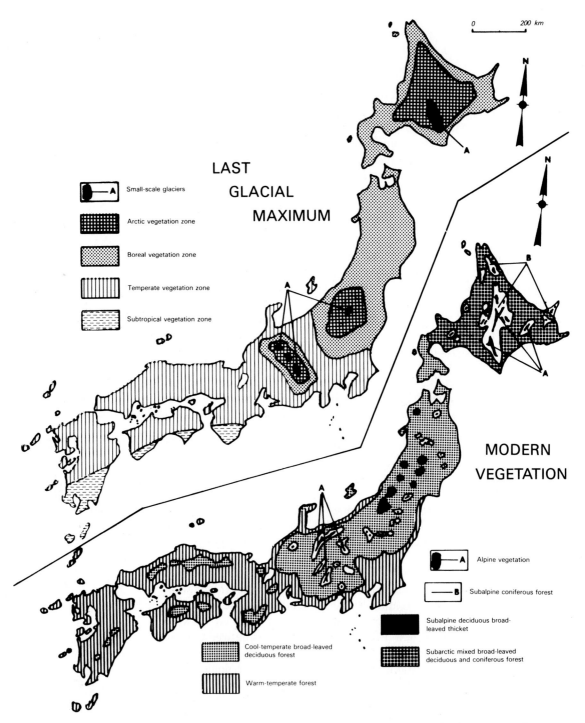

0   200 km

LAST
GLACIAL
MAXIMUM

- Small-scale glaciers ◼──A
- Arctic vegetation zone
- Boreal vegetation zone
- Temperate vegetation zone
- Subtropical vegetation zone

MODERN
VEGETATION

- Alpine vegetation ◼──A
- Subalpine coniferous forest ☐──B
- Subalpine deciduous broad-leaved thicket
- Subarctic mixed broad-leaved deciduous and coniferous forest
- Cool-temperate broad-leaved deciduous forest
- Warm-temperate forest

Figure 2.3 Vegetation patterns in the Japanese islands during the last glacial maximum, and in recent times. (After Kotani 1969: Figure 4 and Yoshioka 1974.)

32

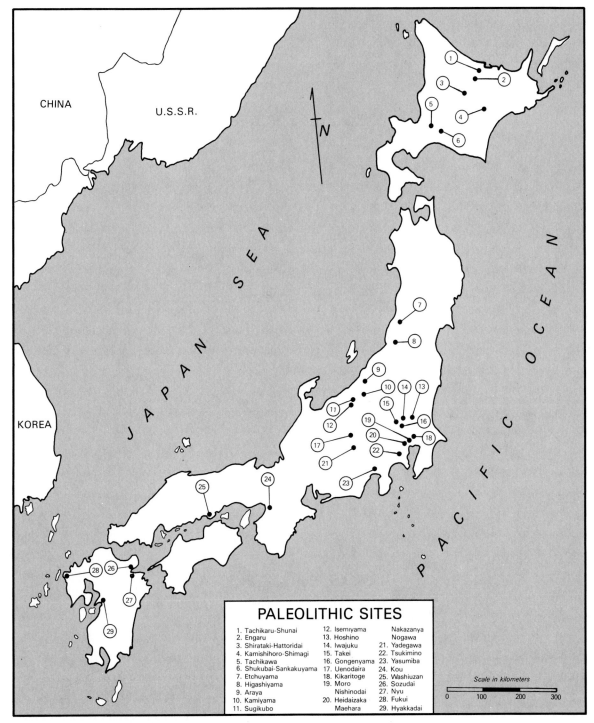

PALEOLITHIC SITES

1. Tachikaru-Shunai
2. Engaru
3. Shirataki-Hattoridai
4. Kamishihoro-Shimagi
5. Tachikawa
6. Shukubai-Sankakuyama
7. Etchuyama
8. Higashiyama
9. Araya
10. Kamiyama
11. Sugikubo
12. Isemiyama
13. Hoshino
14. Iwajuku
15. Takei
16. Gongenyama
17. Uenodaira
18. Kikaritoge
19. Moro
    Nishinodai
20. Heidaizaka
    Maehara
    Nakazanya
    Nogawa
21. Yadegawa
22. Tsukimino
23. Yasumiba
24. Kou
25. Washiuzan
26. Sozudai
27. Nyu
28. Fukui
29. Hyakkadai

Scale in kilometers

0   100   200   300

Figure 2.4 Locations of major Paleolithic sites in Japan. Named sites are those mentioned in text.
(Based on Serizawa 1974: 171.)

33

The Pleistocene epoch, which saw the emergence and submergence of land bridges, and the great volcanic ash falls just referred to, also witnessed episodes of glaciation in the mountains of Japan. Well over 100 glacial cirques are recorded from the summit regions of high mountains in central Honshu and Hokkaido, but these mountain glaciers seem always to have been restricted to the higher elevations. Two and sometimes three sets of terminal moraines in local areas indicate the expansion and contraction of these glaciers during the Pleistocene, but correlations with the continental glaciations of Eurasia and North America are not clearly established.

The islands of Japan lie between 24 and 45 degrees north latitude, spanning a north–south distance of over 1500 km. During the Pleistocene, as now, the country supported distinct northern and southern vegetation communities, and long-term climatic fluctuations caused periodic shifting of the boundary zone between the subtropical southern broad-leaved evergreen forest and the northern hardwood–conifer forest. The altitudinal distribution of species was affected as well.

The Pliocene–Pleistocene temporal boundary is marked in the Osaka region by deposits containing *Liquidambar, Metasequoia,* and other warmth-loving trees now established in Taiwan and southern China. A warm-climate flora with some of the same elements is also known as far north as Sendai, in northeastern Honshu. Subsequent to this stage, a cold Early Pleistocene flora of *Pinus, Larix, Abies, Picea,* and other arboreal species appears at Osaka. Such a floral assemblage now appears only above 1500 m elevation, implying a temperature at that time on the order of 7°C below the present average for the region, if the normal lapse rate of .5°C per 100 m is applied. It is not clear whether this episode is to be dated to the Günz or the Mindel glacial phase in the worldwide chronology. A subsequent interglacial period assemblage of probable early Middle Pleistocene age shows a marked warming of climate, attested by *Syzygium* and *Cinnamonium,* now growing in Kyushu some 500 km south of the fossil locality. Broad-leaved evergreen trees of warm-temperate character dominated this flora, as they dominate the modern flora of the region. Later climatic and environmental stages are not yet well documented in the Osaka region, but data are available from other regions to carry the sequence forward to the end of the Pleistocene.

The later Middle Pleistocene flora of the Tokyo area is characterized at first by cool-temperate species, and subsequently by such subarctic trees as *Picea, Pinus,* and *Abies.* The Late Pleistocene record, established from finds in the Shimosueyoshi Formation and other deposits, indicates that during the last interglacial the region around and north of Tokyo was once again forested by cool-temperate or temperate trees, including *Alnus* and *Cryptomeria,* which imply conditions very like those of the present. South of Tokyo, warm-temperate broad-leaved evergreen forest prevailed, as it does at present.

During the final glaciation of the Late Pleistocene, the record of the Egota peat bed from the Tachikawa Loam indicates the presence of subarctic forest in the Tokyo region, including *Picea, Larix,* and *Scabiosa* as cold-climate indicators. At this time the boundary zone between the northern and southern forest associations, which now lies across central Honshu between Tokyo and Kyoto, would have been displaced much farther south, and the climate of Hokkaido would have had a decidedly subarctic to arctic character (Figure 2.3).

The first people of Japan entered and occupied it at some time during the geological interval just sketched. In the following pages, evidence from a carefully selected series of the most important and informative Paleolithic sites is reviewed, with the aim of summarizing what is known, and identifying questions that remain to be answered, about this initial period of human occupation (Figure 2.4). Since the earliest firmly established evidence of human presence in the Far East—the finds at Choukoutien, China—dates to Middle Pleistocene times, it seems likely that Japan was first occupied after the beginning of that period. And in fact the oldest finds claimed as indicators of human activity in Japan probably belong to the Middle Pleistocene. These are from the site of Sozudai.

Sozudai

The Sozudai site is near the landward end of the Kunisaki Penin-sula, in extreme northeastern Kyushu. It lies on an ancient marine terrace 35 m above the modern level of Japan's Inland Sea, overlook-ing Beppu Bay to the east and south. Less than 2 km away is the mouth of the Kanaidagawa River, adjacent to which is a small modern set-tlement named Hiji-machi.

The site occupies the top and eastern slope of a low knoll, on high ground but only several hundred meters from the sea. A large village site of the Initial Jomon period occurs on the knoll, and it was the remains of this settlement that first attracted archaeologists to Sozudai. In all, excavations have been made at a dozen different localities during a series of field investigations. Trench P, excavated by C. Serizawa, yielded several hundred specimens, which have been described and illustrated in detail in the monograph on which this summary is largely based (Serizawa 1965, 1974).

Trench P was a rectangular excavation 3 × 4 m across and approx-imately 1 m deep. Seven natural strata were recognized; the specimens of archaeological interest came from the fifth layer beneath the sur-

Figure 2.5 Flaked stone specimens from Sozudai, Oita Prefecture, Kyushu, *ca.* 400,000 B.P. Length of specimen at upper left, 10.7 cm. (Shown approximately one-half actual size.) (Courtesy C. Serizawa, Tohoku University.)

face, a bed of andesite gravels. The Jomon period artifacts from the same site occurred only in the topmost layers, separated from the andesite gravel stratum by an intermittent but sterile layer of dark brown volcanic ash up to 15 cm thick, and an unbroken layer of yellowish clay 10–15 cm thick, which graded into the underlying andesite gravel stratum. The stratigraphic situation is clear, and there is no question about any intrusion of later artifacts into the earlier layers.

The bed containing the archaeological specimens was 10–15 cm thick, made up of small and large chunks of soft, weathered andesite. Interspersed among these chunks were angular pieces of quartz rhyolite and vein quartz, all of which were retained for study. Some 225 specimens were mapped in situ, and in all 279 pieces were identified as objects of human workmanship. Another 150 or so items from the collection were not identified as artifacts. No cultural features such as pits, evidence of fire, or conspicuous patterning in the distribution of the archaeological specimens were reported.

The marine terrace on which Sozudai is situated was formed during a high sea level stage of the Pleistocene epoch (Nakagawa 1965). A geological assessment of the site stratigraphy and local geomorphology suggested that the stratum of archaeological interest was probably laid down as the sea level dropped from this high stand. The terrace may mark the same period of high sea level that caused the Shimosueyoshi Transgression in the Tokyo Bay area, and if this interpretation is correct, the andesite gravel bed of archaeological interest was probably laid down about 200,000 B.P.

The investigators also introduce, however, the possibility that the Sozudai deposits were formed late in the preceding Mindel–Riss Interglacial period. They stress that the geological evidence is sufficiently uncertain as to leave the date of the terrace an open question. A Mindel–Riss Interglacial assignment would imply a date of roughly 400,000 B.P. for the Sozudai site, putting it in the same time range as the famed Paleolithic site of Choukoutien, in northern China. Whichever interpretation is accepted, the Sozudai locality is one of the oldest that has been put forward as giving evidence of Paleolithic culture in Japan.

Types defined for the Sozudai collection include split pebbles, flakes, cores, choppers, chopping tools, points, picks, and proto-handaxes. The quartzite of which the objects consist is extemely hard and brittle and full of flaws; the specimens themselves are irregular and varied in form. Flake scars, striking platforms, bulbs of percussion, marginal retouch, and other characteristics exhibited by flaked stone items of known human make are either unrecognizable or identified only with uncertainty on the Sozudai specimens (Figure 2.5). Sozudai is compared to Choukoutien, where many of the flaked stone specimens were also made of quartzite, and similarly lacked such distinguishing features. It is true, however, that at Choukoutien there were also many flaked stone artifacts that did exhibit those characteristics, as well as other evidence such as human bones, hearths, and split and broken bones of animals butchered for food, all of which were lacking at Sozudai.

In short, the case for human occupation at Sozudai rests solely on the lithic specimens themselves, and many archaeologists have expressed doubt that they are artifacts at all. It has been suggested that they are merely naturally fractured stones, shaped and deposited by normal geological processes, although the geological processes that might have been involved have not been convincingly detailed.

In an attempt to resolve the question of the Sozudai specimens' proper identity, Bleed (1977) subjected a series of flakes from the site to a test long ago devised by A. S. Barnes to resolve the question of whether certain artifact-like flaked stones of extreme geological antiquity from Europe (dubbed *eoliths*, or "dawn stones"), were or were not of human make. Barnes established, through hundreds of measurements on specimens of known origin, that stones flaked by natural geological processes commonly had obtuse edges, with flaked edge-angles exceeding 90°. Flaked stones of human manufacture, by contrast, were usually sharper, with acute edge-angles of less than 90°. Bleed measured the edge-angles on a series of flakes from Sozudai, and found them clearly within the range for human artifacts, as established by Barnes.

In a separate test, a sample of 18 flaked stone specimens of various origins was shown to 27 Japanese and American archaeologists who claimed to be familiar with flake characteristics. Five specimens from Sozudai, believed by Bleed to be man-made, were present in this sample. The archaeologists' independent judgments were evaluated statistically, and Bleed interpreted the results as supporting his view that the Sozudai flakes were true artifacts. On the basis of these tests, he concluded that the Sozudai assemblage was clearly of human rather than natural origin.

There are, however, problems with both aspects of this analysis that cast fatal doubts on its validity. The flaked stone specimens selected for measurement of their edge-angles comprised only a small percentage of the items collected from the site, and they were selected expressly because they seemed to Bleed and his collaborators to exhibit the characteristics of man-made flakes. It is possible to pick out of any large collection of crushed and shattered stones some that resemble human artifacts, and it is hardly surprising that measurement of pieces selected for study precisely because they looked like man-made flakes showed them to have edge-angles within the range of human artifacts. The human eye, no less than a pair of calipers, can tell blunt-edged stones from sharp-edged ones. Given the process by which Bleed selected his analytical sample, statistical confirmation of the hypothesis that the flakes were man-made was automatic. No other conclusion was possible, because of the structure of the experiment.

The second test is equally problematical. The specimens measured were originally selected because they seemed to Bleed and his collaborators to exhibit such characteristics of known human artifacts as a striking platform, a point of percussion, and dorsal and ventral surfaces. The statistical tests that compared Bleed's identifications with those made by other archaeologists were said to support his judgments about these matters, yet it is a striking fact that of the 27 archaeologists queried, only 2 identified all five of the specimens from Sozudai as man-made! Unless additional evidence is forthcoming, it seems unlikely that the Sozudai site will be generally accepted as evidence of early human occupation in Japan.

At the site of Nyu, south of Beppu Bay in northeastern Kyushu, and not far from Sozudai, a diverse congeries of flaked stones and some pottery of Jomon and Yayoi types were recovered from a number of different locations. From the artifacts found were defined a chopper culture, a cleaver culture, a flake culture, a blade culture, a point culture, and a microblade culture. The site is believed by its excavators to span a period from Middle Pleistocene to post-Pleistocene times (Zaidan Hojin Kodaigaku Kyokai 1963).   *Nyu*

A geological investigation undertaken to establish the chronology of the site showed that the local deposits were a complex mixture of erosional materials of different ages, which had accumulated over an extremely long period, from Middle Pleistocene to very recent times. This made it impossible to establish a clear geological sequence for the artifacts, and the cultural units described represent not sets of specimens found together in discrete geological units, but simply groups of typologically similar specimens found at many different locations. Since many of the objects, such as choppers, cleavers, and flakes, are of types that, though crude, were made even in Jomon and later times, there is no assurance that the site of Nyu was actually occupied during Paleolithic times, though it remains of course a possibility.

The Hoshino site is on the outskirts of the city of Tochigi, north of Tokyo near the eastern edge of the Kanto Plain (Serizawa 1968). The most important of the several archaeological localities that comprise the site lies at the upper edge of flat agricultural lands at the mouth of a small valley tributary to the Nagano River. Wooded hills rise immediately behind the spot. Pottery of the earlier stages of the Jomon tradition, dating between approximately 4000 and 8000 years ago, occurs in the uppermost soils of some parts of the site. Purely lithic remains, of interest here, lie beneath, to a depth of at least 9 m at Locality 3.   *Hoshino*

The site deposits are made up of volcanic ash layers that have been tentatively correlated with the main Kanto Loam sequence of the Tokyo area. Cultural Stratum 1, which antedated the superficial Jomon deposits and yielded a single well-made stemmed projectile point of the Yuzetsu type, occurs in a volcanic ash layer that has been correlated with the Tachikawa Loam of about 10,000 to 30,000 B.P. Stratum 2 belongs to a local correlative of the Musashino Loam of about 35,000 to 50,000 B.P. Cultural Stratum 3, from which the bulk of the lithic specimens came, as well as lower levels also containing a few specimens, is assigned to a local cognate of the Shimosueyoshi Loam of about 65,000 to 130,000 B.P.

Specimens were collected from Cultural Stratum 3 by four major trenches excavated in Locality 3 of the site. Most of the remains came from 1–2 m below the surface. All lithic materials from the excavations were returned to the laboratory for cleaning and examination. From about 40 cartons of specimens, approximately 2100 items were selected and classified as various types of artifacts. All were made on rolled and battered pieces of quartzite, similar if not identical to the rock of a natural outcrop in the site vicinity.

Most abundant were blocky flakes and cores, each class represented by over 700 objects. Pointed tools, choppers, chopping tools, amorphous tools, pebble points, and hammerstones were less numerous but still common. Specimens identified as picks and proto-handaxes also occurred. The objects were crudely shaped, and did not commonly exhibit bulbs of percussion and concentric rings of force on their flaked surfaces, as is normally the case with chipped stone artifacts. Instead, pieces of stone frequently showed a dendritic series of converging hairline fissures, rather like the pattern formed by many small watercourses flowing into a main channel from both sides. The "downstream" end of this convergent series of flowing lines was taken to be the point of percussion struck in flaking the specimens.

The excavator compares the Hoshino specimens to those from Sozudai and to those from the Middle Pleistocene site of Choukoutien, China. He believes that Hoshino is of the same tradition, and that its choppers and pointed tools suggest a date corresponding to that of the upper levels of Choukoutien. This is congruent with the geological dating of Hoshino, and places it somewhat later in time than Sozudai. These two Japanese sites taken together establish, in the opinion of Serizawa, the excavator, a Paleolithic cultural sequence for Japan that is of comparable age to that known from north China. A time span from about 400,000 to 35,000 B.P. is indicated. The Yuzetsu-type projectile point and Jomon pottery from the Hoshino site indicate that later occupations also occurred there, but they are not continuously linked with the earlier Paleolithic period (Serizawa 1968, 1974).

Hoshino, like Sozudai, has been viewed with skepticism, and subjected to essentially the same criticisms. Although there is no serious dispute about the age of the deposits from which the lithic materials came, the crudity of the specimens and the fact that they do not show the usual hallmarks associated with human lithic technology are urged as cogent reasons for withholding acceptance of Hoshino as an early Paleolithic site.

The site of Gongenyama, only a few kilometers west of Hoshino, *Gongenyama* illustrates an archaeological problem of a different kind than that just described. This site was discovered during earth-moving operations for a housing project, which partially cut away the base of a hill called Gongenyama, exposing flaked stone specimens in three different localities. No ceramics were associated with the stone remains and the three assemblages have been interpreted as representing three consecutive stages of the Paleolithic period.

Of principal interest are three large flaked stone tools said to correspond very closely in typology and technique of manufacture to the handaxes of Late Acheulian type known from the European Paleolithic. The finest specimen is pear shaped, with broad, flat flake scars over both surfaces and secondary flaking near its point. Although the overall flaking is not as extensive or refined as that on some Late Acheulian handaxes, the artifact closely resembles that type. A second specimen, somewhat smaller, is roughly ovate, and bifacially flaked around its edges; the third specimen is more slender, and only crudely flaked. The last two specimens do not so strongly evoke the Acheulian form, and might better be referred to simply as large, roughly flaked bifaces. In addition to these specimens there are a number of rather large, broad flakes, some of which are said to exhibit Levallois-like flaking characteristics. Several, reworked along one edge, are identified as Mousterian-like scrapers. The handaxes and flakes are all from the same locality, and are believed to comprise the earliest assemblage from Gongenyama (Maringer 1956b).

From a second locality came a fist-sized pebble, roughly shaped by the removal of a few large, thick flakes; this exhibited secondary flaking, perhaps from use, along one edge. Another pebble had been bifacially thinned by the removal of large, flat flakes from both surfaces, to form a roughly ovate chopper with steep, blunt edges. Additional tools were rather broad flakes, some unifacially retouched along the sides or ends, apparently to serve as scrapers (Maringer

1956a). The third locality produced a small assemblage of unifacially flaked pebble choppers and flakes. These specimens were relatively small. Several of the flakes were elongate and parallel-sided, apparently lamellar blades (Maringer 1957).

The identification of this series of specimens as true artifacts is not open to serious question, inasmuch as they commonly exhibit well-defined flake scars, bulbs of percussion, fissures, and other characteristics of human lithic technology. The first two assemblages have been compared with the Patjitanian Paleolithic industry of Java, which is said to contain some handaxe-like artifacts as well as simple choppers and flake tools. The third assemblage has been likened to the post-Paleolithic Hoabinhian culture of Southeast Asia; the uniface choppers from Gongenyama are said to closely resemble the Hoabinhian type.

The dating of the artifacts from Gongenyama is not, however, clearly established. The relics were collected at the time of earth-moving operations, and only several years later were the circumstances of their discovery described; the local stratigraphy was recorded from an exposure left by the earth-moving operations. The assemblage that included the handaxes came, it was recollected, from the base of the fifth stratum beneath the surface, a brown loam bed. The pebble choppers were attributed to the upper part of the same bed. Above the brown loam was a sterile stratum of volcanic mud, and over this lay a hard loam bed, from which the Hoabinhian-like assemblage is said to have come. No artifacts were reported from the overlying soft loam and surficial humus bed that completed the stratigraphic series.

This series of volcanic beds is said to correspond to the stratigraphic series established at the site of Iwajuku a few kilometers away, which has in turn been related to the overall Kanto Loam sequence. On this basis, the basal brown loam bed at Gongenyama is thought to be equivalent in age to the Musashino Loam of the Tokyo region, and the overlying strata are roughly correlated with the Tachikawa Loam. Given the dates now assigned to the Kanto Loam series, this correlation implies a date of around 35,000 to 50,000 B.P. for the handaxe assemblage from Gongenyama, and one tens of thousands of years later for the Hoabinhian-like assemblage. The circumstances under which the artifacts were found, however, make a secure conclusion impossible, and the age of the Gongenyama site remains highly speculative.

Iwajuku　　Stone Age remains found at Iwajuku in 1949 comprised the first conclusive evidence of a pre-pottery or Paleolithic culture in Japan. Located in the countryside near Iwajuku railway station, on the edge of the Kanto Plain about 90 km north of Tokyo, the archaeological locality occupies the western slopes of a low saddle between two small hills, and immediately below it is a small swamp a few hectares in extent (Sugihara 1956).

Artifacts had been picked up along an erosion scar on the hillside, and excavations there produced additional specimens in undisturbed geological context within sediments of the Kanto Loam series. This was the first time that unquestionably human artifacts were conclusively demonstrated to occur within the Pleistocene Kanto Loam, and it was an epochal discovery for Japanese prehistory. The discoveries at Iwajuku put Paleolithic research in Japan on a sound footing, and stimulated a great deal of additional research, which has since greatly advanced understanding of the country's early prehistory (Sugihara 1974).

Excavations were conducted at three localities, and four stratigraphic units were recognized. Uppermost was a superficial humus layer, about 50 cm thick. Below the humus was the Azami bed, 1 m thick, which lay conformably on the Iwajuku bed. The Iwajuku bed, about 40 cm thick, in turn graded conformably into the Kompirayama bed, which was about 1 m thick. Beneath this, separated by an erosional unconformity, lay the Inariyama bed of gray pumice, extending to an unknown depth. The Paleolithic artifacts all came from the Azami and Iwajuku beds of Locality A, which roughly correlate with the two middle subdivisions of the Tachikawa Loam. Locality B yielded only a single piece of agate, and Locality C yielded Jomon pottery and other remains, which were confined to the uppermost humus layer.

At the time of excavation, it was clear that the artifacts from Locality A were ancient, and of preceramic age, but it was not possible to supply an absolute date for them in terms of years. Now however, flourishing archaeological and geological research makes it possible to suggest that the artifacts from the Iwajuku bed (Iwajuku I) are probably a bit less than 20,000 years old, and those from the Azami bed (Iwajuku II) about 15,000 years old. A small collection of primarily surface finds (Iwajuku III) is tentatively dated, on the basis of obsidian hydration dating of the specimens themselves, to 14,000 B.P. (Oda and Keally 1975: Chart 2).

The Iwajuku I assemblage consisted of two so-called handaxes, two scrapers, two cores, and a number of flakes and chips (Figure 2.6). The handaxes were flattened tabular ovates of shale, step-flaked around their edges, and rather smooth, as if from much handling and use. Although their size and shape suggest that they may have been used as handaxes, they are clearly not of the same technological tradition as

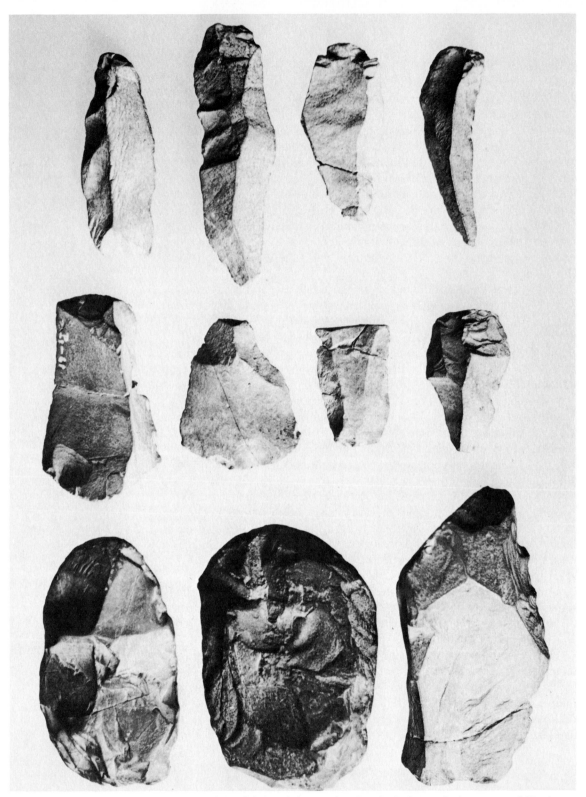

Figure 2.6 Blades, flakes, and choppers from Iwajuku I, Gumma Prefecture, central Honshu, ca. 20,000 B.P. Length of specimen at upper left, 7.8 cm. (Courtesy S. Sugihara, Meiji University.)

the well-known handaxes of Acheulian tradition known from the Paleolithic of Europe and Africa, and they do not closely resemble the specimens from Gongenyama.

The scrapers were made on rather broad, elongate end-blow flakes, which exhibit clearly defined striking platforms, fissures, rings of force, and edge retouch. The flakes and chips show similar characteristics, and there is no doubt that they are objects of human manufacture. Some elongate end-blow flakes with relatively parallel sides and keeled backs clearly resemble the lamellar blades of the Eurasian Upper Paleolithic, though the nondescript cores from Iwajuku do not correspond to the carefully prepared blade cores known from Europe and elsewhere. Because they do not quite attain the ideal form, the specimens are considered to be bladelike flakes, rather than true blades.

The Iwajuku II collection consisted of a few small flake scrapers with side or end retouch; a number of small, irregular cores; and a considerable number of elongate bladelike flakes, mostly rather small and squat. Thick, pointed side-blow flakes were made into knives of a distinctive type by the application of steep unifacial retouch along both edges of the flake. These are referred to as Kiridashi knives (Figure 2.7).

The assemblage designated Iwajuku III included a handful of tiny, slender, parallel-sided microblades, and a beautifully made medium-sized bipoint nicely flaked on both sides. Two of the tiny blades were retouched as scrapers. Agate, obsidian, shale, and andesite were all used to make artifacts at Iwajuku, shale being most common in the earliest period, and agate dominating after that.

The cultural sequence for later Paleolithic times that was adumbrated at Iwajuku has subsequently been much enriched, as will be seen, but its essential outlines stand today as indicative of the course of Japanese cultural development in terminal Pleistocene times. As first shown at Iwajuku, throughout Japan an early culture producing large, bladelike flakes gave way to one producing smaller blades and bladelike flakes, and finally to one producing microblades. Well-made bifacially flaked points appeared at about the same time as the microblades, and both technologies continued into the time of the earliest pottery, when the Jomon tradition was born.

Later excavations at the site, in the deposits beneath the Iwajuku I cultural layer, have produced crude lithic specimens said to include choppers, chopping tools, scrapers, handaxes, cores, and the like, whose age has been estimated at over 50,000 years (Serizawa 1974:109–110). The assemblage is much like those of Sozudai and Hoshino, and it has been accorded the same skeptical reception by

Figure 2.7 Knives from Iwajuku II, Gumma Prefecture, central Honshu, ca. 15,000 B.P. Top, Kiridashi knives; bottom, unnamed type. Length of specimen at upper left, 3 cm. (Shown approximately one and one-half times actual size.) (Courtesy S. Sugihara, Meiji University.)

most Japanese archaeologists. If such specimens are eventually accepted as actual human artifacts, Iwajuku will assume all the more importance as a pivotal site in the annals of Japanese archaeology.

Nogawa   The Nogawa site, in the western suburbs of Tokyo, is on a low bluff overlooking the small stream that gives the archaeological locality its name (Kidder *et al.* 1970; T. Kobayashi *et al.* 1971). The site lies on the Tachikawa Terrace near the base of the Kokubunji cliffs, which rise abruptly to the geologically older Musashino Terrace above. A series of 13 major and minor geological strata were recognized within the Tachikawa Loam and recent humus deposits, which together extended to a depth of about 5 m at the site locality. Over 2000 flaked stone artifacts, and over 7000 fire-reddened stones believed related to cooking, were recovered from a large excavation 30 × 50 m across. The fineness and clarity of its geological stratification, as well as the quantity of its cultural remains, make the Nogawa locality one of the most important Paleolithic sites in Japan.

Eleven cultural levels were distinguished, corresponding to natural divisions within the upper 3 m or so of deposit. The superficial humus layers contained pottery of types extending back in time from the Yayoi period to incipient Jomon, and 10 preceramic levels lay below. After analysis of the artifact types, assemblages seen to be closely related were grouped, resulting in the recognition of three Paleolithic phases at the Nogawa site. The cultural complexes represented are broadly equivalent to those known from Iwajuku, but the more abundant evidence from Nogawa provides a much more detailed record than was available from the Iwajuku site (Figure 2.8).

The relatively meager assemblage of the earliest phase (Strata VIII–V) was dominated by pebble tools and scrapers, with gravers also important. The scrapers and gravers were based on short, broad, bladelike flakes with their tips snapped off. Many such flakes were also apparently put to use as knives, with only minimal retouching. Well-made large, parallel-sided blades also occurred, though they were not common. A few pounding and grinding stones and nondescript cores completed the assemblage.

The middle phase (Strata IV4–IV1) was characterized in particular by cutting tools or knives based on well-made medium-sized blades that were "backed" or blunted along one edge. Common throughout the phase, they were most numerous in its later half. Trapezoidal knives, also highly characteristic of the phase, were made by blunting all but one edge of a thick side-blow flake. These specimens, which are rather like the Kiridashi knives from Iwajuku II, were few in the early part of the phase, but became increasingly abundant later. Small, unifacially flaked points made on blades appeared in about the middle of the phase and increased rapidly toward its end, at which time bifacially flaked points first appeared. Scrapers, gravers, and drills, all made on blades that tended to be pointed at either end, occurred throughout the phase. Prepared blade cores made on truncated pebbles, a few rough pebble choppers, and hundreds of flakes, chips, and core fragments had a similar stratigraphic distribution. Grinding stones were relatively rare, but at least one was found in each level assigned to the phase, with a considerable number present in the earliest layer.

Microlithic tools like those of the Iwajuku III assemblage, now widely known from Late Paleolithic sites throughout Japan, did not occur at the Nogawa site. It is clear from this that a major hiatus in occupation of this particular locus separated its final preceramic phase from the one just described.

The final preceramic occupation at the site (Stratum III) was represented by few artifacts, mostly flakes, chips, and cores. A single well-made bifacially flaked leaf-shaped bipoint and a few large, coarse pebble choppers were the most distinctive specimens. Above this level occurred remains of earliest Jomon times, to which the investigators consider this final phase closely related.

In each layer of the site the artifacts were found in clusters, usually between 4 and 7 m across. Several kinds of clusters were identified.

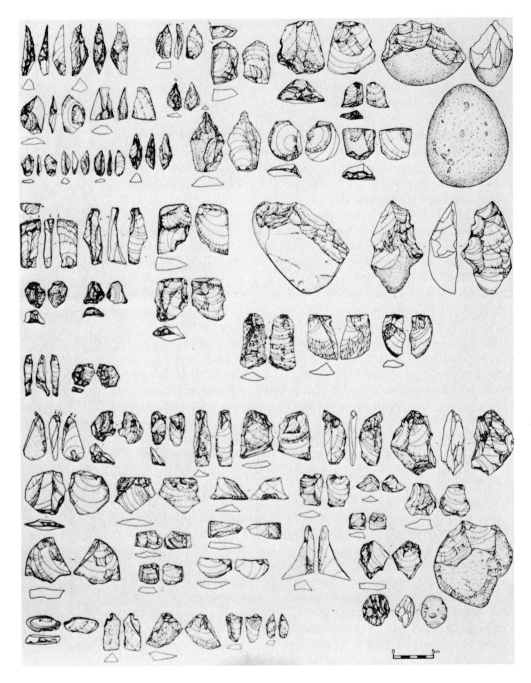

Figure 2.8 Stratigraphic sequence of flaked stone artifacts at the Nogawa site, Tokyo, ca. 20,000–10,000 B.P. Earliest, lower left; latest, upper right. (From T. Kobayashi *et al.* 1971: Figure 4.)

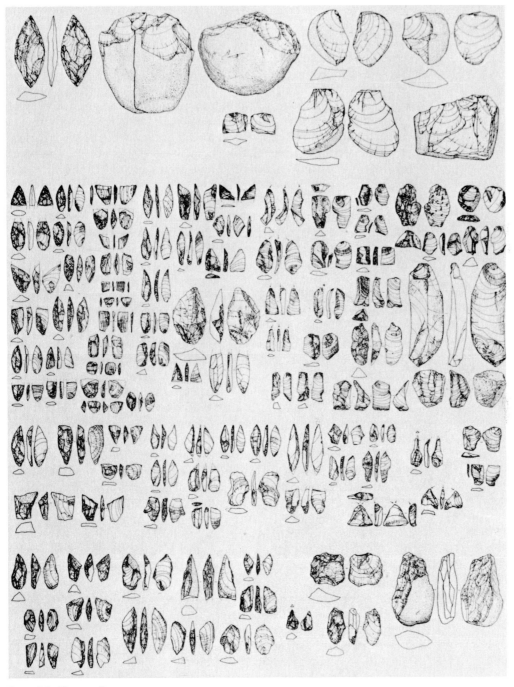

Figure 2.8 (*Continued*)

The simplest ones contained only a few types of tools, or a few tools and a few flakes. These are believed to represent the loci of certain undefined but relatively simple activities. Other clusters were characterized by a few cores and flakes or by tools of relatively few different types, associated with abundant flakes and cores. These spots are believed to have been workshops where tools were made. Clusters consisting predominantly of grinding, pounding, and anvil stones are believed to represent food-processing activities. Finally, there occurred a number of clusters characterized primarily by the great variety of artifacts they contained, which included essentially all the types present in the simpler groups. These were apparently the foci of a range of domestic activities.

Many small scatters of blackened and reddened gravel also occurred at the site, predominantly along its western and southwestern edges, away from the major artifact clusters. In some cases no artifacts at all were associated with these gravel scatters; in others, pounding, grinding, and anvil stones were found nearby. Experimental measurements using an x-ray diffractometer showed that these gravels had been heated to over 600°C, and it seems unquestionable that they are the remnants of ancient hearths.

The detailed mapping of broad horizontal exposures in this way is a promising new emphasis in Japanese Paleolithic research. Other sites in the vicinity of Nogawa, such as Nakazanya, Nishinodai, Heidaizaka, and Maehara, have been subjected to this treatment, and the approach is being applied elsewhere as well. As a corpus of comparative data from many sites is built up, new insights into the patterning of human activities in Japanese Paleolithic sites may be expected to emerge.

The stratigraphic distribution and frequency of clusters of these different kinds suggest that during its earliest phase of occupation the Nogawa site served only as an occasional stopping-place or temporary work area. But during the second phase it evidently became more intensively occupied, consisting then of a central habitation zone flanked by small workshop areas. For several thousand years following the end of this phase, there is no record of occupation, and when the record resumes in late preceramic times, rather ephemeral use is again indicated.

Dates for the cultural sequence have been established by the obsidian hydration method. A date of 18,500 B.P. for the concluding part of the earliest phase, and dates of 18,200, 17,600, 15,100, 14,700, and 14,000 B.P. for the several layers comprising the middle phase, place these occupations firmly in time. The final preceramic occupation is dated by the same method to 9500 B.P., which is barely earlier than the time of the ^{14}C dated Initial Jomon pottery from Natsushima Shell Mound, south of Tokyo (Oda and Keally 1975: Chart 2).

The obsidian most common in the early levels at Nogawa was transported from a source near Mount Hakone, some 80 km southwest of Tokyo. During the middle phase, the most common obsidian was from the Shinshu region in mountainous central Japan near Lake Suwa, about 150 km northwest of Tokyo. Thereafter, Hakone obsidian again dominated. These identifications were established by statistically comparing the uranium content and the density of fission tracks in a series of obsidian samples from Nogawa with similarly obtained values established for obsidians from known outcrops at these places.

Nakazanya

The Nakazanya, Nishinodai, and Heidaizaka sites, a few kilometers from the Nogawa site along the bluffs overlooking the same streamcourse, extend the archaeological record of that vicinity back significantly in time. Detailed reports on the Nishinodai and Heidaizaka excavations are not yet available, but Nakazanya is fully published (Kidder and Oda 1975). The Nakazanya X component, lowermost at that site, yielded over 600 flakes, mostly of chert and agate, a few nondescript cores, a few knives and drills made on broad, short flakes, and a large, heavy scraper. The later preceramic assemblages from Nakazanya were meager, though they did document repeated use of the site over thousands of years, establishing a record that in part parallels that known from the Nogawa site.

Nakazanya X lies stratigraphically below the second black band of the regionally established Tachikawa Loam sequence (the second black band attested at Nakazanya itself), and just above the stratigraphic break between the Tachikawa and Musashino loam beds. A series of five ^{14}C dates for this same black band, established at the Seijo locality, Tokyo, ranges between about 21,500 and 25,000 B.P. A linear regression curve, calculated on the basis of obsidian hydration dates from Nakazanya and other nearby sites, and the cross-checking Tachikawa Loam stratigraphies of these sites suggest that Nakazanya X (upper) probably dates about 28,000 B.P. This is congruent with the stratigraphic position of the assemblage, and the fact that both lines of evidence roughly agree lends credence to the age estimate.

The earliest assemblages from Nakazanya, Nishinodai, and Heidaizaka indicate that the people occupying the Tokyo region during the earlier part of the Tachikawa Stage were not yet practitioners of the elongate flake or blade tool technology recognized from Iwajuku, Nogawa, and many other sites. They instead made their tools on rather short, broad flakes, and on pebbles modified by the removal of only a few chips to produce a sharp cutting or scraping edge (Oda and Keally 1975). This is a very important fact, the implications of which will be returned to in the final pages of this chapter.

Kou   The Kou site, within the city of Osaka in south-central Honshu, was apparently occupied from the Paleolithic into Jomon and later times. The site consists of a number of localities, and has had a long history of excavation, spanning decades. The data are scattered in many sources, making it difficult to compose an overall account of the site, but certain aspects of its Paleolithic assemblage are well known and much discussed (Kamaki 1974).

From a buried but undated context came a number of retouched knives made on elongate flakes that were different from the retouched end-blow blade tools of the Tokyo region. These so-called Kou knives were made on side-blow flakes struck from a uniquely prepared core. The method by which such cores were made has come to be called the Setouchi technique, from its broad distribution around the coasts of the Inland Sea (Setonaikai) of southern Japan. It is believed to be an adaptation to the working of sanukite, a tough, hard volcanic stone common in that region.

A Setouchi core was made by striking off a large chunk from the end of a sanukite pebble, then preparing a striking platform along one edge of this chunk by removing several thick flakes (Figure 2.9). Successive blows at the center of this platform would detach a series of uniform elongate flakes, trapezoidal in shape, with striking platforms and bulbs of percussion along one side. The Setouchi technique, it is believed, was an adaptation allowing artisans of the Inland Sea region to produce elongate flakes that could be used in the same way as the end-blow blades common elsewhere in Japan, out of a locally available stone that was much more intractable than the obsidian and cherts used in the prepared-core blade technologies of other regions.

The trapezoidal Setouchi flakes were made into Kou knives simply by blunting the thick platform side of the flake with steep unifacial retouch, leaving the thin and sharp opposing side unmodified, as a cutting edge. Such cores and knives occur (sometimes with local names) at many sites in southern Japan; they are well known at Washiuzan in Okayama Prefecture, southern Honshu, and at Kiyama in Kagawa Prefecture, Shikoku. The method also seems to be attested in Level 9 of Fukui Rockshelter, in southwestern Kyushu's Nagasaki Prefecture.

The dating of the Paleolithic component at Kou, and of the Kou knife and Setouchi technique, is the subject of a debate that seems to have split along a line between older and younger specialists. A

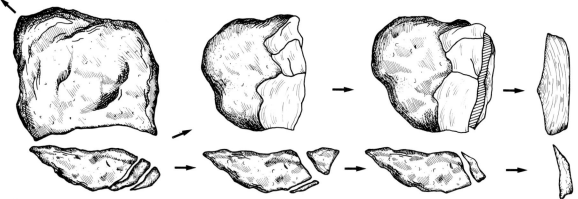

Figure 2.9 Setouchi side-blow flake core preparation technique.

number of younger archaeologists argue that the Kou knife, with its side-blow technology, antedates the blade–knife technologies found elsewhere in Japan. Several leading senior specialists, however, feel that the Kou knife is of about the same age as the other known knife types, and is thus a regional rather than a temporal variant (Watanabe 1977). This debate will no doubt continue until firm dating evidence is obtained, but at present the perspective that sees the Setouchi technique (and hence the Kou knife) as an adaptation to the working of rather intractable volcanic stone seems most reasonable.

Etchuyama is on the continental side of northeastern Japan, about 60 km northwest of the city of Yamagata and 20 km inland from the Japan Sea. The site area consists of a series of Pleistocene and Recent terraces found along the Akagawa River, which drains from the mountainous interior. In a series of campaigns begun in 1958, archaeological investigations were conducted at several localities on terraces of Late Pleistocene age. Excavations at Localities K, A, A', and S yielded well-defined assemblages of chipped stone artifacts typologically distinct from one another. These have been seriated on the basis of comparisons with dated artifacts from elsewhere to yield a Late Paleolithic cultural sequence spanning a period from about 18,000 to 13,000 years ago (Kato 1975; Oda and Kelly 1975). The sequence parallels that from Iwajuku and Nogawa in time, and generally in cultural content as well, but also adds some contrasting details to the archaeological picture for northern Honshu.

Locality K is on a high terrace. Artifacts were excavated from the uppermost part of a volcanic ash deposit of Late Pleistocene age, which occurs throughout the region to a depth of 2 or 3 m. In the

Etchuyama

center of the 10-m-square excavated area was a cluster of small stones, and around this were found many artifacts. The specimens included knives, pointed tools, end- and sidescrapers, boat-shaped scrapers, denticulates, gravers, flakes, and cores. The boat-shaped scrapers are

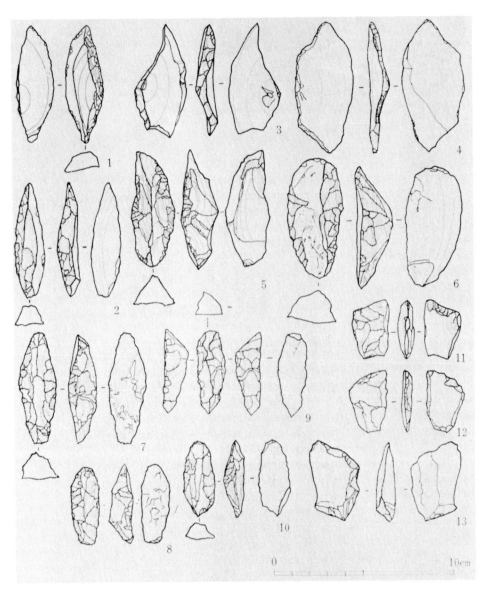

Figure 2.10 Knives, small boat-shaped scrapers, and trapezoidal tools on side–blow flakes, from Etchuyama K, Yamagata Prefecture, northern Honshu, ca. 18,000 B.P. (From Kato 1975: Figure 5.)

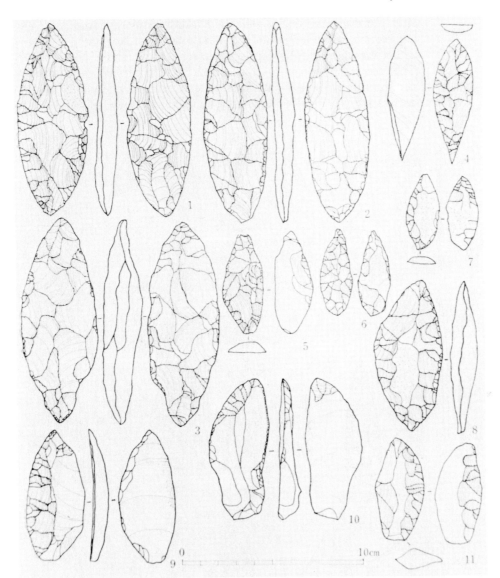

Figure 2.11 Leaf-shaped biface points and uniface knives from Etchuyama A, Yamagata Prefecture, northern Honshu, ca. 14,000 B.P. (Shown approximately one-half actual size.) (From Kato 1975: Figure 2.)

considered particularly characteristic of this industry, as is the fact that most of the knives and other tools are made on large, elongate side-blow flakes 6–7 cm long (Figure 2.10). The retouched knives made on these side-blow flakes are said to be identical with those of the Kou site, and they resemble as well the Kiridashi knives of Iwajuku II and comparable specimens from the middle levels of Nogawa.

Localities A and A' were on a lower terrace, about 120 m apart. This terrace also had been mantled by volcanic ash, the artifacts coming from its upper part, just beneath the recent humus. In both excavations, artifacts were found associated with loose clusters of small

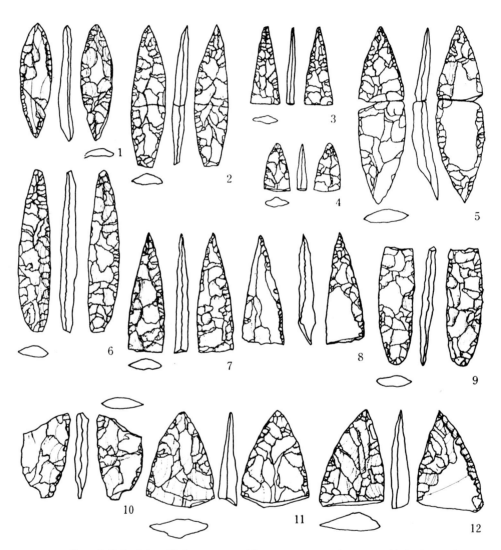

Figure 2.12 Leaf-shaped biface points, and knives, scrapers, and gravers on blades from Etchuyama A', Yamagata Prefecture, northern Honshu, ca. 13,000 B.P. (From Kato 1975: Figures 3.1, 3.2.)

stones, and in Locality A′ a shallow pit over .5 m in diameter containing charcoal and reddened earth was apparently a hearth.

A number of knives made on large, end-struck blades were found at both localities, as were small scrapers and gravers, but the most distinctive specimens recovered were a series of well-made bifacially flaked leaf-shaped points (Figures 2.11, 2.12). Most were pointed at

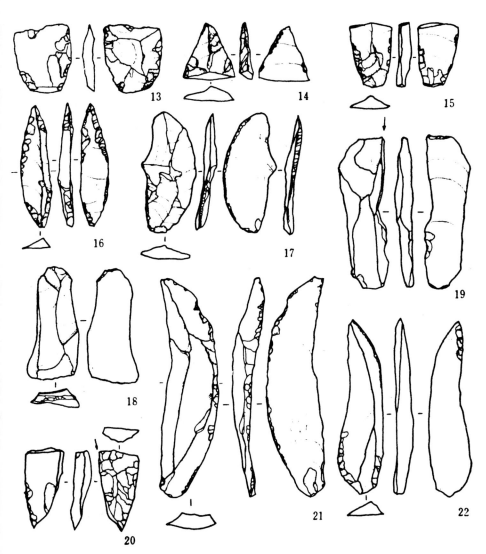

Figure 2.12 (*Continued*)

both ends, though a few had squared-off bases. The larger specimens from Locality A ranged between 8 and 11 cm in length; the smaller ones, between 4 and 6 cm. The points from Locality A' tended toward a more slender form, although broader specimens like those of Locality A were also present. In both areas, these points were made predominantly on end-blow blades, but specimens fashioned from side-blow flakes also occurred.

The artifact assemblages from the two localities differed markedly in the proportion of blades they contained. Such blades amounted to only 5% of the Locality A assemblage, but over 50% of the Locality A' assemblage. Conversely, small scrapers constituted over 50% of the artifacts from Locality A, but less than 5% of those from Locality A'. The relative proportions of points, knives, and gravers were, by contrast, about the same in both assemblages. These variations might be due to minor differences in the ages of the two localities, but it is also likely that the two are essentially contemporaneous, and that functional differences are represented. Locality A' probably was, among other things, a workshop where stone tools were made, whereas Locality A may have been oriented toward some other activity such as hide- or woodworking.

Locality S is on a slope near the edge of the same upper-terrace level on which Locality K occurs. A lithic industry composed of microblades only 1.5–2.5 cm long, distinctive boat-shaped elongate microcores, and scrapers and gravers made on much larger blades occurs there (Figure 2.13). This assemblage was buried approximately .5 m beneath the surface of the recent soil, in contact with the upper surface of the volcanic ash stratum. In several places within the 10 × 12 m excavation, concentrations of small stones were found, the most compact and densest of which was identified as perhaps a cooking area.

Comparisons between the four Etchuyama assemblages and others known from northeastern Japan suggest that the Etchuyama localities probably do not all overlap one another in time. A thread of cultural continuity is clear throughout, as shown by a certain degree of typological overlapping between the assemblages, but transitional assemblages that would fit well between Etchuyama K and Etchuyama A–A' are known from other sites, and there may also be a brief gap in the sequence between Etchuyama A–A' and Etchuyama S. According to a comparative chronology proposed by Oda and Keally (1975), Etchuyama K probably dates about 18,000 years ago, Etchuyama A–A about 13,000 to 14,000 years ago, and Etchuyama S sometime shortly thereafter.

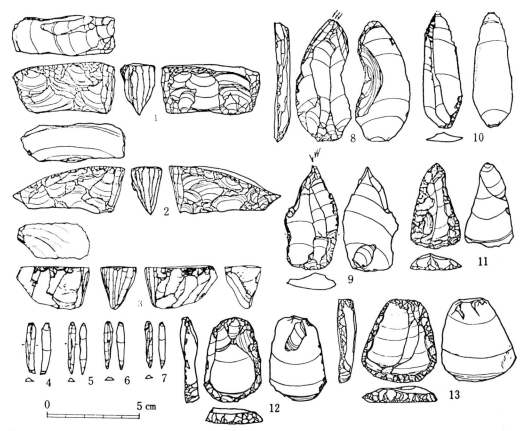

Figure 2.13 Boat-shaped microcores and microblades, and gravers and scrapers made on large blades from Etchuyama S, Yamagata Prefecture, northern Honshu, ca. 11,000–12,000 B.P. (From Kato 1975: Figure 4.)

The Kamishihoro–Shimagi site is near the eastern edge of the town of Kamishihoro, in mountainous central Hokkaido, about 150 km east of Sapporo. Excavations conducted on the forward edge of the 30-m terrace of the Otofuke River produced a series of flaked stone artifacts buried in a clear-cut and informative geological context that establishes them as among the earliest known from Hokkaido (Tsuji 1973).

The gravel-mantled 30-m terrace itself is believed to be Late Pleistocene in age. The artifacts occurred in the upper part of a yellow-brown clay bed, which was separated from the basal gravels by a thin stratum of white clay and an irregularly interrupted layer of pumice. Above the artifact-bearing bed lay a buried soil, a volcanic pumice

Kamishihoro–Shimagi

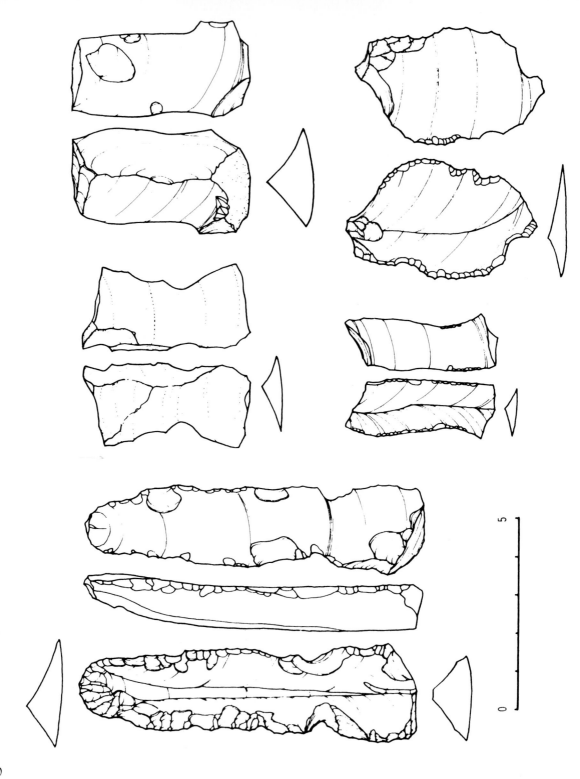

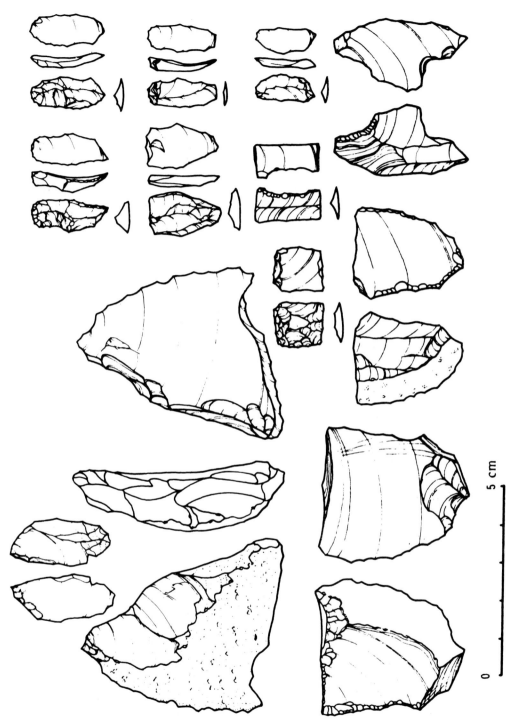

Figure 2.14 Blade and microblade tools from Kamishihoro–Shimagi, Hokkaido, ca. 19,000 B.P. (From Tsuji 1973: Figures 11, 13.)

5 cm

0

61

stratum much folded and distorted by frost action, three more layers of volcanic loam and ash, and a modern humus soil zone. A ^{14}C date of 25,500 B.P. from the lower part of the culture-bearing layer is apparently somewhat older than the artifacts themselves, but does indicate that they belong to the concluding stage of the last glacial period. The buried soil and frost-heaved earth that lay immediately above the cultural stratum suggest that the artifacts were laid down just prior to or during a brief warm interval that was followed by the final cold phase of terminal Pleistocene times.

About 200 artifacts were collected from a series of 2-m-square pits dug at intervals along a roughly east–west line about 150 m long. Specimens included choppers, cores, scrapers, flake tools, gravers, elongate flakes, and knives (Figure 2.14). The choppers were large, irregular flakes or chunks of stone, steeply flaked along one or more sides to form a sharp cutting edge. Cores included split pebbles from which one or two large flakes had been removed; one thick, rectangular block from which a series of elongate flakes had been removed; and other less distinctive pieces of stone from which flakes had been struck. Some of these exhibited marks suggesting that a punch was used to drive off the flakes. The removal of large flakes from split pebbles is considered to represent a Levallois-like technique.

The scrapers were for the most part large, thick, elongate flakes that had been unifacially retouched along one or more edges to serve as sidescrapers. One specimen was disk-shaped, with flaking over most of its convex upper surface, giving it a turtleback appearance. Another was bifacially flaked and might better be termed a knife than a scraper. Several of the scrapers had a tiny retouched projection on one of their edges that would have allowed them to function as gravers, and one small flake had been struck a single blow to give it a burin-like edge.

Knives were made by retouching side-blow and bladelike end-blow flakes along one or more edges. The side-blow specimens, which were the more numerous, tended to be roughly trapezoidal or triangular, whereas the knives made on bladelike flakes were more nearly parallel-sided. It is noteworthy that a few very small blades of microlithic proportions also occurred, and that they were retouched to form tiny knives of the same pattern as the larger elongate flake specimens.

Paleolithic assemblages known from Hokkaido prior to the excavations at Kamishihoro–Shimagi were limited to those displaying a well-developed true blade technology, rather more refined than the grosser end-blow blade and side-blow flake technologies of such sites on Honshu as Iwajuku, Nogawa, and Kou. Because of this, it was for a while accepted that Hokkaido had been remarkably isolated in earliest times from the rest of Japan. The principal importance of the Kamishihoro–Shimagi assemblage is that it first demonstrated the presence in Hokkaido of blade and side-blow flake technologies closely comparable to those of early sites on Honshu, and thereby established the existence of a common early cultural foundation throughout Japan.

Estimates of the age of the Kamishihoro–Shimagi occupation are provided by obsidian hydration measurements of two sets of artifacts, each set containing three specimens. The readings were all closely congruent, and, based on a previously established obsidian hydration rate for Hokkaido, dates of 19,000 and 19,300 B.P. were calculated for the two sets. Such an age accords reasonably well with the ^{14}C date of 25,500 B.P. established for a level just beneath the occupation, and with the dates from Shukubai–Sankakuyama, also in Hokkaido, which has produced similar artifacts.

Shukubai–Sankakuyama

The Shukubai–Sankakuyama site, in the city of Chitose, south of Sapporo, produced a ^{14}C date of 21,450 B.P., and an obsidian hydration date of 21,900 B.P. for an assemblage very like that of Kamishihoro–Shimagi (Yoshizaki 1974). The dated artifacts were recovered from a deeply buried loam stratum that was overlaid by up to 3 m of stratified pumice and sand. Because the site had been greatly disrupted by quarrying operations, the artifacts recovered were relatively few, but they nevertheless confirm the existence in Hokkaido at an early date of elongate flake and knife industries analogous to those previously known only farther south.

Hyakkadai

Near the end of Paleolithic times, evidence from all over Japan attests the appearance of lithic industries that produced ever smaller cores and blades. A stage when relatively small specimens were produced gave way quickly to one characterized by very small, true microcores and microblades. During this time also, bifacially flaked projectile points first appeared at many sites. Large blades and cores continued to be made, but they no longer dominated the lithic assemblages. This progression has been briefly adumbrated in the discussions of the long Iwajuku and Nogawa sequences, but a more detailed treatment is necessary. The record from Hyakkadai will indicate the nature of this concluding Paleolithic phase in extreme southern Japan, after which the discussion will deal with more northerly sites.

The Hyakkadai site is near the middle of western Kyushu's Shimabara Peninsula, which juts into the great shallow enclosed bay known as

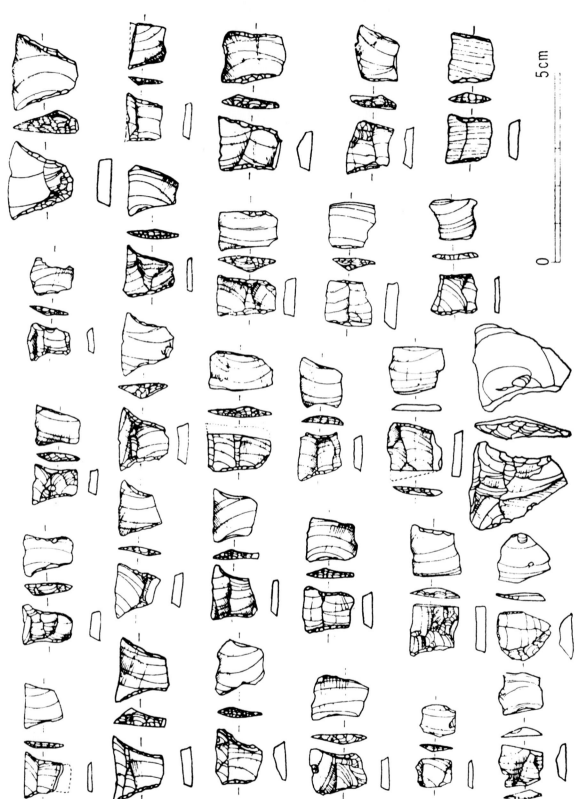

Figure 2.15 Trapezoidal knives made on small blades from Hyakkadai III, Nagasaki Prefecture, Kyushu, ca. 14,000 B.P. (From Aso and Shiraishi 1975: Figure 8.)

5 cm

0

the Ariake Sea, about 40 km east of the city of Nagasaki (Aso and Shiraishi 1975). The archaeological locality lies near the edge of a quite extensive sloping tableland, from which the site takes its name. A tributary to the Ariake Sea runs below the site in a narrow vale, which opens out into a broad alluvial valley a short distance downstream. One trench 20 m in length and two others half as long were ranged side by side to comprise a large, contiguous excavation near the sloping brow of the tableland.

A series of volcanic ash beds of differing color and texture displayed a clear-cut stratigraphic succession through some 2 m of deposit, allowing the recognition of four distinct cultural levels. Immediately beneath the modern stratum of cultivated soil lay a soft bed of yellowish brown volcanic loam that contained stone tools and Jomon pottery, including some of the early stick-impressed Oshigata-mon type. The bed below, a relatively soft black loam containing microblades, was in turn preceded by a very hard, compact black layer of volcanic ash and pumice characterized by trapezoidal knives made on small blades. A culturally barren bed of black sandy loam came next, and then the lowermost culture-bearing stratum, a bed of hard, blackish brown clay. A knife made on a large, elongate flake is considered characteristic of this earliest level.

The earliest assemblage (Hyakkadai IV) can be described quickly. It consisted of a roughly triangular knife made by retouching a large, elongate flake; two large, coarse, bladelike flakes; and a nondescript flake. Though small, the collection is both typologically and stratigraphically important for the linkage it establishes with the industries producing large, elongate flakes, discussed earlier.

The succeeding assemblage (Hyakkadai III) was much larger and more varied. The specimens were clustered in a relatively small area, and as several cores were present and most tools showed little or no evidence of use, it was inferred that the spot was a lithic workshop. The diagnostic cores were split pebbles from which flakes had been driven off in a single direction. The great bulk of the assemblage was made up of short, broad blades of relatively small size, and trapezoidal knives made by snapping off the ends of such blades and blunting the broken edges of the remaining central portion, leaving the original sharp outer edges of the blade unretouched (Figure 2.15). Many of the unretouched blades had one or both ends broken off in the same way, showing that they represent an unfinished stage in the production of trapezoidal knives. A few scrapers and pointed tools made by rough partial retouch of similar blades complete the assemblage.

The latest preceramic assemblage (Hyakkadai II) was dominated by a series of microcores and a large number of microblades (Figure 2.16).

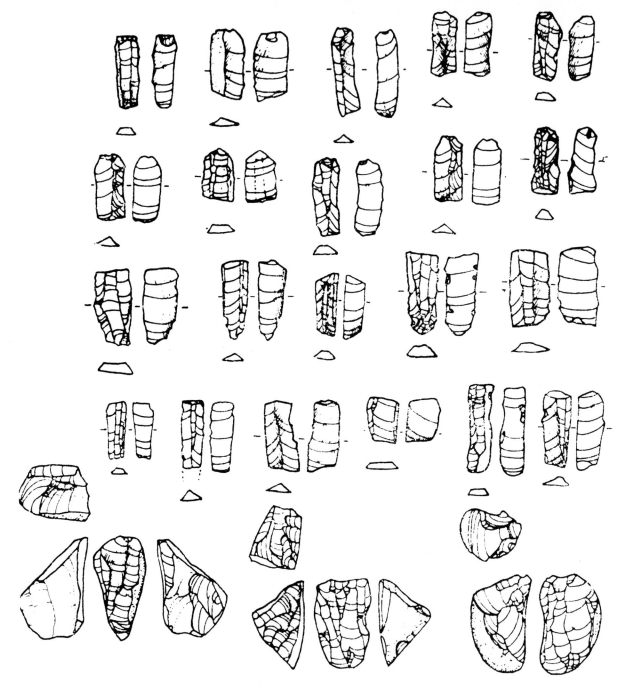

Figure 2.16 Microblades and wedge-shaped microcores from Hyakkadai II, Nagasaki Prefecture, Kyushu, ca. 13,000 B.P. Length of specimen at upper left, 2 cm. (From Aso and Shiraishi 1976: Figure 5.)

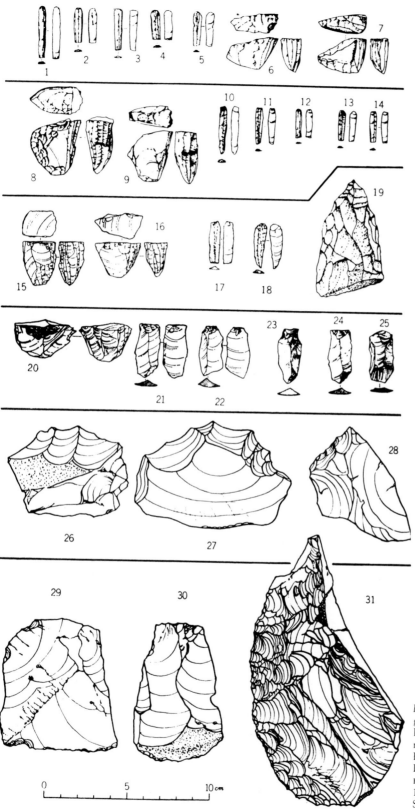

Figure 2.17 Stratigraphic progression from large biface and blade-like flakes, to side-blow flakes, to microcores and microblades at Fukui Rockshelter, Nagasaki Prefecture, Kyushu, from ca. 32,000 B.P. (Level XVI) to 13,500–11,000 B.P. (Levels VII–II). (From Serizawa 1967: Figure 2.)

0   5   10 cm

The cores were boat shaped, made by striking off the end of a pebble to form a flat surface, which was then used as a platform for striking blades off one side of the pebble. Some of these cores were triangular in outline, the blades being struck from one of the apexes of the triangle. Others had both ends of the original pebble broken away, and blades struck off in opposite directions, from both of the striking platforms thus prepared.

The microblades removed from such cores were about 2 cm long and slightly over .5 cm wide. Virtually none were retouched, but many had either one or both ends snapped off, eliminating bulbs of percussion and tapering tail-ends to produce neat, parallel-sided blade segments. Artifacts of other types were not numerous in this assemblage, but a few large knives and trapezoids are of particular interest for the connections they suggest with the earlier assemblages at Hyakkadai.

On comparative typological as well as stratigraphic grounds, the three preceramic Hyakkadai assemblages appear to be relatively close together in time. Comparisons with other sites in the region suggest that Hyakkadai IV may date around 15,000 years ago; Hyakkadai III, around 14,000 years ago. Hyakkadai II, with its well-developed microlithic industry, probably dates around 13,000 years ago. These dates are speculative, since there are few ^{14}C determinations for this general span of time in Kyushu, but similarities between these assemblages and better-dated ones on Honshu leave little doubt that such ages are of the proper order of magnitude (Oda and Keally 1975: Chart 2). Hyakkadai fits well within the developing picture of Late Paleolithic times in Kyushu, as known from a growing number of sites, and exemplifies the presence there of local versions of the blade and microblade industries that flourish farther north.

Fukui Rockshelter, also in western Kyushu, contained a cultural sequence paralleling that found at Hyakkadai, and leading onward into Initial Jomon times. Because of the importance of that site to the question of Jomon cultural origins, however, and to avoid redundancy, detailed discussion of its archaeological record is postponed until the next chapter. Figure 2.17 indicates the essential features of its stratigraphic sequence. Pottery, some of the earliest in Japan, appeared in the upper two levels.

Yasumiba   Yasumiba is an open-air site at the apex of a broad alluvial fan on the south slope of Mount Ataka, about 40 km east of the city of Shizuoka, on the Pacific coast of central Honshu (Sugihara and Ono 1965). The site lies at the juncture of the relatively gentle slope of the fan and the much steeper slope of the mountain itself, on the top of a ridge flanked by low-lying wet areas. A narrow coastal plain fringes the base of the alluvial fan, and the landward end of Suruga Bay is about 5 km west of the archaeological site.

Excavation of the site, which had been initially exposed by a road cut, yielded many microblades and other specimens from the upper part of a brownish volcanic loam stratum buried some 2 m beneath the modern surface. The loam is cognate with the upper part of the Tachikawa Loam series of the Tokyo area, which implies an age for Yasumiba of about 10,000 to 15,000 years, on geological grounds. An independent ^{14}C date of 14,300 B.P. on a hearth and an obsidian hydration date of 11,100 B.P. on an artifact from the site are congruent with the geological evidence for the age of Yasumiba, though none of the evidence allows a precise dating.

Fireplaces, consisting of two small concentrations of charcoal, each partially encircled by large stream cobbles, were found on an occupation surface heavily sprinkled with microblades and associated artifacts. This discovery made Yasumiba, at the time of its excavation, one of the first preceramic finds in Japan to yield unmistakable evidence of domestic cultural features. It has been suggested that these are the remains of an actual habitation, although no other architectural remains were detected within the excavated area, a large square 4 × 5 m across.

Over 4400 artifacts were recovered, of which approximately 1000 specimens represented microblades. Complete microblades, with a bulb of percussion at one end and a pointed tip at the other, were comparatively few. The finding of approximately equal numbers of broken-off bulb ends, pointed ends, and blade midsections showed that both ends were routinely snapped off the blades as originally struck. The parallel-sided blade midsections were undoubtedly the parts intended for use, though the recovered specimens give little evidence of any further modification. Some 20 microcores were also recovered. All were of semiconical form; the boat-shaped microcore seen at Hyakkadai and common elsewhere did not occur at all. A few nonmicrolithic artifacts made on large end-blow and side-blow elongate flakes included endscrapers, sidescrapers, knives, and gravers. About 3200 waste flakes and chips completed the assemblage.

The Yasumiba microlithic industry, with its semiconical microcores, is closely related to that of the Yadegawa site to the north, in mountainous central Honshu, which produced fully conical microcores. The excavators of Yasumiba, in consideration of both chronological and typological evidence, suggested that industries like these preceded those from such sites as Fukui Rockshelter, Araya, and others, which are based on boat-shaped microcores. The single ^{14}C date from Yasumiba indicates that the microblade industry there may be one of the very earliest in Japan. The authors further suggested, on technological grounds, that the boat-shaped microcores were a later improvement on conical or semiconical cores, in that boat-shaped cores can produce straighter, more parallel-sided flakes.

Uenodaira   Uenodaira is a small flat near the tip of a broad, blunt-ended ridge overlooking Lake Suwa, in mountainous central Honshu about 150 km northeast of Tokyo. A broad strip of alluvial flatland below the ridge, now occupied by the city of Suwa, lies along the edge of the lake. The Kakuma River, which drains the high volcanic mountains to the east, crosses this plain and enters the lake a short distance from Uenodaira (Sugihara 1973).

The archaeological excavations at Uenodaira, conducted in the late 1950s, were among the first in Japan to produce large, well-made bifacial projectile points in a well-defined preceramic context. At the famous Iwajuku site, where the existence of a Paleolithic technology in deposits of Pleistocene age was first conclusively established, a single bifacial point had been recovered, but it was a surface find of uncertain age. The excavations at Uenodaira were conducted soon after the breakthrough at Iwajuku by S. Sugihara, its excavator, in an attempt to establish the significance of such a biface point industry within the developing framework of the Japanese Paleolithic.

Test trenches laid across each other at right angles along the top of a small hillock showed that cultural remains were concentrated along its northeastern edge, and a large block excavation was opened in that area. Artifacts were found in the surface soil, in a black humus zone beneath that, and to some extent in the soft upper part of the underlying Hata Loam bed. The Hata Loam is the uppermost layer of the local Shinshu Loam series, which is of Late Pleistocene age. The surface soil and humus bed were apparently metamorphosed from the Hata Loam, and the typologically unified artifact collection is believed to constitute a single contemporaneous assemblage, attributable to the upper part of the Hata Loam.

In two areas of the site occurred clusters or rough alignments of large pebbles and cobbles, associated with many artifacts. The stones were not native to the site, and they must have been brought there by Uenodaira's human inhabitants for some purpose. Though their disposition offered no real clue to their function, stones of such size could have served to contain hearths, or perhaps to weigh down the bases of tentlike structures.

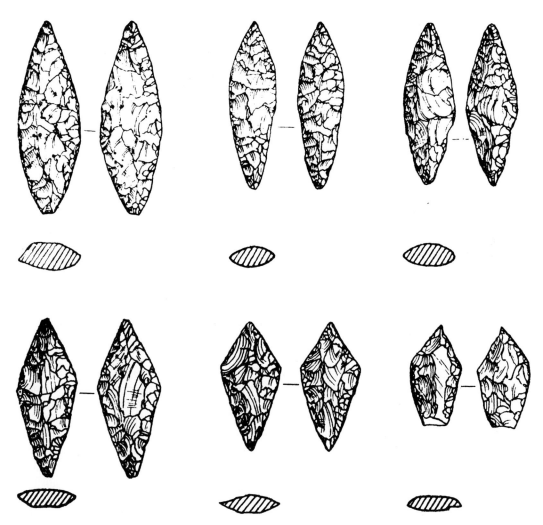

Figure 2.18 Leaf-shaped and diamond-shaped biface points from Uenodaira, Nagano Prefecture, central Honshu, ca. 12,000–14,000 B.P. Length of specimen at upper left, 5.1 cm. (Shown actual size.) (From Sugihara 1973: Figures 12, 14.)

Many bifacially flaked projectile points dominated the artifact assemblage (Figure 2.18). Some of these were quite large and heavy, around 8 cm in length; most, however, were a good deal smaller and lighter, around 5 cm in length. The larger points were of a broad leaf shape, whereas among the smaller ones both slender willow-leaf and diamond shapes appeared. It is thought by the excavator that the larger specimens were probably spearheads; the smaller ones, arrowheads or perhaps cutting segments of a composite spearpoint made by mounting a number of the smaller points in a bone or wooden haft.

A few pseudopoints, similar to but somewhat larger than the smaller leaf-shaped points, were steeply retouched along one edge. They are thought to represent side-blades for composite tools of some sort. Sidescrapers and endscrapers made on elongate flakes may also have been hafted, and small pointed awls, drills, and gravers found at the site may have been used in preparing such hafts.

Elongate bladelike flakes of rather uneven outline were also part of the lithic industry (Figure 2.19). Relatively large, broad specimens up to 5 cm long occurred along with slender microblade-sized ones around 2 cm long. Neither the large nor the small specimens exhibit the regular, parallel sides of true blades struck from well-prepared cores, and the few exhausted cores found at the site are correspondingly nondescript.

The use of pressure flaking in shaping the bifacial points from the site was inferred from a great abundance of small, thin flakes of uniform size found associated with the artifacts. Some 4000 such flakes accounted for nearly 90% of all specimens recovered. Whether or not it is accepted that these flakes specifically give evidence of a pressure-flaking rather than a percussion-flaking technique, they show that the making of stone tools was a major activity at Uenodaira. And in view of the large number of bifacial points found, some finely retouched ones complete, many less refined ones snapped in half as if broken in manufacture, it is reasonable to conclude that stone points were the principal product of the industry. The fact that only a few utterly exhausted cores occurred at the site suggests that the basic artifact forms were roughed out elsewhere, probably near the source of the stone from which they were made, and brought to Uenodaira for finishing. An abundant supply of obsidian is available at Wada Pass, about 12 km from Uenodaira, and it seems likely that the obsidian that made up virtually 100% of the artifacts at the site came from that source.

Two age determinations made by the obsidian hydration method yielded dates of 9100 and 11,000 years ago for the occupation of the site. These dates seem unduly recent, however, in view of the fact that leaf-shaped points very like those of Uenodaira have been dated at the Nogawa, Tsukimino, and Kikaritoge sites near Tokyo to a period between 12,000 and 14,000 years ago, by a series of cross-checking obsidian hydration dates (Oda and Keally 1975: Chart 2). In particular, the date of 9100 years seems unlikely, since pottery had appeared throughout most of Japan by that time, and none was found with the point assemblage at Uenodaira.

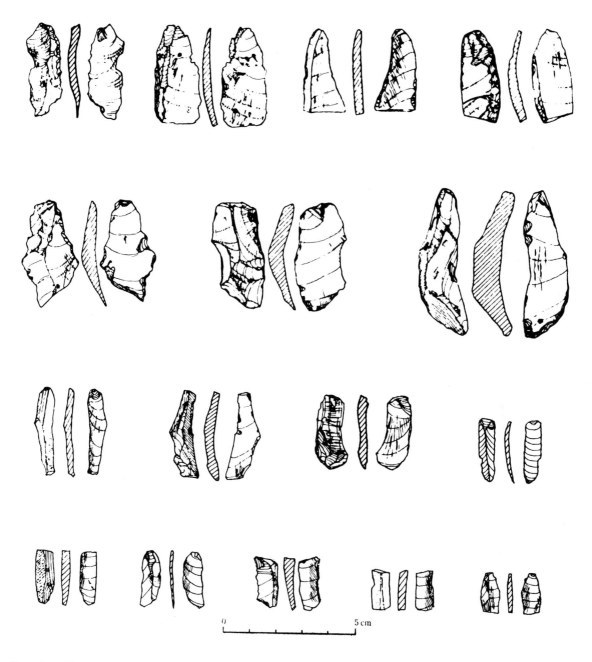

Figure 2.19 Blades and microblades from Uenodaira, Nagano Prefecture, central Honshu, ca. 12,000–14,000 B.P. (Shown approximately three-quarters actual size.) (From Sugihara 1973: Figure 20.)

Araya   The Araya site is in Niigata Prefecture, north-central Honshu, about 75 km south of the city of Niigata, near the juncture of the broad coastal plain of the Japan Sea and the mountainous interior (Serizawa 1959). The stream terrace on which the site occurs is mantled by volcanic ash, and from this ash layer excavations of rather limited extent produced over 2000 lithic specimens. A number of black charcoal lenses suggested that architectural features were possibly present, but excavations were not carried far enough to determine whether or not this was the case.

The lithic assemblage included over 600 microblades; some two dozen boat-shaped or keeled microcores; some 400 highly distinctive gravers or burins made on large, broad blades; over 1000 burin spall

Figure 2.20 Boat-shaped microcore and microblades from Araya, Niigata Prefecture, northern Honshu, ca. 13,000 B.P. (Shown approximately twice actual size.) (Courtesy S. Sugihara, Meiji University.)

Figure 2.21 Araya burins from Araya, Niigata Prefecture, northern Honshu, ca. 13,000 B.P. (Shown actual size.) (Courtesy S. Sugihara, Meiji University.)

flakes; and a few miscellaneous points, choppers, and scrapers. All specimens were made of a hard, fine-grained basalt, probably of local origin. The boat-shaped microcores differ from the more conical forms known from Yasumiba and Yadegawa, but fit well into a general pattern that is widely attested throughout northern Honshu and Hokkaido (Figure 2.20).

The gravers, which have come to be widely known as Araya burins, are the most remarkable specimens from the site (Figure 2.21). They were made by driving off one or sometimes two burin spalls from one end of a large, broad blade, the edges of which had been previously blunted by steep unifacial retouch. The abundance of these distinctive specimens, and the similar abundance of microblades discovered in association with them, make it appear that Araya was a highly task-specific site. It may well have been a workshop where composite tools were manufactured, where bone or wooden haft elements were grooved using the burins and inset with microblade cutting elements. The uniformity of the lithic material and the presence of both micro-cores and burin spalls indicate that the lithic specimens were made on

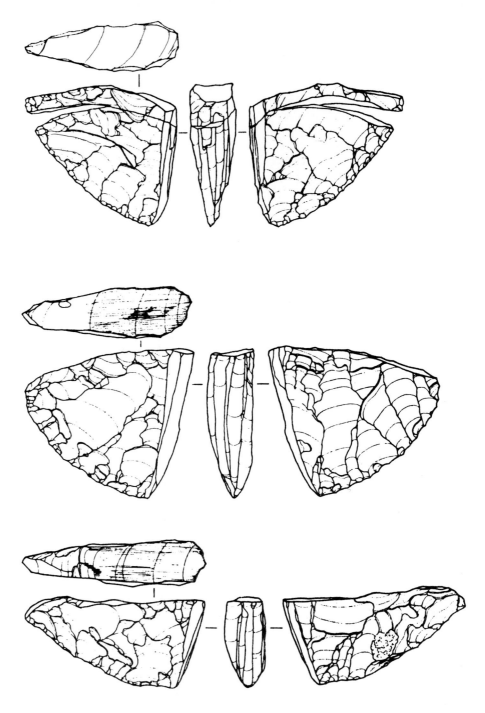

Figure 2.22 Yubetsu-type microcores and microblades from Shirataki–Hattoridai, Hokkaido, ca. 13,000 B.P. Length of microcore at top, 5.6 cm. (From Sugihara and Tozawa 1975: Figure 14.)

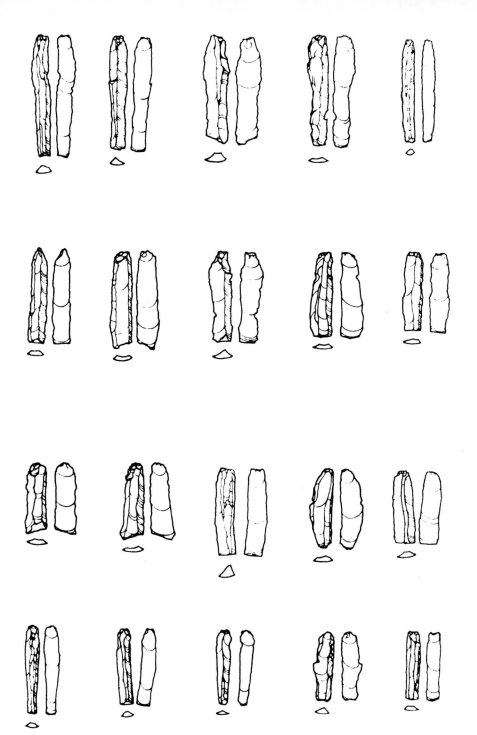

Figure 2.22 (Continued)

the spot, and it is a reasonable surmise that they were put to use in the same place as well.

The Araya site has been ^{14}C dated at 13,200 B.P., giving it an age some specialists believe may be slightly excessive, but which comparative data show to be clearly of the correct order of magnitude (Oda and Keally 1975: Chart 2; Serizawa 1974: endpaper). Since the Araya site was discovered, the distinctive Araya burins have been reported from all over northern Honshu and Hokkaido, and have even been identified from sites in Mongolia, Siberia, and Alaska (Morlan 1967, 1971). They have become, thus, an important Late Paleolithic time horizon marker over a vast area of Northeast Asia.

Shirataki–Hattoridai   The Shirataki–Hattoridai site takes its name from the fact that it is located in northeastern Hokkaido's village of Shirataki, on the edge of a sloping tableland owned by one Mr. Hattori. The site is on the third terrace of the Yubetsu River valley, some 50 km upstream from where the river debouches into the Okhotsk Sea at the town of Yubetsu (Sugihara and Tozawa 1975). Many preceramic sites are known from the hillsides overlooking the river near Shirataki, and research into the terminal Pleistocene microlithic cultures of Hokkaido was pioneered in this area (Yoshizaki 1961).

An area some 25 × 50 m across near the riverward brink of the terrace was sampled by several trenches, and by a large, roughly L-shaped block excavation. The stratigraphy was simple, with artifacts present in the dark surface soil and in an immediately underlying layer of undisturbed yellowish brown clay a few centimeters in thickness. Beneath, several clay–sand and sand-and-gravel layers containing no artifacts overlaid the equally sterile basal gravels of the terrace. No cultural features such as hearths or fire pits were discovered, but the variety of tools found at the site suggested that it was the locus of various domestic activities.

The microlithic industry was based on tiny blades around 1 cm in length, and on microcores made by the highly distinctive Yubetsu or Shirataki technique (Figures 2.22, 2.23). Such microcores were prepared by shaping a large, thin, ovate biface, from which one or more long, curved "ski-spalls" were split off down the long axis. This process produced a half-ovate or boat-shaped core, with a flat upper edge, which was then used as a platform for striking microblades off one end of the core. The resultant microblades tapered to a point at the bottom end (the "keel" of the boat-shaped core), but many archaeologically recovered specimens have had this pointed end snapped off, leaving a relatively parallel-sided blade segment.

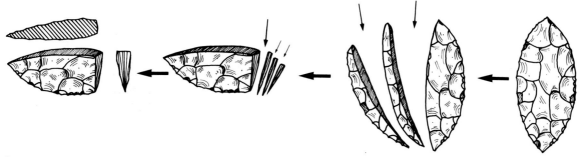

Figure 2.23 Yubetsu technique of microcore production. (After Yoshizaki 1961.)

A number of ski-spalls and large ovate bifaces, and hundreds of random flakes perhaps resultant from biface manufacture, were recovered along with the prepared cores and microblades. It thus appears that the entire manufacturing process took place at the site.

The ovate bifaces of all kinds recovered from the site ranged from roughly flaked specimens about 20 cm in length down to finely flaked ones half that size. Overlapping the lower end of this size range were a number of stemmed bifacial projectile points, undoubtedly made from such ovate blank forms. These are comparable to tanged or stemmed points known from a number of sites in Hokkaido and Honshu (Figure 2.24). Microblades have been found with these points in some, but not all, cases, raising the question of the historical relationship between the two technologies. One of the remarkable results of archaeological investigations in the Shirataki region has been the finding that both the microblades and the projectile points that occur there are organically related as parts of a single lithic industry.

Large blades ranging from 6 to 10 cm in length were common at Shirataki–Hattoridai, and occurred in close association with the microlithic industry. Many of the cores found with the blades were rather irregular, but the best formed of them were subconical, with a flat upper surface that served as a striking platform, and sides that tapered inward (Figure 2.25). Around the circumferences of such cores were overlapping flake scars showing where long, parallel-sided, keeled blades were struck off. Many of the larger tools from the site were made on such blades, especially the endscrapers, sidescrapers, and gravers, ·or burins (Figure 2.26).

A final major artifact class was made up of many heavy, keeled scrapers, triangular in cross section and completely flaked over the two converging upper surfaces but unretouched on the flat or slightly convex bottom surface (Figure 2.27). These are apparently remnants from the process of splitting down large bifaces to form Yubetsu-type boat-

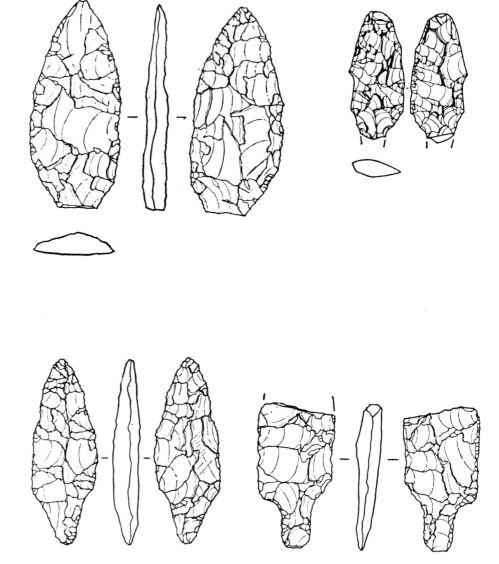

Figure 2.24 Leaf-shaped and stemmed biface points from Shirataki–Hattoridai, Hokkaido, ca. 13,000 B.P. Length of specimen at upper left, 7.5 cm. (Shown approximately three-quarters actual size.) (From Sugihara and Tozawa 1975: Figure 25.)

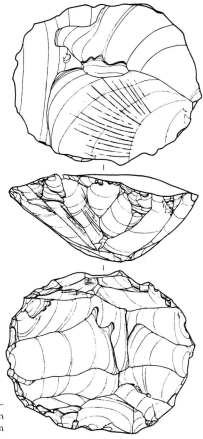

Figure 2.25 Conical blade core from Shirataki–Hattoridai, Hokkaido, ca. 13,000 B.P. (Shown approximately one-half actual size.) (From Sugihara and Tozawa 1975: Figure 42.)

shaped microcores. They correspond in length and thickness to some of the larger bifaces recovered from the site, which were clearly blanks for the making of Yubetsu cores. The keeled scrapers apparently represent the first large spall struck off in the splitting down of a biface, with the distinctive ski-spalls found at the site representing subsequent stages of that process.

A date of approximately 13,000 years ago seems appropriate for Shirataki–Hattoridai, based on the similarity of its artifact assemblage to those of the Shirataki Locality 30 and Oketo–Azumi sites, both dated to this time by the ^{14}C and obsidian hydration techniques (Oda and Keally 1975: Chart 2). A date of 8000 to 10,000 B.P. originally estimated by the excavators of the site does not now seem likely, in view of this evidence.

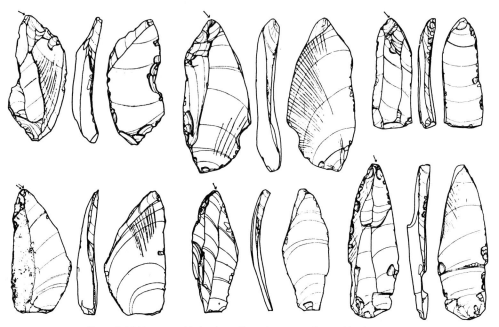

Figure 2.26 Burins on blades from Shirataki–Hattoridai, Hokkaido, ca. 13,000 B.P. Length of specimen at upper left, 6.6 cm. (Shown approximately one-half actual size.) (From Sugihara and Tozawa 1975: Figure 30.)

Shirataki–Hattoridai offers a good glimpse of the lifeway practiced in northeastern Hokkaido in terminal Paleolithic times. Its occupants had placed themselves in a highly favorable location, on the elevated edge of a broad valley overlooking good hunting and fishing grounds along the Yubetsu River. The river, in addition to being a focus of food resources, provided an inexhuaustible supply of water-transported obsidian cobbles for toolmaking. Large leaf-shaped and stemmed points, blades, and scrapers suggest the hunting and processing of game, and the microblades from the site may have provided sharp edges for composite fish-spears and other tools. Scrapers of several types, and gravers, as well as an abundance of obsidian cores and waste flakes, give evidence that the needed tools were manufactured on the spot. Some degree of functional differentiation within the ancient camp is indicated by the tendency of endscrapers and keeled scrapers to occur in separate clusters, and by the fact that microblade cores are largely restricted to one part of the site. Though no evidence of fire or artificial shelter was turned up in the excavations, the kind and variety of activities attested by the archaeological evidence leave little doubt that Shirataki–Hattoridai was a domestic site of some permanence.

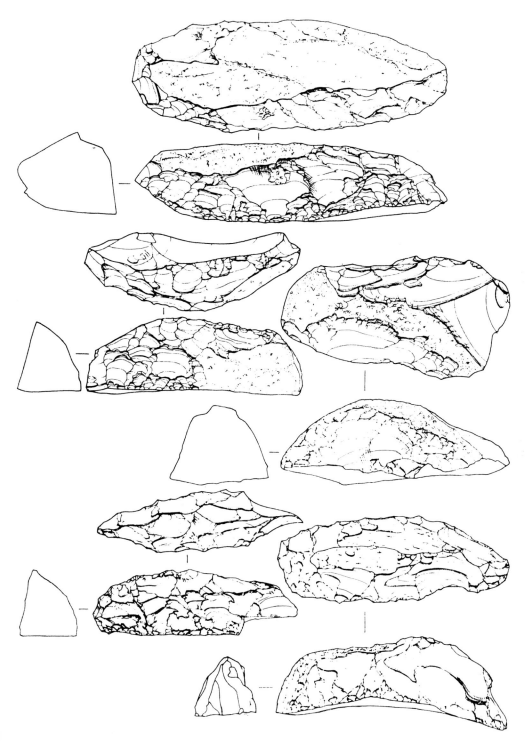

Figure 2.27 Large boat-shaped scrapers from Shirataki–Hattoridai, Hokkaido, ca. 13,000 B.P.
Length of top specimen, 17.2 cm. (Shown approximately half actual size.) (From Sugihara and
Tozawa 1975: Figure 33.)

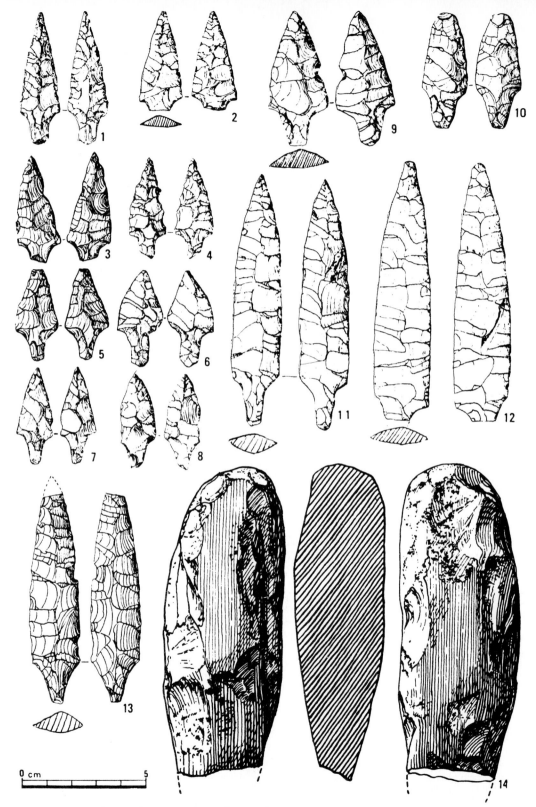

Figure 2.28 Stemmed projectile points and partially ground axe or adze from Tachikaru–Shunai, Hokkaido, ca. 9000 B.P. The smaller points are of the Engaru type; the larger, of the Tachikawa type. (From Yoshizaki 1973: Figure 20.)

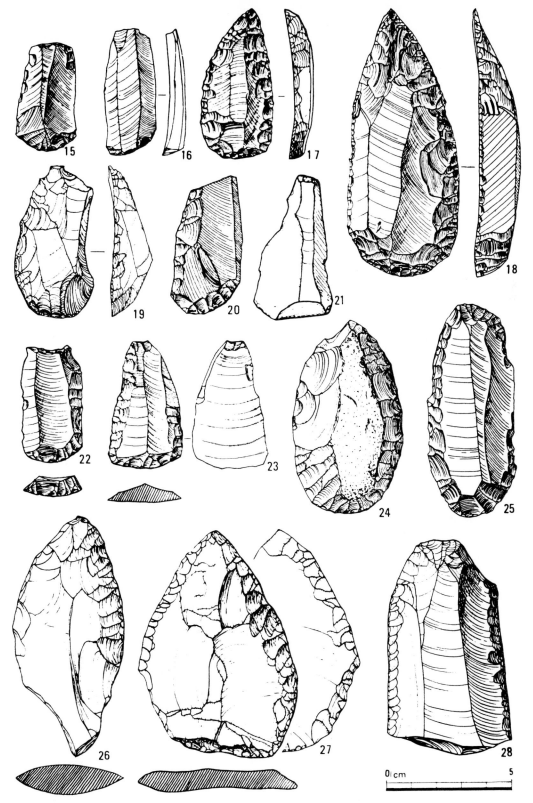

Figure 2.29 Endscrapers, sidescrapers, and knives made on large blades from Tachikaru–Shunai, Hokkaido, ca. 9000 B.P. (From Yoshizaki 1973: Figure 21.)

Tachikaru–Shunai   The Tachikaru–Shunai site is on the edge of the town of Engaru in northeastern Hokkaido, about 25 km from the coast of the Okhotsk Sea (Yoshizaki 1973). It occupies a narrow alluvial terrace overlooking the confluence of two rivers with wooded hills behind and the river plain before. On this terrace, three large block excavations were opened within a radius of about 50 m of one another. The stratigraphy and artifact typology of the three localities were not identical, and the finer details of the cultural sequence remain to be clarified, but on general comparative grounds, it appears that the site was partially contemporaneous with Shirataki–Hattoridai, though extending somewhat later in time. It probably is to be dated between about 12,000 and 9000 years ago, though this is not certainly established.

The earliest assemblage from Tachikaru–Shunai was sparse, consisting principally of large blades retouched to form endscrapers and sidescrapers. Believed to follow it was a similar collection characterized by large blades retouched as sidescrapers, endscrapers, and burins. Blades of microlithic proportions were also found with these specimens, but were rare. Next in the proposed sequence logically come two assemblages, both of which included long, slender blades; Shirataki microcores; endscrapers on blades; and small Araya burins.

The latest and best-represented assemblage was characterized by end- and sidescrapers made on large blades, microblades, gravers, Araya burins, and bifacially flaked projectile points (Figures 2.28, 2.29). Of the last, there were two types. One, the so-called Tachikawa type, had a long, lanceolate blade and a short, broad, tapered stem. Found associated in the excavations were a number of other points of similar shape, but less than half as long, known as the Engaru type. These are believed by many to represent a slightly later period than the Tachikawa type, though this was not confirmed at Tachikaru–Shunai. This assemblage appears to be representative of the very latest stage of the Paleolithic in Hokkaido, inasmuch as projectile points of the same types as found here have been found at other sites in association with the earliest Jomon pottery known for far northern Japan. A nearby site where such an assemblage occurs is Yubetsu–Ichikawa, to be treated in the next chapter.

Conclusion   As shown by the preceding evidence, the Japanese Paleolithic may be broadly segmented into four stages (Figure 2.30). The earliest is not well attested, and is represented by crude, heavy lithic specimens said to resemble the chopper–chopping tools of Middle Pleistocene and later age from Choukoutien, China. Such objects have been found at Sozudai and Nyu in Kyushu, and in the lowest levels of Iwajuku,

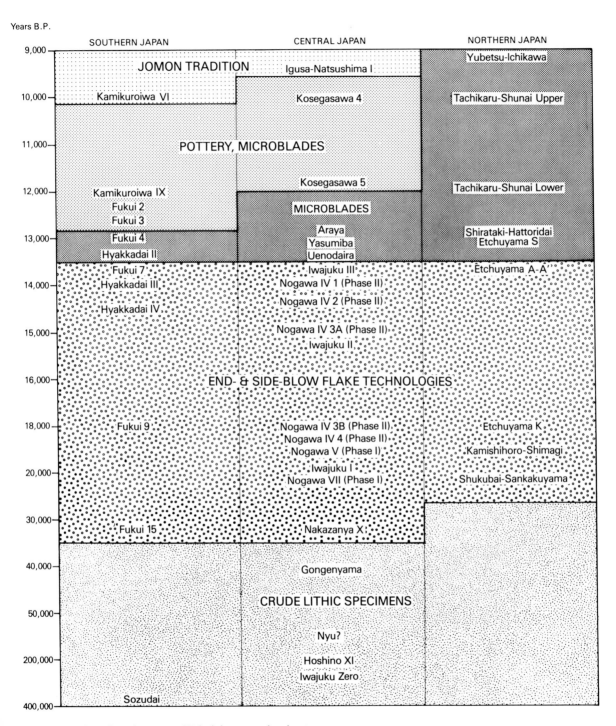

Years B.P.

| | SOUTHERN JAPAN | CENTRAL JAPAN | NORTHERN JAPAN |

9,000 —

JOMON TRADITION

Yubetsu-Ichikawa

Igusa-Natsushima I

Kamikuroiwa VI

Kosegasawa 4

Tachikaru-Shunai Upper

10,000 —

11,000 —

POTTERY, MICROBLADES

12,000 —

Kamikuroiwa IX
Fukui 2
Fukui 3

Kosegasawa 5

Tachikaru-Shunai Lower

MICROBLADES

Fukui 4

Araya
Yasumiba
Uenodaira

Shirataki-Hattoridai
Etchuyama S

13,000 —

Hyakkadai II

Fukui 7
Hyakkadai III

Iwajuku III
Nogawa IV 1 (Phase II)

Etchuyama A-A′

14,000 —

Hyakkadai IV

Nogawa IV 2 (Phase II)

Nogawa IV 3A (Phase II)
Iwajuku II

15,000 —

16,000 —

END- & SIDE-BLOW FLAKE TECHNOLOGIES

Fukui 9

Nogawa IV 3B (Phase II)
Nogawa IV 4 (Phase II)
Nogawa V (Phase I)

Etchuyama K

18,000 —

Kamishihoro-Shimagi

Iwajuku I
Nogawa VII (Phase I)

Shukubai-Sankakuyama

20,000 —

30,000 —

Fukui 15

Nakazanya X

40,000 —

Gongenyama

CRUDE LITHIC SPECIMENS

50,000 —

Nyu?

200,000 —

Hoshino XI
Iwajuku Zero

400,000 —

Sozudai

Figure 2.30 Chronological position of Paleolithic sites referred to in text.

Hoshino, and some other sites. The specimens are large, irregularly broken nodules with sharp edges or points at places on their surfaces, but they lack clearly defined flake scars, bulbs of percussion, and other traits usually considered diagnostic of human workmanship. The various specimens are believed by their discoverers to date between about 400,000 and 35,000 B.P., based on the Choukoutien comparison and on consideration of the available geological evidence. Many specialists do not believe they are artifacts at all, however, and the weight of archaeological opinion is against admitting such uncertain objects as evidence of early Paleolithic occupation.

Several large handaxes or choppers from Gongenyama, of Paleolithic appearance, are undeniably of human manufacture. They resemble the classic Acheulian handaxes of Middle and later Pleistocene age from Europe and Africa, one of them strikingly so. They are believed to have come from a volcanic loam stratum laid down roughly 35,000 to 50,000 years ago, although this geological association is not securely established. Specimens said to be of similar type have also begun to turn up in small numbers at several sites in northern Honshu. At Myojinyama B and Kamiyaji B in Yamagata Prefecture, such artifacts have been assigned dates of 26,000 and 29,600 B.P., but their contexts and associations remain uncertain (Watanabe 1977:96). Such an age ascription puts these sites in the same general time range as is estimated for Gongenyama, but if all these handaxe-like specimens are indeed of that age, then they are many tens of thousands of years younger than the Afro–European paleoliths they resemble. Assessment of their actual significance must await the accumulation of additional evidence, but the specimens are mentioned here because they represent a kind of lithic technology that might well have been present in Japan in early Paleolithic times.

Following the still essentially hypothetical earliest chopper-chopping tool or handaxe stage of the Japanese Paleolithic is a second stage, which is just beginning to become known. The lowest levels of such sites as Nakazanya, Nishinodai, and Heidaizaka, which date between roughly 25,000 and 30,000 B.P., yield artifacts that are undeniably of human make but do not seem to exemplify the prepared core-elongate flake technology that appears later in these and many other sites. A similar assemblage, for which there are ^{14}C dates of 28,700 and 29,300 B.P., has also been reported from the Sanrizuka site, in the eastern part of the Tokyo area.

These artifact assemblages include some fairly large pebble choppers, reminiscent of the so-called "handaxes" of Iwajuku I, and simple cutting and scraping tools made on broad, short flakes. If the subsequent elongate flake technologies of the later Japanese Paleolithic were to be characterized in the European terminology as Aurignacian-like, then these earlier flake industries might with equal justice be termed Mousterian-like. If such a perception of these artifacts is permitted, a highly significant parallelism between the Paleolithic sequences of Japan and extreme western Eurasia begins to come into view. This is an intriguing prospect about which more will surely be heard.

Large end-struck blades and bladelike flakes made from prepared cores appear in the assemblages of the third stage of the Japanese Paleolithic, beginning shortly before 20,000 years ago. These are known from the Tokyo area in Iwajuku I, Nogawa VII, Nishinodai, Takei, and other sites, and from Hokkaido at the site of Shukubai–Sankakuyama. These end-struck blades exemplify a prepared-core technology that is clearly related to that of the Eurasian Advanced Paleolithic. Elongate side-blow flakes, apparently a Japanese-developed variant of the prepared-core technology, first appear soon after. The most famed of these side-blow flake specimens are the ones described earlier from the Kou site, Osaka, which are made by the so-called Setouchi technique. It may be that the side-blow technology was first developed in this region as an adaptation to the tough rhyolitic sanukite stone so common there. A similar side-blow flake technology is also attested in Nogawa V–IV and Iwajuku II in the Tokyo area, Etchuyama K in northern Honshu, and Kamishihoro–Shimagi in Hokkaido. The co-occurrence of both end-blow blades and side-blow flakes in several of these assemblages shows that the two technologies at least partially overlapped in time.

Nuances of formal variation in retouched artifacts made on these two kinds of elongate flakes have been reported from a number of sites, including some not previously mentioned. In particular, several types of knives have been named, which are distinguished on the basis of modes of retouching of the two basic flake types (Morlan 1971). The *Kou knife,* as has been previously described, was made by employing steep unifacial retouch to blunt the thick bulbar edge of a Setouchi-type side-blow flake. The opposing cutting edge was left unmodified, and the resulting knife was trapezoidal, retaining the form of the original flake. *Miyatayama* and *Uwaba knives,* from sites in southern Honshu and Kyushu respectively, are minor variants of this type. Specimens from Etchuyama K, in northern Honshu, are said to be clearly of the same type, and knives made on side-blow flakes from Kamishihoro–Shimagi, Hokkaido, are also highly similar. The *Kiridashi knives* of Iwajuku II were also made on thick, pointed side-blow flakes unifacially retouched along both edges. *Isemiyama knives,* named for a site in central Honshu, were trimmed and blunted at an oblique angle down the long axis of an elongate flake in a way that makes it difficult to establish whether side-blow or end-blow flakes were used in their making.

A variety of knife types made on end-blow blades have also been recognized. *Higashiyama knives*, named for a site near Niigata, in northern Honshu, were made on very large parallel-sided blades. They exhibit slight trimming at the bulbar end, and sometimes have a shallow unretouched notch at the opposite end, made by snapping off a corner of the blade. Their most distinctive characteristics are their large size (up to 18 cm) and the fact that the blades appear to have been made from specially prepared double-platform cores. A round of blades was apparently struck first from one end of such a core; the core was then turned over and another round of blades was struck off in the opposite direction. *Sugikubo knives*, named from a site south of Niigata, are slender blades that were trimmed to a bipointed, willow-leaf form, and blunted along one margin adjacent to one of the tips.

Moro knives, named for a site on the southwestern edge of Tokyo, were made by blunting one edge of a long, roughly formed tapering blade. The bulbar end of the blade was rounded off, and the pointed end and one edge was left sharp and unmodified. *Kyushu knives*, found concentrated in sites along the western edge of that island, are simply elongate bladelike flakes with blunted backs, which resemble Moro knives. *Hyakkadai knives*, from a site of that name also in western Kyushu, were rather different. These were trapezoidal in shape, made by snapping off the ends of a blade and blunting the edges so formed, leaving the original blade edges sharp and unmodified. In appearance, though apparently not in technique of manufacture, they somewhat resemble the Kiridashi knives known from Iwajuku II. They may well, however, be of rather later date than the other knife types mentioned.

Several distinctive types of burins made on blades have also been discovered, of which the best known are the Kosaka and Kamiyama types. *Kosaka burins*, considered part of a Higashiyama complex because they often occur with Higashiyama knives, were made from a blade that was prepared by trimming one end to a slightly concave shape. Burin spalls were then driven off either corner of the trimmed end, by blows directed down the long axis of the blade. *Kamiyama burins*, often associated with Sugikubo knives, are elongate flakes or blades having multiple burin facets at one end. These facets were created by adjacent burin blows directed at an oblique angle, resulting in a steep working surface that often resembles that of an endscraper.

As can be seen, following the initial spread of the end-blow blade and side-blow flake technologies throughout Japan, a good deal of regional variation in artifact types developed. Much remains to be learned about the geographical patterning of this variation, but it is already evident that the northern area developed a greater diversity of types than did the southern. If a boundary line between the northern and southern cultural spheres were to be drawn, it would lie somewhere to the south of Honshu's mountainous midline, in the latitudes between Tokyo and Kyoto. This coincides, not surprisingly, with the general transition zone between the subtropical biotic communities of Kyushu, Shikoku, and southern Honshu, and the north temperate communities of northern Honshu and Hokkaido. It is of great interest that this major cultural divide, well attested ethnologically and linguistically in the folk life and dialect geography of historic times, was already established in the earliest Paleolithic phase for which we have a substantial archaeological record.

Toward the end of this stage, perhaps around 15,000 years ago, there appeared a notable trend toward smaller size in the products of the lithic industry. Specimens 8–10 cm long were common in earlier assemblages, but later tools were smaller and shorter by several centimeters. Iwajuku II and the later levels of the Nogawa site illustrate this tendency for the Tokyo region; Hyakkadai III and IV and Fukui 7 give evidence of the relatively small size of later Paleolithic specimens in Kyushu. The smaller blades of later times grade toward the length range of the microblades that appear in the final Paleolithic stage, but remain much broader than true microblades.

Another change that takes place at about the same time is the appearance of bifacially flaked leaf-shaped projectile points made on large blades or bladelike flakes. These occur after about 14,000 years ago at many sites, including Nogawa and Uenodaira in central Honshu, Etchuyama A and A′ in northern Honshu, and Shirataki-Hattoridai and Tachikaru–Shunai in Hokkaido. It has been suggested that these points evolved from knives made on blades, as the marginal flaking used to shape a blade into a knife form was extended to cover the entire surface of the specimen (Sugihara 1956). At Nogawa, for example, unifacially flaked leaf-shaped points first appeared in the stratigraphic sequence after edge-retouched knives had long been in use, and were followed in turn by bifacially flaked leaf-shaped points. Other sites in central Japan, such as Takei, Yashima, Tsukimino, and Kikaritoge bear out this interpretation, since they too yielded specimens grading between marginally retouched knives and fully retouched bifacial points.

Microlithic industries comprise the last stage of the Japanese Paleolithic, becoming widespread between about 13,000 and 14,000 years ago. Assemblages from the far south include those of Hyakkadai II and Fukui Rockshelter 4, the latter bracketed in time between ^{14}C dates of 13,600 and 12,700 B.P. for strata above and below the bed containing the microlithic assemblage. These microblades were struck from half-cylindrical or boat-shaped microcores made on one end of a split pebble or large flake. Such relatively rude boat-shaped cores are common as far north as central Honshu. In Hokkaido and, to a lesser extent, in northern Honshu, the more sophisticated Yubetsu type of boat-shaped microcore, made on a longitudinally split biface, is the dominant type. Shirataki–Hattoridai, Tachikaru–Shunai, Araya, and Etchuyama S are among the sites that have produced such specimens.

It is a fact of considerable interest that this north–south division in microcore technology corresponds quite precisely with that noted for the preceding stage of elongate-flake industries. Cylindrical or conical microcores also occur widely, but only sporadically, and not as a well-defined complex. Yasumiba, near the city of Shizuoka, and Yadegawa, in the mountains of central Honshu, produced some roughly conical cores rather like specimens from Fukui Rockshelter, in association with a number of small boat-shaped or half-cylindrical specimens.

Microblade tools as such, doubtless because of their tiny size, do not exhibit the kind of formal variation seen in larger artifacts. Microblades were rarely retouched. The only common modification was the snapping off of one or both ends of the blade to eliminate the bulb of percussion and pointed tip. The straight-sided blade segments thus produced were probably mounted as cutting edges in bone or antler hafts to make a variety of different composite tools, but of these no traces survive. Where unmodified blades survive, broader forms reflect the generally southerly distribution of the boat-shaped cores from which they were struck. More slender forms with sharply pointed tips reflect the more northerly distribution of the Yubetsu-type cores from which they were produced.

The distinctive burin type described from the Araya site in northern Honshu also belongs to the final stage of the Japanese Paleolithic. It has been found associated with microblades and Yubetsu-type microcores at many sites in northern Honshu and Hokkaido, and has been reported outside Japan from sites as far away as Mongolia and Alaska. The distribution of the Araya burin is predominantly northern, with little to indicate that it ever became significant to the microlithic industries of southern Japan.

Bifacially flaked projectile points, which first appeared in the context of earlier elongate flake assemblages, continued to occur in association with microblades in central and northern Japan. Yasumiba, Uenodaira, Etchuyama, Shirataki–Hattoridai, and Tachikaru–Shunai are among the sites that have yielded such associations, and there are many others as well. It is fascinating that not only are the two kinds of artifacts found physically associated, but that a very interesting linkage is vividly established between the microblade and biface technologies by the fact that Yubetsu-type microcores were made directly from large bifacially flaked points.

The way of life indicated by the Paleolithic sites described in this chapter can be characterized simply. Passing over the earliest stages, for which the evidence is still too dubious or scanty to warrant interpretation, the period from about 20,000 to 12,000 B.P. or so seems to have been one in which cultures much like those of the late Advanced Paleolithic and early Mesolithic in western and northern Eurasia flourished in Japan. Evidence indicates the repeated occupation of certain localities by people who were undoubtedly skilled and technologically sophisticated hunters and gatherers. In earlier times the elephant and other Pleistocene animals probably still roamed in Japan, and the bones of deer, boar, and smaller creatures found at a few later sites suggest something of the human hunters' diet then. Evidence of plant food remains in the archaeological sites is nil, but this is surely due to poor conditions for the preservation of such remains rather than to the neglect of plant foods by the human population. It seems likely that a rather different cultural milieu developed in the mountains and conifer–hardwood forests of northern Honshu and Hokkaido than that which evolved in the broad-leaved evergreen forests and around the warm shores of southern Japan's Inland Sea, but so far the details remain to be learned.

Scatters of fired pebbles and charcoal, a broad range of pounding, chopping, cutting, scraping, and piercing tools, and detritus from the making of stone artifacts indicate that many of the known sites were domestic settlements. Most of these were in the open air rather than in caves, which suggests that some sort of artificial shelter was also in widespread use. Detailed study of the internal variation within Paleolithic sites in Japan is still in its infancy, but such studies have been inaugurated at Nogawa and elsewhere, and there is promise of a much more detailed interpretation to come of this early lifeway.

It seems appropriate to bring this chapter to a close by making brief reference to a study that directly demonstrates the considerable geographical scope and scale of human interaction in Paleolithic Japan. As indicated in the preceding summary of findings at the Nogawa site, long-distance transport of obsidian for tool use was early established. A pioneering synthesis for the Tokyo region, which analyzed over 2000 obsidian specimens from some 130 archaeological sites of Paleolithic and later times, has shown that raw material from two main source areas in the mountains around Tokyo was being transported over distances of 150 km or more by as early as 20,000 years ago (Suzuki 1974).

Major sources of obsidian in the Shinshu region, around Lake Suwa 150 km northwest of Tokyo, and in the Hakone Mountains about 80 km southwest of Tokyo, have long been known. Another important source is the small island of Kozujima, in the Pacific Ocean south of Tokyo Bay, some 50 km offshore from the tip of the Izu Peninsula. These obsidian flows were geologically characterized by an ingenious technique that combined measurement of uranium content, petrographic analysis, and fission-track dating of the flows themselves. Using these data it was possible to identify the ultimate sources of the obsidian used for artifacts at a large number of archaeological sites with a high degree of confidence.

In addition to demonstrating that a far-flung obsidian distribution system was early established and maintained throughout the following millennia, the evidence also indicates that watercraft must have been in use from very early times. Obsidian from the Kozujima source has apparently been used on adjacent Honshu since 15,000 or 20,000 years ago, and the seafloor in the region is deep enough that the archipelago of which Kozujima was a part was probably not fully connected with Honshu even during the lowest sea level stage of the terminal Pleistocene.

This highly informative technique of analysis, which is also important as an essential step in the obsidian hydration dating process, is being carried on elsewhere in Japan as well. Within a few years it should be possible to map exchange spheres for the country as a whole, an exciting prospect. Already the broad scope of direct social interaction attested for the Tokyo region during the Paleolithic period is a notable datum.

3 : The Jomon Period

During the closing phases of the terminal Pleistocene, pottery appeared in Japan, first in Kyushu and a little later in Shikoku and central Honshu. This event marks the beginning of the Jomon tradition, which dominated the Japanese islands for over 10,000 years. The pottery appeared at first in the context of microlithic and large-biface-point industries that were not significantly different from those known from latest Paleolithic times in various parts of Japan, but soon the nature of the lithic industries underwent a change. The micro-blade technology was abandoned and a characteristic set of small triangular arrowpoints, chipped and ground stone axes or adzes, grinding stones, and other tools was adopted. This complex of pottery and stone tools persisted throughout the long Jomon period with only minor stylistic and incremental change through time, and this, with other evidence, reveals the Jomon tradition as a rich and successful hunting–fishing–gathering adaptation of remarkable stability and continuity.

A framework of broadly defined cultural periods, based on changes over time in ceramics, has been developed for the Jomon tradition as a whole. Very roughly, the Initial Jomon is characterized by pottery with linear-relief, appliqué, and nail-impressed decoration; Early Jomon, by simple cord-marked vessels with conoidal bottoms (*Jomon* means "cord-motif"); Middle Jomon, by deep vessels with a variety of cord-marked and elaborate sculptured motifs; Late Jomon, by a variety of pots and bowls embellished with zoned cord-marking; and Final

Jomon, by an even larger range of forms exhibiting zoned cord-marking, broad-line incision, and plain polished surfaces (Figure 3.1). There is also an Epi-Jomon period recognized in northern Honshu and Hokkaido, which represents a persistence of Jomon ceramic techniques into a time when the new Yayoi culture had replaced Jomon throughout southern and central Japan. This terminology, as can readily be seen, developed along with the process of discovery. Although ideally it is less than desirable to have a chronological system in which "early" and "late" do not designate the ends of the temporal continuum, this usage is based directly on the firmly established Japanese terminology, and it seems unwise to rename the periods simply for the sake of logical nicety.

These cultural periods have come to be well dated by a large number of ^{14}C determinations on organic matter found associated with pottery of diagnostic types (Figure 3.2). Though future work will certainly produce additional ^{14}C dates and further refinement of the details of the ceramic chronology within each of the major periods, it is unlikely that the broad outlines of the overall temporal framework

Decorative Modes (all pottery types)	Periods				
	Initial	Early	Middle	Late	Final
Incising			x	x	x
Grooving	x	x	x	x	x
Diagonal cord-marking	x	x	x	x	
Zoned cord-marking		x	x	x	
Herringbone cord-marking		x		x	
Bamboo stick-marking	x	x	x		
Woodgrain pattern cord-marking			x		
Knotted cord-marking		x			
Knotless cord-marking		x			
Net-shaped cord-marking		x			
Wheat pattern cord-marking		x			
Oblique variant cord-marking		x			
Shell-scraping	x	x			
Shell-impressing	x	x			
Shell-imprinting	x	x			
Punctuation	x	x			
Zigzag rouletting	x				
Lattice rouletting	x				
Elliptical rouletting	x				
Nail-marking	x				
Linear relief	x				

Figure 3.1 Principal decorative modes in the Jomon pottery of the Tokyo region. (Based on Kidder and Esaka 1968:282–283.)

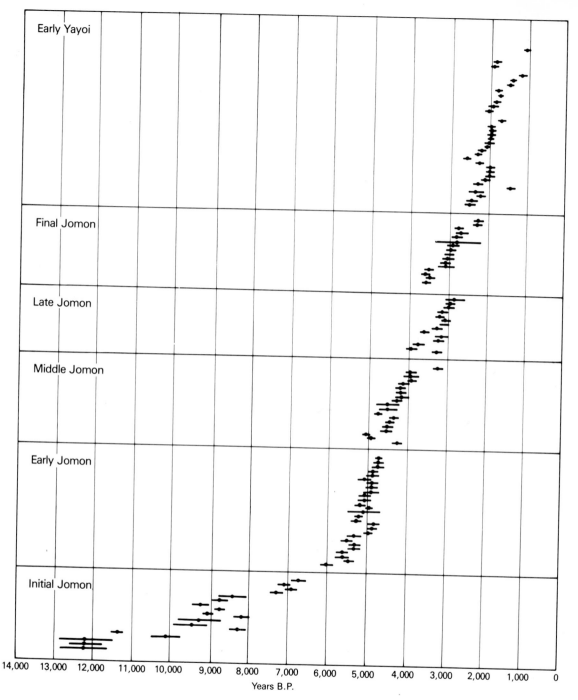

Figure 3.2   Carbon-14 dates associated with Jomon and Yayoi pottery. (Redrawn from Watanabe, in Serizawa 1974:Figure 285.)

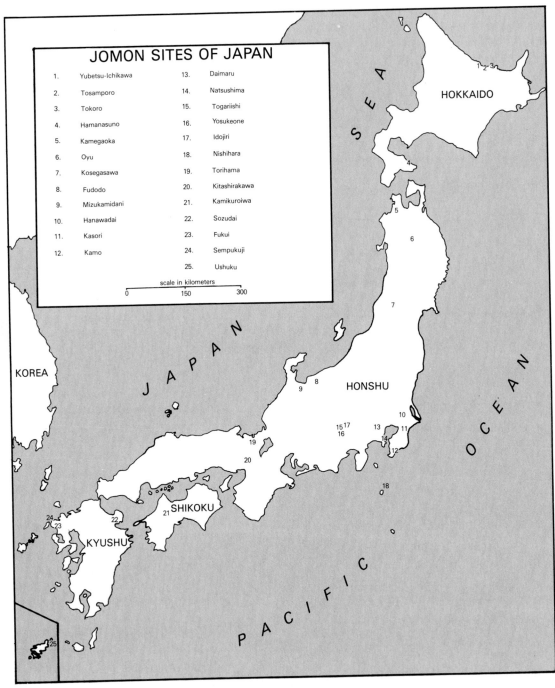

JOMON SITES OF JAPAN

1. Yubetsu-Ichikawa
2. Tosamporo
3. Tokoro
4. Hamanasuno
5. Kamegaoka
6. Oyu
7. Kosegasawa
8. Fudodo
9. Mizukamidani
10. Hanawadai
11. Kasori
12. Kamo
13. Daimaru
14. Natsushima
15. Togariishi
16. Yosukeone
17. Idojiri
18. Nishihara
19. Torihama
20. Kitashirakawa
21. Kamikuroiwa
22. Sozudai
23. Fukui
24. Sempukuji
25. Ushuku

scale in kilometers
0   150   300

Figure 3.3 Locations of principal Jomon sites mentioned in text.

shown in Figure 3.2 will be much altered. There would, however, seem to be some warrant for subdividing the very long Initial Jomon period, and indeed the earlier end of this period has been set off as a separate unit by Sugao Yamanouchi, late dean of Japanese archaeologists. This subdivision has not yet won complete acceptance among specialists involved with the Jomon culture, but as evidence continues to accumulate, it may well become accepted. If such a period were to be established, it might reasonably be referred to as Incipient Jomon.

In the following pages are described a series of sites selected as exemplars of the most significant temporal and regional developments within the Jomon tradition (Figure 3.3). Although, of course, archaeological details and nuances of interpretation could be multiplied almost indefinitely by a more exhaustive survey, the sites chosen for review are some of the best known and most discussed in Japanese archaeological circles, and they are believed to provide a good general perspective on most important aspects of the Jomon culture.

Fukui

Fukui Rockshelter is in extreme western Kyushu, about 60 km north of the city of Nagasaki (Kamaki and Serizawa 1965, 1967). It is a medium-sized overhang at the base of a sandstone outcrop, open and well lighted, with a southwestern exposure looking out over the Fukui River. Other small shelters occur nearby along the base of the same outcrop, and archaeological remains are present at some of them as well. In the past, as now, the area was apparently an ideal residential location.

Fukui Rockshelter is particularly significant because cultural continuity between the preceramic and ceramic stages of prehistoric Japanese culture was first directly demonstrated there. Potsherds of very early type occurred in Strata 2 and 3 associated with microblades and boat-shaped microcores; in the preceding stratum, 4, the microblade industry occurred without pottery. Microlithic industries are known from many Late Paleolithic sites throughout Japan, and it was at Fukui Rockshelter that the late Paleolithic and Jomon cultures were first convincingly linked in a single continuous stratigraphic and typological succession (Figure 3.4).

A trench dug from the front to the back of the shelter cut down through 15 natural strata in penetrating to a depth 5.5 m beneath the surface, where bedrock was finally encountered and excavation halted. The cultural remains came from Strata 1–4, 7, 9, and 15. Stratum 1 was a disturbed mixture of Jomon and protohistoric materials that need not be discussed further, and Strata 5, 6, 8, and 10–14 were essentially barren.

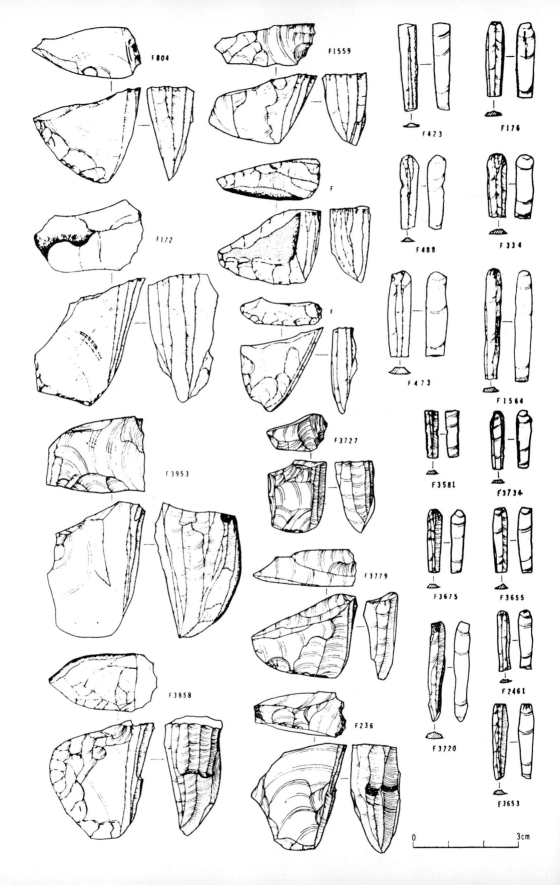

F804

F1559

F172

F

F

F423

F176

F488

F334

F473

F1564

F3727

F3779

F3953

F3858

F236

F3581

F3734

F3675

F3655

F2461

F3720

F3653

0   3cm

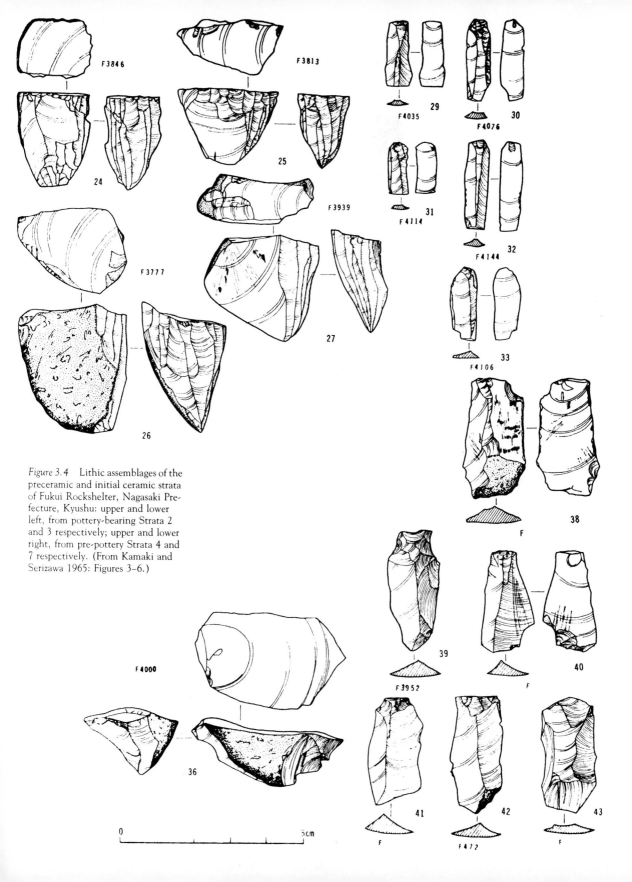

Figure 3.4 Lithic assemblages of the preceramic and initial ceramic strata of Fukui Rockshelter, Nagasaki Prefecture, Kyushu: upper and lower left, from pottery-bearing Strata 2 and 3 respectively; upper and lower right, from pre-pottery Strata 4 and 7 respectively. (From Kamaki and Serizawa 1965: Figures 3–6.)

Figure 3.5 Pottery vessel with linear-relief Decoration, of the Initial Jomon from Ishigoya Cave, Nagano Prefecture, central Honshu. This is one of a very few complete Initial Jomon vessels known. Sherds of a similar linear-relief ware from Fukui Rockshelter, Nagasaki, are among the earliest ceramics known from Japan. Height, 25 cm. (Shown one-half actual size.) (Courtesy K. Higuchi, Kokugakuin University.)

Among the earliest artifacts, which came from Stratum 15, were a broken piece of a large, well-flaked biface, and a smaller bifacially flaked axelike implement. A number of large, elongate end-blow flakes or blades also occurred. The assemblage from Stratum 9 included several large, heavy flakes, of which two were apparently the remnants of cores from which smaller flakes had been removed by a side-blow technique. From Stratum 7 came a number of small parallel-sided end-blow blades and the roughly cylindrical and half-cylindrical cores they were struck from. The blades were rather short and broad, and the cores prepared only roughly. The archaeological record up to this point was sparse, but adequate to show that the site was occupied well back into Late Paleolithic times.

Microblades and boat-shaped microcores first appeared in Stratum 4. The microblades were of roughly the same length as the small blades of Stratum 7, but only about half the width. The microcores were more refined, smaller versions of the half-cylindrical core type of Stratum 7, some sufficiently elongate to be termed boat-shaped cores (Hayashi 1968). A large, leaf-shaped bifacially flaked point and some unifacially retouched scrapers made on large, broad flakes were associated with the microliths. The microblades of Strata 3 and 2 were slightly longer and slimmer than those of Stratum 4, but all three assemblages may reasonably be characterized as closely related stages of a single industry. Scrapers were also present in Strata 3 and 2, but bifacially flaked points were not.

The pottery that first appeared in Stratum 3 in association with microblades is among the earliest known from Japan. The finds included a number of small sherds ornamented with relatively broad modeled bands of linear-relief decoration (Figure 3.5). These were present only in Stratum 3. Sherds with fine-line linear-relief decoration and fingernail-impressed decoration occurred in both Stratum 3 and the overlying Stratum 2. The fingernail-impressed motif increased in abundance over time, becoming the dominant type in the upper part of Stratum 2.

The ^{14}C dates obtained for the Fukui sequence as a whole are somewhat confused (Table 3.1). The dates were determined by two different laboratories, and it is of interest to note that the ages obtained by Gakushuin University (GaK-949, etc.) are all in consistent

TABLE 3.1
Carbon-14 Dates from Fukui Rockshelter[a]

Stratum	Age determination (B.P.)	Laboratory Number[b]
2	12,400 ± 350	GaK-949
3	12,700 ± 500	GaK-950
4	14,400 ± 400	I-945
7	13,600 ± 600	GaK-951
9	13,130 ± 600	I-947
12	10,700 ± 300	I-946
15	>31,900	GaK-952

[a] From Kamaki and Serizawa 1967.
[b] GaK, Gakushuin University; I, Isotopes Laboratory.

stratigraphic order, whereas those produced by the Isotopes Laboratory (I-945, etc.) are in precisely the reverse of the order that would be expected according to their stratigraphic provenience.

Various speculations could be advanced to account for the discrepant dates, but for present purposes the problem can simply be avoided. It is enough here to note that the inconsistencies arise in the lower part of the archaeological sequence, and do not affect the strata that record the initial appearance of pottery. Moreover, the dates of 12,400 and 12,700 B.P. for the linear-relief pottery of Strata 2 and 3 agree very well with an independent ^{14}C date of 12,165 B.P. for similar pottery from the site of Kamikuroiwa in Shikoku, reinforcing confidence in their accuracy.

Sempukuji   Sempukuji Cave, in northwestern Kyushu's port city of Sasebo, amplifies the record of the Paleolithic–Jomon transition in southwestern Japan (Aso and Shiraishi 1975). Preliminary reports describe extensive excavations in the large open cave or rockshelter, revealing the occurrence of microlithic tools and very early pottery in an orderly stratigraphic sequence. The discovery of a new variety of linear-relief pottery decorated with bean-shaped appliqué fillets, in a layer beneath one containing linear-relief pottery like that of the first ceramic-bearing stratum of Fukui Rockshelter, suggests that the initial Sempukuji pottery may be the oldest yet discovered.

Thirteen natural strata were recognized within 2 m of cave deposit. Pottery sherds with bean-appliqué decoration appeared in the first cultural layer, immediately above a sterile bed of angular sandstone derived from the underlying bedrock. A massive rockfall stratum divided the bed containing this pottery into upper and lower layers. Accompanying the ceramics both above and below the rockfall were many microblades and boat-shaped microcores, along with large, thick biface "blanks" and spall flakes, which may represent stages in the preparation of boat-shaped microcores. Endscrapers and rough percussion-flaked axes also were present. These beds were, in all, over .5 m thick, and yielded a large sample of both ceramic and lithic specimens.

A second series of beds conformably overlying the first, also about .5 m in thickness, produced pottery with yet another variety of linear-relief decoration. The bean-appliqué and linear-relief varieties overlapped slightly in stratigraphic distribution, suggesting an unbroken transition. Microblade cores and microblades were common in these layers. Nail-impressed pottery occurred in an overlying stratum, which was separated from that yielding the linear-relief ware by a layer of massive rocks that had fallen from the shelter ceiling. A fireplace near the front of the cave was associated with this level.

Pottery with roller-impressed decoration occurred in a subsequent level. Stick-impressed and streaked ceramics are also said to occur in the sequence between the nail-marked and roller-impressed wares, but their stratigraphic placement and relative abundance are unclear. The roller-impressed ware was associated with a stone-paved area and three stone-lined fire pits toward the front of the shelter, and related stone tools included a large, stemmed scraper and several bifacially flaked points. One large, leaf-shaped specimen had been reworked, giving it a series of burin facets at one end. Two smaller points were triangular in outline, with deeply indented bases, and two broken specimens were probably of the leaf-shaped type.

The archaeological record of Initial Jomon times ends near the surface of the deposit, the final few centimeters of fill producing only scattered items of Late Jomon, Final Jomon, and Heian period culture. The inner part of the shelter, which yielded the early remains, was apparently abandoned as the accumulating deposits neared the ceiling, eliminating the well-protected living space that had sheltered the site's early occupants.

The age of the earliest Sempukuji pottery is not precisely established. Because it stratigraphically precedes pottery of a type ^{14}C dated to 12,400 and 12,700 B.P. at Fukui Rockshelter, and 12,165 B.P. at Kamikuroiwa, it should be at least 12 millennia old, and presumably older. Yet an analysis of obsidian associated with the bean-appliqué pottery at Sempukuji gave a date of only 10,500 years ago. It seems unlikely, however, that such a late date will gain general acceptance, in view of the earlier ^{14}C dates for similar pottery elsewhere, and the well-recognized tendency, in Japan at least, for the obsidian dating method to yield dates younger than those derived by the ^{14}C technique for comparable specimens. If the bean-appliqué ware is considered as only a variant form of linear-relief ware, as indeed appears reasonable since both use the appliqué technique (Y. Suzuki 1977), a date on the order of those from Fukui and Kamikuroiwa would seem appropriate for Sempukuji as well.

It is of special interest that by the time roller-impressed pottery appeared in the archaeological sequence, the microlithic industry that was a legacy of Paleolithic times no longer occurred at Sempukuji. In its place was a very different stone tool assemblage, one clearly related to the lithic industry of the mature Jomon tradition. Leaf-shaped and triangular biface points, and a stemmed scraper of a highly distinctive type known to persist until the very end of Jomon times, were among the finds associated with the roller-impressed ceramics.

Kamikuroiwa   The rockshelter site of Kamikuroiwa, located in the interior of western Shikoku about 30 km east of the city of Matsuyama, is also of major importance to the understanding of Jomon origins. The shelter is at the base of a limestone bluff long ago undercut by the Kuma River, which has now shifted its course farther out onto the alluvial plain that the site overlooks. Several trenches were dug under the shelter, sectioning 2 m of deposit (Esaka and Nishida 1967).

A thin surface stratum containing Kofun period artifacts and some quite early Jomon burials was sealed off from the underlying Initial Jomon horizon by a thick rockfall layer, a thin bed containing a few artifacts, another rockfall layer, and a laminated bed of water-deposited clays and gravels. A ^{14}C sample collected from this alluvial bed yielded a date of 10,700 B.P. Below these culturally sterile layers were alternating bands of brown clay and darker earth, amounting to about .5 m in thickness, which contained the Initial Jomon artifacts that give Kamikuroiwa its special importance.

Charcoal found in the Initial Jomon deposits produced a ^{14}C date of 12,165 B.P. The pottery from this level was essentially identical to that from Fukui and the earlier levels of Sempukuji. It was embellished with parallel bands of fine-line linear-relief decoration, and the shapes of recovered fragments suggest that the vessels were deep, round-bottomed pots (cf. Figure 3.5). Accompanying the pottery sherds were several triangular projectile points with tanged bases, shaped like the Yuzetsu points known from preceramic and early ceramic times in northeastern Japan, but smaller and thinner than most. Two roughly flaked, thick, heavy bifaces, a crude chopper, and other lithic specimens also occurred.

Microblades were not present at Kamikuroiwa, as they were at Fukui and Sempukuji. Instead, bifacial projectile points were the diagnostic elements of the lithic industry here associated with the early linear-relief pottery. The projectile points and other stone artifacts give the Kamikuroiwa lithic assemblage a composition like that of the postmicrolithic period at Sempukuji. Yet the postmicrolithic Sempukuji stone tool assemblage seems to be significantly later in time than the comparable one from Kamikuroiwa, as shown by its association with roller-impressed pottery, which comes well after linear-relief ware in the stratigraphic sequence at Sempukuji. In this connection it is interesting to note that the earliest pottery to appear farther north also occurs with biface projectile points, as illustrated by the following example of Kosegasawa Cave. The evidence thus suggests that pottery was spreading from south to north at the same time that the new lithic industry was spreading from north to south.

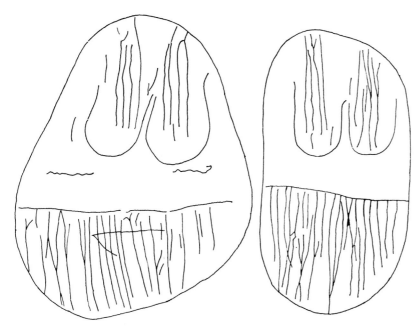

Figure 3.6   Incised stones with possible female representations, of the Initial Jomon from Kamikuroiwa, Ehime Prefecture, Shikoku. (From Esaka and Nishida 1967.)

Before turning from Kamikuroiwa, notice must be taken of some remarkable specimens that could be considered the first representatives of the long-enduring and continuously evolving tradition of Jomon charms and talismans. Seven river pebbles of naturally ovate, flattened form, engraved with parallel, crosshatch, and curvilinear lines, were found associated with the linear-relief pottery. Two of them seem to represent bare-breasted women with long hair, wearing skirts made of hanging cords (Figure 3.6). This interpretation is somewhat imaginative, since none of the specimens bear marks clearly indicating a head, arms, or legs. Nevertheless, they are clearly symbolic objects, and an anthropomorphic interpretation is defensible.

Kosegasawa Cave is in steep, mountainous country near the Japan Sea Coast, about 60 km south of the city of Niigata, in northwestern Honshu. The site is on the middle slopes of Mount Kosegasawa, overlooking the narrow valley of the Muroya River. A warm southern exposure, a small stream for culinary use close by, and ready access to the trout, salmon, dace, and other natural resources of the river valley

Kosegasawa

below made the sheltered site a highly favorable spot for human habitation (Nakamura 1960).

A stratified rocky deposit up to 2 m deep choked the portal of the cave at the time of its discovery, and spilled out onto a small terrace in front of it. The uppermost meter or so of the cave fill lacked cultural remains, but lying below were three beds comprising a cultural stratum about 1 m in thickness, which yielded several hearths and nearly 12,000 artifacts.

Approximately 1000 small fragments of pottery were recovered. The lowest bed contained relatively few sherds, all of types better represented in the two higher levels. Fine-line linear-relief pottery analogous to that known from the sites in Kyushu and Shikoku was not abundant at the site, but most of that which occurred was found in the lower two beds. Comb-pattern and stick-impressed ware were most abundant in the middle level, whereas fingernail-impressed ware, appliqué-design ware, and pottery decorated by rouletting with a cord-wrapped stick were about equally distributed between the upper two levels. Roller-impressed and incised sherds were concentrated in the uppermost bed. All of these types belong to the very beginnings of the Jomon ceramic tradition in northern Japan, as determined not only by the excavations at Kosegasawa, but by archaeological work elsewhere as well. Documentation of their occurrence in stratigraphic order at Kosegasawa was one of the most important fruits of the excavation there.

Large, well-made bifacially flaked projectile points made on elongate bladelike flakes were associated with the ceramics in all three cultural layers. Over 500 such specimens, complete or broken, were recovered. Slender leaf-shaped and stemmed points were more common in the earlier levels, and broader leaf-shaped ones somewhat more prevalent later, but all types occurred throughout the Initial Jomon occupation. Many of the slender points were very thick in cross section, to the extent that they are characterized as cylindrical. Many of the broader points lacked the fine retouch seen on the more slender specimens, and were perhaps blanks or preforms that had not been rendered into final shape.

Over 500 additional flaked stone points of quite different character are believed to be arrowheads. Leaf-shaped and stemmed forms occurred, but they were much shorter, thinner, and lighter than their large counterparts. A number of triangular specimens with deeply indented bases had no larger counterparts at Kosegasawa, but they are highly reminiscent of the projectile points from the later part of the Initial Jomon period at Sempukuji and from many sites of subsequent Jomon periods.

Associated with the bifacial artifacts was a core-and-blade technology represented by several hundred specimens. Straight, parallel-sided blades up to 10 cm long were retouched to form side-blades for knives, perforators, gravers, burins, sidescrapers, and endscrapers. From some were fashioned highly distinctive stemmed scrapers of a type that first appeared widely at about this time and persisted to the end of the Jomon cultural tradition. Some tiny, thick, bladelike flakes of microlithic size also occurred. Cores were extremely rare, but a few utterly exhausted fragments suggest that roughly prepared cylindrical or half-cylindrical cores were used to produce the larger blades. Some fragments of longitudinally split bifacial points may be discards from a process by which boat-shaped microblade cores were formed, but this is uncertain.

A substantial number of heavy, unifacially beveled percussion-flaked adze blades, over 100 in all, complement the collection of endscrapers, gravers, and the like, to suggest that woodworking was an important industry at Kosegasawa Cave. These specimens, made on elongate pebbles or very large parallel-sided flakes, ranged between about 10 and 20 cm in length. They were usually flaked all over their upper surfaces, and were occasionally ground and polished at their tips. Several fragmentary specimens ground and polished over all of their extant surface may represent completely ground and polished celts. A few pieces of ground stone, perhaps whetstones, and a single milling stone or quern fragment complete the list of ground stone artifacts.

A number of fragments of split and broken bone included three pointed specimens, perhaps tools of some kind. Species represented by the bones included deer, boar, bear, rabbit, squirrel, and ermine, all of which occur in the surrounding countryside today.

The Initial Jomon occupation at Kosegasawa Cave probably spans a period between about 12,000 and 9000 years ago. Pottery with rouletted string-impressed designs, which appears in the upper levels, is like a ware that is ^{14}C dated to about 9500 B.P. at the Natsushima site, near Yokohama, and pottery with linear-relief decoration, which appears in the lower levels, is of a type known to be older than 12,000 B.P. at Fukui and Kamikuroiwa in southwestern Japan.

The Kosegasawa occupation belongs entirely to the Jomon period, since no levels lacked ceramics. However, its transitional character is clearly shown by the fact that the pottery is of the earliest types known from Japan, while the large bifacial points and blades of the lithic assemblage are unquestionably continuous with those of industries known from terminal Paleolithic times. Partially ground stone celts, known elsewhere from both Paleolithic and Jomon contexts, also oc-

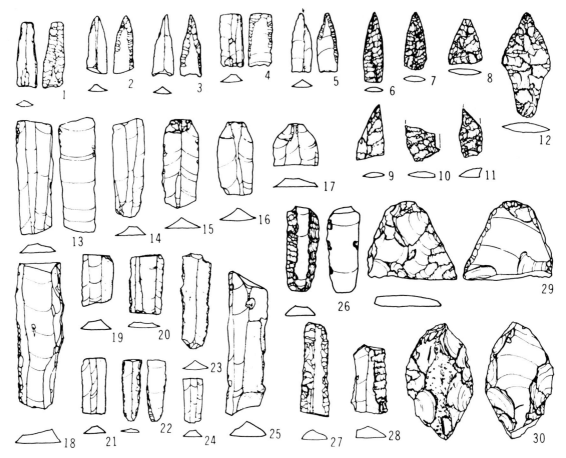

Figure 3.7 Points made on blades, biface points, and blade tools and blade cores found with earliest Jomon pottery at Yubetsu–Ichikawa, Hokkaido. (Shown one-half actual size.) (From Yubetsu–Ichikawa Chosa Dan 1973:Figure 31.)

cur, as do arrowheads and hafted scrapers of types that continue well into Jomon times, long after the disappearance of the earlier lithic industry based on prepared cores and blades.

Yubetsu–Ichikawa   Yubetsu–Ichikawa, about 25 km northeast of the Late Paleolithic site of Tachikaru–Shunai on the edge of the Okhotsk Sea, continues the regional archaeological sequence for northeastern Hokkaido into the beginning of Jomon times (Yubetsu–Ichikawa Chosa Dan 1973). The site lies on the 5-m terrace of the Okhotsk seaboard, within 1 km of the mouth of the Yubetsu River. The terrain is grassland, with

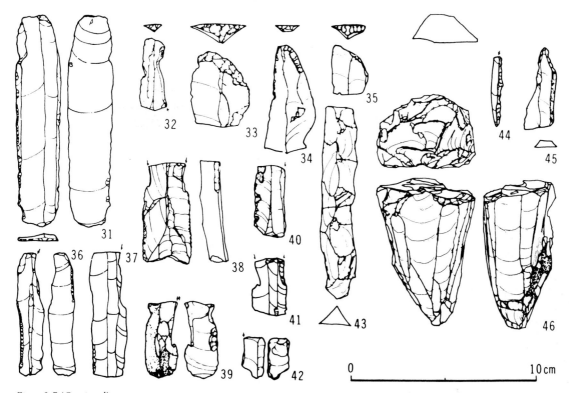

Figure 3.7 (Continued)

willow, birch, and reeds along the little streams that flow from the higher ground behind the site into the sea.

Several localities where blades, blade cores, pottery, and other specimens were observed on the surface occur within a few hundred meters of one another along the marine terrace. Previous excavations, only partially reported, showed the potential of the area for providing information on the juncture between Paleolithic and Jomon times, and the study summarized here was carried out in the hope of elucidating this transition.

The main excavation at Yubetsu–Ichikawa consisted of a trench 2–3 m wide, which extended for over 150 m along a small drainage channel that cut through the site. The soil stratigraphy was complicated by differential rates of deposition from place to place within the site due to minor topographic variation, and by heaving of the soil by repeated freezing and thawing. These conditions precluded the establishment of a refined stratigraphic framework, but as later analysis based on roughly established stratigraphic divisions showed, there was no consistent variation in artifact types and frequencies from bottom to top of the cultural deposit. Though other possibilities cannot be rigorously excluded, it seems likely from internal evidence and the dating considerations to be presented that a single period of occupation is represented at the site.

Of principal interest at Yubetsu–Ichikawa is the association of long, slender lanceolate arrowpoints made on blades, with Jomon pottery of the earliest type known for Hokkaido (Figure 3.7). The Initial Jomon ceramic specimens, all badly fragmented, included both plain and cord-marked varieties. A few sherds from near the surface of the site were recognized as being of the well-known Hokuto type, which belongs to a later period and is believed to postdate the main occupation. Other items of blade tool technology included many knives, endscrapers, and sidescrapers, some of which were found in the bottom of a shallow aboriginally dug pit directly associated with cord-marked pottery. Most of the reworked blades had been broken into segments 4–8 cm long, but some nearly complete specimens ranged between 15 and 19 cm in length. Blades in the microlithic size range were present but rare, and all the blade cores found were large, roughly conical or cylindrical specimens.

Stone artifacts not of the blade tool tradition were also well represented. Among them were a few leaf-shaped biface points, and some large triangular points with tapering stems, like those of the Engaru and Tachikawa types at the nearby preceramic site of Tachikaru–Shunai. Polished stone axeheads, notched sinker stones, milling or grinding slabs, and some broken tools that appear to have been hafted scrapers were all of types familiar from Jomon period sites, and they complement the ceramic evidence to underscore the transitional character of the Yubetsu–Ichikawa assemblage.

The date of the sites' occupation is believed to lie between 7000 and 8500 years ago, since its pottery and its blade arrowheads are essentially identical to specimens ^{14}C dated to that time range at several other northern Hokkaido sites. Three ^{14}C samples of charcoal from Yubetsu–Ichikawa gave dates between about 4000 and 5500 B.P., considered much too recent in view of the comparative typological evidence. This dating anomaly remains unexplained, though it has been suggested that much later charcoal may have been carried down to the lower levels of the site by postoccupation frost-heaving phenomena.

The excavators of Yubetsu–Ichikawa point out striking similarities in both typology and overall composition between its artifact assemblage and that of the Novopetrovka culture of the Middle Amur River in Manchuria. Both inventories are characterized by long, slender arrowheads made on blades, bifacially flaked stemmed points, scrapers, gravers, and knives made on large blades, notched sinker stones, grinding slabs, and stone axes. Small amounts of plain and surface-manipulated pottery also occur in both cultural inventories, but the wares are quite different typologically. Squarish semisubterranean pithouses with rounded corners, known from the Novopetrovka culture, are reminiscent of Initial Jomon pithouses known from several northeastern Hokkaido sites, though no dwellings were identified at Yubetsu-Ichikawa itself. A ^{14}C date of about 4200 B.P. from a site of the Novopetrovka culture suggests that it is later than the beginnings of the blade arrowhead phase of Initial Jomon in Hokkaido, but of course there may well be earlier manifestations yet to be discovered in the Amur region.

Many sites in addition to those just sketched are known to have been occupied during the incipient phase of Initial Jomon times. Since the first discoveries at Kosegasawa, Fukui, and Kamikuroiwa, evidence has accumulated rapidly (Suzuki 1977). Regrettably, ^{14}C dates for this period are still few, but evidence is already sufficient to indicate that between approximately 12,500 and 10,000 years ago, pottery spread throughout the southern islands of Japan, from southwestern Kyushu to northern Honshu (Figure 3.2). In Hokkaido, at the northern end of the Japanese archipelago, the Jomon age dawned later, with the earliest ^{14}C dates for pottery falling around 8500 B.P. Typological and stratigraphic evidence supports the conclusion to be drawn from the ^{14}C dates, in that the first ceramics to appear in central and northeastern Japan were of slightly later types than those that were the first to appear in southern Japan. When the evidence from Hokkaido is considered, this tendency is still clearer. The earliest pottery known there is less similar to the Initial Jomon types known farther south than to the types of the subsequent Early Jomon period of central and northern Honshu.

The stone tools found with the earliest ceramics also differ from north to south. As seen in the preceding chapter on the Paleolithic period, microlithic industries were present throughout the Japanese islands in late glacial times. Bifacially flaked projectile points were an integral part of many of these industries, and became increasingly common toward the end of the microlithic phase, especially in central and northern Japan. In the mature Jomon tradition bifacially flaked projectile points, though radically reduced in size, continued as an important element, but the microblade technology was abandoned. It is significant, therefore, that the first Initial Jomon pottery of Kyushu

The Paleolithic–Jomon Transition

appears in association with a microlithic industry, whereas at Kamikuroiwa in Shikoku and north, the first Initial Jomon ceramics occur not with microblades but with lithic assemblages dominated by bifacially flaked projectile points. This is true of Hokkaido as well, although there the picture is complicated by the considerably later appearance of pottery and the occurrence of distinctive arrowheads made on large blades, clearly of Northeast Asian affinities.

These distributions, straightforwardly interpreted, suggest that ceramics were introduced from the continent via Korea and spread northward among societies then in the process of modifying and expanding some aspects of their indigenous lithic technology and abandoning others. When it is considered that this same interval was also a time of major climatic and environmental change coincident with the end of the Pleistocene glacial age, it becomes clear that the shifts noted in artifact assemblages were part of a major cultural readaptation. The character of the latest Paleolithic and incipient Jomon lifeways that formed the basis of this readaptation is not yet understood in detail, but by the latter half of the Initial Jomon period, relative residential stability, shellfish gathering, fishing, hunting of a wide variety of birds and mammals, processing of plant foods, and the construction of substantial semisubterranean pithouses were well attested. The site of Natsushima, which was first occupied about the middle of Initial Jomon times, will introduce most of these developments.

Natsushima   Natsushima is a small island near the western edge of Tokyo Bay, a few kilometers south of Yokohama (Sugihara and Serizawa 1957). It has been much modified in recent times and is now joined to the mainland, but it was formerly a low wooded islet several hundred meters across, its highest point about 45 m above sea level. The shell midden that was subjected to archaeological excavation lies on a sloping point near the southern end of the island. A number of well-known Jomon sites occur on the adjacent bayshore and on nearby islands, including the Hirasaka shell mounds, the Daimaru site, and others,

The Natsushima excavations, made shortly after World War II, contributed importantly to shaping a new understanding of Jomon archaeology. The stratigraphic succession within the shell mound demonstrated a close sequential relationship between the earliest pottery types then known from the Tokyo area. Furthermore, one of the first few ^{14}C determinations to be obtained for Japanese archaeological materials was from Natsushima, providing the first (and surprisingly early) absolute date for the beginning of the Jomon cultural sequence. Additionally, the stone, bone, and shell artifacts, and the occurrence of fish, bird, and mammal bones not often preserved in Jomon sites, concretely demonstrated the existence of a remarkably rich and mature fishing and hunting lifeway for Initial Jomon times.

Approximately half of the Natsushima shell midden, which was roughly 15 m in diameter and 1.5 m deep, was excavated. Four main stratigraphic units were traceable throughout the midden, and in some places further subdivision of the deposit was possible. The archaeological beds were faulted in several places, evidently from the tectonic disturbances so common in the Tokyo region. A bed of shell resting on sterile volcanic soil formed the base of the mound. This was overlaid by a bed of humus mixed with shell, another bed of shell, and another bed of humus mixed with shell, which extended to the surface. Artifacts occurred throughout these layers, but with one exception no cultural features other than artifacts were discovered.

Lying on the volcanic soil surface beneath the earliest shell bed was a hearth, which consisted of many large pebbles strewn beside a roughly circular concentration of ash, charcoal, and burned earth. A ^{14}C determination on charcoal from this fireplace gave a date of 9450 B.P., establishing what was then an unexpectedly great age for Initial Jomon culture. So surprisingly early was it—about twice the generally accepted age estimate for Initial Jomon—that it was at first widely disbelieved. As more and more ^{14}C dates on Jomon sites have accumulated, however, the Natsushima date has been seen to fit well into the overall framework of Jomon chronology, and is no longer seriously doubted.

Over 10,000 pottery sherds were excavated at Natsushima. The few completely restorable vessels were all conical with pointed or rounded bottoms, as were all but a handful of some 90 vessels whose base shapes could be determined from fragmentary evidence. Decorative techniques seen on the pottery included cord-impressing of various kinds, incising, shell-stamping, and some appliqué. Impressions made by rolling a cord-wrapped stick over the wet clay of a vessel before firing produced the so-called Yoriitomon motif, which characterized the earliest pottery from the site (Figures 3.8–3.11).

The stone tool assemblage accompanying the earliest ceramic types at Natsushima was dominated by a large number of roughly flaked axe- or adzeheads, some of them partially ground at the bit. These became rare in the later levels. Milling stones were few but occurred throughout; both grinding slabs and mortars were represented. Small triangular flaked stone arrowheads, also few, similarly occurred throughout but were most numerous in the later levels. Bone arrowheads, points,

Figure 3.8 Pot with string-rouletted (Yoriitomon) decoration of the Initial Jomon from Natsushima, in Tokyo Bay, central Honshu. Height, 32 cm. (Shown approximately one-half actual size.) (Courtesy S. Sugihara, Meiji University.)

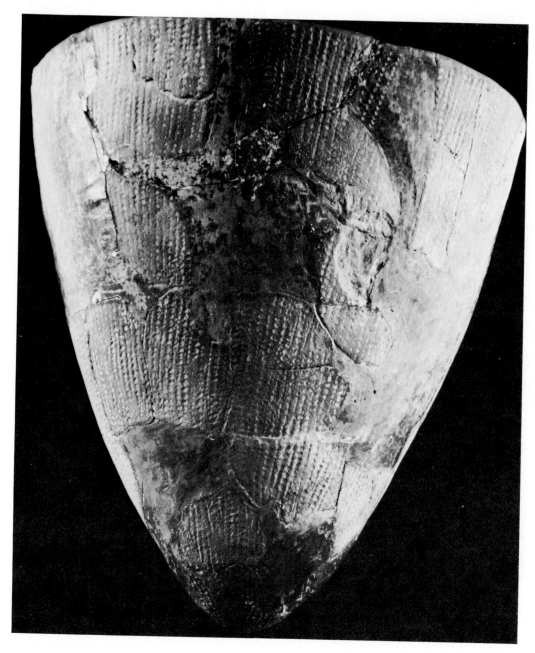

Figure 3.9 Pot with cord-impressed (Jomon) decoration of the Initial Jomon from Natsushima in Tokyo Bay, central Honshu. Height 22 cm. (Courtesy S. Sugihara, Meiji University.)

Figure 3.10 Pot with sculptured rim and appliqué decoration of the Early Jomon from Natsushima, in Tokyo Bay, central Honshu. Sekiyama type. Height, 20 cm. (Shown approximately three-quarters actual size.) (Courtesy S. Sugihara, Meiji University.)

Figure 3.11 Pot with zoned cord-marking and appliqué decoration, of the Early Jomon from Natsushima, in Tokyo Bay, central Honshu. Sekiyama type. Height 22 cm. (Shown approximately three-quarters actual size.) (Courtesy S. Sugihara, Meiji University.)

needles, fishhooks, and other tools of unknown use were found throughout the stratigraphic sequence (Figures 3.12–3.15). Bird bone was favored for the making of these tools in the earlier period, with deer bone and antler coming into use later. A small axe made of a boar tusk is attributed to the latest part of the occupation.

The faunal remains from Natsushima included 34 species of oysters, clams, and other shellfish, 17 species of large and small marine fishes, 7 species of land and sea birds, and 11 species of mammals, including boar, hare, the raccoon-dog (*Nyctereutes*), dog, and dolphin. Oysters were most abundant in the early levels of the midden, later decreased in number, then again became abundant in the upper layers. This phenomenon appears also in other shell mounds around Tokyo Bay, and is believed to indicate a deepening of the bay's waters in Early Jomon times, followed by a recession to the modern level by Middle Jomon times. The vertebrate species showed no conspicuous trends in changing abundance over time. In fact, the occurrence of most species from top to bottom of the site deposits suggests that the local environment remained stable in most respects throughout the time that the Natsushima shell mound was occupied.

Since no architectural remains were found at Natsushima, it is not completely clear whether the site should be considered a stable residential location or a campsite. The varied food and artifactual remains, however, suggest relatively long-term occupation. Stable resi-

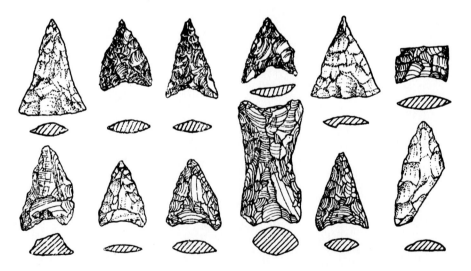

Figure 3.12 Small triangular arrowpoints and scraper of the Initial Jomon from Natsushima, in Tokyo Bay, central Honshu. (Shown actual size.) (From Sugihara and Serizawa 1957:Figure 24.)

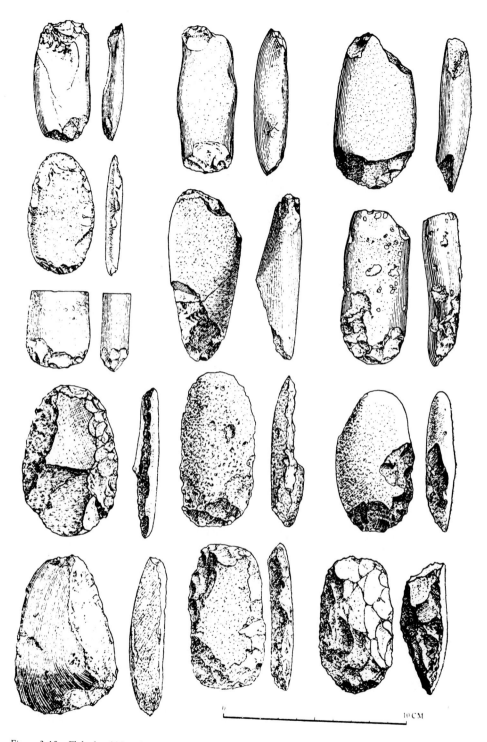

Figure 3.13 Flaked pebble adzes of the Initial Jomon from Natsushima, in Tokyo Bay, central Honshu. (Shown approximately one-half actual size.) (From Sugihara and Serizawa 1957:Figure 21.)

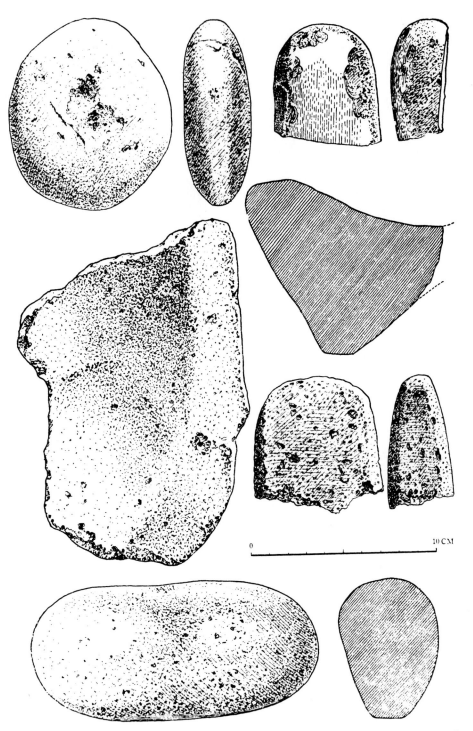

0   10 CM

Figure 3.14   Grinding stones of the Initial Jomon from Natsushima, in Tokyo Bay, central Honshu. (Shown approximately one-half actual size.) (From Sugihara and Serizawa 1957:Figure 23.)

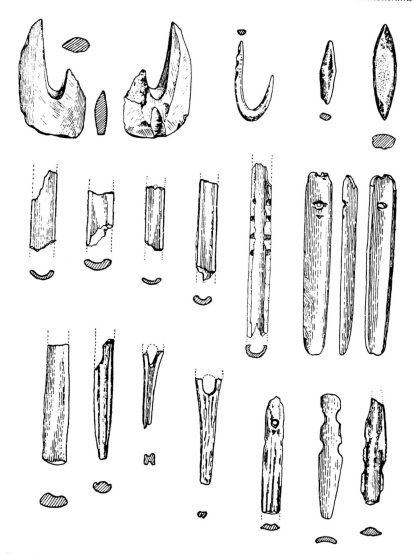

Figure 3.15 Bone fishhooks, fish gorges, needles or net shuttles, and unidentified specimens of the Initial and/or Early Jomon from Natsushima, in Tokyo Bay, central Honshu. Length of specimen at upper left, ca. 3.2 cm. (Shown approximately actual size.) (From Sugihara and Serizawa 1957:Figure 26.)

dential sites with pithouse architecture were in fact established in the region at this time, as indicated by findings at Hanawadai, in Ibaraki Prefecture, and dwellings may have also been present at Natsushima, in unexcavated areas adjacent to the shell midden.

At Hanawadai, the traces of five shallow semisubterranean

pithouses were discovered, giving a picture of Initial Jomon dwellings as fairly substantial rectangular structures, about 3.5 × 6.5 m across, with roof-support posts in each corner and down the midline of the floor. Internal fireplaces were lacking. Burned areas and charcoal found between the Hanawadai structures suggest that cooking took place outside rather than indoors as in later times (Tsuboi 1971:114–115). The open hearth found at Natsushima could reflect a similar pattern.

Kamo   The Kamo site, which was occupied during Early Jomon and to some extent Middle Jomon times, demonstrates a strong continuity with the preceding Initial Jomon, supporting and amplifying the cultural and environmental record from Natsushima. Kamo is near the southern tip of the Boso Peninsula, on the side facing the Pacific Ocean (Matsumoto *et al.* 1952). This massive peninsula bounds Tokyo Bay on the east, and the site lies about 70 km south and slightly east of Tokyo itself. The site is at the base of a low range of hills, on the edge of a small, wet, alluvium-filled basin used in recent times for paddy field cultivation. Earlier, as the archaeological excavations showed, the basin was a swampy inlet, and the excellent preservation of normally perishable organic remains for which Kamo is noted is a function of their having been buried in a continuously wet geological context, where normal processes of decay were inhibited.

A large block excavation, opened at the base of the hill, extended to shale bedrock at a depth of about 3 m. Upon this base lay a bed of blue clay, one of peat, and a second one of blue clay, all devoid of artifacts. These layers give a record of the inlet's gradual filling in prior to the time of occupation. In a second peat bed, which overlay this series, and in a bed of gray clay immediately above it, were a number of wooden artifacts and other specimens associated with pottery of Early Jomon type. A subsequent bed of blue clay contained no artifacts, but it was in turn succeeded by a white clay bed and the modern soil, both of which contained artifacts of the Middle Jomon period. Near the surface of the modern soil, some pottery of the late prehistoric Kofun period was also encountered.

Most striking of the finds at Kamo were the remains of a dugout canoe found embedded upside down in the peat layer of Early Jomon age. The surviving remnant is about 4.8 m long. One end is present, the other missing, and it appears that the original vessel may have been considerably over 5 m long. The canoe, hollowed out of a split log of *Apananthe* wood, apparently had squarish ends, and it may have been rather shallow, with little freeboard. Adze marks are visible on the interior surfaces, which are well worked. A fragment of the wood was ^{14}C dated at about 5100 B.P., a date that fits well within the known time range for the Early Jomon pottery types found at the site.

A few other wooden artifacts were recovered from the peat stratum containing the canoe. Most significant of these were six canoe paddles, two with large, broad blades and four with smaller, more slender blades. The longest complete specimen, about 130 cm in length, was of the smaller, lighter variety. The large-bladed specimens were probably half again as long. A curved limb about 38 cm long and 2 cm in diameter, broken at one end and carefully notched at the other, is believed to be a fragment of a small hunting bow. The function of a large rectangular fragment of a flat, well-smoothed board is obscure.

The pottery from Kamo was analytically subdivided into 10 different types, but for present purposes these need not be summarized in detail. It is enough to mention that the sherds found with the canoe and other wooden specimens were generally of the broadly defined Moroiso type, characterized by nail-marked and cord-marked ornamentation. Such traits are characteristic of the later half of the Early Jomon period, as is fiber-tempering of the clay of the vessel, which also was observed in some of the Kamo specimens. Middle Jomon ceramics from the upper layers of the site were broadly of the Kasori E type, with such decorative features as sculptured rims and ridges, broad- and fine-line incised patterns, zoned cord-marking, and zoned-erased cord-marking. A handful of these sherds had been painted with a brownish red lacquer. This proved, on analysis, to be an organic substance, probably resin, to which oxides of iron had been added.

Stone artifacts from the Early Jomon strata were rare, and included only a triangular arrowhead, two grinding stones, three grooved net floats of pumice, an earring, and a pendant, the last two specimens both made of talc. The Middle Jomon layers produced many arrowheads, which were made of obsidian microscopically determined to be the kind occurring in the Hakone Mountains, about 100 km to the west. Grinding stones were also quite numerous, and several specimens each were recovered of mortars, notched net sinkers, roughly finished axes, and pitted stones that may have served as nutcracking anvils.

Seventeen animal species were identified from Kamo. Deer, boar, dolphin, and otter occurred in the Early Jomon deposits, along with four kinds of fish and one avian species. From the Middle Jomon deposits came deer, boar, dog, hare, dolphin, and whale, two kinds of fish, and two species of birds. Plants probably used as food are represented by the nuts, seed stones, cupules, or fruit coats of 11 species, including oak and chestnut. From other plant macrofossil evidence, four species of coniferous trees and 13 species of dicotyledons were identified, and a pollen analysis of the Early Jomon peat layer verified the occurrence of 12 arboreal species, including most of those represented by macrofossil remains.

With no major exceptions, the biota identified from the archaeological strata at Kamo is that characteristic of the modern Boso Peninsula, where the site occurs. Only the pollen analysis provided quantitative data on the relative abundances of different species, but these data reinforce the impression gained from the other species lists, that in Early and Middle Jomon times the climate and biota of the region were much as they are today. The most important change between then and now would seem to be a local one, the gradual filling in of the marshy inlet that lay before the Kamo site. This was culminated by its conversion to rice paddy fields in historic times. The minor differences between the animal species lists for Early and Middle Jomon times could be at least partially related to this phenomenon.

Whether Kamo was a residential settlement or an occasionally visited hunting–gathering camp cannot now be surely determined, but, as in the case of Natsushima, it is tempting to think of it as a relatively stable domestic settlement. The excavations were confined to what was, clearly, the water's edge at the time of the site's occupation, and if houses were present they would no doubt have been on the higher, drier ground nearby. Even without houses as part of the archaeological record from the site, however, it is evident that Kamo was ideally situated to have served as a base settlement from which to exploit the rich local environment. All the major natural resource zones of the immediate region—marshland, seashore, wooded hills, rivercourses—lay within a radius of 1 or 2 km. A village centrally located with respect to these zones could be relatively stable, exploiting them all in turn, and the biotic as well as artifactual evidence found at Kamo indicates that a wide range of local resources were in fact gathered and used, and the remains discarded at this site.

The dwellings of the Early Jomon period, as known from several other sites in the Tokyo region, were similar to those of Initial Jomon times. Usually rectangular or squarish with rounded corners, the pithouse floors had rows of wall posts around the edges and two or more major roof-support posts near the center. Formalized interior fireplaces, either stone-lined pits or large ceramic pots set into the floor toward one end of the house, were present in these structures (Okamoto and Tozawa 1965:110). As has been noted, it is purely conjectural whether such dwellings were present at Kamo itself, but they were at any rate in wide use in the region during the period of the Kamo occupation.

Initial and Early Jomon occupation in the Kyoto region of south-central Honshu is strikingly represented by the Torihama Shell Mound, which is near the coast of the Japan Sea in Fukui Prefecture, about 60 km north of the city of Kyoto. Torihama is in a low-lying area along an old rivercourse, and its waterlogged deposits have preserved an abundance of wood, bone, fibers, and other items in strata dated by their pottery to the Initial and Early Jomon periods. A brief preliminary report on the work indicates that about 300 cartons of pottery sherds, 200 cartons of bones, 70 cartons of wooden specimens, and well over 1000 stone and bone artifacts were recovered (Morikawa 1976).

Torihama

From a stratum believed to date quite early in Initial Jomon times was recovered a well-worked wooden adze handle. This had been made by trimming and shaping a tree branch and a section of the trunk from which it had stemmed at a near-right angle, to create an L-shaped handle. The slender branch became the grip, and a flattened platform to which a stone celt could be lashed was shaped at the distal end of the piece. Two similar, complete specimens, and over 40 other partially worked items believed to be uncompleted adze handles, were recovered from subsequent Early Jomon deposits. This series of objects showed evidence of having been shaved down with stone scrapers. In many cases it appeared that the wood was first deliberately charred, in order to facilitate the reduction process.

Over 30 wooden fragments believed to represent hunting bows were recovered from the Early Jomon level. These pieces ranged from 80 to 120 cm in length, and showed evidence of careful shaping. One finely made specimen, skillfully wrapped with cherry bark, was among the finds. A number of sharply pointed poles, about 3 cm in diameter, may have been spears. All were broken or burned at one end, however, so their original length is not known. A wooden fragment that quite clearly represents the prow of a dugout canoe, and three paddles, one of which was a 1.2-m-long complete specimen, demonstrate the use of watercraft at Torihama in Early Jomon times.

A number of simple wooden bowls from 20 to 50 cm in diameter, and a wooden comb with nine teeth about 2.5 cm long, were beautifully coated with bright red or black lacquer. The use of this decorative technique was well attested in the Early Jomon assemblage; lacquered fragments of pottery also were discovered.

In addition to finished items of this sort, a great many pieces of wood, either split and shaved into planks, or smoothed and pointed as posts or poles, were recovered. These were apparently building materials, suggesting that architectural features also existed at the site.

Fragments of woven grass and bark indicated the presence of basketry at Torihama, although no complete objects were retrieved. Numerous specimens of cordage, including individual strands and tangled masses of material, ranged in weight and diameter from thread to string to rope. Some of the material clearly represented netting. That cordage and textiles were in widespread use among the Jomon people has of course long been inferred from the cord-marking that is the preeminent characteristic of Jomon ceramics, but the specimens from Torihama revealed a variety of types that was quite surprising.

Stone tools included projectile points, hafted scrapers, drills, polished stone axe- or adzeheads, sinker stones, milling stones, and mortars. Bone sewing needles with eyes, shell bracelets, and shell ornaments were also part of the artifact inventory.

Food remains included large quantities of fish, bird, and mammal

Figure 3.16   Nail-impressed and cord-marked pot of the Initial Jomon from the Kitashirakawa site, Kyoto, south-central Honshu. Kitashirakawa Lower Type II. Height, 18.5 cm. (Shown approximately one-half actual size.) (Kyoto University Museum.)

Figure 3.17 Cord-marked bowl of the Initial Jomon from the Kitashir-akawa site, Kyoto, south-central Honshu. Kitashirakawa Lower Type II. Height, 22 cm. (Shown approximately one-half actual size.) (Kyoto University Museum.)

Figure 3.18 Small bowl with incised and cord-marked decoration, of the Initial Jomon from the Kitashirakawa site, Kyoto, south-central Honshu. Kitashirakawa Lower Type II. Height, 6.4 cm. (Shown actual size.) (Kyoto University Museum.)

bone. Vegetal foods were represented by seeds, nuts, and other materials. The biotic remains, not yet identified as to species, were abundant and varied, and promise to provide the fullest picture yet available of Early Jomon subsistence.

Other Initial and Early Jomon sites have been discovered in the Kyoto region, but the record obtained up to now has not been rich. The Early Jomon site of Kitashirakawa, on the campus of Kyoto University, has long been a major pillar of Jomon ceramic chronology in the region, and the occurrence of Kitashirakawa-type pottery at Torihama establishes an important link between the two sites (Figures 3.16–3.18). The Early Jomon site of Sakuragaoka, in Nara Prefecture south of Kyoto, has yielded evidence of irregular, roundish pithouses with hearths, and the Kou site in the city of Osaka has produced Jomon burials, but a detailed record of the Early Jomon culture is yet to be developed for this region (Okada 1965). Torihama, when fully reported, will be a highly significant new addition to our knowledge.

Sozudai   At Sozudai, overlooking Beppu Bay in northeastern Kyushu, is one of the earliest known Jomon villages of southern Japan (Yawata and Kagawa 1955). The putative Paleolithic site of the same name, mentioned in Chapter 2, occupies the same spot. Sozudai is an old place-name signifying that the locality is a tableland plentifully supplied with small springs. These have long attracted human occupation. Several other Initial Jomon sites comparable in age to that at Sozudai occur nearby, and later Jomon, Yayoi, and Kofun period sites are also present in the vicinity.

Pottery sherds, stone projectile points, and other artifacts were found over the entire top of the small eminence on which the site occurred, an area some 200 × 300 m across. Several long trenches and a number of test pits were laid out where artifacts were thickest, and their excavation produced an abundance of potsherds and stone tools. Many small pits dug by the aboriginal inhabitants, and other evidence, indicated the former presence of a number of dwelling structures.

The pottery from the site was of two basic types, both belonging to the latter half of the Initial Jomon period. Sherds bearing rouletted impressions made with a cord-wrapped stick were found from bottom to top of the excavated culture-bearing stratum at the site, but were most abundant at the deeper levels. The vessels from which these fragments came were deep, widemouthed pots with pointed bottoms. Pottery decorated by rouletting with a carved stick also occurred throughout the site, but was most abundant at intermediate depths. These vessels too were predominantly deep, widemouthed pots with pointed bottoms. Undecorated sherds occurred as well, but their form, composition, and pattern of occurrence within the site were the same as for the stick-impressed ware, and they are believed to represent either an undecorated variety of that type, or simply undecorated segments of stick-impressed vessels.

Stone tools were recovered in unusually large quantities at Sozudai. Large pebble choppers with a few flakes struck off along one or more edges were common. Even more abundant were large flakes of roughly ovate to triangular outline, flaked predominantly over one surface and given a cutting or scraping edge by retouch along one or more sides. Tools commonly termed sidescrapers, endscrapers, and knives are all well represented among these specimens.

Bifacially flaked points, also numerous, were segregated into 11 different types. Several of these types, comprising points that are rather large, thick, and coarsely flaked, seem to represent progressive stages in the refinement of rough initial forms into completed projectile points. They are too thick and bulky to be considered finished forms. The completed specimens vary somewhat in size and quality of finish, but are of remarkably uniform shape, all being triangular with very deeply notched bases. This is a typical Jomon style, which is widespread in Japan and persisted for millennia.

Among an abundance of cores and flakes from the site were a few specimens clearly representative of a prepared-core-and-blade technology. One piece of stone about 5 cm long exhibited several long, parallel scars showing where elongate flakes or blades had been removed from it. A number of long, keeled end-struck flakes were also found. These specimens were quite broad and long, small blades rather than microblades in the usual terminology. They are suspected of representing a pre-Jomon occupation at the site.

In contrast to the abundance of flaked stone specimens, ground stone artifacts were only scantily represented. Several roughly rectangular flaked stone axeheads had partially ground bits, and several flat, fist-sized stones of circular outline exhibited grinding around the edges. Flat pebbles with a small depression pecked into one or both faces also occurred at the site, represented by two examples.

The remains of dwellings have not often been found in sites of the Initial Jomon period, and the excavation at Sozudai was among the first in southern Japan to produce evidence of the house structures of this time. Many small round pits 20–60 cm in diameter and up to 40 cm deep were observed in the excavations. These were not recognized as house remains at first, because they did not occur within large house pits of the sort well known from later times as characteristic Jomon dwellings. But when a shallow saucer-like depression, fire-reddened and associated with ash and charcoal, was found, the possibility was established that Initial Jomon house floors at Sozudai might have been built directly on the ground surface rather than excavated into it. Excavations pursued in examination of this possibility turned up remains of what apparently had indeed been a house built on the surface of the ground. Two postholes occurred west of the hearth, and a low earthen bank about 20 cm high occurred along one edge of an artifact-rich occupation floor. Unfortunately, the area east of the hearth had been previously excavated and no further details were learned about the feature.

Much better evidence came from another excavation unit. Here a series of small pits was found that neatly formed the outline of what would have been a rectangulate structure with pointed ends. Three pits along the centerline, and three pits placed on each side of, and parallel to, this centerline, suggest the former existence of posts supporting a steeply pitched roof that probably sloped directly to the ground. The area enclosed would have been of fair size, as the distance from end to end along the centerline measured 5 m, and that between the two rows of postholes along either side measured nearly 3 m. Several pits that do not conform to this projection may have held auxiliary support posts; they may not have been postholes at all, but may have served as storage receptacles. There was no formal fireplace, but a patch of fire-reddened earth in one quarter of the structure probably attests the location of the hearth.

Among the many posthole-like pits revealed in other excavation units, similar rectangular house outlines may be visualized. But here the pits are more numerous, and repeated superimposition of sequent structures seems indicated. Thus, although the existence of other structures at the site is probable, the evidence for their precise form is equivocal. At the site of Senzuku, in Kyushu's Saga Prefecture, circular semisubterranean pithouses about 2.5 m in diameter and 40 cm deep have been reported from the following Early Jomon period (Otomasu 1965:253).

The evidence from Sozudai shows that the basic pattern of Jomon village life was already established in Kyushu by the middle of Initial Jomon times. The houses seem to have had less formalized interiors than those of later periods, but they were substantial structures. Apparently the site, which covers a considerable area, consisted of a number of households. The situation of Sozudai, on high ground near permanent water, overlooking the edge of the sea, is also like that of later Jomon settlements. Both hunting and the gathering of vegetal foods is suggested by the artifactual remains, although hunting may at that time have been relatively more important than it later became, to judge by the abundance of projectile points and scrapers, and the rarity of grinding stones for processing vegetal foods.

Tosamporo

The Initial stage of Jomon occupation in Hokkaido is so far documented only by fragmentary evidence. A fuller record is available for Early Jomon times, from sites found along the Pacific shore, at the extreme northeastern corner of the island. On the hills around Lake Tosamporo, near the coastal fishing town of Nemuro, occur many large groupings of prehistoric house-pit depressions. The mapping of two such groupings, one on either side of a broad estuary connecting the lake to the nearby sea, produced a tally of 171 probable house structures. Excavations in four of these depressions revealed pithouses containing stick-impressed pottery of the Early Jomon period. Other subsidiary excavations revealed pottery and a bronze artifact dating to the Kofun period, leading the investigators to suggest that the sites observed were not Early Jomon settlements exclusively, but were probably occupied over a long period of time (Yawata 1966).

The four excavated structures were strikingly similar to one another in both form and artifact content. A description of House 30, which was rich in specimens, suffices to illustrate the character of the Early Jomon remains. The house floor was ovate in plan, measuring 6.5 × 8 m. It was dish shaped in cross section, excavated a few centimeters below the level of the old, sloping ground surface. The earth that had been removed from the floor had been banked up along the downslope edge of the structure. An unlined ovate hearth occurred slightly off-center, toward the southern end of the dwelling. A large number of rather small, shallow pits, which presumably once held roof-support poles, formed an ovate pattern corresponding to the shape of the floor, but set in about 80 cm from its edge. The structure had apparently burned while in use, as indicated by an abundance of charcoal and several areas of fire-reddened earth. Two ^{14}C determinations on this charcoal gave dates of 3460 and 4020 B.P., which seem perhaps as much as 1000 years too young in view of the conventional dating of Early Jomon elsewhere in Japan.

Most of the pottery found during excavation of the house pit was of a stick-impressed rouletted ware corresponding to Early Jomon types known from northern Honshu. No complete vessels were found, but fragments showed that the basic form was a pointed-bottom pot with a wide mouth and straight, unmodeled rim. Several sherds and a nearly complete deep, cylindrical vessel of the so-called Hokuto type were found in the house fill, but they were quite obviously later discards, not directly associated with the Early Jomon occupation.

The lithic assemblage included small, slender lanceolate and triangular unstemmed projectile points, as well as bulkier diamond-shaped points with broad contracting stems. Several much larger specimens, well flaked and extensively retouched, may have been knives or spearheads. Distinctive hafted scrapers were represented by a number of specimens, most of them made on large end-struck blades. End-scrapers and sidescrapers were also made on such blades. A large pebble chopper, several small, beautifully ground and polished stone adzeheads, and many fragments of sharp, flat, ground stone "saw blades" apparently served for heavier cutting tasks. A number of flattened or dished-out stone slabs were apparently used as milling or grinding stones; one specimen had been worn completely through.

Tokoro   A rich site representative of Hokkaido's Middle Jomon is the Tokoro Shell Mound, on the Tokoro River near where it flows into the Okhotsk Sea, about 120 km northwest of the Lake Tosamporo region (Komai 1963). The site consists of a series of five overlapping shell middens extending for about 150 m along a hillside parallel to the river. Trenching of these middens produced an abundance of Middle Jomon pottery, stone tools, and faunal remains, as well as a shell sample that was ^{14}C dated at 4150 B.P.

The pottery was of the so-called Hokuto type widespread in Hokkaido, characterized by tall, cylindrical vessels having cord-marked bodies and modeled rims. Among the stone tools were slender lanceolate and triangular stemless projectile points, thicker and heavier diamond-shaped projectile points with broad contracting stems, and large ovate bifaces that may have been knives or spearpoints. A series of slender, thin lanceolate points made by retouching the edges of end-struck blades were also recovered, mostly from the lower levels of the excavation (Figure 3.19). They are believed by the excavators to

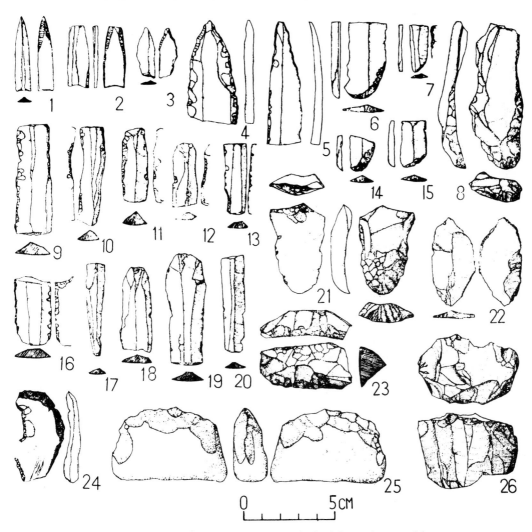

Figure 3.19 Arrowheads made on blades, and knives, scrapers, and other lithic implements of the Early Jomon from Tokoro Shell Mound, Hokkaido. (Shown approximately one-half actual size.) (From Komai 1963:Figure 46.)

antedate the Hokuto ceramic phase, although the pottery they were found with was cord-marked and not notably different from the Hokuto type. The other stone tools from the same levels of the trenches that produced tbe points made on blades are also like the specimens found associated with Hokuto pottery in higher levels of the deposit. A high degree of continuity from the preceding Early Jomon is evident in this assemblage.

Other tools recovered include stemmed scrapers made on blades, large and small blade cores, large blades with edge retouch, end- and sidescrapers, gravers, and drills. A few large pebble choppers were also in evidence. Ground stone tools included partly and completely polished celts, grinding stones with grooves apparently resulting from their being used to sharpen stone celts or bone tools, and flat, slightly dished milling stones.

Bone and antler artifacts were not abundant, but several kinds of specimens were nevertheless recovered. Several small bipoints, and sections of cut and shaped bone, appear to be parts of a simple type of composite fish-spear head. Slender bone sewing needles with eyes, bone and antler flakers and spatulas, and small bone pendants were also found.

Faunal remains from the middens clearly reflect the site's location on an estuary, with low coastal flats before, wooded upland behind, and the sea only a short distance away. The middens were themselves composed predominantly of oyster shells. Seal, sea lion, and whale were well represented, as were halibut, mullet, and dog salmon. Mallard, teal, and crow were the most common birds. Dog was very well represented, and the remains of brown bear surprisingly common, especially in view of the paucity of evidence of other large land mammals. A wide range of smaller species, including rodents and marine vertebrates, further indicate that the occupants of Tokoro Shell Mound enjoyed a broadly based food economy.

No dwellings assignable to the Middle Jomon period were discovered in the excavations. A pithouse of a much later period was discovered in one spot, and some apparently early postholes and other structural remains in another, but clear evidence of structures in use at Tokoro during the principal period of occupation is lacking. It seems unlikely, however, that a site so rich in domestic leavings was not a residential location, and the apparent lack of houses may be only a reflection of the relatively limited extent of the excavations. Probably house structures much like those known from Lake Tosamporo were in use.

From early times, as illustrated at Tosamporo and Tokoro, the Jomon culture of Hokkaido displayed minor divergences, which set it slightly apart from the Jomon of the southern islands of Japan. Most apparent are differences in the stone tool industries and of these the most important is the long retention in Hokkaido of core–blade lithic technology. This Paleolithic technique essentially disappeared with the advent of Jomon culture throughout most of Japan, but continued in Hokkaido well into the Middle Jomon period. Hokkaido also comprised a distinctive ceramic subarea throughout the Jomon age. In overall lifeway, however, in Hokkaido as elsewhere, a pattern of broad-spectrum hunting, fishing, and gathering was established in Early Jomon times, and continued for millennia thereafter without fundamental change.

A peak of cultural maturity and richness was achieved during the Middle Jomon period, especially in central Honshu (Figures 3.20–3.33). The Togariishi site, which is an excellent representative of this development, is one of many large Middle Jomon settlements scattered across the gently sloping western flank of Mount Yatsuga, overlooking Lake Suwa (Miyazaka 1957). The area is in the so-called Japanese Alps, 150 km west and somewhat north of Tokyo. The foot of Mount Yatsuga is veined with many small watercourses, which join a larger stream that empties into Lake Suwa a few kilometers below Togariishi. The small streams trend generally east–west, and between them are long, finger-like ridges. Several hundred prehistoric sites have been found upon these ridges, along the river flowing into Lake Suwa, and at the northwestern end of the lake itself. All these locations are still favored spots for human habitation, with present-day farming hamlets scattered along the ridgetops and modern urban concentrations occupying the lakeshore.

Archaeological investigations at Togariishi, and at its satellite of Yosukeone a short distance away on an adjacent ridgetop, were pursued with great dedication for more than 25 years by a local public school teacher, Eiichi Miyazaka. During this time four major excavation programs were undertaken, with the aid and support of the local community. Extensive areas were dug at both sites, 33 pithouses being cleared at Togariishi and 28 at Yosukeone. Excavations of such scope are extremely rare, and this work furnishes one of the fullest records available for the large sites characteristic of Middle Jomon times in the mountainous regions of central Honshu.

The temporal position of the two sites is established by the pottery types they yielded. Some deep, cylindrical vessels with appliqué relief and stick-impressed decoration were probably made near the beginning of Middle Jomon times. Most of the pottery, however, was of

Togariishi

 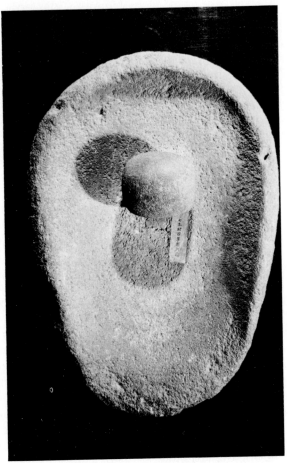

Figure 3.20 Grinding stone of the Early Jomon from Mogusaen, Tokyo, central Honshu. Left: obverse, pitted surface for cracking nuts; Right: reverse, scooped-out milling surface. Length, 45 cm. (Kyoto University Museum.)

deep urn and jar forms with the modeled and zoned decoration characteristic of the later part of that period.

The pithouses of both sites were relatively small, measuring 4–5 m, with their floors excavated about .5 m below the then-existing ground surface. In plan they varied from nearly circular to nearly square, most of them being rather irregular but verging on a circular outline. Stone-lined fireplaces about 1 m square and .5 m in depth were placed about midway between the centers and the north walls of the structures. A number of large postholes, roughly .5 m deep and a little less in diameter, occurred near the walls. Usually a dwelling had four to six

Figure 3.21 Indented-base and stemmed arrowpoints from Minami Akita-gun, Akita Prefecture, northern Honshu. Such specimens occur over most of Japan, throughout most of the Jomon period. Length of specimen at upper left, 3 cm. (Shown approximately twice actual size.) (Kyoto University Museum.)

main roof-support postholes, and a number of other pits, large and small, dug into the floor. Some of these may have been additional postholes; others undoubtedly served for storage or perhaps for burial.

Small pits about 1 m in diameter and 1 m deep were found in the open space between houses, particularly at Togariishi. Small postholes

Figure 3.22 Stemmed scrapers from the city of Akita and Minami Akita-gun, Akita Prefecture, northern Honshu. Similar specimens occur from pre-Jomon times throughout the Jomon period. The broader specimens are more typical of central and southern Japan; the elongate specimens are more typical of northern Japan. Length of specimen at lower left, 11 cm. (Shown actual size.) (Kyoto University Museum.)

Figure 3.23 Polished stone axe or adze blades from various sites in northern Honshu. Similar specimens were made throughout Japan from Early Jomon times onward. Length of specimen at left, 15.5 cm. (Shown approximately one-half actual size.) (Kyoto University Museum.)

encircling these pits may have held the bases of poles positioned to form a superstructure over them, and it is suggested that these may have been storage huts.

The economic base of the settlement is not directly attested by plant or animal remains, but well-worn grinding slabs, mortars, and abraded pebbles that probably served as handstones for such mills suggest that roots, tubers, nuts, and seeds were major dietary items. Roughly flaked artifacts often referred to as axeheads but more probably the tips of hoe-like digging tools used to recover roots and tubers were abundant. Triangular projectile points and hafted scrapers give evidence of hunting. Abundant ceramic remains, mostly of deep pots, indicate that food was prepared by boiling, and a cookery based on vegetable and meat stews can be easily imagined.

In the largest pithouse excavated at Togariishi, a structure about 7 m in diameter, was an unusually large, deep fire pit well over 1 m across. In one end of this pit was another large hole, dug still deeper into the ground. This continued a large lump of red earth, which had apparently been refined by straining and filtering. Near one side of the pit, a hollow space under a hearthstone was found to contain some

Figure 3.24 Notched stone and pottery weights from Jomon sites of varying age in central and south-central Honshu. Longest specimen, 7.2 cm. (Shown actual size.) (Kyoto University Museum.)

powdery, oxidized iron. Some heavily burned, crumbly pieces of granite were also found in the fire pit, and a large quantity of broken pottery occurred near one wall of the structure. It is believed by the excavator that this hearth and the associated materials were used in the manufacture of pottery.

In addition to the ceramic craft so abundantly attested by pottery sherds and the possible workshop discovered at Togariishi, a stone-flaking industry is attested by both finished items and obsidian flakes. No major lithic workshop area was identified, however. Woodworking tools, obviously a necessity for the construction of houses, and no doubt used in the crafting of smaller items as well, included polished stone axe or adzeheads, drills, and scrapers.

A number of pithouses exhibited unusual installations believed to be ceremonial. At Togariishi, a pottery vessel buried upright under a pile of stones associated with a fireplace was found to contain a beautifully polished stone axehead. In one corner of a pithouse at

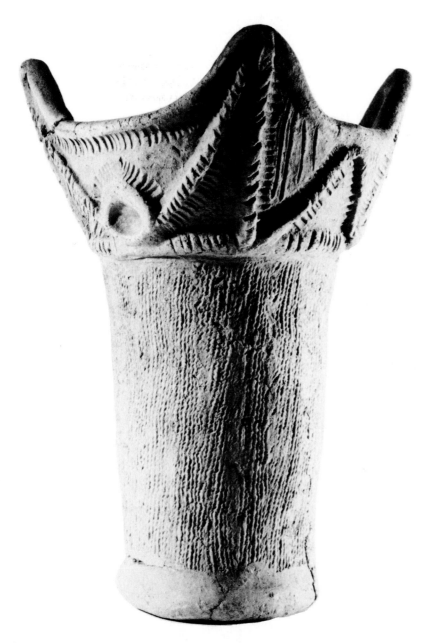

Figure 3.25 Deep cylindrical pot with peaked rim, of the Middle Jomon from the Kaido site, Nagano Prefecture, central Honshu. Katsuzaka type. Height, 31 cm. (Shown approximately one-half actual size.) (Kyoto University Museum.)

Figure 3.26 Deep cylindrical pot with peaked rim, of the Middle Jomon from the Kasori Shell Mound, Chiba Prefecture, central Honshu. Kasori E type. Height, 41 cm. (Shown approximately one-half actual size.) (Courtesy S. Sugihara, Meiji University.)

Figure 3.27 Deep cylindrical pot with sculptured body and rim, of the Middle Jomon from the Nakahara site, Yamanashi Prefecture, central Honshu. Katsuzaka type. Height, ca. 28 cm. (Shown approximately one-half actual size.) (Courtesy S. Sugihara, Meiji University.)

Yosukeone, inside one of three pottery vessels found stacked upon one another, the broken remains of a number of typical Jomon clay figurines had been placed. A cache of broken figurines was also found in another structure. Conspicuously, no caches of unbroken, complete specimens were found.

In a pithouse at Togariishi, two large ceramic urns were buried in the floor, and a number of paving stones laid around them. Next to this feature was a large flat stone, over 1 m long, which formed a small

Figure 3.28 Large, deep pot with sculptured body and rim, of the Middle Jomon from the Kaido site, Nagano Prefecture, central Honshu. Katsuzaka type. Height, 48.5 cm. (Shown approximately one-fourth actual size.) (Kyoto University Museum.)

platform protruding slightly above the level of the floor. It also was surrounded by paving stones. On this low platform was a complete obsidian projectile point, and behind it on the floor was a sharp spoonlike object of flaked stone and a small, uncompleted axehead of polished stone. This whole arrangement partially flanked the fireplace of the house, and it is believed possibly to represent an offering place, or altar.

In one of the pithouses at Yosukeone there was found a slender, elongate stone that had been erected in the middle of a low stone platform, around which were a number of vertically set stone slabs. The central pillar, a phallic shape that was battered and abraded on its

Figure 3.29 Small cylindrical pot with sculptured body, of the Middle Jomon from the Kaido site, Nagano Prefecture, central Honshu. Katsuzaka type. Height, 18.8 cm. (Shown approximately one-half actual size.) (Kyoto University Museum.)

edges and tip, protruded approximately .5 m above the surface of the platform. The arrangement occupied a narrow space behind the fireplace, along one wall of the house, and around it were many obsidian flakes. In another house was discovered a similar low stone platform, next to which was found a phallic stone broken in two. This had evidently once been erected on the stone dais, beneath which were found three polished stone axeheads and three flaked stone axeheads. The phallic stone of a comparable altar in still another house had been removed, but the hole in which it had been placed gave evidence of its former presence. Polished stone axes were also found near this feature, as were two mortars. Finally, in addition to these examples, well-made phallic stones were found in two other houses at Yosukeone, where they evidently had been placed in a corner behind a roof-support pillar.

A number of pithouses contained large pots buried in the floor and covered with stone lids. All were identically situated, centered between the main roof supports on the south side of the houses in which

Figure 3.30 Large, deep pot with sculptured body and rim, of the Middle Jomon from the Kaido site, Nagano Prefecture, central Honshu. Kasori E 1 type. Height, 39 cm. (Shown approximately one-third actual size.) (Kyoto University Museum.)

they occurred. Since this would have been an area of heavy traffic into and out of the houses, it is speculated that these vessels may have served some special purpose other than routine storage.

All these finds, some of them readily understood and others enigmatic, make it clear that household ceremonialism flourished at Togariishi and Yosukeone. The phallic altars, caches of broken female figurines and polished stone axes, and other more obscure caches,

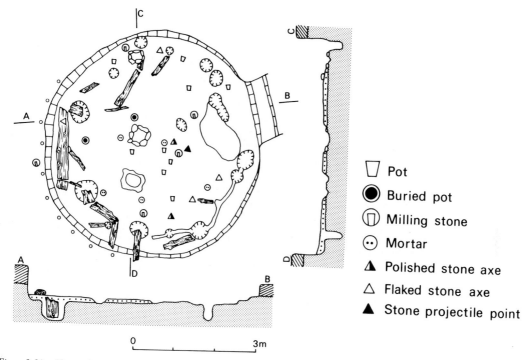

Figure 3.31   Plan and section of Middle Jomon circular house pit from Idojiri, Nagano Prefecture, central Honshu. (Redrawn from Fujimori 1965: Figure 2.)

offer loose analogies to ceremonial practices that survive to this day in folk observances of rural Japan.

Small pits about 1 m in diameter and 1 m deep, found in the open spaces between houses in clusters of five or six, may represent burials. It has been suggested that ash and charcoal found in and around these pits may reflect a custom of building fires near new graves, such as still survives locally in parts of Japan. No human bones or burial offerings were found in any of the pits, but clearly identifiable burials are generally rare in Jomon sites, which undoubtedly reflects poor conditions for preservation of bone rather than a lack of burials.

Lying just beneath the modern soil at Togariishi, at a level corresponding to the Middle Jomon occupation surface, was found a series of about two dozen stones of roughly uniform size, which extended in a line for about 10 m. The stones were placed at uniform intervals, as if they might have been stepping-stones. Excavations under several of the stones revealed the existence of large pits, which, however, contained no artifactual remains. A few meters beyond the end of this

Figure 3.32   Reconstructed Middle Jomon dwelling of rectilinear plan from Shijimizuka, Shizuoka Prefecture, central Honshu. (C. M. Aikens photo.)

path lay a large, angular boulder, under which a very large ceramic vessel was buried in an upright position. The vessel contained black soil, flecks of charcoal, and a single large elongate flake of andesite. The boulder itself, pointed at the top, is described by the Japanese term *togariishi*, which has become the name of the site.

The boulder, stepping-stones, and possible burial pits lie in a large open area, which yielded no pithouses. The excavated portion of the site lies to the south of this space, and test excavations have turned up many hearths, pits, and artifacts to the north and west. The evidence clearly indicates that the village of Togariishi surrounded this open space on three sides, and the area is given an unmistakable ceremonial and social character by the cultural features found there. It is reasonable to consider this central ground as a focal point of the communal life of the settlement.

The settlement of Togariishi–Yosukeone was obviously stable and long occupied. About 100 dwellings are attested either by actual house-pit floors or by hearths discovered during test excavations, and surficial indications over a large area suggest that many more dwellings may have been present. The pottery types suggest that the heaviest occupation occurred near the end of Middle Jomon times, over a span

Figure 3.33 Series of overlapping house pits of the Middle Jomon, buried under midden deposit at Kasori Shell Mound, Chiba Prefecture, central Honshu. (Courtesy S. Sugihara, Meiji University.)

of perhaps 300 years. That occupation actually continued throughout this period is suggested not only by the pottery types found but also by indications of much rebuilding. Some house pits contained many more postholes than normal, suggesting that their superstructures had been repeatedly repaired or rebuilt. Furthermore, many abandoned house-pits had been cut into by the construction of later dwellings on the same spot.

If an average useful life of 50 years is assumed for an individual house, and it is assumed on this basis that about one-sixth of the known dwellings might have been occupied at any one time, a population of 16 or 17 families, perhaps 60 to 80 persons, could be inferred. Such an estimate establishes only an approximate order of magnitude, and there is other evidence suggesting some growth and shifting of population over the life of the settlement, rather than a completely static situation.

Yosukeone, it appears, was a daughter village of Togariishi. The pottery at Yosukeone is of types belonging to the very end of Middle Jomon times, whereas Togariishi produced not only these types but somewhat earlier ones as well. A further indicator of such a relationship is that Yosukeone gave much less evidence of repeated house rebuilding than did Togariishi, again implying that it was the younger and shorter-lived of the two residential aggregations.

Idojiri   Farther south along the western flank of Mount Yatsuga, about 15 km from Togariishi, the Idojiri group of sites has also been subjected to intensive investigation (Fujimori 1965). Of about 50 known archaeological localities in this area, 24 were investigated by surface survey and partial excavation. Of the sites investigated, 17 proved to belong to the Middle Jomon period, and 7 to the Late Jomon period. About 90 pithouses were excavated, and a large number of pottery vessels, stone tools, and ceremonial objects were recovered. Large, thriving settlements comparable to those at Togariishi and Yosukeone are indicated, and the high density of sites shows that this area too supported a relatively dense population during Middle Jomon times.

The Idojiri sites essentially duplicate the architectural and ceremonial features of Togariishi and Yosukeone, but they also provide important new data bearing on the economic and social life of the Middle Jomon villages. One important feature of the investigation, and the subject of emphasis in this summary, was the compiling of information on the natural food potential of the vicinity. The broad, southwest-facing flank of Mount Yatsuga is, because of its slope and the direction of its exposure, a good deal warmer than the average for the mountainous region of which it is a part. The biota thus includes warmer lowland elements not usual in the mountains, along with the typical local species that flourish in the cooler microenvironments of the vicinity.

The land on which the archaeological sites occur is now in agricultural plots, and away from the cultivated fields, the native forest cover has been replaced by silviculturally valuable coniferous species. In the ravines and bottoms, however, native deciduous forest still occurs, in a relict distribution into which it has been forced by the planting of conifers on the more accessible uplands. In earlier times deciduous forest, with its abundance of edible plant and animal species, must have covered the flanks of Mount Yatsuga, and would have provided an extremely rich environment for a hunting and gathering people.

A tabulation of the edible species still to be found on the slopes of Mount Yatsuga shows about 150 items, with seasons of availability covering the annual round. Many kinds of large and small mammals, birds, fish, shellfish, turtles, snakes, snails, insects, nuts, fruits, grass seeds, roots, shoots, greens, and medicinal flowers make an impressive list of forest products. Many of them—for example, acorns, chestnuts, walnuts, and various roots, available in large quantities in the fall of the year and easily preserved—could provide stores to carry people through the winter. Insects and their larvae could provide, as they still do in some farm households, a highly nutritious and flavorful contribution to the diet of early spring and summer, which would have been the season of least abundance in this region. And the sheer range and variety of plants and animals available would ensure a reliable food supply, despite the normal short-term cyclical fluctuations in relative abundance that many species are prone to. Many wild foods are exploited as seasonal delicacies by the people of the region even today.

Several thick, flat cakes, apparently of finely ground meal, were recovered from a pithouse of the Idojiri group. Their outer surfaces were charred, and one bore the imprint of a large leaf. They were found on and around a milling stone that lay beside the fireplace of the house, and it is inferred that such cakes, wrapped in leaves, were probably cooked or dried for storage. Since the original discovery, more specimens have been found in the same region, suggesting that the production of such cakes was general.

To identify the vegetal substance of which the cakes were made, a number of possible materials were ground, mixed, and heated beside an open fire. The products were then compared with the archaeological specimens. Sticky, potato-like roots could not readily be made into cakes resembling the originals, but, interestingly enough, it was found in experiments with other materials that if a portion of root meal was *not* added during processing, cakes made from other materials would not hold together. In order, the foodstuffs that yielded cakes most closely resembling the original artifacts were rice, wheat, corn, and chestnut. However, none of the preparations resulted in a really good replica of the archaeological specimens, and it must be concluded that the original primitive recipe has not yet been learned. It scarcely needs to be added that these experiments are not a sufficient basis from which to conclude that rice and wheat were under cultivation in Middle Jomon times.

Milling stones and mullers, suitable for use in shelling and grinding such food products as acorns, chestnuts, and seeds of all kinds, were common in the Idojiri sites. They were deeply worn from much use, and open at one end, which would allow ground-up meal to be pushed out onto a mat or tray as the grinding process continued. Other obvious food-getting and processing implements were flaked stone projectile points, knives, and scrapers, which were also well represented.

The projectile points were of a familiar small, triangular, indented-base form. Scrapers and knives included simple tools made on flakes as well as the more sophisticated hafted scrapers so typical of the Jomon culture everywhere.

Roughly flaked stone celts were remarkably abundant at the Idojiri sites. Experiments with these specimens, hafted as the tips of digging sticks, showed that they were highly effective for excavation in the loamy soils of the region. It has often been speculated that these tools were hafted as hoe blades, which remains a clear possibility, but experiments show that well over twice the amount of earth could be moved in a given amount of time when they were mounted in the straight digging-stick configuration. Additional experiments showed that these rough celts could also serve other purposes effectively, and that it would probably be a mistake to interpret them only as digging-stick tips. Held in the hand, they proved efficient in the digging of small pits such as the postholes and storage pits found in the aboriginal house floors, and when hafted as axes they were capable of cutting down a small tree in just a few minutes.

Flat, fist-sized stones with one or more small depressions battered into both surfaces were also extremely common. It has been suggested that these were used as pivots for the upper end of fire-drill shafts, a function that experiments showed they were suited for. However, so abundant are they, many specimens often being found in a single pithouse, that this explanation can hardly account for them all. Experiments also showed that two such stones, used in conjunction as a press, were effective in quickly and cleanly splitting open walnuts. If processing walnuts is reckoned as having been a family chore, the large number of such stones is easily understood.

The principal investigator of the Idojiri project, Eiichi Fujimori, has suggested that the prosperous hunting–gathering economy of the Middle Jomon period in this region may have also included an incipient form of slash-and-burn horticulture. The abundance of stone celts suggests that digging and the cutting down of trees were common activities, and Fujimori raises the possibility that land was deliberately cleared and fired in order to foster the growth of native grasses, roots, and other foods. Many edible species grow in the region, and these might have been deliberately cared for or managed so as to increase the natural yield. Grass grows luxuriantly on recently fired land, and even walnut and chestnut trees that have been licked by flame produce nuts more abundantly. Furthermore, selective firing of parts of the landscape would have been an effective tactic for hunters in pursuit of game.

Against this interpretation it has been objected, with proper logic, that an abundance of digging and cutting tools does not by itself prove the existence of cultivation or of management of natural vegetation by the use of fire. The same tools would have been useful in a purely hunting–gathering economy. To establish the existence or nonexistence of the incipient horticultural practices suggested is, of course, inherently difficult, and the problem of obtaining unequivocal archaeological evidence is intertwined with the difficulty of defining the nature of the transition from hunting–gathering to horticulture. Nevertheless, it is a well-established fact that the regional population grew markedly during the Middle Jomon period, and the thesis that certain techniques of resource management boosted the output of the traditional woodland economy at that time is an attractive one.

Very large communal structures have been discovered at several Middle Jomon sites. The Fudodo and Mizukamidani sites in Toyama Prefecture, on the Japan Sea side of central Honshu, exemplify these exciting finds. Only brief, preliminary reports are so far available, but they make it clear that these structures add a new dimension to our knowledge of Jomon social life (Toyama-ken Kyoiku Iinkai 1974a, 1974b).

Fudodo is on a low terrace in old river delta lands not far from the large, well-sheltered arm of the Japan Sea known as Toyama Bay. Mizukamidani lies about 30 km west of Fudodo, in a narrow tributary valley a few kilometers inland. A number of other localities shown by their pottery to have been occupied at the same period occur in the vicinity of each of these sites, but earlier occupations are virtually unknown. It appears that Fudodo and Mizukamidani were part of a general florescence of human settlement around Toyama Bay during the Middle Jomon period.

Excavations at Fudodo, which sampled an area about 60 m square, disclosed the remains of 19 pithouse structures scattered along a northwest–southeast axis. More or less complete excavation of several structures showed that both small and large buildings were present. One well-preserved smaller structure, which had been built over another of roughly the same size, was ovate in plan, 5 × 6 m across. It had been excavated a few centimeters below ground level, and had a rectangular, stone-lined fireplace situated somewhat off-center. A deep storage pit nearly 1 m in diameter had been dug against the end wall of the house pit, and a plethora of large and small pits in the house floor presumably included both pillar holes for roof supports, and storage caches. This seems to have been a single-family dwelling, not significantly different from hundreds of others of the Middle

Fudodo and Mizukamidani

Jomon period, and perhaps representative of most of the houses at Fudodo.

Near the center of the site were the remains of one very large building, ovate in plan, 17 m long and 8 m wide. It was of semisubterranean construction, though only a few centimeters deep. Four stone-lined hearths were placed equidistant along its central axis, and 16 large, deep postholes were ranged down either side and across the ends of the floor, about 1 m or so inside the edge of the encircling house-pit wall. A large, ceramic urn was buried in the floor adjacent to each of the two most centrally located hearths, and a number of small pits occurred here and there in the floor. One very large, shallow pit cutting through one wall of the house is believed to be unrelated to the main occupation.

Adjacent to the main building was a small version of it, 7.5 m long and 5 m wide, with two hearths placed along its central axis. It apparently had eight major roof-support pillars, although the confusing multiplicity of pits in the floor make this less than certain.

At Mizukamidani several structures similar to the lesser communal building of Fudodo were found, along with a number of smaller pithouse dwellings of conventional Middle Jomon type. In all, 16 structures were recognized in the excavations, but only a few were completely uncovered. Also of interest at Mizukamidani were several small monoliths that had been erected in the open central ground around which the larger buildings were clustered, suggesting public or ceremonial functions.

The occurrence of both large and small buildings at these sites during the same occupation period implies social patterning not concretely attested in previously known Jomon settlements, but the evidence can be interpreted in more than one way and it will probably be some time before a consensus is reached. Nevertheless, without attempting to specify too closely the nature of the groups that used the great hall at Fudodo, or the cluster of large buildings around the open common at Mizukamidani, it is legitimate to recognize in those precincts an expression of societal centralization. Whether they are best interpreted as the quarters of dominant families or the meeting halls of sodalities of some kind is difficult to decide, though perhaps when detailed reports, including descriptions of the associated artifacts, are published, understanding will be advanced.

Kasori   In the Tokyo region, as in the mountains of central Honshu, the Middle Jomon period was a time of markedly increased population. This growth carried over into the Late Jomon as well. Hundreds upon hundreds of localities bearing Middle and Late Jomon pottery have been recorded, and especially along the beaches and inlets of Tokyo Bay there occur many sites of very large size. Typically these sites consist of an extensive shell midden, either circular or U-shaped, beneath or near which are buried artifacts and the remains of pithouses (Figures 3.34–3.43).

Kasori Shell Mound, in the eastern part of the city of Chiba near the northeastern edge of Tokyo Bay, is a good example of such a site, which was occupied in both Middle and Late Jomon times (Sugihara 1977; Takeda 1968; Takiguchi 1977). It occupies two adjacent low hillocks on the edge of what was once an inlet and later a stream flowing into Tokyo Bay, but is now a long, meandering belt of rice paddy fields, which occupy the rich alluvial bottom. Kasori is several kilometers inland from the bay now, but in earlier times, before the inlets around Tokyo Bay became so heavily silted in, it could have, and undoubtedly did, have immediate access by boat to the saltwater bay.

The natural setting is such that the varied food products of forest, river, and sea were immediately at hand. The bones of duck, geese, pheasant, deer, boar, hare, and raccoon-dog (*Nyctereutes*) represent forest and stream species that might have been taken at the very edge of the settlement. The remains of bass, rayfish, bream, sea turtle, and porpoise, and the shells of about 30 species of mollusks, demonstrate that both the nearby inlet and the bay into which it emptied were regularly exploited. In earlier archaeological deposits the small *Corbicula* was abundant, suggesting an emphasis on the gathering of shellfish in the brackish waters about the mouth of the inlet. A subsequent increase in other kinds of shellfish relative to *Corbicula* suggests that a broader range of bayshore microenvironments was exploited in later times.

A typical Jomon tool kit related to food-getting activities included notched sinkers made of small stones or pottery sherds, perforated net floats of pumice, antler fishhooks and fish-spear points, and flaked stone arrowpoints. The harvesting of vegetal foods is also suggested by the recovery of many roughly flaked stone axe- or hoe-heads, and many grinding and nutcracking stones. Deep, cylindrical pots with flaring mouths, some of them fire-blackened, seem to have served for cooking and storage.

The main occupation areas of the site are marked by two large, irregular rings of shell debris, each about 150 m from edge to edge, which encircle the tops of adjacent low rounded knolls and spill down their flanks. The shell deposits vary between .5 m and 2 m in thickness, and in both cases enclose a central area where few archaeological

Figure 3.34   Pitted nutcracking stones of the Jomon period from central Honshu. Circular specimen, Late Jomon from Yoyama Shell Mound, Chiba Prefecture; Elongate specimen, period
undetermined, from Nagao site, Kanagawa Prefecture. (Kyoto University Museum.)

remains have been found. Kasori Shell Mound has been dug intermittently since it was first presented to the world of scholarship in 1888,
and the two shell rings had been thought to be essentially independent
sites; the northern one was attributed to Middle Jomon and the southern one was attributed to Late Jomon times. Ceramic evidence recovered by extensive modern excavations now shows, however, that the
two localities were closely related, apparently as a mother and a
daughter village. In brief, the dominant pottery types of the northern
locality are Middle Jomon and those of the southern locality are Late

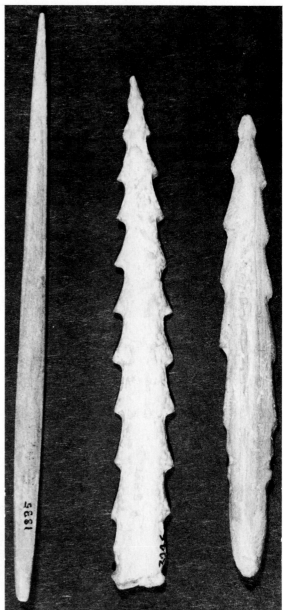

Figure 3.37 Bone fishhook and bone points of the Late Jomon from Yoyama Shell Mound, Chiba Prefecture, central Honshu. Length of fishhook, 4.7 cm. (Shown twice actual size.) (Kyoto University Museum.)

Figure 3.38 Bone inflation nozzles for skin floats, of the Late Jomon from various sites in central Honshu. Upper left, Tatsugi Shell Mound, Ibaraki Prefecture; upper right, Yoyama Shell Mound, Chiba Prefecture; lower left, Shimomunabe Shell Mound, Tokyo; lower right, Nakazuma Shell Mound, Ibaraki Prefecture. Length of specimen at upper left, 3.9 cm. (Kyoto University Museum.)

Figure 3.39 Miniature teapot of the Late Jomon from the Fukuda site, Ibaraki Prefecture, central Honshu. Kasori B II type. Height, 7 cm. (Shown approximately actual size.) (Kyoto University Museum.)

Figure 3.40 Small wide-mouthed jar of the Late Jomon from Nakazuma Shell Mound, Ibaraki Prefecture, central Honshu. Height, 7.8 cm. (Shown approximately one-half actual size.) (Kyoto University Museum.)

Figure 3.41 Conoidal cord-marked pot with appliqué decoration and sculptured rim, of the Late Jomon. Provenience unknown. Angyo 1 type. Height, 37 cm. (Shown approximately one-half actual size.) (Courtesy S. Sugihara, Meiji University.)

Figure 3.42 Incised pot of the Late Jomon from Soya Shell Mound, Chiba Prefecture, central Honshu. Horinouchi type. Height, 19 cm. (Shown approximately one-half actual size.) (Courtesy S. Sugihara, Meiji University.)

Figure 3.43 Pot with sculptured rim and zoned cord-marking, of the Late Jomon from the Oyaba site, Chiba Prefecture, central Honshu. Kasori B. type. Height, 21 cm. (Shown approximately one-half actual size.) (Courtesy S. Sugihara, Meiji University.)

Jomon, but Late Jomon remains are also well represented in the older northern mound, indicating that occupation continued there after the southern settlement was established.

The conventional interpretation of such sites as Kasori has been that they represent large, planned villages arranged in orderly fashion around a great open plaza that was either completely encircled by dwellings or open at one end. Many sites, including Kasori, do display such an arrangement. It is increasingly doubted, however, whether the observed archaeological patterns are representative of such settlements as they existed at any given time.

Extensive excavations in the northern mound at Kasori have identified 47 pithouses, and if a comparable density of structures exists elsewhere in and around the mound, a total several times as large is implied. Detailed ceramic and stratigraphic evidence shows, however, that relatively few of the houses were occupied at any one time. The great shell ring is in fact made up of many lesser shell deposits associated with individual houses or groups of houses, and detailed analysis of the pottery from such spots shows that at least three subphases of occupation are represented among these smaller middens. Furthermore, excavation of one such area revealed the remains of 7 houses, but they overlapped and crosscut one another in a way that suggested the repeated rebuilding of just two residences on the spot.

These data show clearly that the impressive size of the archaeological site that now meets the eye at Kasori is a reflection of continuous occupation over a long period of time, rather than of particularly large village size. Whether the smaller aggregation that would have been occupied at any one time was arranged in circular fashion around a central plaza as originally thought no longer seems certain, although clearly a spacious village commons was present in one form or another throughout the life of the settlement.

Approximately three-quarters of the many Jomon sites known to occur along the eastern shore of Tokyo Bay are dated to Middle and Late Jomon times. A high density of sites around the bay during this time span is attributed to a florescence in the marine economy of the region. As seen at Kasori, settlements were usually so situated as to allow exploitation of the whole range of marine and inland environmental zones. The Shomyoji Shell Mound in Yokohama, on the western edge of the bay, gave abundant evidence of deep-sea fishing and sealing as well, in addition to the taking of many inshore species and land mammals. Numerous inland settlements are also known from this era, though they do not reach the density known along the bayshore (Groot and Sinoto 1952; Okamoto and Tozawa 1965:118, 124).

With the close of Late Jomon times, the population of the Tokyo

Bay region seems to have decreased markedly. Perhaps the same post-Pleistocene evolution of the bay itself, which had brought it to a height of productivity during the Middle and Late Jomon periods, underlay the decline. Silting in of the bay, over thousands of years, has resulted in the gradual sedimentation of many of its inlets, and it may be that a crucial juncture was reached in this infilling at about the end of the Late Jomon period. Kasori Shell Mound, along with many others, was abandoned at this time, perhaps because of increasing difficulty in obtaining the marine resources that were a major component of its economy.

Kamegaoka   In the Final Jomon period, developments in central Honshu maintained a high level, but northern Honshu became the region of greatest cultural elaboration (Figures 3.44–3.64). Kamegaoka, one of the richest Jomon sites ever discovered, is illustrative. Kamegaoka has been known as an archaeological locality since at least the early 1600s. It has been plundered for decades, if not centuries, and has yielded thousands of artifacts, now scattered in collections throughout Japan and beyond. The site is at the extreme northern tip of Honshu, about 40 km west of the city of Aomori, on the inland side of a range of low hills flanking the coast of the Japan Sea.

The principal archaeological locality is near the tip of a low ridge, the local name of which has been applied to the site. Around the base of the ridge is low, wet alluvial land now converted to rice paddy fields, but formerly a marsh. Artifacts have been excavated both from the ridgetop and from the old swamp, where normally perishable organic specimens were preserved in buried peat layers. Little is known of the ancient village itself, apparently long destroyed by the repeated digging to which the site has been subjected. The objects recovered, however, give an impression of a particularly rich and thriving settlement, which the Obora series of pottery types indicates was occupied throughout several phases of the Final Jomon period.

The setting of Kamegaoka, on a wooded ridge with a marsh below and the sea only several kilometers behind, a major river just beyond the marsh, and a large bay a few kilometers downstream, would seem to have been particularly favorable to the taking of a wide variety of natural resources. Modern archaeological investigations at the site (Shimizu 1959) recovered 16 species of plant remains, most of them woods probably used in artifact making. Edible plants included horse chestnut and walnut. The remains of deer, boar, waterfowl, dolphin, fish, and shellfish were also recovered. Pollen from a peat layer just below the major culture-bearing stratum revealed the presence of pine, beech, alder, willow, and two kinds of chestnuts, suggesting that environmental conditions very like those of the present prevailed at that time.

Artifacts associated with the food quest and household industries included small stemmed and leaf-shaped arrowpoints, scrapers, and awls or drills of stone, all apparently made for hafting into wood or bone shafts. Barbed bone harpoon points, and notched stones probably used as net sinkers, have also been found. Polished stone celts of different sizes could have served as axes and gouges, and pieces of battered and abraded stone may have been hammers, grinding stones, and the like. Sandstone slabs having many broad, elongate grooves worn into their surfaces seem to have been used in the manufacture of stone beads. The widths of the grooves, and their curvature, correspond well to the sizes and shapes of beads actually recovered from the site. Bone awls and needles suggest the tailoring of clothing and other articles.

A social order that placed much emphasis on ceremony, and perhaps on status distinctions among members of the group, is indicated by the wealth of finely made objects for which Kamegaoka is famous. Most remarkable are the numerous large hollow ceramic figurines depicting goggle-eyed anthropomorphs apparently dressed in ornamental tunics and plain leggings. Many wear elaborate headdresses, and some display necklaces and pendants. Breasts indicate that most specimens are female representations. Smaller, solid-bodied figurines with facial features rendered in a quite different style are also common. These too are usually female.

Shallow bowls, dishes and bowls on high circular bases, jars, bottles, and spouted teapots seem to represent a complex of ceremonial vessels. All are finely crafted, most are well polished, and some were painted with red and white lacquer. Many such vessels have been found at Kamegaoka, though they are nevertheless few in proportion to the much more abundant jars and pots of lesser elegance representing the utilitarian wares of the settlement. It is no doubt indicative of societal differentiation within the village that the finer wares and figurines have usually been found in groups in only certain parts of the site. Fragments of basketry, lacquered like some of the ceramic pieces, probably belong to the same complex of ceremonial items.

Engraved pottery plaques, engraved pottery balls or disks perforated for suspension, ceramic earplugs, spherical stone beads, curved elongate *magatama* beads of stone, bone hairpins, bone combs, bone bracelets, and finely made stone scepters, usually of phallic shape, are items of personal adornment that no doubt served to indicate relative wealth and social status among the villagers.

Figure 3.44 Deep cord-marked pot of the Final Jomon from Nakazuma Shell Mound, Ibaraki Prefecture, central Honshu. Horinouchi II type. Height, 20 cm. (Shown approximately one-half actual size.) (Kyoto University Museum.)

Figure 3.45 Deep bowl with peaked rim, of the Final Jomon from the Shigasato site, Shiga Prefecture, south-central Honshu. Shigasato type. Height, 26 cm. (Shown approximately one-half actual size.) (Kyoto University Museum.)

Figure 3.46 Teapot of the Final
Jomon from Higashikananoi Shell
Mound, Chiba Prefecture, central
Honshu. Kasori B 1 type. Height, 11
cm. (Shown actual size.) (Kyoto
University Museum.)

Figure 3.47 Pedestaled offering dish of the Final Jomon from Sunazawa, Aomori Prefecture, northern Honshu. Sunazawa type. Height, 12 cm. (Shown approximately three-quarters actual size.)
(Courtesy S. Sugihara, Meiji University.)

Figure 3.48 Footed offering cup of the Final Jomon from Takashugi Onoe, Aomori Prefecture, northern Honshu. Obora B C type. Height, 8 cm. (Shown actual size.) (Kyoto University Museum.)

Figure 3.49 Small incised jars of the Final Jomon from Kamegaoka, Aomori Prefecture, northern Honshu. From left, Horinouchi II, Obora C2, Obora C1 types. Height of specimen at left, 11 cm. (Shown approximately one-half actual size.) (Kyoto University Museum.)

Figure 3.50 Zoned cord-marked bowl of the Final Jomon from Takashugi Onoe, Aomori Prefecture, northern Honshu. Obora C1 type. Height, 7.5 cm. (Shown approximately three-quarters actual size.) (Kyoto University Museum.)

Figure 3.51 Small, deep bowl of the Final Jomon from the Shigasato site, Shiga Prefecture, south-central Honshu. Shigasato type. Height, 16 cm. (Kyoto University Museum.)

Figure 3.52 Solid clay anthropomorphic female figurine of the Late Jomon from from Nakazuma Shell Mound, Ibaraki Prefecture, central Honshu. Length, 10.8 cm. (Kyoto University Museum.)

169

Figure 3.53 Solid clay anthropomorphic male (?) figurine of the Final Jomon from central Honshu. Angyo II type. (T. Higuchi photo.)

Figure 3.54 Hollow clay anthropomorphic female figurine of the Final Jomon from the Kamegaoka site, Aomori Prefecture, northern Honshu. Height, 17 cm. (Shown approximately one-half actual size.) (Courtesy S. Sugihara, Meiji University.)

Figure 3.55 Solid clay anthropomorphic female figurine of the Final Jomon from the Amataki site, Aomori Prefecture, northern Honshu. Height, 13 cm. (Shown one-half actual size.) (Courtesy S. Sugihara, Meiji University.)

Figure 3.56 Hollow clay figurine in the form of a tortoise shell, of the Final Jomon from the Ebarada site, Chiba Prefecture, central Honshu. Length, 14 cm. (Shown approximately one-half actual size.) (Courtesy S. Sugihara, Meiji University.)

Figure 3.57 Ornamented clay earspools of the Late Jomon from Shinpukuji Shell Mound, Saitama Prefecture, and Horinouchi Shell Mound, Chiba Prefecture, both central Honshu. Diameter of largest specimen, 7.5 cm. (Shown actual size.) (Kyoto University Museum.)

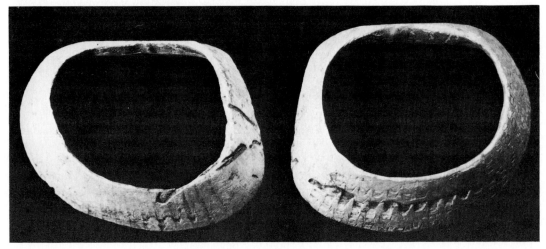

Figure 3.58 Shell bracelets of Late Jomon style from Todori Shell Mound, Kumamoto Prefecture, Kyushu. Greatest diameter of specimen at right, 8.2 cm. (Kyoto University Museum.)

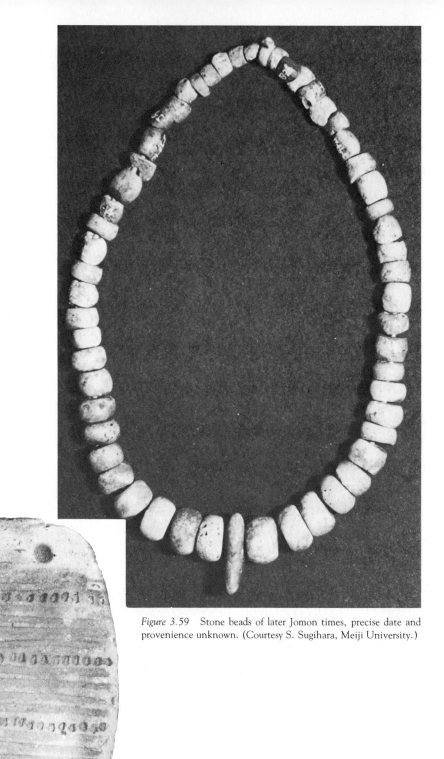

Figure 3.59 Stone beads of later Jomon times, precise date and provenience unknown. (Courtesy S. Sugihara, Meiji University.)

Figure 3.60 Clay plaque or stamp of the Final Jomon from the Sanno site, Miyagi Prefecture, northern Honshu. Length, 9 cm. (Shown actual size.) (Courtesy S. Sugihara, Meiji University.)

Figure 3.61 Curved *magatama*-like beads of stone and clay of the Final Jomon from the Amataki site, Iwate Prefecture, northern Honshu. Length of specimen at far right, 3 cm. (Shown approximately actual size.) (Courtesy S. Sugihara, Meiji University.)

Figure 3.62 Curved *magatama* and *magatama*-like beads. Top row, clay *magatama* of the Late Jomon from the Osagata site, Ibaraki Prefecture, central Honshu. Bottom row, stone *magatama*-like beads attributed to the Final Jomon from the Kou site, Osaka Prefecture, south-central Honshu. Diameter of largest specimen, 4.4 cm. (Shown actual size.) (Kyoto University Museum.)

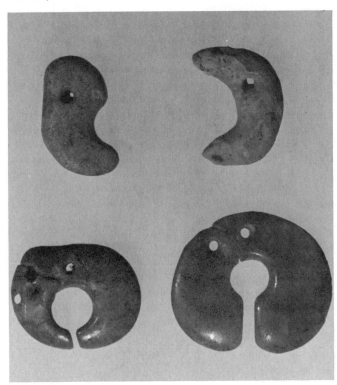

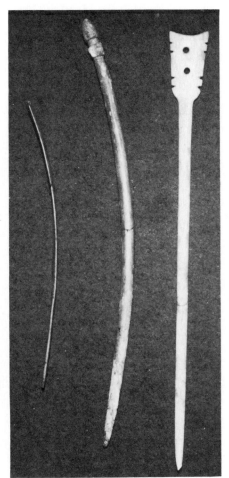

Figure 3.63 Bone hairpins of the Final Jomon from various sites in central Honshu. Length of specimen at right, 18 cm. (Shown approximately two-thirds actual size.) (Courtesy S. Sugihara, Meiji University.)

Figure 3.64 Phallic stones representative of Late and Final Jomon types from central and northern Honshu. Left, from Kofukusaka Shell Mound, Saitama Prefecture; center, from Tomizakibata, Miyagi Prefecture; right, from Suginodo, Iwate Prefecture. Length of specimen at right, 34 cm. (Shown approximately one-half actual size.) (Kyoto University Museum.)

Evidence of one kind of ritual system within which objects such as
those found at Kamegaoka may have functioned is widespread in
northern Japan. At a number of localities in northern Honshu and
Hokkaido, circular stone alignments of clearly ritual character, dating
to Late and Final Jomon times, have been found. Two such sites,
perhaps the largest and best described of their kind, occur within 100
m of one another in the town of Oyu, near the northern tip of Honshu. The individual sites are named Manza and Nonakado, respectively, after the two small hamlets where they occur (Bunkazai Hogo
Iinkai 1953).

The monuments are on a high river terrace, at the time of investigation brushy and partly wooded, but believed to have been open
parkland when they were made long ago. The structure at Manza, with
an outside diameter of about 45 m, was slightly larger than its companion, but aside from variation in measurements the two are essentially
identical, and a description of one will serve for both.

The Manza site was composed of two concentric circular zones or
bands, each made up of many small concentrations of river cobbles
(Figure 3.65). These small concentrations were so abundant in some
places that they formed a nearly continuous stone pavement; in other
places their distribution was less dense. The width of the outer band
was about 8 m; that of the inner band, about 2 m. Between them was
an open strip about 8 m across, and encircled by the inner band was a
clear space about 8 m in diameter. Near the middle of the northwest
quarter of the monument, in the clear strip between the two concentric circles, was a special stone feature that may have functioned as a
sundial. A similar feature at Nonakado, Manza's companion site, occupied the same relative position within the larger monument.

A feature discovered only at Nonakado was a double alignment of
stones outlining a passageway leading up to an opening in the southern
edge of the outer stone circle. Owing to recent disturbance and the
incompleteness of the excavations, it is uncertain whether or not the
monument at Manza had such an entryway.

The small individual stone clusters, usually circular to ovate, measured between 1 and 2 m across. They were composed of large, smooth
river cobbles, no doubt from the stream at the base of the terrace on
which the sites occur. A large proportion of the stones were elongate,
and in many clusters one or more of the elongate stones were placed
on end, in an erect position. The other stones of the clusters lay in
disorder, but it may be that many of them were once erected and later
toppled to the positions in which they were found by the archaeologists.

Excavations beneath a number of the stone clusters revealed ovate

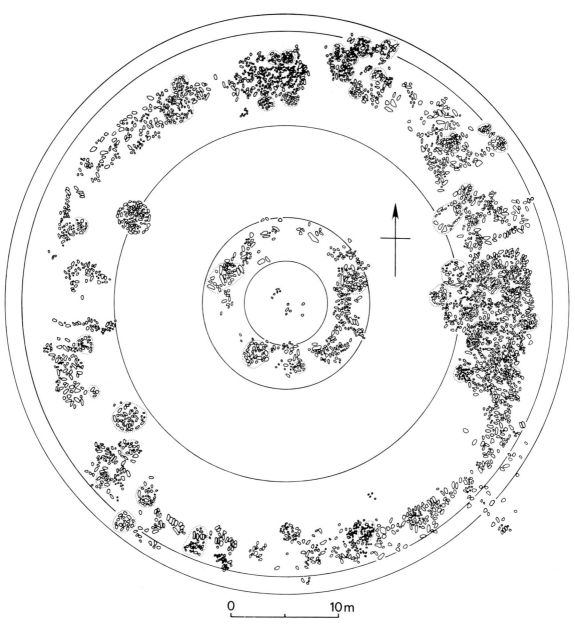

Figure 3.65 Plan map of the concentric stone circles of the Final Jomon at the Manza site, Oyu, Aomori Prefecture, northern Honshu. (Redrawn from Bunkazai Hogo Iinkai 1953:Figure 94.)

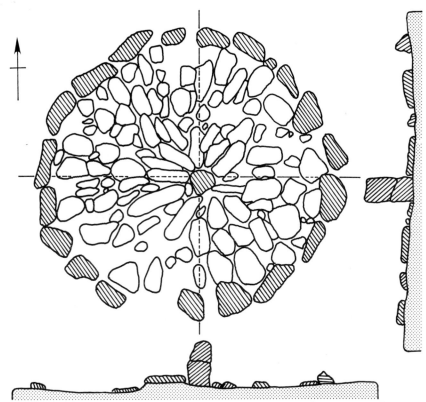

Figure 3.66 Sundial-like feature from the northwest quadrant of the circular monument at Manza (Figure 3.65). Diameter, ca. 2.5 m. (Redrawn from Bunkazai Hogo Iinkai 1953: Figure 16.)

pits about 1 m long, and half that wide and deep, of ample size to have contained human burials placed in the fetal position. Soil from one of the pits contained a relatively large amount of phosphorus, suggesting that it once contained bones, but several other samples showed no difference between the soil of the pits examined and that of their surroundings. Neither did any of the suspected grave pits contain burial offerings, though that is not unusual for Jomon times. The case is thus not particularly strong, but in the absence of a more compelling alternative interpretation, it is believed that these pit features were graves.

The previously mentioned sundial-like feature at Manza was slightly ovate, and a little less than 2.5 m in maximum diameter. At its center was a monolith that stood somewhat less than .5 m above the ground surface (Figure 3.66). The one at Nonakado was circular, 2 m in diameter, and had a central monolith close to 1 m tall. In both cases the perimeter of the feature was clearly defined by a single row of large, elongate cobbles aligned end to end, and the stones within the enclosure were laid with their long axes pointing toward the central monolith. This pattern was particularly crisp at Nonakado, where carefully selected elongate stones of about the same size and shape were used.

The antiquity of the Oyu monuments is established by stratigraphic and ceramic evidence. Excavations around the bases of the stone features showed that they had originally been set in a black soil that was subsequently covered by a thin stratum of volcanic ash, in turn covered by the modern surface layer of black humus. Pottery and other artifacts found beneath the unbroken ash layer clearly belong to the time of the monuments' construction, and are of types that establish the sites as being of Late Jomon age.

The investigators early considered the possibility that the stone circles at Oyu were some sort of special ceremonial centers, but subsequently came to favor the interpretation that they were cemeteries. The passageway leading into the monument at Nonakado indeed suggests a special ritual entrance, and a ritual function for the sundial-like features is implied by their uniqueness and particular placement. But few items that could be interpreted as ritual offerings were found, and the presence of apparent burial pits beneath the small stone features of the monument was stressed in the final interpretation. Too much should not be made of this distinction, however, since death and burial are everywhere accompanied by ceremonialism, and it does not seem strange to think of a cemetery as also being a ceremonial precinct.

Similar monuments occur widely in northern Honshu and in Hokkaido. At Taira-mura, Nagano Prefecture, in the mountainous center of Honshu, was discovered a group of small stone clusters, in the middle of which was a series of vertically set elongate cobble monoliths. At Kabayama, Iwate Prefecture, in northern Honshu, was found a large group of stone clusters, some of which had elongate cobbles still standing erect at their centers. A well-defined small sundial-like feature very similar to those at Oyu has also been reported from Nishizakiyama–Oshoro, Hokkaido. Adjacent to it were a number of stone clusters with what were apparently burial pits beneath. None of these sites constituted large circular monuments like those at Oyu, but a very small circle, several meters across, of erect stone monoliths from Jichinyama–Oshoro, Hokkaido, represents the stone-circle concept.

Outside Japan, burial monuments of similar form are known from several places in Northeast Asia. The Hokuei site on the Soviet island

of Sakhalin, north of Hokkaido, produced small stone enclosures 1 m
or so across, which were filled with small cobbles. These enclosures
covered pits in the ground, which yielded such apparent burial offerings as perforated stone beads and pendants. From Khongkhor–Obo,
in Mongolia, is reported a burial site consisting of a pit overlaid by a
cluster of stones, in the center of which was an erect stone monolith.
Other such sites are said to exist in Siberia as well. It remains to be
seen how strong a connection can be established between the continental and Japanese features, but it is evident that a cultural relationship of some sort existed.

From the Kyoto region on south and west, the archaeological record
for Middle and Later Jomon times is not as well developed as it is
farther north and east. This is probably to some extent due simply to a
lag in Jomon research, as the archaeologists' attention has been heavily competed for in southwestern Japan by the many important Yayoi
and Kofun period sites to be found there. It is also becoming clear,
however, that the Jomon way of life may not have flourished quite so
abundantly in the broad-leaved evergreen forest environment of the
south as it did in the deciduous mixed forests of the north. This is one
possible reason, in addition to the general lag in Jomon research, for
the relatively poorer archaeological record of southwestern Japan.

Southwestern Japan

The Middle Jomon period of the Kyoto region opened with pottery
types showing a strong relationship to the wares common along the
Inland Sea to the south, but later in the period the pottery came to
reflect the styles of eastern Japan. During the Late Jomon period,
southwestern influence once again became dominant, and this pattern
continued to the end of Final Jomon times. In general the lifeway
represented seems to follow the typical Jomon pithouse-dwelling,
hunting–gathering pattern, but little detailed information on these
aspects of the regional archaeology is yet available.

A number of surveys conducted in parts of southern Honshu indicate that Jomon occupation there was concentrated along the coasts of
the Japan and Inland seas, and along the mountainous spine of the
island (Esaka 1972; Kamaki 1965; Makabe and Shiomi 1965). Most of
the known sites date to Late and Final Jomon times, though evidence
of earlier occupation is present in the region. Ceramic types were
relatively uniform throughout the area, suggesting that it constituted a
single major interaction sphere.

Occupation sites known from the mountains are found where hunting, gathering of acorns and nuts, and the taking of salmon from rivers
debouching into the Japan Sea all would have been possible. At the

site of Maeike, in Okayama Prefecture, as well as at other places in southwestern Japan, large, deep, storage pits filled with acorns and capped with clay have been found.

Sites found along the seashores and on small coastal islands show that the typical Jomon fishing–shellfishing economy prevailed on both the Japan Sea and Inland Sea coasts. A common pattern was one of small groups of sites clustered around small bays, adjacent to sandbars or reefs. On the Inland Sea side of southern Honshu it is apparent that this pattern represents a shift from relatively sparse occupation of the higher tablelands in the Early Jomon period to much denser occupation of the coasts in the Late and Final Jomon periods.

Many of the sites known from the Inland Sea coast, especially in Okayama Prefecture, have yielded pottery of a number of different types, indicating that they were long occupied. Some locations appear to have been used either intermittently or continuously throughout the Middle, Late, and Final Jomon periods. It has also been observed that, outside of a relatively few favored areas in the Inland Sea region, the density of known Jomon sites is very low. A clue to the environmental factors that may be involved is supplied by work on the island of Shikoku.

It had earlier been believed that Shikoku, which bounds the Inland Sea on the east, had supported very little Jomon occupation. Surveys have now shown, however, that sites are well represented at low elevations along the coast, and at elevations above 450 m in the mountains. The upland distribution corresponds to the zone of mixed deciduous forest; the intermediate elevations, which in semitropical Shikoku harbor broad-leaved evergreen forest, were apparently not much occupied. It thus appears that in the southwest, as in the northeast of Japan, the Jomon way of life was best adapted to the coasts and temperate woodlands, and did not flourish in the warmer and biotically quite different evergreen forests of the south (Esaka 1972:132).

Many more Jomon culture sites have been recorded for Kyushu than for southern Honshu and Shikoku, but even here most of the reported data refer to ceramics or to surface surveys, with only limited information from excavated sites so far reported in detail.

Beginning in Late Jomon, and continuing into Final Jomon times, the ceramic inventory took on an increasing variety of forms, perhaps as a reflection of growing continental influences. The deep and shallow pot forms, which are very old in the Jomon tradition, continued, but new shapes appeared, including large kettles, pouring vessels, dishes, and pedestaled bowls. In the Final Jomon period, there spread widely throughout Kyushu a thin, well-made, polished deep-brown or blackware pottery with clear affinities to the polished blackware of the continental Lungshanoid horizon. Some such specimens were even footed in the continental manner, with tripod or four-legged bases (Kagawa 1965).

The Oishi site in northeastern Kyushu, extensively excavated using modern techniques but not yet fully reported, is an apparently typical Final Jomon settlement of this blackware pottery phase. Flat, percussion-flaked and partially ground stone celts believed to have functioned as plow and hoe blades were abundantly represented in the Oishi assemblage. Fully ground and polished reaping knives of a form well known from the following Yayoi period were also well represented. These implements account for 60% of the stone artifacts recovered at Oishi, suggesting that breaking ground and reaping seeds were activities of considerable importance there. A number of small seeds were excavated from the same general area that produced the stone celts, but they have proven very difficult to identify, and it is uncertain whether they represent cultivated species.

Other sites in northwestern Kyushu have, however, yielded quite clear, though not universally accepted, evidence of cultivated grains from Final Jomon contexts. At the site of Wakudoishi some rather convincing examples of probable rice-grain impressions on Final Jomon pottery are known, and at Tsuko and Harayama actual preserved rice grains have been recovered from the latest phase of Final Jomon times. Wheat and millet may also have been present in Japan by this time, but firm identification and dating of suspected remains are proving elusive (Esaka 1972; Kagawa 1965).

The settlement of Oishi, of considerable size, was situated on a broad tableland. Near its middle was a large pit about 8 m in diameter, in the center of which was a smaller elevated "stage." Three steps cut into the earth led down into this pit. It is supposed that this curious construction was an open-air community ceremonial center, and it may have functioned in connection with rites of cultivation. Interestingly, on this sunken stage and elsewhere, curved *magatama* beads were found. These occur very commonly in clearly ceremonial contexts in the subsequent Yayoi and Kofun periods, lending some credence to the speculations about ceremonialism at Oishi.

The indicators of increasing continental influence noted at Oishi seem to be quite general throughout Kyushu in Final Jomon times. In addition to the items already noted, there appear in significant quantity at this time pottery spindle whorls like those of the following Yayoi period, suggesting that spinning and weaving, well attested in the Yayoi period, were introduced into Kyushu during the Final Jomon. Cemeteries containing multiple burials, in large jars or in stone cists, appear as additional precursors of the new Yayoi culture soon to follow.

Conclusion   Jomon culture developed out of the Late Paleolithic tradition of Japan, becoming recognizable archaeologically as a new cultural entity with the introduction of pottery into the Japanese islands from the south, via Kyushu. Between about 12,500 and 10,000 years ago, Jomon pottery came into use throughout the three southern islands, and was established in Hokkaido by at least 8500 B.P. This was during the earlier part of which the stone tool technology of the Paleolithic persisted along with the newly introduced ceramics. The way of life of these incipient Jomon people is not yet well understood, but at least by the later part of the Initial Jomon period, soon after 10,000 B.P., the pattern of life that was to continue with little change throughout the remaining 7000 years of the Jomon age was fully established.

Jomon culture was a remarkably successful adaptation to the biotic diversity fostered by Japan's highly mountainous topography, numerous rivers, and heavily indented coastline. It flourished most richly in the regions covered by north temperate deciduous forest, but was less well suited to the semitropical broad-leaved evergreen forests of the south. The close juxtaposition of mountains, rivers, and coasts throughout most of the long, narrow Japanese archipelago meant that the economic resources needed to sustain local groups could usually be obtained within just a few kilometers, making it possible to maintain a predominantly sedentary pattern of residence on the basis of a hunting–gathering–fishing–shellfishing economy (Figure 3.67). Small villages of substantial semisubterranean pithouses are known to have existed from Initial Jomon times onward, and the pottery types and other evidence from some sites show that particularly favorable locations were occupied intermittently or continuously for hundreds or even thousands of years.

Vegetal foods were clearly an important, perhaps dominant, part of the economic base. In spring and summer the Japanese mountainsides abound in edible roots, shoots, and greens, and in autumn the forests produce acorns, walnuts, chestnuts, and other seeds, which can be gathered in huge quantities and stored for long periods. Grinding and cracking stones, hoe or digging-stick tips of flaked and ground stone, large storage pits, and much evidence of cracked and broken husks archaeologically attest the extensive use of nuts and seeds. Roots and greens are not directly attested, but starchy cakes found at a number of sites may be evidence of root harvesting. In the mountains of Nagano

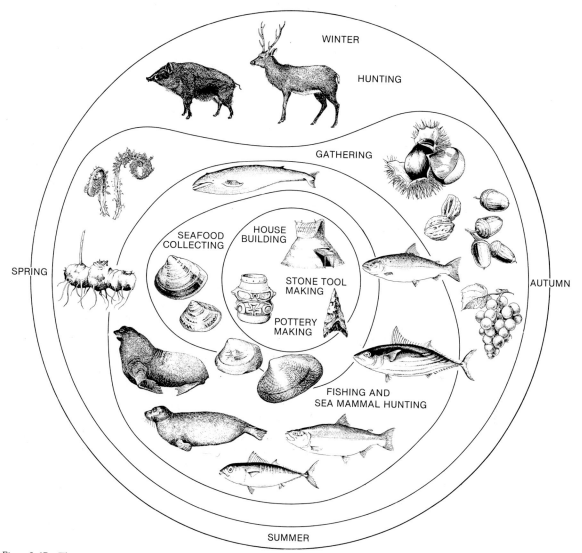

WINTER

HUNTING

GATHERING

SEAFOOD
COLLECTING

HOUSE
BUILDING

STONE TOOL
MAKING

POTTERY
MAKING

SPRING

AUTUMN

FISHING AND
SEA MAMMAL HUNTING

SUMMER

Figure 3.67 The Jomon seasonal hunting–gathering cycle. (Adapted from the original of Tatsuo Kobayashi by Gordon Miller. By permission of the Museum of Anthropology, University of British Columbia, Vancouver, Canada.)

Prefecture today, and no doubt elsewhere as well, such plants are still gathered as special seasonal treats.

Fish and shellfish, as well as a variety of other marine organisms, were then as now abundantly available the year around in the thousands of kilometers of bays, estuaries, and inlets of the rugged

Japanese coastline. Shell mounds by the thousands everywhere in Japan give evidence of the exploitation of these marine resources. In northern Honshu and Hokkaido, salmon and other fish ascended the many short rivers in vast numbers during the spring and summer. Woodland game animals such as deer, boar, and badger were for the most part rather small and solitary of habit, but they were everywhere available, and their bones in archaeological sites indicate that they made up a significant portion of the Jomon diet. A rich technology for getting and processing fish and game included dugout canoes, fish-spears and leisters, nets with floats and sinkers, hook and line, bow and arrow, stone knives and scrapers, and, of course, ceramic cooking pots.

The occurrence of Jomon pottery on small islets off the main islands of Japan shows that Jomon people were accomplished sailors from quite early times. Sado Island, 30 km off the western shore of northeast Honshu in the Japan Sea, and the Oki Islands, in the Japan Sea, 40 km off the west coast of southern Honshu, were occupied by the end of the Initial Jomon period. The Izu Islands, 50 km and more offshore in the Pacific south of Tokyo Bay, were occupied prior to and during Initial Jomon times. The island of Tsushima, lying midway in the strait between Japan and Korea, has yielded Early Jomon pottery, and Late Jomon wares occur as far away as the islands around Okinawa, about 600 km south of extreme southern Kyushu's port city of Kagoshima (Kamaki 1965; Makabe and Shiomi 1965; Pearson 1969).

Coastal areas where the resources of mountain, sea, and river were closely juxtaposed were biotically richest and most varied, and this is reflected in the high density of Jomon occupation around Tokyo Bay, Matsushima Bay near Sendai, and similar places. Favored interior regions also existed, however, as in mountainous Nagano Prefecture west of Tokyo, in the Japanese Alps.

Although it has been suggested that there may have been some seasonal alternation of occupation between coast and interior, such a pattern of transhumance would seem hardly to have been necessary in most settings. No doubt in Jomon as in recent times, there were both coastal and interior peoples, well established and quite self-sufficient within their particular small regions. Such a pattern actually seems to be reflected in the ceramic type distributions of the Tokyo region during Middle Jomon. The correspondence between pottery distributions and environmental zones is not exact, but in a general way the Atamadai series dominates the coastal areas, and the contemporaneous Katsuzaka series covers the inland zone, extending up into the central mountains (Okamoto and Tozawa 1965).

The rich and settled way of life that is especially well attested in the mountains of Nagano Prefecture at Togariishi, Yosukeone, and Idojiri has led Fujimori (1965; Esaka 1972) and others to believe that an indigenous pattern of slash-and-burn cultivation arose there in Middle Jomon times. This interpretation is not based on the finding of actual cultigens—no demonstrable cultigens have yet been found in these sites—but stems in essence from the fact that the Jomon people of this region (and others) did indeed live like Neolithic farmers. That is, they dwelt in substantial, comfortable houses arranged in stable, long-occupied villages, practiced a rich ceremonialism involving phallic altars and female figurines, and possessed a variety of fine ornamental and ceremonial objects. At such sites as Fudodo and Mizukamidani in Toyama Prefecture, they are known to have erected some buildings of considerable size, centrally located and no doubt communally built and utilized.

Soon after the beginning of Jomon times, the pottery began to show the existence of regional style zones that correspond in a rough way to geographical areas that even today are recognized by the Japanese as comprising distinctive cultural–environmental entities. Apparently this reflects the settling in of the country, and the consolidation of rather well-defined regional spheres of interaction between sets of local groups. Although the shape and size of the various interaction spheres varied over time to some extent, their existence is strong testimony to the early establishment and long persistence of regional folk traditions within the Jomon culture.

During the first part of the Initial Jomon period, linear-relief pottery spread from Kyushu to the southern marches of northeastern Honshu. Later in the period, nail-marked pottery occurred from Kyushu to central Honshu, and impressed-design ware occurred in northeastern Honshu. The Tokyo region, where the distribution of these two decorative motifs overlapped, also saw the appearance of rouletted cord-marked designs. Subsequently two major style zones of impressed and incised wares can be recognized, spanning northern and southern Japan respectively, and overlapping in the area of central Honshu and Tokyo.

By the Early Jomon period, six ceramic style zones can be recognized: eastern Hokkaido, western Hokkaido–far northern Honshu, the southern portion of northeastern Honshu, central Honshu including the Tokyo region, southwestern Honshu and Shikoku, and Kyushu. Middle Jomon saw the shifting of some of the boundary lines, but essentially the same pattern prevailed. In the Late Jomon period eastern and western Hokkaido comprised two separate style zones; northeastern and central Honshu largely coalesced into a single zone, but the Tokyo region maintained its own identity. Southwestern Honshu and Shikoku remained a unit, about as before, and Kyushu broke down into northern and southern zones.

The Final Jomon period saw significant restructuring of the earlier patterns. Northeastern and southwestern Japan were dominated by two overriding style zones, both involving finely made dark burnished wares in a variety of forms. Within the northeastern zone, which extended from central Honshu to Hokkaido, local foci of lesser intensity can be recognized in eastern Hokkaido, western Hokkaido–northeastern Honshu, and the Tokyo region. The southwestern zone from central Honshu southward, incorporating both Shikoku and Kyushu, was relatively more uniform internally. It is evident that during the Final Jomon, a major new spread of ceramic style and technique swept across the whole country, being absorbed into and submerging to a considerable extent (though not completely, especially in the northeast) the earlier regional pottery traditions (Kamaki 1965; Kidder and Esaka 1968; Tsuboi and Kobayashi 1977).

This far-reaching current of change in ceramic styles during Final Jomon times was one of the harbingers of further changes, to come from the direction of Korea and China to the southwest. In southwestern Japan, and especially in Kyushu, there appeared in the Final Jomon period such features as jar burials, stone cist graves, spindle whorls for weaving, ground stone reaping knives, and even actual grains of rice, which presaged the development of new cultural and economic patterns that were to become dominant in the following Yayoi age.

4 : The Yayoi Period

The Yayoi period saw the establishment of the traditional Japanese rural economy in essentially the form that was to persist right down to modern times (Figure 4.1). Wet-rice agriculture based on paddy field cultivation; semilunar stone reaping knives; wooden hoes, rakes, shovels, and pestles; loom weaving; iron tools; halberds, spears, swords, and mirrors of bronze; ornamental glass beads; and a new style of pottery making—these are some of the principal archaeological elements by which the new complex is recognized. All are items that clearly were initially imported from the continent, or inspired by continental prototypes.

These conspicuous new items so changed the appearance of the archaeological complexes by which the prehistoric inhabitants of the Japanese islands are known that many have seen in them evidence of a massive replacement of the preceding Jomon culture and its people by a wave of continental immigrants. In the late nineteenth century, after discoveries at Yayoi-cho in Tokyo had given a name to the new cultural manifestation, a common conception was that Yayoi culture marked the arrival of the true Japanese people in the home islands. The more ancient Jomon culture, which could be seen to have retreated northward before the Yayoi advance, was attributed to the Ainu, who by historic times had been crowded into the northern island of Hokkaido and the remoter regions of northern Honshu by the dominant Japanese.

Later interpretations have stressed continuity between Jomon and

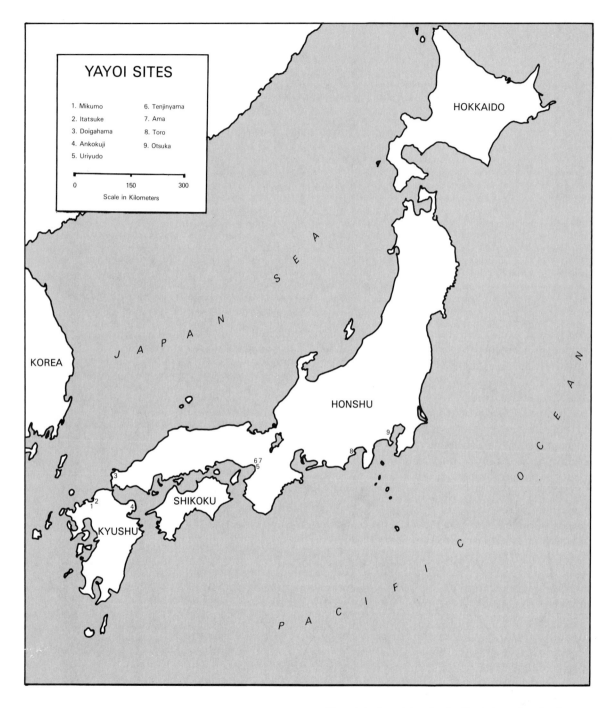

Figure 4.1 Locations of major Yayoi sites referred to in text.

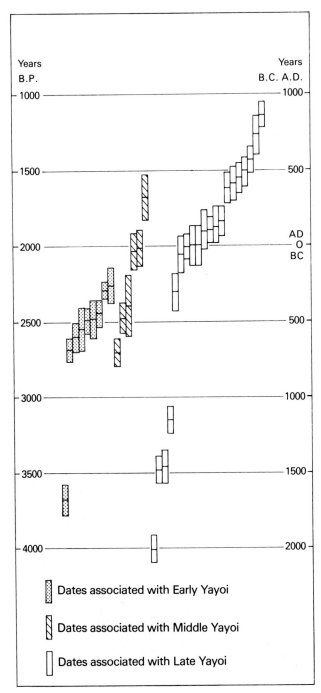

Figure 4.2 Carbon-14 dates associated with Yayoi pottery.

189

Yayoi culture, as shown in stratigraphically and stylistically overlapping ceramic traits, and the appearance in Japan of rice, paddy fields, and other elements as early as Late and Final Jomon times. The importance of continental contributions is not doubted, but the archaeological evidence—and the linguistic and biological considerations discussed in Chapter 1 are of importance here as well—indicates that continental immigrants were few in number, and appeared only in those parts of northern Kyushu and southwestern Honshu closest to the mainland.

According to the established interpretation of Yayoi chronology that has been developed over many decades of research, the new pattern developed rapidly. Bronze mirrors of Chinese manufacture, made in the later part of Former Han times, have been found in pottery vessels of Middle Yayoi type at several sites in Kyushu. Based on the historical Chinese dates for such mirrors, and allowing time for

Figure 4.3   Pottery from the Early Yayoi site of Itatsuke, Fukuoka Prefecture, Kyushu. Specimen at left is of the Final Jomon Yusu type; that at right is of the Initial Yayoi Itatsuke type. Height of specimen at left, ca. 27 cm. (Shown approximately one-third actual size.) (Courtesy T. Okazaki, Kyushu University.)

the mirrors to have been carried to Japan, treasured for a while by local chieftains, and buried with them upon their deaths, it has reasonably been estimated that such mirrors—and the Middle Yayoi ceramic types associated with them—probably date between about 100 B.C. and A.D. 100. Early Yayoi pottery, which is known to precede stratigraphically the types dated by association with Chinese mirrors, is assigned a like duration of 200 years, from 100 B.C. back to 300 B.C. Correspondingly, Late Yayoi pottery is dated by the same reasoning to the interval A.D. 100–300. Radiocarbon dates suggest that Yayoi culture emerged earlier and persisted longer than the conventional dates indicate (Figure 4.2), but the matter is controversial, and the conventional chronology remains in general use.

The Yayoi pattern seems to have spread through Japan in two stages. During Early Yayoi, the culture appeared throughout southwestern Japan as far north and east as the Kyoto–Nagoya region, and during Middle Yayoi, it spread through mountainous central Honshu, the Tokyo region, and northern Honshu. During Late Yayoi, though it became more fully established in northern Honshu, it apparently never did cross the Tsugaru Strait into the island of Hokkaido. Figures 4.3 through 4.15 picture the main Yayoi ceramic types associated with

Figure 4.4 Deep pot of the Early Yayoi from the Karako site, Nara Prefecture, south-central Honshu. Karako I type. Height, 27.5 cm. (Shown approximately one-third actual size.) (Kyoto University Museum.)

Figure 4.5   Large jar of the Early Yayoi from the Karako site, Nara Prefecture, south-central Honshu. Karako I type. Height, 42.5 cm. (Shown one-half actual size.) (Kyoto University Museum.)

Figure 4.6 Decorated jar of the Early Yayoi from the Karako site, Nara Prefecture, south-central Honshu. Karako I type, Height, 28.6 cm. (Shown approximately one-third actual size.) (Kyoto University Museum.)

Figure 4.7 Jar of the Middle Yayoi from Hakuraku, Yokohama, Kanagawa Prefecture, central Honshu. A transitional type, of Yayoi form with Jomon cord-marked decoration. Height, 31.3 cm. (Shown approximately one-third actual size.) (Kyoto University Museum.)

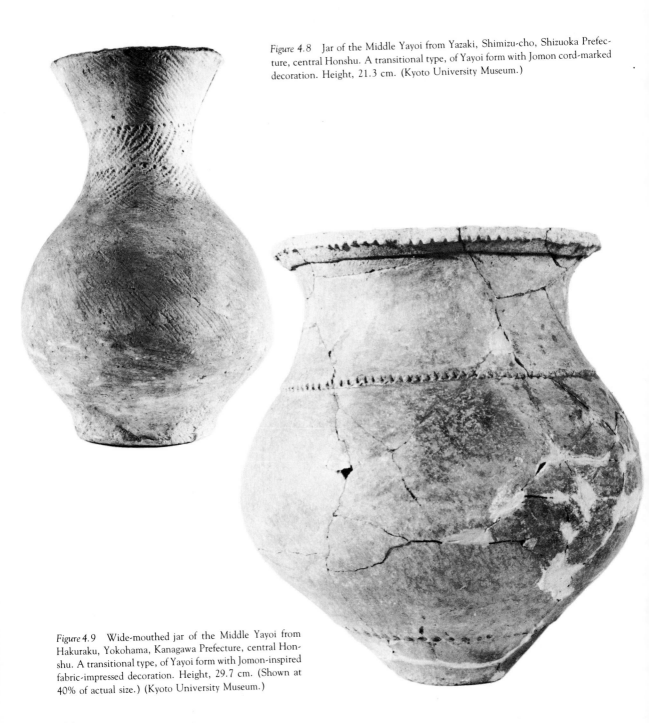

Figure 4.8 Jar of the Middle Yayoi from Yazaki, Shimizu-cho, Shizuoka Prefecture, central Honshu. A transitional type, of Yayoi form with Jomon cord-marked decoration. Height, 21.3 cm. (Kyoto University Museum.)

Figure 4.9 Wide-mouthed jar of the Middle Yayoi from Hakuraku, Yokohama, Kanagawa Prefecture, central Honshu. A transitional type, of Yayoi form with Jomon-inspired fabric-impressed decoration. Height, 29.7 cm. (Shown at 40% of actual size.) (Kyoto University Museum.)

Figure 4.10 Beaker of the Middle Yayoi from Minami Oyama, Fukushima Prefecture, central Honshu. A transitional type, with zoned cord-marking of Jomon inspiration. Minami Oyama I type. Height, 28 cm. (Courtesy S. Sugihara, Meiji University.)

Figure 4.11 Large jar of the Middle Yayoi from the Izuruhara site, Tochigi Prefecture, central Honshu. A transitional type, with Jomon-like incised and cord-marked decoration. Suwada type. Height, 49 cm. (Shown one-third actual size.) (Courtesy S. Sugihara, Meiji University.)

Figure 4.12 Burial urn of the later Middle Yayoi from Nozoe, city of Ogori, Fukuoka Prefecture, Kyushu. Height, 120 cm. (Kyoto University Museum.)

Figure 4.13 Jar of the Late Yayoi from Kakeyama Shell Mound, Aichi Prefecture, south-central Honshu. Kakeyama type. Height, 22.6 cm. (Shown approximately one-half actual size.) (Kyoto University Museum.)

Figure 4.14 Compound jar of the Late Yayoi from Kakeyama Shell Mound, Aichi Prefecture, south-central Honshu. Kakeyama type. Height, 16.5 cm. (Shown approximately one-half actual size.) (Kyoto University Museum.)

Figure 4.15   Pedestaled bowl of the Late Yayoi from Kakeyama Shell Mound, Aichi Prefecture, south-central Honshu. Kakeyama type. Height, 20.3 cm. (Kyoto University Museum.)

this expansion, and illustrate as well the development of Yayoi pottery over time.

The site summaries that follow illustrate the most important cultural characteristics and developments of the Yayoi period, with attention focused on Kyushu, where the culture first appeared, and the Kyoto–Osaka region, where it reached its highest development. The concluding pages of the chapter address aspects of cultural change and societal evolution, and close with a partial account of Yayoi period culture as seen through the eyes of early Chinese historical chroniclers who knew the Japanese as frontier barbarians.

The Itatsuke site, in the city of Fukuoka, northern Kyushu, is generally recognized as the type locality for the initial phase of Early Yayoi culture. Some bronze swords and halberds were discovered near the village of Itatsuke in 1918, and systematic excavations have been

Itatsuke

conducted intermittently at the site since 1949 (Mori and Okazaki 1961; Otsuka 1973).

South of the Gokasa River, which empties into Hakata Bay a few kilometers away, a narrow tableland about 10 m high and 500 m long rises out of the broad, low floodplain. This is the site of a modern farming community surrounded by rice paddies. In the northwestern sector of the modern settlement, which is favored by a number of especially good wells, have been found the remains of ancient Itatsuke. The existence of the modern settlement has imposed limitations on excavation at the archaeological site, and disturbances incident to the long historical occupation there have obscured portions of the record. The character and content of the ancient site are thus incompletely known—the residential area has not been found, for example—but the place has nevertheless yielded extremely important information bearing on the appearance of Early Yayoi culture.

Excavations centered on the northwestern portion of the elevated tableland have revealed a number of small pits, several deep wells, and three ditches, all of which contained or were stratigraphically associated with pottery of both the Yusu and Itatsuke types. Yusu ware is known, from a nearby site of the same name, as the latest pottery type of the Final Jomon period, whereas Itatsuke ware is recognized as the initial Early Yayoi type. Both Yusu and Itatsuke wares were made in the form of deep pots, globular jars, and pedestaled bowls. Brushed and combed surfaces were common on both, as were vessel profiles exhibiting a gentle incurve between the rim and the angled shoulder of the vessel. The types differ only in minor nuances of form and decorative technique, and their close kinship is clearly evident (Figure 4.3). The fact that they co-occur throughout the Itatsuke excavations is important evidence that Itatsuke was occupied very near the time of the Jomon–Yayoi transition.

Many small pits, varyingly of circular, elliptical, rectangular, and trapezoidal plan, were found within the arc of a long, curving ditch that seems to have bounded the Itatsuke site along its western edge. The pits differed in size, but most were between 1.6 and 2.6 m across, and approximately 1 m deep. When discovered they contained pottery fragments and other trash, but it is surmised that their original use was probably food storage.

Several filled-in ancient wells were discovered in the same area, and were found to contain Early Yayoi pottery. Two wells, which were completely excavated, proved to be of similar dimensions, approximately .8 m in diameter and 6 m in depth. Both contained pottery sherds and other remains.

The long, curving ditch at the western edge of the site, and two other channels that were later dug at right angles intersecting it, apparently attest community efforts at water control. The main ditch,

Figure 4.16 Stone reaping knives (*ishibocho*) typical of those in use throughout the Yayoi period, from Fukuoka Prefecture, Kyushu. Upper, from Undojominami, city of Izuka; lower from Sugu Okamoto, city of Kasuga. Length of lower specimen, 13 cm. (Shown actual size.) (Kyoto University Museum.)

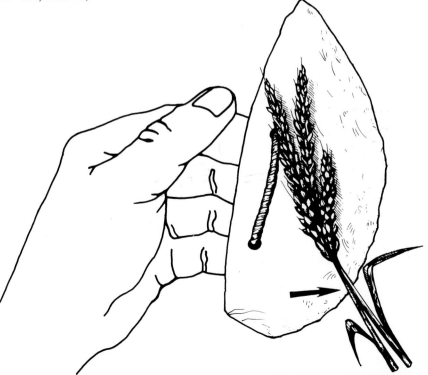

Figure 4.17 Yayoi-type *ishibocho* stone reaping knife in use. Similar tools were used in this manner for stripping seed heads from rice plants until very recent times in Southeast Asia.

of which a segment about 110 m long was cleared archaeologically, varied in width from about 2 to 4.5 m, and in depth below the modern surface from about .5 to 1.5 m. The straight ditches that crossed the curving one were both shorter and narrower. It is not clear whether these three channels served for irrigation, drainage, or flood protection. Because the earliest ditch seems to have bounded the occupation area of the site, it has been suggested that most probably the system was created to afford protection to the residential portion of the village.

Evidence that Itatsuke was from its inception a farming settlement came from the excavated fill of these ditches, and from some of the storage pits. Charred grains of rice were found at several spots, and the

Figure 4.18 Clay and stone spindle whorls typical of the Yayoi period, from the city of Fukuoka, Fukuoka Prefecture, Kyushu. Exact provenience unknown. Diameter of largest specimen, 5.8 cm. (Kyoto University Museum.)

"ghosts" of rice grains that had been accidentally embedded in the bases of clay vessels during manufacture show that rice was common at the site as early as the time the first Itatsuke ware was made there. The sizes and length–width ratios of the Itatsuke rice grains and impressions show that Early Yayoi rice was similar to modern Japanese rice, sufficiently so as to be assignable to the same species, *Oryza japonica*.

Ground stone knives of semilunar shape, usually perforated with two holes through which a cord might be passed as a device for helping to grip the implement, are another indicator of rice cultivation at Itatsuke. Similar specimens have been found in continental China associated with rice cultivation perhaps several millennia earlier, and they are common in the ancient rice-growing areas of coastal China and southern Korea as well (Chang 1977:95); the type has also been identified from the Burzahom Neolithic site in India. Modern ethnographic examples from Southeast Asia that attest the use of similar small, hand-held knives for harvesting the seed heads of rice offer additional assurance that the interpretation of these semilunar knives, or *ishibocho,* as reaping knives is reliable (Figures 4.16, 4.17).

Confirmation of the thesis that agriculture was well established at Itatsuke appeared in Japanese newspapers in the early summer of 1979, with reports that actual ancient paddy fields had been uncovered there. At the time of this writing few details of the discovery are available, but it can be noted that the new finds are not particularly surprising, in view of the other evidence from Itatsuke and elsewhere.

The *ishibocho* reaping knives and the flooded paddy field form of cultivation are clearly of continental origin, and must have entered Japan together as elements of the wet-rice complex. The art of loom weaving, as attested by disk-shaped perforated clay and stone spindle whorls and wooden loom parts, may have entered Japan at about the same time (Figure 4.18). A number of spindle whorls have been recovered from Itatsuke, although so far no specimens identifiable as loom parts have been found at this particular site. Tanged points of ground slate, and a portion of a double-keeled ground stone blade of the same material, are of forms that indicate clearly that they were copied from metal prototypes. Metal tools clearly assignable to the Early Yayoi have not been found at Itatsuke, but the sharpness of some of the cutting marks on the banks of the ditches there has been adduced as an indication that metal tools were in fact used at the site. Specimens from other sites show that utilitarian iron tools of continental make were certainly present in Japan during Early Yayoi times, though they may have been rare.

Evidence of cultural continuity between Early Yayoi and the preceding Final Jomon period includes most notably the typological and stratigraphic overlap previously mentioned between Yusu (Final Jo-

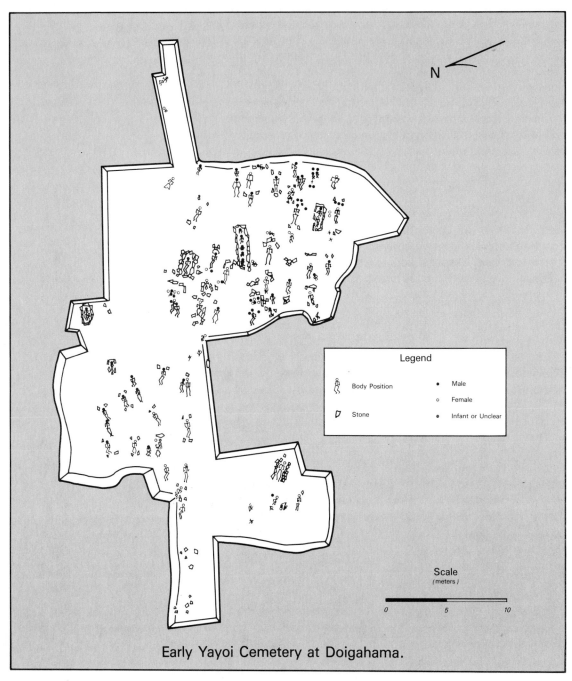

Early Yayoi Cemetery at Doigahama.

Figure 4.19 Cemetery of the Early Yayoi period at Doigahama, Yamaguchi Prefecture, southern Honshu. (Redrawn from Kanazeki *et al.* 1961:Figure 1.)

mon) and Itatsuke (Early Yayoi) pottery types at the site. Additionally, small, triangular arrowpoints with incurved or deeply indented bases from Itatsuke are of traditional Jomon forms attested as far back as Early Jomon times in Kyushu and elsewhere. They suggest not only the persistence of Jomon traditions of stoneworking, but also the continued importance of hunting in the new Yayoi culture. Roughly flaked stone hoe or digging-stick blades and well-made polished stone axe- and adzeheads are yet other carry-overs from Jomon to Yayoi at Itatsuke.

Doigahama is a cemetery of the Early Yayoi period. It is on the northwesternmost tip of southern Honshu, in Yamaguchi Prefecture (Kanazeki *et al.* 1961). The site occupies one end of a long, stabilized sand dune that crests about 5.5 m above the level of the nearby sea. The dune is now partially forested, and low-lying areas on either side of it are occupied by rice paddy fields. Excavations carried out over a period of several years have exposed remains of the historic, Kofun, and Yayoi periods. The Yayoi burials, of interest here, are assignable on the basis of associated pottery types to the later part of Early Yayoi, with a few belonging to early Middle Yayoi. Cemetery burial on a significant scale was a development of Yayoi times in Japan, and Doigahama offers a good example of Early Yayoi burial practices.

Doigahama

The cemetery measured approximately 60 × 70 m, with burials most densely concentrated in one area of about 20 m² (Figure 4.19). In all, the remains of 175 individuals were recovered by systematic excavations, and many other burials have come from the site over the years. Of the skeletons for which age determinations were possible, 62% were elderly, 18% were adults of mature years, 15% were infants or small children, and 5% were young adults. This age distribution suggests that Doigahama was a normal community cemetery. It is puzzling, however, that of 156 cases where sex could be determined, 106 individuals turned out to be male, whereas only 50 were identified as female. This may be simply an artifact of sampling error, but could genuinely reflect a higher mortality rate for males. It is suggestive in this connection that all the projectile points found at the site were recovered from among the bones of human beings.

Four types of burials were found. Many skeletons simply lay in the sand, with no traces of any kind of coffin or enclosure. They may have been placed in simple pits, although the finding of what were apparently iron nails in one spot suggests that perishable wooden coffins were in use. Many other skeletons had a few large stones placed around each individual, often arranged with one stone on either side of the head, and one on either side of the feet. The third burial type consisted of several interments made inside rough stone enclosures, and the fourth type was a refinement of the third, consisting of interments in large, rectangular chambers that were made up of vertically set stone slabs. After the burials were put in place, these rough enclosures were roofed over as chamber graves by laying stone slabs across the tops of the enclosing walls. The third and fourth types were relatively uncommon, represented by only a few specimens each.

Multiple interments occurred in a number of instances, the most usual such case being one in which a single individual was accompanied by two or more separate skulls. A particularly striking multiple case was the finding of five complete individuals, all adult males, buried within a large, well-made stone chamber about 3 m long, .5 m wide, and .7 m high.

Burial goods from the cemetery included such items as a glass bead, round beads of jadeite, tubular beads of jasper, disk beads of shell, and shell bracelets and finger rings. A number of ceramic vessels were recovered in the course of the excavations, but only in one case did it appear that a pot had been emplaced as a burial accompaniment. Burial of individuals within large pottery jars, a very common form of interment throughout the Yayoi period, was not attested at Doigahama. No conspicuous patterning in the distribution of grave goods by age or sex was noted, but there was a major division in the cemetery between the few interments in stone chambers and the many found without coffins. This division and the finding of what may have been trophy heads associated with some burials suggest a certain degree of status differentiation within the Early Yayoi society represented by the remains at Doigahama.

Mikumo   The Middle Yayoi site at Mikumo, about 15 km southwest of the modern city of Fukuoka in northern Kyushu, has been known since the early 1820s. It is reported that a jar burial discovered at the site contained a wealth of Chinese bronze mirrors of the Early Han period, 35 in all. Along with them were found a sword and some spearpoints of bronze, and a number of stone beads. Years later, from another jar burial in the vicinity were recovered 21 more bronze mirrors, along with other metal artifacts. The first finds at Mikumo preceded by over 60 years the discoveries at Yayoi-cho in Tokyo that gave more or less formal recognition to the Yayoi culture as an archaeological entity, and they have long figured importantly in discussions of its continental connections (Figures 4.20–4.22).

The site was finally excavated on a large scale in 1975 and 1976, when several impending construction projects threatened its continued existence (Fukuoka-ken Kyoiku Iinkai 1975, 1976). Preliminary reports show that it was a major settlement not only during Yayoi times but during the Kofun and medieval periods as well. A Kofun period burial tumulus there indicates that at one time Mikumo may have been a minor political center of sorts, but it is at present only a relatively small farming village like many others in the region.

The site occupies an area of very slightly elevated ground in the midst of a broad alluvial floodplain. It occurs on the natural levee between two rivers, which follow parallel courses about 1 km apart in the vicinity of Mikumo, watering a rich agricultural region now entirely in rice paddy fields as far as the edges of the distant hills.

Large horizontal exposures revealed postholes, hearths, and other features of many houses, buried only a few centimeters beneath the modern ground level. The floors had been sunk into the ancient surface, giving the houses a typically semisubterranean character. Because the overlying soil had been disturbed by centuries of cultivation, the level of the surface from which they were dug, and hence their original depth, could not be determined. The Yayoi period houses were generally either round or square with rounded corners. Square houses of the Kofun period showed that occupation continued for a long time on the same spot, but most of the cultural features were of Yayoi age. Some individual building plans could be traced more or less completely, but there was a great deal of overlapping of earlier and later structures, leaving details of form and construction uncertain.

Middle and Late Yayoi period burials were found in several places not far from residential areas. In each such place clustered a number of interments, an individual burial typically consisting of a large ceramic funerary urn capped by a smaller one of similar shape. These lay not far beneath the surface in shallow pits that were either circular or ovate, depending on whether the burial urns had been set upright or laid on their sides.

Several small stone-lined chambers or loosely constructed stone coffins, reminiscent of those known from Doigahama but much smaller, were also found. They were rectangular, about 1 m long and 20 cm or so across, with floors made of several flat stones, and walls and ends consisting of a number of unshaped, vertically set slabs. They were roofed or covered by two or more large flat slabs laid across the tops of the walls. At one place, two such chambers occurred close together, and one of these was a double coffin, partitioned by several slabs set on edge down the centerline of the interior. These two stone chambers were not closely associated with any interments of the more common jar burial type, but a third did occur among a group of jar burials.

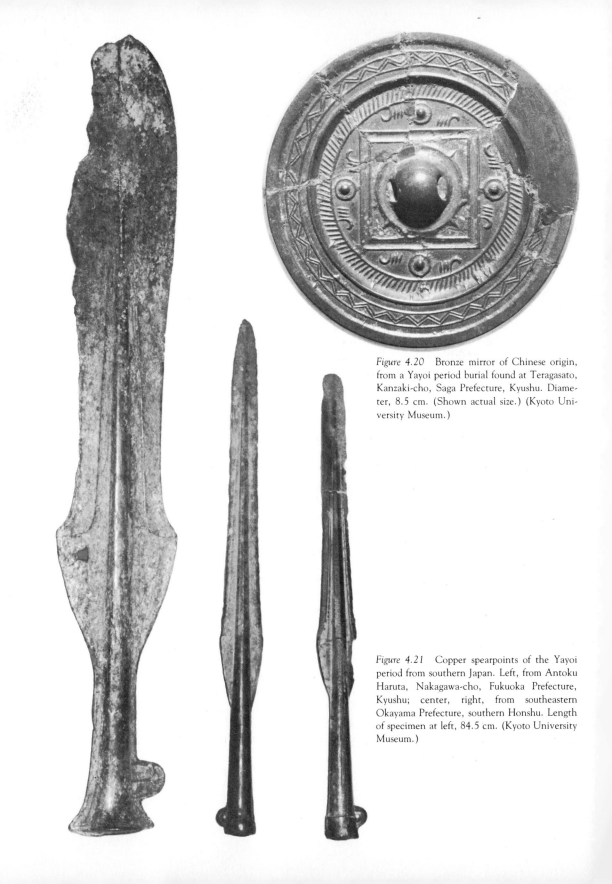

Figure 4.20 Bronze mirror of Chinese origin, from a Yayoi period burial found at Teragasato, Kanzaki-cho, Saga Prefecture, Kyushu. Diameter, 8.5 cm. (Shown actual size.) (Kyoto University Museum.)

Figure 4.21 Copper spearpoints of the Yayoi period from southern Japan. Left, from Antoku Haruta, Nakagawa-cho, Fukuoka Prefecture, Kyushu; center, right, from southeastern Okayama Prefecture, southern Honshu. Length of specimen at left, 84.5 cm. (Kyoto University Museum.)

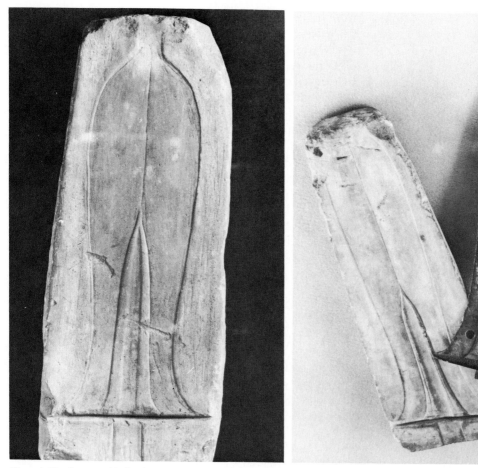

Figure 4.22 Stone molds for the casting of bronze blades, and a blade cast from such a mold, Yayoi period (far right). (T. Higuchi photo.)

Many of the graves contained few or no burial offerings, but several were quite rich, in particular two burials that had been excavated prior to the 1975–1976 work. Their location and the types of fragmentary artifacts recovered at the spot correspond well to the historically recorded facts of the initial digging at Mikumo during the early 1820s. Fragments of one mirror recovered by the recent digging have actually been fitted together with pieces of a formerly discovered specimen. This implies that the spot is indeed the very same, and to the wealth of mirrors, glass beads, and metal artifacts from the previous excavations may thus be added many more glass beads, a number of iron arrowpoints, some gilded bronze ornaments, one complete

Chinese bronze mirror, and the fragments of many more. One of the burial urns had been removed, leaving only the pit it had occupied, but the other was of a type belonging to the later part of the Middle Yayoi period. This probably dates both burials, which were close together and yielded the same types of artifacts.

Among all the burials discovered, no others approached these two in abundance of associated artifacts, from which it is clear that the people interred here were of special importance. The bronze mirrors of Chinese make, and other metal specimens in these graves, also make clear the importance of continental status symbols and weaponry to the embryonic Yayoi aristocracy, establishing a pattern that was to persist and expand throughout Yayoi and Kofun times, and well into the historic period. Many other finds support this conclusion, especially those from the nearby Sugu site, which duplicates and adds important nuances to the record from Mikumo.

Ankokuji   As a final example of Yayoi culture in its Kyushu homeland, the Late Yayoi site of Ankokuji may be described (Kyushu Bunka Sogo Kenkyujo 1958). Located at the northeastern corner of the island in old delta lands where the Tabuka River flows into the Inland Sea north of Beppu Bay, it offers an excellent illustration of the factors determining the location of most Yayoi settlements. A geological survey showed that the modern Tabuka River flows on top of a widespread conglomerate stratum of Pleistocene age. This it has covered with more recent alluvial deposits, in the process leaving many abandoned meander loops scattered over the floodplain. The site of Ankokuji is on one of these old meanders, which is filled with a black, muddy soil naturally irrigated by groundwater.

Four ancient ditches at the site, which contained Early Kofun period pottery sherds, probably originated near the end of the Yayoi period after the site had been occupied for quite some time. All were about 1.5 m wide and 1 m deep. Three of them seem to have been drainage ditches dug to lead excess water from the old cutoff meander into the living Tabuka River, which apparently then followed much the same channel that it does now. The courses of these ditches overlapped at one point, and the stratigraphy there showed that they were dug at successive periods, only one having been in use at any one time. The fourth ditch, which followed an arc parallel to the course of the modern river, may have carried water tapped off far upstream, though where it was ultimately used is unknown.

Older members of local farming families, interviewed at the time of the archaeological investigations, recounted that, decades before, their elders had regularly farmed the old streamcourse, planting rice by direct sowing. Later, modern irrigation and drainage works were built and the local fields redistricted into a rectilinear pattern, but until that time an agricultural technique prevailed that was probably as old as the pioneer Yayoi settlement there.

That people occupied the vicinity of this natural paddy field in Late Yayoi times was abundantly attested by many ceramic and wooden artifacts of that vintage, which had come to rest in it. These had been covered and preserved by layers of wet peat and mud. That the old streambed was the scene of actual farming in those times was indicated by the finding of many rice grains along with the artifacts, and by rows of wooden stakes that had probably been used to shore up footpaths across the spongy fields. Other fruits, nuts, and seeds associated with the rice grains included those of peach, persimmon, walnut, chestnut, acorn, and pine. These food products are still gathered from wild trees, so that, broadly speaking, the modern rural economy still strongly reflects the subsistence base established at ancient Ankokuji.

The residential portion of the village was adjacent to the old field. No individual house alignments were discernible among the hundreds of postholes found there; nor, with one dubious exception, were any hearths or other house floor features discovered. The excavators con-cluded that the swarms of posts must have supported structures with raised floors, and they suggested that each series of posts may have supported a large platform serving as a common floor for a number of dwellings. The building of individual houses upon such platforms is known to occur in Southeast Asia, but whether the postholes at An-kokuji represent a communal platform or the repeated rebuilding of individual structures cannot readily be determined.

A further problem in the interpretation of these archaeological features is that, at other sites, Yayoi structures that are identifiable as dwellings are either semisubterranean or built directly on the ground surface. Whether the architectural remains at Ankokuji were actually dwellings rather than elevated storage houses of the kind known from other Yayoi sites cannot be established beyond a reasonable doubt. However, the finding of such artifacts as pottery, flaked stone pro-jectile points, and broken bone discarded as food refuse in the same areas as the posthole clusters strongly suggests human habitation.

The stone and wooden tools found associated with the posthole clusters have a plainly domestic character. Stone tools were not nu-merous, but several ground and polished axeheads, a number of flaked stone arrowpoints, a ground stone reaping knife, and a number of milling stones give evidence of a variety of functions. A carved wooden cup and some spoons were obviously individual eating utensils; such agricultural tools as wooden mallets, spades, and plowshares attest the labors of the fields. Several wooden frames held together by mortise-and-tenon joinery demonstrate craftsmanship in woodworking, but are of uncertain function. A great many poles, logs, and rough boards were no doubt the remains of the buildings that once stood on the site. It is inferred from the sharp, clear cutting marks on the many wooden objects that metal tools were regularly used at Ankokuji, though none were found. Of course the same wet-soil conditions that preserved the wooden specimens so well would be inimical to the long-term survival of metals.

A detailed study of the pottery from Ankokuji showed it to be of conspicuously uniform character. Most of the vessels were urns, though pedestaled bowls and other forms also occurred. The decorated pieces were marked with comb-incised patterns to the virtual exclusion of other motifs. Most of the pottery was of Late Yayoi type, though some pieces of Haji ware, which flourished in the Kofun and later periods, were also found. The Yayoi and Haji pieces were all but indistinguishable, and it is believed that Ankokuji was occupied just at the time of transition between the two ceramic types. Haji ware is generally considered to have been mass-produced on the potter's wheel, and the high degree of uniformity noted in the Late Yayoi ware from Ankokuji indicates that it too was produced by standardized tools and techniques, if not actually wheel-made.

The investigators point out that the pottery from Ankokuji shares very detailed similarities with that of other sites all along the coasts of the Inland Sea. Highly similar ceramics are found even in the distant Osaka and Nara regions, attesting close communication and sharing of craft lore over a broad area. The geographical position of Ankokuji, on a major peninsula at the western edge of the Inland Sea, places it as much within the cultural orbit of that area as of Kyushu, and it must have been from similar coastal sites that Early Yayoi culture had begun its northeastward expansion centuries before. At any rate, ceramic comparisons indicate that close communication between the Kyushu homeland and areas beyond was maintained even in latest Yayoi times.

Ama   At the eastern end of the Inland Sea is the Ama site, located in west-central Honshu about halfway between the modern cities of Kyoto and Osaka (Takatsuki-shi Shi Hensan Iinkai 1973; Takatsuki-shi Kyoiku Iinkai 1977). A broad corridor of alluvial land traversed by meandering streams extends between these two cities, and the Ama site occupies a long, low rise on the floodplain, 1 km or so out from the hills that bound it on the north.

Ceramics taken from limited excavations at the Ama site in the late 1920s were pivotal in the first recognition of Early Yayoi settlement in the Kyoto–Osaka region, and in understanding the northeastward spread of Yayoi culture from its original homeland in Kyushu. Detailed comparisons showed that the comb pattern and other motifs of one of the main Ama types were clearly the same as those of pottery assigned to about the middle of the Early Yayoi period in Kyushu, and helped to show that during what is now called the Ongagawa phase there was a general northeastward extension of Yayoi culture along both sides of the Inland Sea. This expansion came to a temporary halt a short distance northeast of the Kyoto–Osaka region, marking the initial stage in the dissemination of the new agricultural way of life throughout Japan. Ama was, thus, one of the first farming settlements to be established in the area that later became the heartland of historic Japanese civilization.

The region has long been in rice paddies, but with the growth of suburban communities serving metropolitan Osaka, a number of construction projects encroaching on the old fields have created occasion for a series of archaeological excavations. One report identifies 11 archaeological localities, all found on a strip of land approximately .5 km wide and 1.5 km long. Evidence from excavations at these spots suggests that the whole expanse is one site, occupied throughout the Yayoi and Kofun periods and on into historic times. Several Yayoi villages and a number of Kofun period burial mounds also occur on higher ground along the edge of the hills to the north.

The Early Yayoi occupation seems to have been relatively limited and was concentrated in the central portion of the site area. During Middle Yayoi times, after a major flood buried the early occupation surface under a thick stratum of sand and gravel, the village expanded both east and west. By Late Yayoi times the center of activity had shifted still farther east. At each subperiod the residential areas were apparently encircled by moatlike ditches. The full extent of the boundary ditches is not clear, but it is known that during Early Yayoi times the settlement was encircled by two concentric canals, each 3–4 m wide and slightly over 1 m deep. The outer one enclosed an oval area 90 × 150 m, the inner one an oval 70 × 110 m. The paddy fields no doubt lay on lower ground beyond, as suggested by pollen analyses from excavations in several areas.

Numerous pits, postholes, and cuttings found within the inner enclosure were clearly the residue of architectural units, but it has proved difficult to sort structural patterns out of the complexity of overlapping features. A single relatively small squarish structure with rounded corners shows the character of at least one type of Late Yayoi period house. Its perimeter was outlined by a narrow groove, apparently to take the bases of vertical walls, and a centrally located fireplace and a number of roof-support-pillar holes were excavated into its floor. Continuing excavations at the site will undoubtedly clarify the nature of its architectural remains.

A wealth of ceramic, stone, and wooden artifacts has been recovered from the many seasons of excavation at Ama. Detailed comparative analysis may alter the picture somewhat, but it now appears that, changing pottery styles aside, there was no essential change in the basic technology of the settlement throughout the Yayoi period.

Household equipment presumably involved with food preparation included deep pots, bowls, jars, and cups of pottery, and wooden spoons, ladles, and trenchers. Pedestaled ceramic bowls, and carved wooden ones of the same style, were probably special serving or offering dishes. Flat stones with broad, shallow depressions worn in their upper surfaces may have been used for crushing or grinding seeds or nuts, and large, double-ended wooden pestles about 1 m long were undoubtedly rice-pounders of the type depicted in use on the decorated sides of bronze *dotaku* bells cast during the Yayoi period. (*Dotaku* are discussed in detail in the next section on *Tenjinyama*.)

Agricultural instruments were mostly of wood, which was well preserved in the waterlogged soils of the site. Several long-handled wooden spades with roundish points were remarkably like modern steel gardening spades in form. Square hoes, some with short forklike tines at the end of the blade such as are still to be seen in rural Japan, were also recovered. Elongate semilunar reaping knives of ground stone, the *ishibocho* so familiar in Yayoi sites, complete the basic list of planting and harvesting tools.

Artisans' woodworking tools and evidence of lithic manufacturing activities were well represented. A number of stout wooden shafts, perforated at one end to hold a tapered stone head, were complemented by many axeheads of both flaked and ground stone. Adze handles were skillfully carved from forked poles—one arm of the fork was cut off short and flattened on one side so that a stone celt could be lashed to it, and the longer arm served as a handle. That these artifacts were probably manufactured at the site was suggested by the finding, in the encircling ditches, of many scraps of worked wood, including some unfinished tools. Flaked stone drills and gravers, of which a number of specimens were found, no doubt served as woodworking implements. Rough flaked stone forms that correspond closely to the shape of *ishibocho* suggest that these tools also were made at the site.

Though Ama was plainly at all times principally an agricultural settlement, hunting activities were also attested by the artifact inventory. A number of small hardwood bows somewhat less than 1 m in length were found in good condition. Projectile points included ovate and triangular chipped stone forms, some with tapering stems. Several long-stemmed points of ground stone, obviously made in imitation of metal prototypes, were also found, as was a single long-stemmed bronze point. Other flaked stone specimens included several large spearheads, and a number of thick flakes and large, thick bifaces that appear to have been discarded remnants of lithic manufacturing activities.

The burials found at Ama, which were principally of the Middle Yayoi period, suggest the existence of certain social divisions within the village of that time. Several small cemetery areas, separate but all very similar, occurred around the edge of the village. They are believed to reflect the existence of self-consciously differentiated corporate groups within the settlement, a pattern common in rural Japanese villages throughout historical times. It further seems likely that the burials in these cemeteries were of individuals of relatively high status, presumably the most influential members of their respective groups. This is inferred from the special construction of the burial areas, and from the fact that they contained very few actual interments considering their area and the overall size of the site they belonged to.

All of the cemeteries were subdivided into several square plots, each 8–9 m across and outlined by a ditch perhaps 2 m wide and 1 m deep. Within these plots were found one, two, or more interments, in wooden coffins buried in simple rectangular pits. There were few or no burial offerings in the graves themselves but a number of pottery vessels were taken from the ditches surrounding the burial plots. The coffins were well made, of four long planks for top, bottom, and sides, and had carefully shaped end pieces fitted into grooves in the bottom and side boards. A few jar burials found scattered about the site are presumed to represent the type of interment accorded to common villagers, but in fact far too few burials of any kind have been found to account for the population of a whole settlement. It is possible that common folk were for the most part buried beyond the village boundaries in areas not yet investigated.

At the Higashi Nara site in the nearby city of Ibaraki, a burial plot similar to those at Ama has been found, apparently associated with Early Yayoi period remains. A detailed report is not yet available, but the find seems to suggest that special burial arrangements for persons of status go back to the very beginning of Yayoi occupation in the region. Further excavations at the Ama site will no doubt help elucidate this matter.

Within 2 km of the Ama site are at least a dozen more settlements, all of the Middle and Late Yayoi periods (Haraguchi 1977). Most

Tenjinyama

occupy the edges of the hills immediately north and west of Ama, overlooking good agricultural lands but themselves situated high and dry, above any danger of flooding. Their position, proximity, and later dates of origin as compared to the Ama site make it seem likely that they are daughter villages that hived off from the main settlement as time passed. One important stimulus affecting these daughter communities' choice of location was no doubt the episode of flooding that covered the Early Yayoi occupation level at Ama. Some of the people driven from the Ama site by high water at that time probably stayed on in the newer locations, but others returned, for the mother village was rebuilt during the Middle Yayoi period and grew larger than before. It probably continued to contribute to the growth of surrounding communities throughout the remainder of the Yayoi period; several new settlements appeared in the vicinity even in Late Yayoi times.

Tenjinyama, on a point extending out from the hills about 1 km west of Ama, is perhaps the earliest and nearest of these apparent daughter villages, formed early in the Middle Yayoi period (Takatsuki-shi Shi Hensan Iinkai 1973). The site, damaged by modern activities of various kinds, was not fully excavated. Field observations nevertheless indicate that it was of fair size, occupying a U-shaped area about 500 m across, with cultural remains concentrated on three adjacent points of land.

Excavations conducted at one locality uncovered a great many artifacts of the same types as those found at Ama and traces of seven shallow, semisubterranean house floors that overlapped, in a way indicative of repeated rebuilding. Structures either circular, ovate, or square with rounded corners were outlined by deep, narrow trenches, in which the bases of the house walls were presumably footed. Centrally located fire pits and a number of probable storage caches and pits for roof-support posts were dug into the floors, but because of the overlapping of structures the layout of the floor features in any given house is not clear. One structure well enough defined to measure was roundish, about 4.5 m in diameter. A rectilinear building, partially damaged by a road cut but still clearly much larger than any of the others, was about 6.5 m long. It may have been a communal structure of some sort; the smaller units were presumably dwellings.

Tenjinyama and its neighboring ridgetop settlements exemplify a type of upland village that became common all around the shores of the Inland Sea during Middle and Late Yayoi times. Some of these, such as Tenjinyama and its neighboring site of Benitakeyama, were large, several hundred meters across. Others, such as nearby Nariai or Haginoshiyo, were much smaller, perhaps hamlets of only a few houses. What significance is to be attached to this widespread flores-

Figure 4.23 Hilltop residential sites, some with moats and palisades, became increasingly common in Middle and Late Yayoi times. Shown is the Middle Yayoi Otsuka site, Kanagawa Prefecture, central Honshu. (Courtesy J. Okamoto.)

cence of upland sites, whether it reflects mainly a simple practical avoidance of flood-prone terrain as seems to have been the case around Ama, or whether it had to do with a growing need for defense from marauders, is a question of great interest. The case of the recently excavated Otsuka site in Yokohama, on a hilltop ringed by a fortification ditch and earthwork, shows rather clearly that defensibility was a very important consideration, at least in some places, by Middle Yayoi times (Figure 4.23).

Other finds made at Tenjinyama bear on an additional issue of general interest for Yayoi cultures. In the early nineteenth century, a bronze ceremonial bell, or *dotaku,* was discovered near the site. In the early 1950s, another was found on a hilltop west of a nearby modern Shinto shrine. In neither case are the precise circumstances and location of the finds known, but it seems evident that both *dotaku* had been deliberately buried in isolated spots; it is possible that they were cached near one another, though that must remain only speculation.

These *dotaku* are typical specimens of their kind. They are made in the shape of a truncated cone, with an exterior flange extending lengthwise along both sides and across the top of the body. This flange is perforated at the top, and wear marks seen there on many specimens show that *dotaku* were customarily suspended in bell-like fashion from a cord passed through this opening. Holes in the top of the body from which a tongue or clapper could be suspended are characteristic, and occasional specimens have been found with the actual tongues still associated. From such evidence it seems clear that *dotaku* were in general used in bell-like fashion, though the manner of their construction, with perforations in their sides due to the casting technique used, would have precluded their producing a clear, bell-like tone. The "voice" of the *dotaku* was no doubt a metallic rattling sound, akin to that produced by the thin metal bells attached to a long rope over offering boxes in modern Japanese shrines and temples, to be shaken when a contribution is made.

The first specimen discovered at Tenjinyama, in the early 1880s, is 109 cm tall, making it one of the largest *dotaku* known. The second is about 59 cm tall, near the middle of the known size range. Both are of the same type, with rectilinear panels on their sides outlined by low-relief castings, and circular fillips attached at intervals along the flanged edges of the body. The details of these features indicate that both specimens were made near the end of Late Yayoi times.

Over 350 *dotaku* have been found so far in southwestern Japan, and new discoveries are still being made (Figures 4.24–4.27). They have been found almost exclusively in remote places, buried on hills or cached under ledges, away from human habitations. They are found

Figure 4.24 Copper bells, or *dotaku,* of the Yayoi period from south-central Honshu. Left, from Kono-cho, city of Kishiwada, Osaka Prefecture; center, from Nara Prefecture, precise location unknown; right, from Shinamachi, city of Kusatsu, Shiga Prefecture. Height of specimen at left, 43.4 cm. (Shown approximately one-quarter actual size.) (Kyoto University Museum.)

Figure 4.25 Copper bell, or *dotaku,* of Late Yayoi type from Mikawauchi, Nodagawa-cho, Kyoto Prefecture, south-central Honshu. Height, ca. 110 cm. Replica of original. (Kyoto University Museum.)

Figure 4.26 Details of designs on copper bells or *dotaku* of the Yayoi period. (T. Higuchi photo.)

Figure 4.27 Yayoi period copper bells (*dotaku*) and bronze blades from various sites. (T. Higuchi photo.)

sometimes singly, sometimes in groups of many specimens. Their distribution is centered along the eastern edges of the Inland Sea, and many have been found within the Kyoto–Osaka region. The Tenjinyama *dotaku* seem in every way typical of the usual circumstances of occurrence, even in the point that they were finally left hidden away, and thus passed out of use and knowledge. Although it has been argued that *dotaku* remained in use during the Kofun period, informed opinion is virtually unanimous that their casting and use ceased with the end of Yayoi times. It has been suggested that these events were related, and tied in turn to major social developments occurring at the same time—an intriguing idea, which will be taken up in its own right in the concluding chapter of this book.

Uriyudo   The Uriyudo site, in the eastern quarter of present-day Osaka, is one of many settlements in that vicinity occupied from Early Yayoi times onward (Uriyudo Chosa Kai 1971, 1973). It is a low-lying area, the ancient plain of Kawachi, where the old Yamato River broke up into five major streams as it approached its eventual outlet at Osaka Bay. Geological evidence shows that this was a flood-prone region, with the local landscape undergoing continual change. No doubt it is because of periodic major flooding that occupation of the Uriyudo site, though it spans many centuries, was not continuous.

The site's contents are known from archaeological excavations performed in conjunction with the building of modern canals across the area. A long-term excavation project is being carried out within the canal rights-of-way, long narrow swaths about 5 m wide that cut the site at many angles. From these excavations it is known that the Yayoi occupation covered a zone about 1 km in length and .5 km in width.

Early Yayoi remains at the site were found buried under alluvial sands and clays. After a period of abandonment the spot was reoccupied, and a large village flourished there during the Middle Yayoi period. Discontinuous deposits of alluvial clays laid down during this time show that occasional minor flooding occurred throughout the Middle Yayoi occupation, which was brought to an end by a series of floods that left over 2 m of interbedded sands and gravels over the site area. These events initiated a period of human abandonment lasting until Early Kofun times, and after a brief occupation the area was once again flooded and abandoned, to be reoccupied during the historic Nara period. With the canalization and drainage works of later times the land became continuously habitable, and it is now becoming ever more thickly covered by metropolitan Osaka.

The same environmental conditions that led to the Early Yayoi farmers' being periodically driven from Uriyudo were also responsible for its continuing attractiveness to them. Abundant flowing water, and the rich alluvial soils it carried in, provided ideal conditions for rice cultivation. The slightly raised natural levees along the streams provided dry land for human occupation. Uriyudo is in fact only one of several hundred sites of Yayoi and later times known to exist on and around the plain of Kawachi, and it is evident that by the Middle Yayoi period the plain was a major center of population. The agricultural wealth of the region must have been great, and ever-expanding.

Clusters of pits, large and small, were excavated at several different localities. Some of the pits were elongate; others were round and undercut, with a bell-shaped cross section; yet others were quite small and had vertical sides. In some of the last were found the stumps of wooden posts. The various kinds of pits may represent storage cells and remnants of the roof-support pillars of dwellings, but only in rare cases could actual house patterns be picked out of the confusion of archaeological features. It seems that structures were built and rebuilt on the same spots until the archaeological record of the activity became so complicated as to defy precise interpretation.

Domestic artifacts recovered included disk-shaped spindle whorls of both pottery and stone, many large ceramic jars and pots, and carved wooden serving bowls. Wooden artifacts were well preserved in the waterlogged deposits of the site, and many were recovered. Large, double-ended wooden pestles more than 1 m in length, closely resembling those used in historic times for pounding glutinous rice in a wooden mortar, were also household artifacts.

Agricultural tools were represented by two-piece wooden hoes having handles socketed at acute angles through wooden blades, by the remains of wooden paddy field clogs, and by a remarkably well preserved shovel. The shovel was 1.3 m in length, with a long narrow blade and flaring-ended handle; the whole was carved from a single piece of wood. Stone reaping knives, or *ishibocho,* were also common finds.

Specimens of stone were relatively few, but varied. Ground stone artifacts included the just-mentioned *ishibocho* and several ground stone celts. Flaked stone artifacts included stemmed and leaf-shaped arrowpoints, a number of sidescrapers or simple knives, and several drills and gravers. Although metal items were not found in the Uriyudo excavations it is clear from evidence elsewhere that iron was in use for the making of edged tools from Early Yayoi times onward. The paucity of stone tools at the site may well have been due to common use of iron tools, which have rusted entirely away.

Remains of actual cultigens recovered from the excavations included charred grains believed to be rice and wheat, fragments of melon rinds, and peach or plum pits. Analysis of pollen from a series of sediments at the site confirmed the presence of rice and wheat. Walnuts, acorns, and other specimens attest the gathering of foods from the nearby forest.

Pollen stratigraphy showed that the site area was originally a forest of broad-leaved trees, but became a grassy, weedy clearing during Middle Yayoi times. This no doubt reflects the needs of Uriyudo's occupants for building-timber and firewood, for with the ends of the several human occupation cycles, the pollen record typically indicates regrowth of the forest. Changes in the composition of the pollen record over time also suggest a slight warming of the local climate after the Middle Yayoi period. However, it is difficult to separate the effects of human and climatic impacts on the local vegetation with any assurance.

Of special interest from a societal point of view are the burials discovered at Uriyudo. Early in the excavation project, one of the main trenches cut through an area about 100 m long in which were found a cluster of 5 burial mounds and more than 20 individual jar burials in simple pits. The mounds lay east of the pit burials, separated from the nearest of them by about 10 m. The entire cemetery was of the Middle Yayoi period, and there is no doubt that the differences between the graves represent differences in the social status of their occupants rather than a change in burial customs over time.

The individual pit graves each consisted of a large ceramic jar or pot, capped with another, smaller vessel. These pit burials often occurred in little clumps of three or four, separated from other, similar clumps by a short distance. No funerary offerings were discovered, and there was no significant differentiation among the burials. From the number of interments exposed within the narrow confines of the archaeologists' trench, it appears that a village cemetery of hundreds of graves might be represented.

The burial mounds adjacent to the common graveyard were at first only partially exposed, the limits of archaeological exploration being strictly defined by steel caissons driven into the ground along the boundaries of the excavation right-of-way across the site. The northern edges of three mounds and the southern edges of two others were exposed, from which it could be observed that all five were oriented to the cardinal directions and were square or rectangular. The largest measured 12 m across, the smallest 8 m, and all were 1 m or so high. Around their bases were rather poorly defined shallow ditches 1 m or so in width, which probably had contributed some at least of the earthen fill of the mounds. In their rectilinear outlines and boundary ditches, these earthworks are rather similar to those known from the Ama site, but the examples from Uriyudo are significantly greater in actual mound volume.

On a later occasion, Mound 2 of this group was completely uncovered, to reveal that 6 extended burials in wooden coffins, and 1 bundle burial in a large pottery jar, lay in an orderly arrangement about the center of the mound. Around the periphery of this group were 6 more jar burials. It is evident from the placement of the 13 burials, and the intrusion of some upon others, that all were not made at the same time. Stratigraphic evidence indicates, however, that some probably were. It is conjectured that such mounds may have been the sepulchers of preeminent family groups, used over a considerable period of time.

There was a general lack of burial offerings within the graves themselves, but around the mounds were found various pottery jars, including pedestaled offering vessels. These came mostly from the surrounding ditches, where they may eventually have come to rest after being placed on the tops or around the edges of the burial mounds. It has been pointed out that this practice seems to presage a ceremonial observance common in the following Kofun period, of placing large, specially made ceramic *haniwa* figures around the tops of burial tumuli as offerings and guardians. *Haniwa* are discussed in detail in Chapter 5.

Investigations continue at the time of writing. Over 20 burial mounds and many more pit burials have been found, from more than one locality, but detailed reports are not yet available. It remains to be seen how these mounds with their multiple burials of two strikingly different types may be plausibly interpreted when all the data are analyzed, and what significance may be attributed to the resemblance between the jar burials of the mounds and those of the adjacent cemetery of individual pit graves. At a minimum, the existence of social class differentiation at Uriyudo must be affirmed, and the practice of some form of immolation burial seems a good possibility.

Repeated flooding terminated the Middle Yayoi period occupation of ancient Uriyudo and left over 2 m of laminated sand and gravel covering it. This flooding was not a purely local phenomenon, for deeply buried Middle Yayoi sites have also come to light beneath the flood deposits of other rivers east of Osaka Bay, and elsewhere in the country as well.

In time, this major episode of flooding in the Osaka region corresponds to the worldwide Flandrian stage of slightly raised sea level, and pollen studies from Uriyudo, as previously mentioned, suggest that this was also a period of slightly higher local temperatures. One widespread result of a rise in sea level would be the raising of the base level of rivers flowing into the sea. This in turn would naturally increase the frequency of flooding across such low-lying plains as those east of Osaka Bay, until the sluggish rivers gradually built up their natural levees sufficiently to contain the waters once again. This would take place even if there was no increase in precipitation, but it is also possible that the higher local temperatures, by causing increased evaporation from the nearby sea, may have brought about increased precipitation over the land.

Obviously not all the settlements along these rivers would have been equally vulnerable to flooding, due to local topographical variations. But inevitably some amount of localized flooding out and resettling of refugees must have gone on from earliest times, given the nature of the lands settled by the Yayoi farmers. As time went on, with settlements becoming larger and the land more densely settled, the problems of the dispossessed would have become increasingly severe. If, at such a stage in the history of a region, there came a marked increase in the frequency and severity of flooding, matters might quickly become critical. The displacement of even a few settlements the size of Uriyudo, forcing their hundreds of occupants to find new lands, or to try to join other collectivities, might well have occasioned important sociopolitical adjustments within the region as a whole. It has been suggested that such factors may have offered important new opportunities for expansion of the managerial powers of the social elites attested at Uriyudo and elsewhere. Certainly by the beginning of the following Kofun period, a strong and prosperous managerial class had arisen in the Kawachi region.

Toro   The Middle to Late Yayoi Toro site, located within the boundaries of the city of Shizuoka about 150 km southwest of Tokyo, was discovered in 1943 during the construction of a light-metals plant. Wartime conditions limited its archaeological study then, but the site's enormous wealth and significance for Japanese cultural history was recognized by a number of prominent scholars, who returned to examine it more fully in 1947. In 1948, the Japan Archaeologists' Association was formed, with the study of Toro as one of its first objectives. The research at Toro was multidisciplinary, with specialists in archaeology, geology, geography, zoology, botany, the history of agriculture, and architecture all cooperating in the investigation. Two large monographs embody their detailed results (Nihon Kokogaku Kyokai Kenkyukai 1949, 1954), and are the source of the information summarized here.

Toro is in the delta region of the Abe River, which flows from mountainous central Japan into the Pacific Ocean. The site is on the natural levee of an old channel, and overlooks low, swampy land to the southeast. The cultural remains lay about 1 m beneath the surface of modern rice paddy fields. A stratum of fine blue sand incorporating extensive lenses of gravel covered a humus zone, which contained the archaeological features of the site. It is believed that a flood, represented by the sand-and-gravel stratum, abruptly terminated the life of the settlement in full career. It seems unlikely that the many artifacts

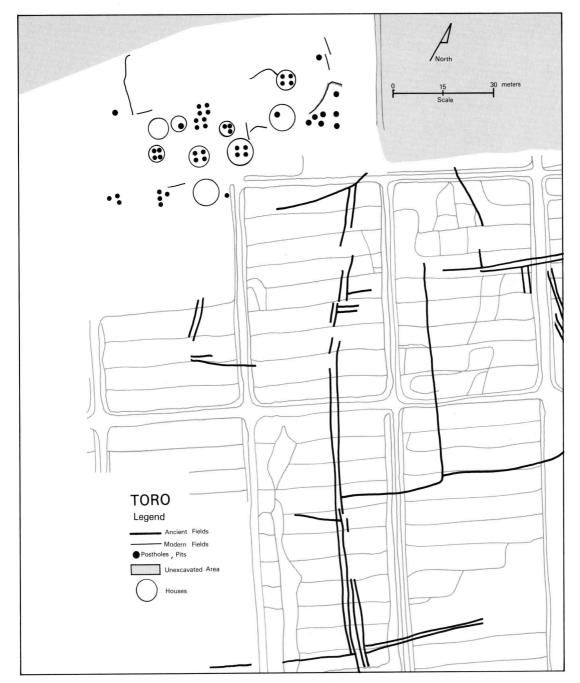

Figure 4.28 Map of the main portion of the Middle Yayoi Toro site, Shizuoka Prefecture, central Honshu, showing the village remains and associated paddy fields. Yayoi period plots lay buried beneath modern rice fields. (Redrawn from Nihon Kokogaku Kyokai Kenkyukai 1954:Map 2.)

Figure 4.29 Reconstructed Middle Yayoi dwelling from the Toro site, Shizuoka Prefecture, central Honshu. (C. M. Aikens photo.)

Figure 4.30 Reconstructed Middle Yayoi granary from the Toro site, Shizuoka Prefecture, central Honshu. (C. M. Aikens photo.)

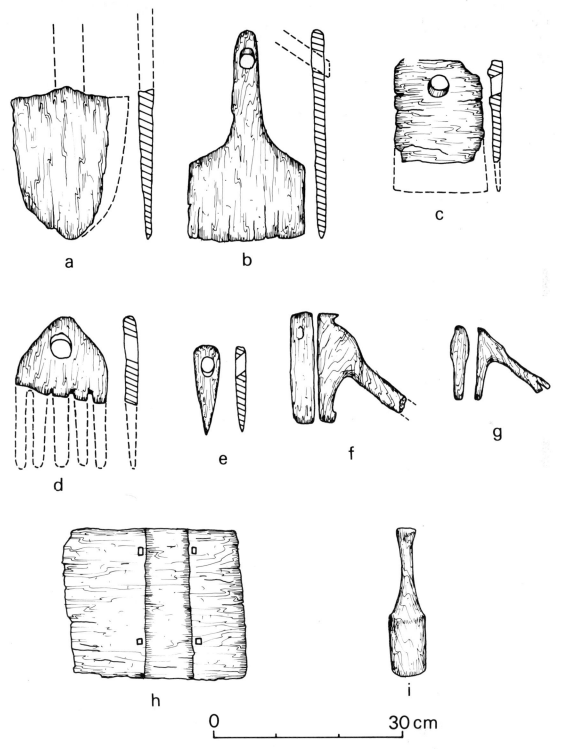

Figure 4.31 Wooden tools of the Middle Yayoi from the Toro site, Shizuoka Prefecture, central Honshu: (a) spade; (b, c), hoes; (d), toothed hoe or rake; (e), pick; (f, g), adze handles; (h), part of a paddy field clog; (i), pounder or pestle. (Selected specimens redrawn from Nihon Kokogaku Kyokai Kenkyukai 1954:Figures 34, 35, 36.)

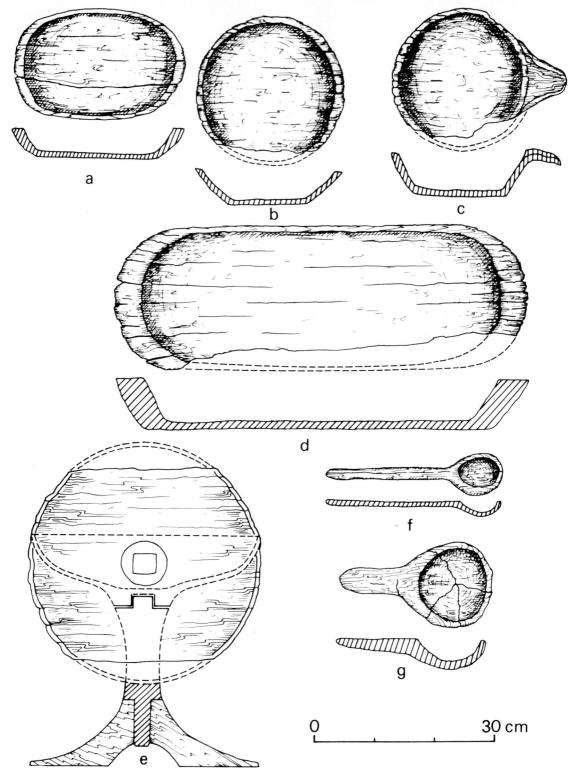

Figure 4.32 Wooden eating utensils of the Middle Yayoi from the Toro site, Shizuoka Prefecture, central Honshu: (a, b) bowls; (c) bowl with pouring lip; (d) trencher; (e) composite pedestaled bowl; (f, g) serving spoons. (Selected specimens redrawn from Nihon Kokogaku Kyokai Kenkyukai 1954:Figures 30–33.)

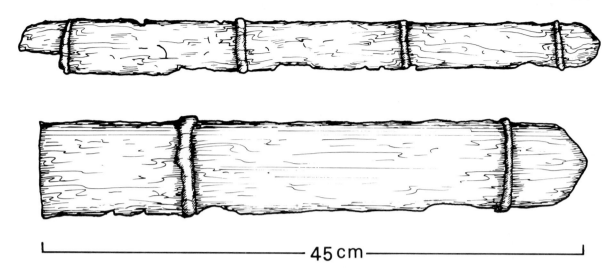

45 cm

Figure 4.33   Wooden sword and scabbard of the Middle Yayoi from the Toro site, Shizuoka Prefecture, central Honshu. (Redrawn from Nihon Kokogaku Kyokai Kenkyukai 1954:Plate 70.)

recovered in still functional condition had simply fallen gradually into disuse.

The ancient village of Toro was occupied from the end of the Middle Yayoi through the beginning of the Late Yayoi period. Twelve dwellings, two storage buildings, and a series of rice paddies were excavated, along with animal and vegetal food remains and thousands of artifacts of pottery, wood, and textiles. Though a large area 60 × 120 m was systematically trenched, and longer exploratory trenches extended out from this center, the boundaries of the site were not fully defined, and the total size of the old village is unknown. In any event, its richness in normally perishable cultural remains, owing to its rapid burial and the waterlogged condition of its deposits thereafter, make Toro a remarkably complete and exciting document of early domestic farm life in Japan (Figures 4.28–4.36).

The settlement was built on slightly elevated ground, overlooking its paddy fields immediately to the south. Nine of the dwellings, and both storage structures, formed a compact cluster from which the other three dwellings were separated by 25–50 m (Figure 4.28).

The houses were all markedly similar in form, size, and method of construction, so that one description, with very little qualification, can serve for all (Figure 4.29). The structures were oval to somewhat squarish in plan, built on the existing ground surface. Their floors measured between 6 and 7.5 m across, most falling in the middle of the range. Sturdy roof supports are indicated by deep postholes, usu-

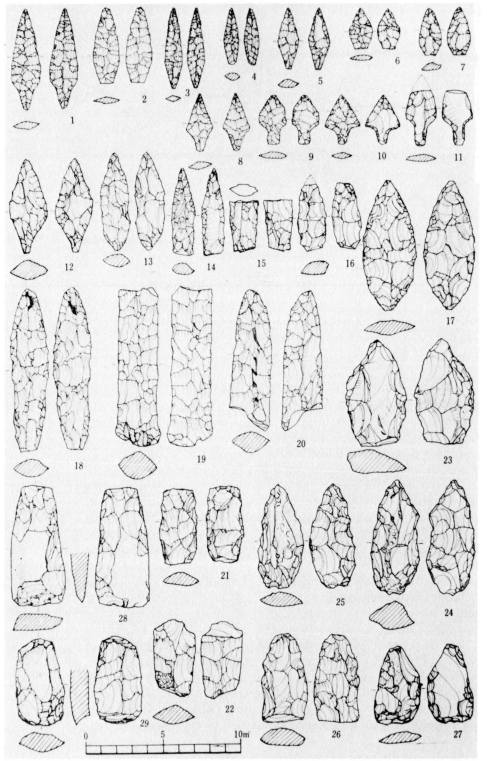

Figure 4.34 Flaked stone tools typical of the Middle Yayoi from the Uriyudo site, Osaka Prefecture, south-central Honshu. (From Uriyudo Iseki Chosa Kai 1973:Figure 68.)

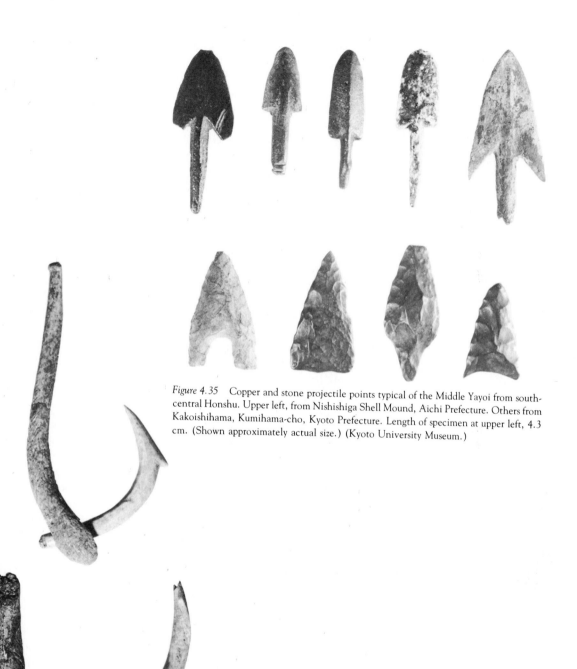

Figure 4.35 Copper and stone projectile points typical of the Middle Yayoi from south-central Honshu. Upper left, from Nishishiga Shell Mound, Aichi Prefecture. Others from Kakoishihama, Kumihama-cho, Kyoto Prefecture. Length of specimen at upper left, 4.3 cm. (Shown approximately actual size.) (Kyoto University Museum.)

Figure 4.36 Composite bone fishhooks typical of the Yayoi period from Makomodani Shell Mound, Okayama Prefecture, Southern Honshu. Length of upper specimen, 8 cm. (Shown approximately actual size.) (Kyoto University Museum.)

233

ally placed equidistant from one another in a four-square pattern centered on a clay-lined fire pit in the middle of the floor.

Encircling the living floor was a raised bench 30 cm high and 1 m or more wide, the inner and outer edges of which were retained by flat, adze-cut panel boards and stakes driven vertically into the ground. It appears that the lower walls of the house superstructure came to the ground around the outer edge of this earthen bench, allowing the bench to serve as a dike against seepage of water into the house interior, and as an interior shelf for domestic equipment. The typical house superstructure is believed to have been made of poles and thatch, though one house, in which many adze-cut boards up to 3 m in length were found, apparently had walls of vertically set planks. A flat, adze-cut board found at the southern edge of the floor in two of the houses may have served as an entrance step; its position suggested that doorways faced south toward the cultivated fields.

Two storage buildings occurred close together, in the midst of the main cluster of dwellings (Figure 4.30). The evidence for them consisted of two sets of sturdy wooden pillars, the buried portions of which were preserved upright in their original postholes. One structure was attested by adze-squared posts set in a square pattern 2 m across. The other, of the same size and shape, was outlined by one unshaped pole at each corner, with a fifth at the center. A ladder made of slender logs, and a perforated flat board made to fit around one of the supporting pillars as a guard to prevent rats from climbing it, indicate that these were raised, high-floored structures. A mass of rice straw found near one of them may have been part of its contents or may have been a remnant of its thatched covering.

The paddy fields were constructed on slightly lower ground immediately adjacent to the settlement, and were marked by a series of narrow embankments laid out in a rough rectilinear pattern (Figure 4.28). A series of plots occupied an area about 200 × 300 m across, and continued an unknown distance beyond the limits of the excavation. Over 30 individual plots of varying size were indicated, the smallest being about 30 m square and the largest about 30 × 60 m. Artifacts typical of the occupation site, found buried in and near these embankments, clearly establish an organic relationship between the human settlement and the fields.

The earthen embankments that divided the fields were retained by long alignments of thousands upon thousands of wooden stakes driven into the ground along both their sides. These embankments served as dikes for water control, and no doubt as pathways for people working the plots, just as in modern paddy fields. A striking comparison of the ancient and modern field systems is afforded by the site map, which shows both the ancient Yayoi period field boundaries and those of the modern rice paddies under which the Toro site lay. The older fields are smaller and less regular, but of clearly similar pattern.

Man-made watercourses also occur at the site, as indicated by long, parallel alignments of stakes that do not seem to mark paddy boundaries, but appear rather to be ditch-bank retaining walls. It is not clear, however, whether these ditches may have been primarily for irrigation, as suggested by the sites' excavators, or for drainage, as suggested by the naturally low-lying, swampy condition of the area in general. They do not form a complete, interconnected system that is easily interpretable, but one major channel running the length of the excavated area had a feature suggestive of a sluice gate midway along its length, suggesting that it, at least, was an irrigation ditch.

Subsistence was based primarily on cultivated wet-land rice, but dry-land farming, hunting, and gathering are also attested. In addition to the evidence of the paddy fields themselves, many rice grains were recovered, and bundles of rice straw were commonly observed in the excavations. Millet seeds indicate that dry farming was practiced on higher, drier land, and the seeds and rinds of gourds and melons suggest the cultivation of household gardens, perhaps on the natural levee near the dwellings. Peach stones from the excavations may indicate either the gathering of wild fruits or the cultivation of orchards; the evidence does not establish which.

Skeletal remains from the site indicate that a variety of mammals, fish, and shellfish complemented the vegetable diet. The cow was clearly a domestic species. Deer and boar could have been taken in the mountains only a few kilometers away; raccoon, which may not have been a food species, would have been native to the immediate local habitat. Fish were available both in the nearby Abe River and in the sea several kilometers away, and 12 species of freshwater and marine forms show that both sources were exploited. The same is true of mollusks. The shells of 11 species, mostly but not entirely marine forms, were identified from the excavated collections. A number of insects were also found, but these were probably pests rather than dietary items.

Agricultural tools were of several kinds, their functions readily identifiable by reference to the traditional farming equipment of historic times (Figure 4.31). A small dugout canoe, of which only one end was preserved, was probably used in the paddy fields for carrying material and equipment used in cultivation, as is still the practice today. The vessel was approximately 50 cm in width and an estimated 3–4 m in length. Many large wooden clogs, virtually identical to those worn today by people working the muddy fields, were found both in the dwelling areas and in the paddies themselves.

Two-piece wooden hoes, with the blade fitted at an oblique angle to the handle, were recovered in some numbers. Wooden hoes with forked ends, some with tines so long that they might better be called rakes, were also in common use. A few large, sharpened flat wooden blades are interpreted as ploughs, and a number of pointed wooden stakes with hafting holes like those of the hoes at one end are thought to be the heads of picks. Fragments of wooden spades were also recovered.

Several wooden bows, bone fishhooks, and grooved-stone net-sinkers represent the fishing and hunting component of the village economy. These artifacts seem relatively few in comparison to the abundance of other tool types at the site. Considering the existence of considerable skeletal evidence for fishing and hunting, it may be speculated that such foods were gained mainly by exchange with other settlements, and that the people of Toro did not engage themselves very actively in these pursuits.

The domestic utensils, like the farming implements, are of remarkably familiar forms, despite their age of nearly two millennia (Figure 4.32). Bamboo trays and baskets, probably used in harvesting and food preparation, were represented by a number of partially complete specimens and fragments. Simple over-and-under weaves, generally like those seen in bamboo trays made today, were most common. Coarsely woven mats, probably household furniture, were also found. Grinding tools included small flat milling stones and long wooden pestles or pounders; the latter were fairly common. Actual mortars were not recovered, but it seems likely that large, cylindrical blocks of wood with concave upper surfaces functioned as mortar bases.

Fire was produced by the fire-drill method, as shown by the recovery of small boards having a number of charred cylindrical pits worn into their upper surfaces. Cooking ware consisted of pottery jars and bowls, many fire-blackened fragments of which were recovered. Water and storage jars are no doubt also represented among the abundant ceramic remains. Large wooden ladles and wooden spatulas probably functioned then, as now, in the preparation of boiled dishes and the serving of steamed rice.

Dining ware and utensils, all of wood, were well represented in the Toro collections. Small, simple three-piece benches about 30 cm high may have functioned as individual serving tables. Some had dished-out upper surfaces, clearly suggesting their use as eating utensils. Large, pedestaled bowls of skillfully joined, three-part composite construction (bowl, pedestal shaft, and base) seem to have served a similar function, and nicely carved spoons, bowls, and large trenchers in a variety of shapes and sizes completed the table service.

Household chores apparently included spinning and weaving.

Quite a few fragments of coarse woven cloth were found, as were several perforated stone disks, no doubt spindle whorls. Some long wooden shafts, carved like elongated spools with thickened ends, are thought to have been bolts for rolling up the products of the loom. Other manufactures included of course the agricultural, hunting, and household items previously mentioned. Probably all were made locally, though this surmise is not certainly established by the available evidence.

The woodworking industry especially is noteworthy, both for its unusually full preservation, and for the technical mastery and versatility in application of a few simple techniques that it displays. A few polished stone axe or adze blades were found, but it seems clear that most of the wood products were shaped with metal adzes now decomposed. A fragment of badly oxidized iron was found, but the best evidence comes from the shallow, regular marks made with sharp tools on thousands of pieces of wood at the site. Experiments with a modern metal-bladed adze of traditional form produced similar cutting marks, and of course there is evidence from other sources that such metal tools were in use during the Yayoi period.

Many objects, such as bowls, trenchers, and spoons, were simply carved from a single block of wood, but well-executed mortise-and-tenon joinery was also employed in the making of benches, clogs, pedestaled bowls, and other artifacts. Both square-cut holes, apparently made with chisels, and round holes, obviously drilled, are evident in the products of the woodworking industry. Some of the wooden pounders, or mallets, found in the excavations may have been used to drive chisels, though this is only speculation. An industry in products of tree bark is also attested at Toro by many fragments of cut or laced bark, but because identifiable products are nil, little can be said of the craft other than to note its existence.

Artifacts that functioned as ornaments and/or indicators of social status are few. Corroded bronze rings recovered from the excavations, rare and hence valuable, must have been the property of persons wealthier than most. The same might be said of a few glass beads of deep cobalt blue. These objects were clearly not products of the village, and offer concrete evidence of wider networks to which the local society belonged. A number of nicely made wooden swords and daggers, some with wooden scabbards, seem to symbolize a certain authority, ritual and perhaps secular as well, that was presumably invested in their bearers (Figure 4.33). They were at any rate certainly not functional fighting weapons. Two curved *magatama* beads of serpentine, perforated for suspension at one end, may have had a similar meaning.

Kasajima

At a number of places along the Inland Sea, and to a lesser extent on the Pacific coast, Yayoi settlements are coming to light in shoreline settings that bespeak a primary concern with the resources of the sea rather than those of the land. No doubt the earlier littoral traditions of Jomon times were never wholly lost, but little attention has been accorded to the Yayoi period evidence for maritime exploitation. The site of Kasajima, at the very tip of the Kii Peninsula 170 km south of Kyoto, is illustrative of a considerable number of sites that indicate the importance of a marine orientation during Yayoi times (Yasui 1969).

The archaeological remains were found on the landward edge of a small island about 1 km off the tip of the peninsula. A low sandbar connecting the island to the peninsula has probably existed in some form, perhaps intermittently, since the Yayoi occupation or before, but its history is not known in detail. Many artifacts were found on what must have been an old shoreline, but no houses were discovered. If houses had been built at that elevation, high water during storms might well have destroyed them, but in any case residential quarters would presumably have been situated on the higher ground behind the site.

The artifacts give indications of maritime pursuits, but the strongest evidence of the site's function is simply its location, on a point of land washed by the tropical and biotically rich Japanese Current that sweeps the eastern coasts of Japan. The area has been famed throughout historical times for its excellent harbor and rich bays, and has long been a productive fishing center.

In this connection, perhaps the most interesting of the archaeological finds at Kasajima were the remains of a small boat. The most informative of the fragmentary specimens was a thick adze-cut board, pointed at one end and bowed in the middle, which had been the bottom of a built-up plank boat. The fragment recovered was slightly over 4 m long. A notched rib piece, part of the interior bracing of the hull, and the flared ends of two paddles were also recovered. High-prowed, gondola-like vessels are known to have existed in Yayoi times—such a craft was illustrated on the side of a bronze *dotaku* from Kyushu—but the Kasajima specimens were the first to be recovered archaeologically.

Elongate clay cylinders perforated at both ends, and long sticks drilled through at one or both ends, are believed to represent a set of floats and sinkers for use with a gill net. Clay sinkers of this same type are known from several sites of the Late Yayoi and Kofun periods, which occur along the shores of the Inland Sea. A number of sharply pointed slender wooden shafts are thought to have been fish-spears or arrows, though their lack of barbs would make them less than ideal for such a use. Fragments of hunting bows were also found, and it is speculated that they were used in fishing as well as in the hunting of land animals. Bones of bream, bonito, shark, rayfish, and sea turtle, and the shells of several kinds of marine mollusks represent the catch of the Kasajima fisherfolk. The bones and teeth of boar and deer show that land hunting was practiced as well.

A related industry, logically complementary to the fishing economy, was saltmaking. A few footed ceramic vessels were found, of a type known to have been used elsewhere along the Inland Sea in the production of salt through evaporation of seawater. A number of large, thick, widemouthed pots of a very coarse ceramic fabric probably served the same function.

The occupation at Kasajima is believed to date to terminal Yayoi times. This is based, of course, on the ceramic specimens, most of which belong to Late Yayoi types. A few vessels seem to be transitional to the Haji ware of the Kofun period, and they are the basis on which the occupation is assigned to the very end of the Yayoi period. That the island had been earlier occupied is indicated by Middle Yayoi pottery collected from the surface at a nearby locality, but the nature of this earlier occupation was not established.

The initial spread of the new lifeway in Early Yayoi times was limited to the semitropical warm-temperature regions of Kyushu, Shikoku, and southwestern Honshu, about as far north as the modern city of Nagoya. While Early Yayoi culture was spreading throughout southwestern Japan, Final Jomon culture persisted in the Tokyo region and lands farther north. It was not until Middle Yayoi times that the new cultural elements appeared in central and northern Honshu, and Yayoi culture did not spread into Hokkaido at all.

Middle and Late Yayoi ceramics from Tokyo north have a distinctively Jomon-like character. Vessel forms are predominantly like those known from the Yayoi to the south, but decoration is mainly in the northern Jomon tradition of cord-rouletting and zoned cord-marking (Figures 4.7–4.11). Strong continuities with preceding local Jomon ceramic types are evident in a number of cases, and regional differentiation in Middle Yayoi ceramics generally followed lines established in the Final Jomon period.

In the earlier days of Yayoi research in northern Japan, many believed that the new ceramics and other elements appearing there represented a simple diffusion of a few material culture traits among Jomon people who for long continued the older hunting–gathering way of life. Considerable evidence now shows, however, that the

The Tokyo Region and Northern Honshu

rice-cultivating economy and its characteristic tool kit were also a part of this cultural spread. At the site of Inakadate, in Aomori Prefecture near the very tip of northern Honshu, over 200 charred rice grains were found in association with pottery of later Middle Yayoi type. Furthermore, pottery from this site and a number of others in northern Honshu exhibits rice-grain impressions, and distinctive *ishibocho* reaping knives and stone hoes are even more widely attested (Ito 1966).

Fishing and hunting of course continued to be important. A series of sea caves on the Miura Peninsula at the mouth of Tokyo Bay, occupied during Late Yayoi times, contained shellfish remains, bone fishhooks, and harpoons. The same sites were evidently manufacturing stations as well, since both complete and partly finished shell bracelets and *ishibocho* reaping knives were found there. Salt may also have been extracted from seawater by an evaporative technique, an inference suggested by the occurrence of an unusual number of large ceramic kettles and thick beds of highly oxidized white ash. Around Matsushima Bay near Sendai also, there was Late Yayoi occupation of sea caves, and open middens in the vicinity give evidence of both shellfish gathering and the hunting of deer and boar (Ito 1966; Kanzawa 1966).

A number of Yayoi villages and cemeteries are known to occur in Tokyo and northern Honshu, but they are far less common than are Yayoi sites in southwestern Japan. Furthermore, only a few sites have as yet yielded much detailed information on settlement layout and architecture. The available evidence nevertheless suggests the existence of both large and small villages of squarish semisubterranean pithouses, situated variously on the edges of elevated tablelands and in low-lying areas near rivers. In the Tokyo region it appears that the earlier farmers established themselves on the more elevated ground, and later sites, occupied as local populations continued to grow, came more and more to be founded in the wet lowlands.

Extensive excavations at the Otsuka site in Yokohama afford the fullest perspective yet available on a Yayoi settlement of the Tokyo region, even though the results of the work have been reported only in summary fashion (Tsude 1979). Excavation of the village, situated on the flat top of a low hill overlooking the Hayabuchi River, has revealed the remains of over 90 structures occupied during later Middle Yayoi times (Figure 4.23). Around the edges of the hilltop, encircling the settlement and enclosing an area about 130 × 200 m wide, was a fortification ditch up to 2 m deep and 2–4 m wide. Some traces suggest that an earthwork formerly encircled the outer edge of the ditch, which would have enhanced its effectiveness as a barrier between the village and any unwelcome outsiders.

House structures were semisubterranean, squarish to circular, with four main roof-support posts placed in the floor and a hearth near one wall. Most were of modest size and were apparently single-family dwellings. From stratigraphic overlapping of house floors and other evidence, archaeologists involved with the site estimate that perhaps 30 of the structures were in use at any one time. Three clusters of dwellings are recognized, and associated with each were one or two especially large structures, and one or two linear sets of postholes probably representing high-floored storage houses, which may have had some sort of public character.

About 100 m southeast of the Otsuka site was found a cemetery belonging to the same period and obviously related to the village. Excavations at this, the Saikachido site, revealed about 25 graves, each of which consisted of a small, low, flat-topped earthen mound flanked by shallow ditches on all four sides, and having at its center a human burial. These low mounds were arranged adjacent to one another in an orderly fashion, and from the fact that there were so few such graves adjacent to such an obviously populous village, it seems clear that this must have been an elite cemetery where only people of high social status were buried. These graves are very similar to the Middle Yayoi burial mounds known from Ama, Uriyudo, and other sites in the Kyoto region, and their appearance at Saikachido establishes the extension of the pattern into the Tokyo region as well.

No Yayoi cultural period as such is recognized in the farthest north. In Hokkaido this general time range is represented by a complex known as Zokujomon, or Epi-Jomon, and pottery of Epi-Jomon type is also known from parts of northernmost Honshu. As its name implies, the Epi-Jomon is believed to represent essentially a continuation of the ancient Jomon way of life, which apparently persisted in the remoteness of the north throughout the time during which Yayoi culture was spreading elsewhere in Japan.

Hokkaido

A very good example of an Epi-Jomon dwelling and its cultural contents is afforded by House 13 from the Sakaeura II site in northeastern Hokkaido. There, on a long sand ridge between the Tokoro River estuary and the Okhotsk Sea, exist traces of about 200 house-pit depressions, which apparently represent several successive archaeological periods. House 13 was originally a Final Jomon structure, which architectural and ceramic evidence suggests was rebuilt and reoccupied during the Epi-Jomon period (Komai 1963; Tokyo Daigaku Kokogaku Kenkyushitsu 1972).

House 13 was visible on the surface as a large depression about .5 m deep. Excavation showed that the first pithouse to be made on the spot was roughly ovate, having flattened ends and measuring about 6.5 × 7.5 m. From one of the long sides of the pit, a passageway about 2 m wide projected outward in a roughly straight line for almost 8 m. Small postholes, which occurred at intervals along the edges of the passageway and continued around the circumference of the house pit, marked the positions of vertical poles that apparently framed the aboveground superstructure of the house. Six much larger postholes, rather irregularly clustered about the center of the floor, held the main roof-support pillars. At the center of the floor, surrounded by the main support postholes, was a large reddened area that marked the location of the structure's hearth.

Overlying this occupation floor, which pottery and other artifacts showed to be of the Final Jomon period, were three additional hard-packed living surfaces. These were laid down after the end of the original occupation, and belonged to the Epi-Jomon period. Each successively later surface was separated from the one beneath it by a few centimeters of fill, and each was smaller than the last, as successive occupations took advantage of the area used previously. Only the uppermost of these later house floors could be traced in its entirety, and it was seen to be in effect a half-sized version of the original structure, aligned on the same axes.

The Epi-Jomon house floor was basically ovate, somewhat flattened at one end and along one side. The structure was 4.5 m long and 4 m wide, and from the flattened side there extended a passageway about 2 m in length and 70 cm in width. Five large postholes aligned along each side of the floor .5 m or so from its edges probably held the main roof-support pillars. A circular area of reddened earth near one end of the floor marked the position of the hearth, and a large, irregular burned area extending from it to the end wall may perhaps have been the result of a fire that got out of control.

On the floor of the house was found a small, flat-bottomed pot, deep and widemouthed with slightly bulging sides. Lugs perforated to take a cord for suspension protruded from opposite sides of the vessel just below the rim. Rows of punctates decorated the rim and upper part of the pot, and the body as a whole was cord-marked. A considerably larger pot, with more markedly excurvate sides and a slightly constricted rim, was found on one of the underlying floor surfaces. It too was cord-marked, and was decorated around the rim with punctates and horizontal cord-impressions. Both were of Epi-Jomon type, as were a number of sherds found in the excavations. Stone tools from the Epi-Jomon floors were few, comprising only several end- and sidescrapers, a graver, a small milling stone, and a pounding stone.

Several small, lanceolate projectile points and one larger diamond-shaped spearpoint with a contracting stem, found during excavation, are also believed to relate to this occupation.

This so-called Epi-Jomon culture is not well defined or understood. Essentially, Epi-Jomon complexes are recognized on the basis of pottery types that combine certain features of Yayoi vessel form with characteristically Jomon decorative techniques. Such complexes are stratigraphically preceded by assemblages containing pottery assigned to the Final Jomon period, and succeeded by assemblages assigned to the Satsumon culture. The Satsumon, which will be discussed more fully in the following chapter, is also characterized by ceramic forms clearly related to the Yayoi tradition, but architecture, evidence of metals, and other considerations indicate that it is largely, if not completely, contemporaneous with the Kofun period, which succeeded the Yayoi farther south. Clearly the northward spread of Yayoi culture was ultimately felt in Hokkaido, but the details and precise chronology of the process remain unclear.

Conclusion

The cultural and economic patterns that came together during the Yayoi period comprised the fundamental basis of traditional Japanese society as we know it today. The advent of Yayoi was in northern Kyushu, where it emerged from the Jomon tradition during its Late and Final periods with the appearance of rice cultivation, a new ceramic style, and other elements. The Late and Final Jomon periods were a time of strong influence from the continent, reflected in the archaeological record by the appearance of new ceramic forms and techniques, notably large kettles, teapots, and footed bowls made of a thin, dark, well-polished ware that is reminiscent of the Chinese Lungshanoid horizon. The earliest accidental rice-grain impressions on clay pots are attributed to the Late Jomon period, and the earliest actual rice grains to be found in Japan belonged to the Final Jomon.

The transition from Jomon to Yayoi, though quite rapid, was not abrupt. The site of Itatsuke, type locality for the new Yayoi culture, is the earliest yet known that yields, as one complex, finds of actual rice grains, the remains of paddy fields and ditches, *ishibocho* reaping knives, disk-shaped clay spindle whorls, and indications of the use of metal tools. All these items, with the possible exception of metal tools, have been sporadically recovered from Late or Final Jomon contexts, but Itatsuke first brings them together into the pattern recognized as definitive of Yayoi culture.

Significantly, and reflective of the same gradual process of Yayoi crystallization just noted, the pottery complex from Itatsuke displays strong continuity with the Jomon ceramic tradition. So much is this the case that only one versed in the nuances of ceramic typology can appreciate the minor differences that distinguish the earliest Yayoi Itatsuke type from the latest Jomon Yusu type, both of which occur in association at the site.

As the Yayoi complex spread, first throughout southwestern Japan and later through central and northern Honshu, minor regional variations appeared in the pottery (Figure 4.37). These are believed to reflect divisions previously existing among Jomon societies that took up the new pattern of life, and it was only after the Yayoi culture became well established that the boundaries of ceramic style zones departed significantly from those drawn in Jomon times.

The Yayoi shift to wet-rice cultivation was of revolutionary significance, supporting rapid population growth and providing an economic base for the development of ever-increasing societal complexity. The density of Yayoi sites in southwestern Japan is many times greater than that known for Jomon sites in the same area, despite the fact that the Yayoi period was so much briefer than the Jomon. Some of this difference must of course be attributed to the destructive effects of time on the Jomon record, but the contrast is surely real, and of major scope.

The patterning of architectural and artifactual remains, ditches, and paddy fields, as well as general attributes of village location at sites such as Itatsuke, Toro, and Ankokuji, show the persistence of a similar pattern of stable village farming life throughout the Yayoi period. The workaday world of the Yayoi villager is illustrated in rare detail at Toro, for example, with its thatched single-family dwellings, above-ground storehouses, banked and ditched paddy fields, and wealth of agricultural tools and domestic utensils.

The record equally shows a progressive growth in the political realm of society. This is reflected in measures taken to enhance the defensibility of villages, in weapons of war, and in rich burials attesting the coalescence of an elite social stratum able to acquire such costly status symbols as bronze blades and mirrors. The hilltop location of the Otsuka site, and its surrounding fortification ditch and earthwork, exemplify a pattern that became increasingly common in Middle and Late Yayoi times. Special burial plots such as those from Ama, Uriyudo, and Saikachido were clearly not for common folk, and the rendering of this grave type into tumulus form at Uriyudo clearly foreshadows the great mounded sepulchers of the succeeding Kofun period's warlords and kings.

An intriguing division of probable sociopolitical and/or religious significance can be seen within southwestern Japan in the more or less mutually exclusive archaeological distributions of bronze blades and

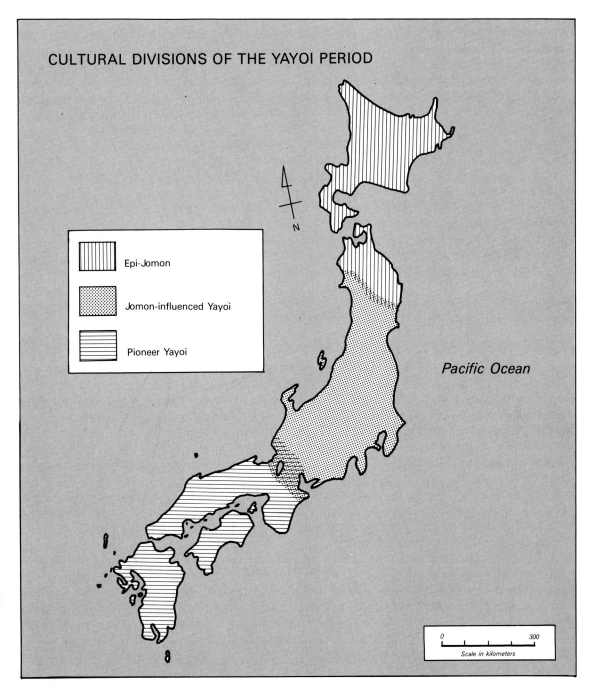

Figure 4.37 Yayoi period regional variation. The boundary zones in central and far northern Honshu coincide closely with present-day climatic–vegetational divisions.

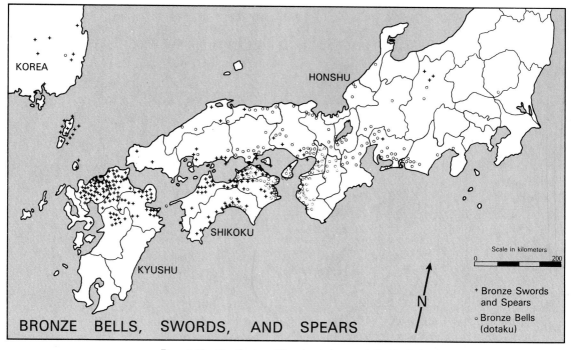

Figure 4.38   Distribution of Yayoi period copper bells (*dotaku*) and copper spearpoints, haberds, and swords. (After T. Higuchi 1974:Figure 277.)

dotaku bells (Figure 4.38). Finds of bronze blades—swords, spears, and halberds—are concentrated in Kyushu, southern Honshu, and Shikoku, and finds of *dotaku* cluster in the Kyoto–Nara–Osaka region and along the northern reaches of the Inland Sea. Both classes of objects were clearly of local manufacture, inasmuch as stone and clay molds for their casting have been found in each of the respective distributional zones. In historic Japanese tradition, swords and spears are symbolic of governmental authority, and bells were important in religious observances. It has been suggested, based on this analogy, that society in the Kyushu–southern Honshu sphere may have been dominated by secular authority, whereas spiritual authority was more important in the northern Inland Sea–Kyoto region. This is an interesting thesis worthy of consideration, but it cannot be elaborated further in the present context.

The ancient Chinese dynastic histories offer a fascinating glimpse of certain aspects of Japanese culture during Late Yayoi times. The people of Japan, or Wa, as it was called by the early Chinese, were among the "eastern barbarians" who occupied the frontiers of the empire, and they entered the Chinese historical record many centuries before writing and a historiographic tradition appeared in Japan itself (Figure 4.39). These chronicles illuminate, and are illuminated by, the archaeological record in a very interesting way.

The *Wei Chih*, or *Record of Wei* (A.D. 221–265), completed in A.D. 297, is the most important early source for Japanese history. Chinese traditional historiography stressed fact, emphasizing events and overt acts, and the writing of history ideally consisted of setting down this factual material exactly and dispassionately (Gardner 1938:69–70). The *Wei Chih* was written in this tradition, and its essential veracity is widely accepted. The *Hou Han Shu*, or *History of the Later Han Dynasty* (A.D. 25–220) ostensibly pertains to an earlier period, but its compilation was completed much later, in A.D. 445. A good deal of its descriptive content appears to have been simply copied from the *Wei Chih*, making it of relatively less interest as an ethnographic source (Young 1958).

The historic account of the *Wei Chih* clearly reflects, as will shortly be seen from an excerpt, the achievement of a significant level of sociopolitical complexity by the Japanese of Late Yayoi times. The chronicle speaks of class distinctions, rulers, vassals, ambassadors, foreign missions, taxes, and granaries and markets supervised by officials. It also records (in sections not quoted here) the existence of many populous little "countries," variously described as consisting of from 1000 families to probably more than 70,000 households.

A major debate rages among Japanese archaeologists and historians over the locations of some of the Japanese countries mentioned in the *Wei Chih*, especially over that of Queen Himiko's country of Yamatai, which figures prominently in the *Wei Chih* account. Discussion of this problem will be deferred to Chapter 5, since data from the Kofun period are also relevant and for present purposes it is enough to note that whatever the facts of exact location, no serious party to the debate doubts that the scenes and events described occurred somewhere within southwestern Japan. In other words, there is no real doubt that the chronicle is in a general way descriptive of the Japanese culture of Yayoi times, which is the point of interest here.

According to the *Wei Chih*,

> The people of Wa dwell in the middle of the ocean on the mountainous islands southeast of [the prefecture of] Tai-fang. They formerly comprised more than one hundred communities. During the Han dynasty, [Wa envoys] appeared at the Court; today, thirty of their communities maintain intercourse [with us] through envoys and scribes. . . .
> The social customs [of the Wa] are not lewd. The men wear a band of cloth around their heads, exposing the top. Their clothing is fastened around the

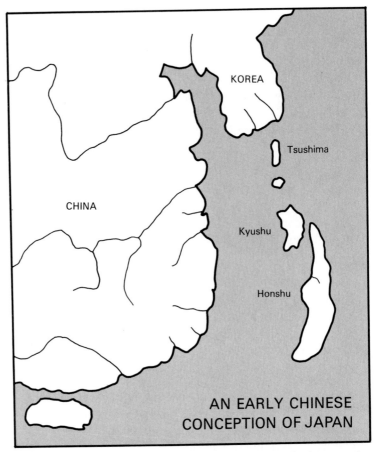

Figure 4.39 Japan, the land of Wa in the early Chinese chronicles, was mistakenly conceived as extending from the island of Kyushu toward the south, rather than toward the northeast, as is the case. Some early maps either do not show the island of Hokkaido or include it as part of northern Honshu. (Redrawn from Mizuno *et al.* 1960:Figure 354.)

body with little sewing. The women wear their hair in loops. Their clothing is like an unlined coverlet and is worn by slipping the head through an opening in the center. [The people] cultivate grains, rice, hemp, and mulberry trees for sericulture. They spin and weave and produce fine linen and silk fabrics. There are no oxen, horses, tigers, leopards, sheep, or magpies. Their weapons are spears, shields, and wooden bows made with short lower part and long upper part; and their bamboo arrows are sometimes tipped with iron or bone. Thus in what they have and what they lack, they are similar to the people of Tan-erh and Chu-yai. . . .

The land of Wa is warm and mild [in climate]. In winter as in summer the people live on vegetables and go about barefooted. Their houses have rooms; father and mother, elder and younger, sleep separately. They smear their bodies with pink and scarlet, just as the Chinese use powder. They serve meat on bamboo and wooden trays, helping themselves with their fingers. When a person dies, they prepare a single coffin, without an outer one. They cover the graves with sand to make a mound. When death occurs, mourning is observed for more than ten days, during which period they do not eat meat. The head mourners wail and lament, while friends sing, dance, and drink liquor. When the funeral is over, all members of the whole family go into the water to cleanse themselves in a bath of purification.

When they go on voyages across the sea to visit China, they always select a man who does not arrange his hair, does not rid himself of fleas, lets his clothing [get as] dirty as it will, does not eat meat, and does not approach women. This man behaves like a mourner and is known as the fortune keeper. When the voyage turns out propitious, they all lavish on him slaves and other valuables. In case there is disease or mishap, they kill him, saying that he was not scrupulous in his duties. . . .

In their meetings and in their deportment, there is no distinction between father and son or between men and women. They are fond of liquor. In their worship, men of importance simply clap their hands instead of kneeling or bowing. The people live long, some to one hundred and others to eighty or ninety years. Ordinarily, men of importance have four or five wives, the lesser ones, two or three. Women are not loose in morals or jealous. There is no theft, and litigation is infrequent. In case of violation of law, the light offender loses his wife and children by confiscation; as for the grave offender, the members of his household and also his kinsmen are exterminated. There are class distinctions among the people, and some men are vassals of others. Taxes are collected. There are granaries as well as markets in each province, where necessaries are exchanged under the supervision of the Wa officials. . . .

When the lowly meet men of importance on the road, they stop and withdraw to the roadside. In conveying messages to them or addressing them, they either squat or kneel, with both hands on the ground. This is the way they show respect. When responding, they say "ah," which corresponds to the affirmative "yes."

The country [of Yamatai] formerly had a man as ruler. For some seventy or eighty years after that there were disturbances and warfare. Thereupon the people agreed upon a woman for their ruler. Her name was Himiko. She occupied herself with magic and sorcery, bewitching the people. Though mature in age, she remained unmarried. She had a younger brother who assisted her in ruling the country. After she became the ruler, there were few who saw her. She had one thousand women as attendants, but only one man. He served her food and drink and acted as a medium of communication. She resided in a palace surrounded by towers and stockades, with armed guards in a state of constant vigilance. . . .

In the sixth month of the second year of Ching-ch'u (A.D. 238), the Queen of Wa sent the grandee Nashonmi and others to visit the prefecture [of Tai-fang], where they requested permission to proceed to the Emperor's Court with tribute. The Governor, Liu Hsia, dispatched an officer to accompany the party to the capital. In answer to the Queen of Wa, an edict of the Emperor, issued in the twelfth month of the same year, said as follows: "Herein we address Himiko, Queen of Wa, whom we now officially call a friend of Wei. The Governor of Tai-fang, Liu Hsia, has sent a messenger to accompany your vassal, Nashonmi, and his lieutenant, Tsushi Gori. They have arrived here with your tribute, consisting of four male slaves and six female slaves, together with two pieces of cloth with designs, each twenty feet in length. You live very far away across the sea; yet you have sent an embassy with tribute. Your loyalty and filial piety we appreciate exceedingly. We confer upon you, therefore, the title 'Queen of Wa friendly to Wei,' together with the decoration of the gold seal with purple ribbon. The latter, properly encased, is to be sent to you through the Governor. We expect you, O Queen, to rule your people in peace and to endeavor to be devoted and obedient.

"Your ambassadors, Nashonmi and Gori, who have come from afar, must have had a long and fatiguing journey. We have, therefore, given to Nashonmi an appointment as Lieutenant Colonel in the Imperial Guard, and to Gori an appointment as Commandant in the Imperial Guard. We also bestow upon them the decoration of the silver seal with blue ribbon. We have granted them audience in appreciation of their visit, before sending them home with gifts. The gifts are these: five pieces of crimson brocade with dragon designs; ten pieces of crimson tapestry with dappled pattern; fifty lengths of bluish-red fabric; and fifty lengths of dark blue fabric. These are in return for what you sent as tribute. As a special gift, we bestow upon you three pieces of blue brocade with interwoven characters, five pieces of tapestry with delicate floral designs, fifty lengths of white silk, eight taels of gold, two swords five feet long, one hundred bronze mirrors, and fifty catties each of jade and of red beads. All these things are sealed in boxes and entrusted to Nashonmi and Gori. When they arrive and you acknowledge their receipt, you may exhibit them to your countrymen in order to demonstrate that our country thinks so much of you as to bestow such exquisite gifts upon you." . . .

When Himiko passed away, a great mound was raised, more than a hundred paces in diameter. Over a hundred male and female attendants followed her to the grave. Then a king was placed on the throne, but the people would not obey him. Assassination and murder followed; more than one thousand were thus slain.

A relative to Himiko named Iyo, a girl of thirteen, was [then] made queen and order was restored. Cheng issued a proclamation to the effect that Iyo was the ruler. Then Iyo sent a delegation of twenty under the grandee Yazaku, General of the Imperial Guard, to accompany Cheng home [to China]. The delegation visited the capital and presented thirty male and female slaves. It also offered [to the Court] five thousand white gems and two pieces of carved jade, as well as twenty pieces of brocade with variegated designs [Tsunoda and Goodrich 1951].

As both the archaeological record and the Chinese chronicles show, local elites had achieved a significant measure of political and economic power by the later part of the Yayoi period. The following Kofun period saw a burgeoning of this strength, which continued to grow along the lines drawn in Yayoi times.

5 : The Kofun Period

The Kofun period is set off from the Yayoi, out of which it emerged, by a major expansion in the political sector of society. The earliest *kofun*, the burial mounds the period takes it name from, seem to have appeared in the Kinai region between present-day Osaka, Kyoto, and Nara, and spread outward from that center (Figure 5.1). This is the traditional homeland of the Japanese imperial family and the Japanese state, and prevailing archaeological opinion traces the expansion of Yamato hegemony outward from this region by marking the distribution of the earliest Kofun mounds to appear in other parts of the country.

The Kofun period is usually placed between about A.D. 300 and 700. The earlier date is inferred from the occurrence in Kofun burials of Chinese bronze mirrors bearing dates of manufacture in the mid-third century; the later date roughly corresponds to the appearance of the first native written history of Japan, the *Kojiki* or *Record of Ancient Matters,* which was completed in A.D. 712. The Kofun period has been chronologically subdivided in various ways by archaeologists. Most commonly encountered in the literature are two schemes—one defining Early, Middle, and Late subperiods (with reference often made to the early and late halves of each), and the other describing Early and Late phases, each with internal subdivisions. A highly refined version of the latter scheme subdivides Early Kofun into four numbered subphases, and Late Kofun into three (Otsuka 1966). Such refined seriation is made possible by the wealth and diversity of material goods as-

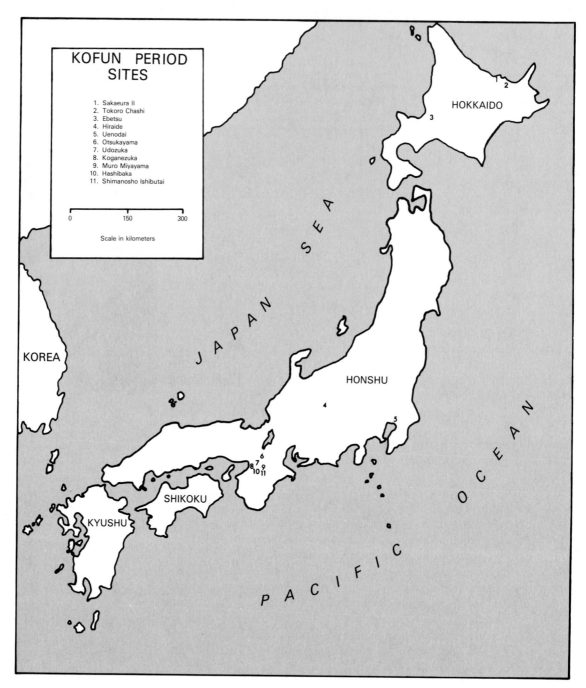

Figure 5.1   Locations of principal Kofun period sites mentioned in text.

sociated with Kofun burials, and by architectural changes in the Kofun mounds themselves. The system allows Kofun period specialists to speak of events or developments in terms of roughly half-century units, and in the following discussion a combination of the Early–Late framework and absolute chronology is used. For example, an individual site may be referred to as belonging to the end of the Early Kofun period, and also attributed a date in the last half of the fifth century A.D.

The entire Kofun period is protohistoric rather than prehistoric, in the sense that written Chinese and Korean chronicles of the time periodically make some mention of Japanese affairs; the Japanese *Kojiki,* and the *Nihon Shoki* that followed it (in A.D. 720), purport to tell the history of the times based on unwritten tradition. The age is not considered fully historic, however, because the foreign references to Japan are so limited, and the native Japanese accounts so obviously a compound of origin myth, invention, and reality contrived for the purpose of legitimizing the political claims of the Yamato house, which commissioned their writing.

The written sources refer to powerful clan groups and their leaders, to many kinds of greater and lesser titled officials, to guilds and corporations of artisans, fishers, farmers, and soldiers attached to the clans, and to repeated political embassies, strifes, and wars. The chronology and details of many of the events related in the histories are confused or in dispute, but there is sufficient agreement between parts of the Chinese, Korean, and Japanese writings to show that the period was indeed one of great political and military ferment within a generally feudalistic society, during which rival Japanese clans jockeyed for position and some of the more powerful alliances even managed to achieve short-lived conquests in the Korean peninsula. The archaeological record confirms this general picture, and extends our understanding of the period in many ways, as will be seen.

The ensuing discussion focuses on the archaeology of the Kyoto–Nara–Osaka region, since that area was central to the growth of political power that fostered the rise of the earliest Japanese state. There are many important Kofun sites in other parts of Japan, most notably in Kyushu, in Okayama Prefecture on the Inland Sea, and in the Tokyo region, but these are brought into the discussion only as they bear on the poltical developments out of which the Yamato state grew. The lifeways of the aristocracy, and of the common people who ultimately supported the aristocracy, are also treated, as are cultural developments beyond the northern frontier in Hokkaido, where the power of the Japanese state was never fully established until the nineteenth century.

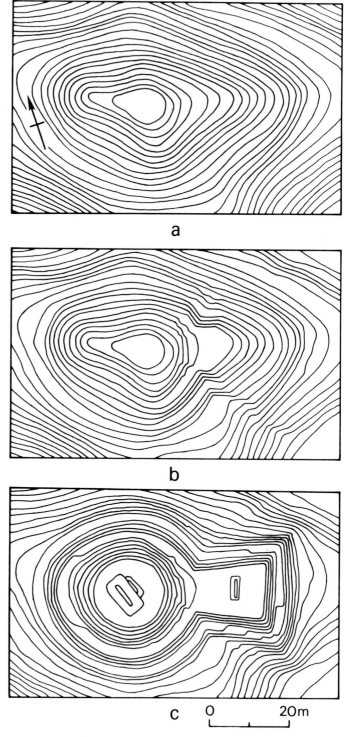

Figure 5.2 Formation of a keyhole-shaped *kofun* by modification of a natural hill. (Redrawn from Tsuboi and Machida 1977:162.)

Tsubai Otsukayama Kofun, approximately 25 km south of Kyoto near the city of Nara, is considered typical of the burial mounds of the Early Kofun period (Umehara 1964). It is the northernmost of a group of three large tumuli built on the tips of ridges immediately overlooking the Kizu River plain. During construction of the Kyoto–Nara railway in 1894, a deep cut was made through the Otsukayama tumulus. When this was later widened in 1953, the discovery of artifacts spilling from one of its sides prompted an emergency investigation of the site by T. Higuchi.

Otsukayama Kofun is of the so-called *zenpo-koen* form, meaning that it consists of a square platform before, with a round mound behind. Such mounds have been referred to in English as keyhole-shaped, a term that will no doubt survive because of its convenience, even though the type of lock from which it takes its meaning is no longer part of everyday experience. The rounded eminence of the rear of Otsukayama Kofun was originally a natural hillock on the tip of a mountain ridge, which was manually shaped to the desired form by removing earth at some points and piling it up at others (Figure 5.2). The flat, rectangular apron before this mound was originally the lower, gentler basal slope of the ridge, also manually graded and shaped to the desired form. Evidence of an ancient ditch at places along the sides of the tumulus suggests that it was originally surrounded by a dry moat. The rounded rear mound, the top of which was artificially raised about 5 m above the original surface of the hillock on which it was based, stood about 30 m above the apparent base level of the frontal apron.

Because the builders of the *kofun* so artfully made use of natural topography, its boundaries are not precisely delimitable. Roughly, it can be seen as having an overall length of about 185 m, and a width, across the middle of the rear mound, of about 75 m. Because of its situation on a natural eminence, however, it appears to be even larger than these measurements suggest, and in fact the name of the locality itself refers to the large size of the mound.

At a point that would have been the approximate center of the rear mound before it was sectioned by the railroad cut, a long, narrow subterranean chamber was found in a deep pit. It was 4.9 m long, 1.1 m wide, and 3 m high in interior dimensions, its floor lying perhaps 4 m below the original surface of the mound. The walls were made of thick, flat slabs of stone, irregularly coursed, without mortar. They rested on a layer of gravel that had been put down before they were made, and gravel had also been subsequently poured into the space between the stone walls and the sides of the pit in which they were constructed.

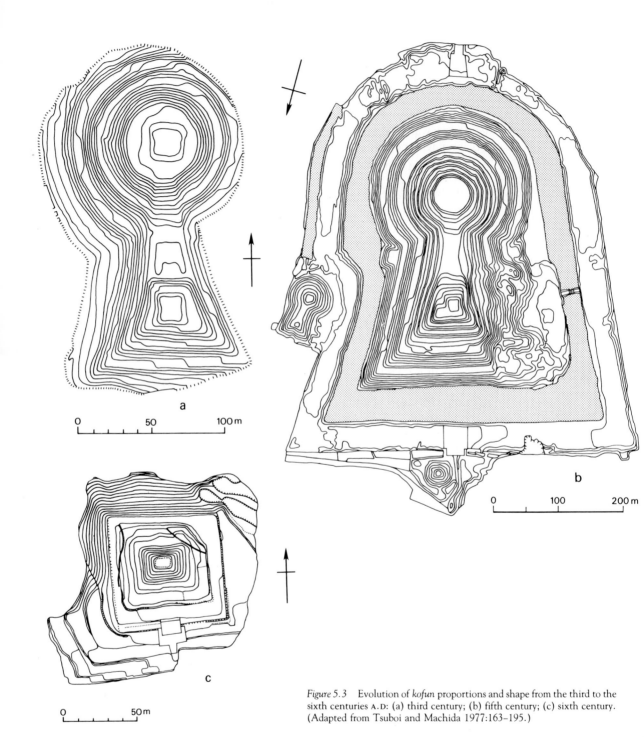

Figure 5.3 Evolution of *kofun* proportions and shape from the third to the sixth centuries A.D: (a) third century; (b) fifth century; (c) sixth century. (Adapted from Tsuboi and Machida 1977:163–195.)

Figure 5.4 Development of stone coffin types. Upper, log-shaped coffin of the Early Kofun period from Chausuyama Kofun, Kyoto Prefecture, south-central Honshu. Length, 3.1 m. Middle, composite coffin of the Middle Kofun period from Kurumazuka Kofun, Kyoto Prefecture. Length, 2.6 m. Lower, composite coffin of a style that first appeared in the late Kofun period. Specimen shown is of the following Asuka period, from the Fukunishi tumulus, city of Kyoto. Length, 2 m. (Kyoto University Museum.)

A

B

C

258   *Figure* 5.5 (Legend on facing page.)

D

E

Chinese and Japanese bronze mirrors:
A, Chinese, of the Latter Han period, from Hyotanyama Kofun (Early Kofun period), Shiga Prefecture, south-central Honshu. Diameter, 15 cm. B, Chinese, of the Latter Han period, from Terado Otsuka Kofun (Early Kofun period), Kyoto Prefecture, south-central Honshu. Diameter, 17.5 cm. C, Chinese, of the Latter Han period, from Tanaka Choshizuka Kofun (Early Kofun period), Fukuoka Prefecture, Kyushu. Diameter, 21.7 cm. D, Japanese, of the Early Kofun period, from Terado Otsuka Kofun, Kyoto Prefecture. Diameter, 22 cm. E, Japanese, of the Early Kofun period from Tanaka Choshizuka Kofun, Fukuoka Prefecture. Diameter, 21.1 cm. (Continued on p. 260)

Figure 5.5 (Continued). F, Japanese, of the Early Kofun period, from Terado Otsuka Kofun, Kyoto Prefecture. Diameter, 15.4 cm. G, Japanese, of the Middle Kofun period, from Kodo Kofun, Kyoto Prefecture. Diameter, 12.2 cm. H, Japanese, of the Late Kofun period, from Shidami-Otsuka Kofun, Aichi Prefecture, south-central Honshu. Diameter at rim 11.2 cm. (Kyoto University Museum.)

The floor of the burial chamber was paved with a thick layer of clay, in which there was a depression where a long, cylindrical wooden coffin had rested. The ceiling was formed by eight large, rectangular stone slabs laid across the tops of the walls, closely fitted together and also covered with a thick layer of clay. The chamber was strong and well made, apparently built with due consideration for keeping the interior dry, and was intact when found except for damage done to it by the railway excavations.

All that remained of the wooden coffin were several fragments, and no traces of its former occupant were preserved. The coffin had been covered with a layer of clay before the tomb was closed, and this was extended to form a second layer over the whole floor of the chamber. There is no evidence that burial offerings were included within the coffin itself, but a number of extremely important artifacts were found arranged along the walls of the stone chamber.

Weapons of war were prominent among the burial goods. Several iron swords up to 90 cm long, and spearpoints or knives up to 45 cm long, were placed to one side of the coffin. Also found were a number of iron and bronze points, presumably hafted to now decomposed wooden arrowshafts when deposited. Three types were represented: one of triangular shape with flaring tangs, a second of lanceolate form, and a third of modified spatulate outline. Other martial equipment included fragments of an iron helmet and many small, thin, rectangular plates of iron, perforated to permit their being sewn together to form flexible body armor. Apparently they were part of a mailed shirt or vest when deposited. The cords that held the metal plates together had long since vanished by the time the archaeaologists found the armor, but many of the plates remained rusted together to suggest something of the original shape of the garment.

Iron tools among the burial offerings included sickles, axe- and adzeheads, wood chisels, and woodcarving knives. One of these wood-carving implements, the distinctive *yariganna*, was a beveled blade sharpened from the underside only, and mounted at the end of a long shaft. The name indicates that it is a spearlike planing tool, and paintings of early historic times show that this device, held in both hands, functioned as a kind of drawknife used in planing down lumber. Other iron tools included barbed iron harpoons, small fish-spears, and a fishhook.

The most remarkable and interpretively useful specimens from Ot-sukayama Kofun were more than 30 bronze mirrors, all of Chinese manufacture and historically dated to about the last half of the third century A.D. They were arranged along both sides and at the head of the burial chamber, all set on edge leaning against the base of the stone walls. In addition to these were three specimens that had been buried separately, which were found during the railway excavations.

With few exceptions the mirrors were all of one style, and in several cases two or three specimens had been made after the same model. From these circumstances it is clear that Chinese bronze mirrors were shipped to Japan in wholesale lots from continental factories, and comparable though less abundant evidence from other Kofun sites supports this interpretation. These mirrors were widely exchanged within Japan, probably in the context of diplomatic exercises and alliance making among local and regional nobles.

In a brilliant piece of typological and distributional research, Kobayashi (1961, 1976) has traced the occurrence throughout much of Japan of bronze mirrors made from the same models, thus showing the far-flung network of exchange relationships that existed among the chieftains of Kofun times. Otsukayama Kofun occupies a central place in this study, its trove of mirrors having produced specimens of which duplicates are known from 19 other places around the country. The Otsukayama mirrors had mates at several relatively nearby sites in the Kyoto–Nara–Osaka region, but direct connections are also attested as far away as Fukuoka and Oita prefectures in Kyushu; Tottori, Hiroshima, and Okayama prefectures in southwestern Honshu; Aichi,

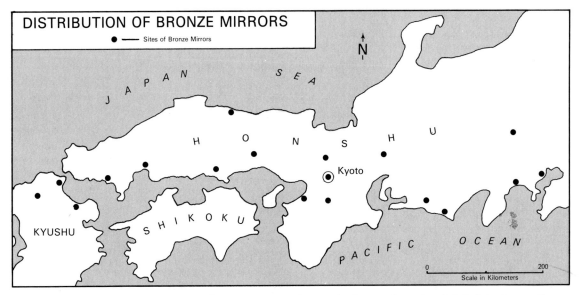

Figure 5.6 Geographical distribution of Kofun period sites directly linked, by sharing of bronze mirrors made from the same models, to Tsubai Otsukayama Kofun, Kyoto. (Based on Y. Kobayashi 1976.)

Shizuoka, and Gifu prefectures in central Honshu; and Kanagawa and Chiba prefectures in the Tokyo region (Figure 5.6). Other connections indirectly link many more sites, reflecting an intricate web of relationships and shared interests among the Kofun period nobility throughout Japan.

Some archaeologists think, because of its early age, great size, and far-flung connections, that Otsukayama may be the burial place of the very person who first established Yamato hegemony over the whole of Japan. This opinion is not widely held, however, principally because there is no certainty that Otsukayama is the earliest Kofun mound to be constructed in Japan, and because it is somewhat away from the main centers of Early Kofun construction near Nara and Osaka. Neither side's arguments are necessarily conclusive, but Otsukayama is in any case extremely important as evidence of the network of ties that existed between the early ruling elites throughout the country.

Koganezuka Kofun, which also dates to the Early Kofun period, is in southern Osaka on the broad alluvial plain east of Osaka Bay (Suenaga *et al.* 1954). The name of the site, which might be translated as "gold hill," derives from a local legend of golden treasures buried in its tombs. Yayoi period sites are numerous in the region, and many tumuli of the fifth through the seventh centuries also exist there.

Koganezuka Kofun

Koganezuka Kofun lies on the relatively flat top of a low, elongate natural hill. This rises about 15 m above the surrounding plain, the natural elevation enhancing the grandeur of the tumulus built up on it. The tumulus measured 85 m in overall length; the rear mound was 57 m in diameter and the front platform was 28 m long by 34 m wide. The rear mound was built up to a height of 8 m, the front platform to a height of 6 m. Virtually the entire volume of this structure consisted of earth excavated nearby and piled up to form the desired shape. It was encircled by a borrow ditch that might also be thought of as a kind of moat, although it was not graded to one level and could not have functioned as a water barrier. The great size of the tumulus seems remarkable for such an early stage of the Kofun period, and it vividly attests the truly monumental labor that the chieftains of the time were already able to command.

Along the crest of the rear mound and the edges of the frontal platform, large, low-fired earthenware cylinders were arranged in close-set rows. These represent the earliest form of the fascinating *haniwa* figures that were emplaced apparently as guardians of the burial tumuli, and became increasingly elaborate over time. Fragments of a clay *haniwa* model of a house were also found. These fragments were embedded in the surface at the center of the rear mound, in a position that turned out to be directly above the coffin of the principal personage buried at the site.

Three burial chambers were discovered about 1 m beneath the surface of the rear mound. A long, slender vault about 2.5 m wide and 10 m end to end lay in the center, aligned with the long axis of the *kofun*. Adjacent to the vault on the east was a similar but slightly smaller structure, and west of it, a little farther away, lay a third one, much smaller. The discovery of multiple burials in Early Kofun mounds is not uncommon, and it suggests emulation of the contemporary Chinese practice of sending retainers or guardians along with a dead chieftain to the afterworld.

The central vault was entirely of clay, with massive walls nearly 1 m thick. It was made to accommodate a long, cylindrical coffin hewn from a large log, and had been sealed with a thick layer of clay after the coffin was emplaced. The vault rested on a thick bed of gravel, probably intended to provide drainage and thus help preserve the buried remains. Despite these efforts, the casket and its occupant had almost entirely decomposed, leaving only a few fragments of the coffin to suggest its original shape, and the inorganic artifacts that had been provided as burial offerings.

A number of objects had been placed inside the coffin of the principal personage. A bracelet of polished jasper was found at either side of the coffin, about where a wearer's wrists would have been. Groups of tubular and curved *magatama* beads of jade, jasper, and alabaster were found about the neck and body region, and others had been placed near the feet. Associated with one of the bead groups was a bronze mirror of Chinese make. The objects within the coffin were entirely ornamental or magical; no weapons of war or mundane tools were among them. Outside the coffin, however, emplaced on the ground beside it before the final clay cover was added to the burial vault, were many long and short swords of iron and a number of iron axes, sickles, and other tools. Among these offerings was a single Chinese bronze mirror, which bore its continental maker's name and a date corresponding to A.D. 239 in the Christian calendar.

The tomb on the east side of the central burial was quite differently made and furnished. It lacked the massiveness of its companion; the relatively thin clay of the vault walls was apparently merely a coating plastered against a long, rectangular boxlike coffin of wood, now decomposed. The burial goods were also radically different, running heavily to weapons, almost all of which were placed inside the coffin itself.

Of the coffin's occupant, only the skull remained. Three bronze

Figure 5.7 Pedestaled offering bowls of Sue ware, Late Kofun period. Left, from Kamoinariyama Kofun, Shiga Prefecture, south-central Honshu. Height, 44 cm. Right, from Kinzaki Kofun, Shimane Prefecture, southern Honshu. Height, 54.2 cm. (Shown one-third actual size.) (Kyoto University Museum.)

Figure 5.8 Pedestaled offering vessels of Sue ware, Late Kofun period. Left, lidded cup. Height, 12.1 cm. Right, jar with lid missing. Height, 29.6 cm. Both from Kinzaki Kofun, Shimane Prefecture, southern Honshu. (Both shown approximately one-half actual size.) (Kyoto University Museum.)

Figure 5.9 Jar of Sue ware, Late Kofun period. From Kinzakiyama Kofun, Shimane Prefecture, southern Honshu. Height, 16 cm. (Shown approximately one-half actual size.) (Kyoto University Museum.)

Figure 5.10 Composite set of lidded offering bowls of Sue ware, Late Kofun period. From Yamaguchi Shinjocho, Nara Prefecture, south-central Honshu. Diameter, ca. 34 cm. (Shown approximately one-half actual size.) (Kyoto University Museum.)

Figure 5.11 Rough miniature clay effigies of *magatama* beads, spherical beads, mirrors, pot, and mortar, probably used as ceremonial offerings. Of the Middle or Late Kofun period, from Kisami-Araida, city of Shimoda, Shizuoka Prefecture. (Kyoto University Museum.)

Figure 5.12 Ground and polished stone bracelets of the Early Kofun period, from Hyotanyama Kofun, Shiga Prefecture, south-central Honshu. Largest specimen, 15.5 cm. long. (Shown approximately one-half actual size.) (Kyoto University Museum.)

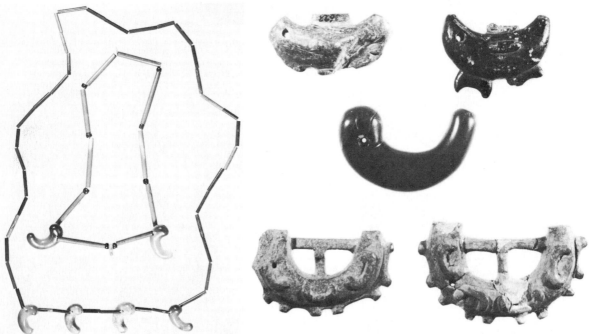

Figure 5.13 Necklaces of cylindrical and *magatama* (curved) beads, of the Middle Kofun period, from Ubusunayama Kofun, Kyoto Prefecture, south-central Honshu. Cylindrical sections range in length from 1.7 to 5.1 cm. (Kyoto University Museum.)

Figure 5.14 Stone *magatama* beads of various types, all Late Kofun period. Left, from Kinzaki Kofun, Shimane Prefecture, southern Honshu. Center and lower right, from Ichinodai site, Ibaraki Prefecture, central Honshu. Upper right, from Naraba, city of Sakai, Osaka Prefecture, south-central Honshu. Length of specimen at lower left, 7.7 cm. (Shown approximately one-half actual size.) (Kyoto University Museum.)

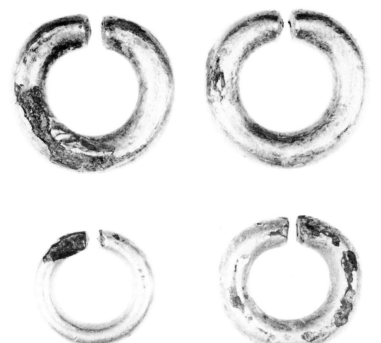

Figure 5.15 Gold earrings of the Late Kofun period, from the city of Tomioka, Gumma Prefecture, central Honshu. Diameter of largest specimen, 3 cm. (Shown one and one-half times actual size.) (Kyoto University Museum.)

Figure 5.16 *Haniwa* horse of the Late Kofun period, from Kurihama, city of Yokosuka, Kanagawa Prefecture, central Honshu. Height, 66 cm. (Kyoto University Museum.)

Figure 5.17 Human *Haniwa* figure of the Late Kofun period, from the Unemezuka site, city of Kamakura, Kanagawa Prefecture, central Honshu. Height, 28.8 cm. (Kyoto University Museum.)

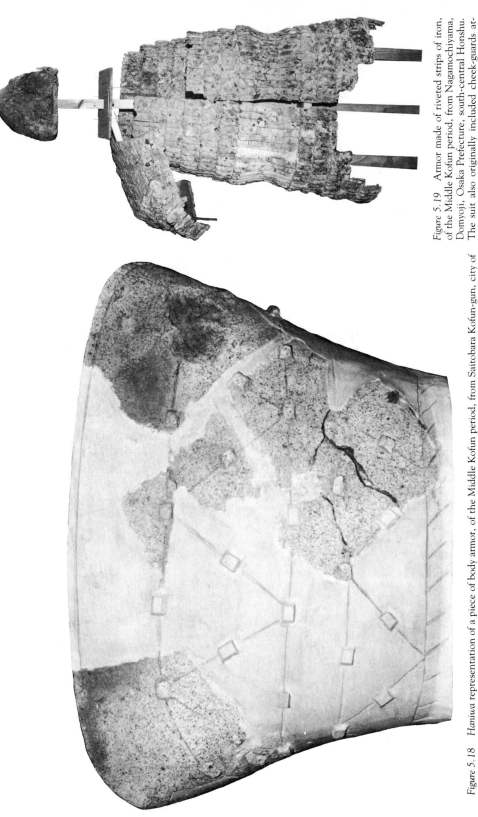

Figure 5.18 Haniwa representation of a piece of body armor, of the Middle Kofun period, from Saitobaru Kofun-gun, city of Saito, Miyazaki Prefecture, Kyushu. Height, 30.5 cm. (Shown approximately one-third actual size.) (Kyoto University Museum.)

Figure 5.19 Armor made of riveted strips of iron, of the Middle Kofun period, from Nagamochiyama, Domyoji, Osaka Prefecture, south-central Honshu. The suit also originally included cheek-guards attached to the helmet, and upper and lower leg-guards. (Kyoto University Museum.)

Figure 5.20 Replica of a metal helmet of the Kofun period, from Nishikoyama Kofun, Osaka Prefecture, south-central Honshu. Height, 31 cm. (Kyoto University Museum.)

mirrors had been placed around it, the largest leaning against the skull itself. In the upper end of the coffin beyond the mirrors were a set of iron body armor with helmet, a handful of iron knives, a bronze coin, some tubular stone beads, and a large "hoe-type" stone bracelet, so called because in its rectangular outline, with a circular opening in the center, it resembles the blade of a traditional Japanese hoe. All the smaller objects had apparently been wrapped in silk. About the neck of the interred personage was a cluster of beads, and at either side was a pair of iron swords. Iron tools, including axeheads, knives, and a saw, were at one side, and in the lower end of the coffin were a number of additional axeheads and two more swords. Outside the coffin, on the side adjacent to the central burial, were a shield with bronze ornaments, four short swords, and 110 iron arrowheads.

The third tomb, on the west side of the principal interment, was like that just described in structure and content, but little more than half its size and less abundantly furnished. At the head of the coffin were three iron swords and 110 iron arrowheads. The occurrence of

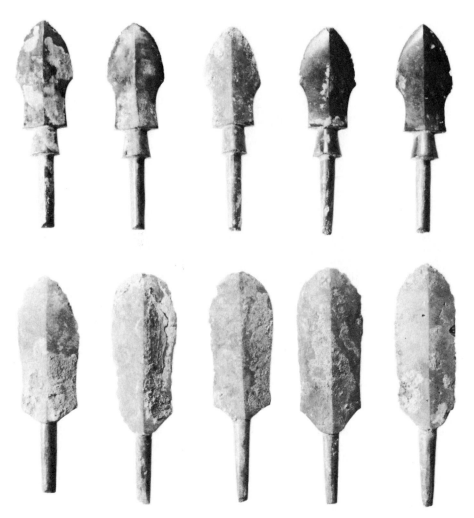

Figure 5.21   Nickel alloy spearpoints of the Early Kofun period, from Hyotanyama Kofun, Shiga Prefecture, south-central Honshu. Length of specimen at lower right, 6.5 cm. (Shown actual size.) (Kyoto University Museum.)

exactly the same number of iron arrowheads in both subsidiary graves indicates that this may have been a standard set, or some multiple of a standard quiver-lot. Next to the arrowheads was a bronze mirror, on which rested a cluster of curved and tubular stone beads, apparently once a necklace. Three more iron swords laid along one side of the coffin must have been next to the body, and on either side were clusters of very small tubular beads, which had probably been worn as

Figure 5.22 Effigy blades made of talc for use as burial offerings, of the Middle Kofun period, from Kurumazuka Kofun, Kyoto Prefecture, south-central Honshu. Longest specimen, 5.7 cm. (Kyoto University Museum.)

bracelets. At the foot of the coffin was placed a set of iron armor and a helmet.

From the contents of the three graves at Koganezuka Kofun, the investigators inferred that the personage of the central tomb was a woman, and those of the graves flanking her were men. This is based on the fact that the central tomb contained no weapons except those contributed just before the grave was finally sealed, whereas weaponry was prominent in the other two. Because of the lesser size and wealth of the westernmost burial it has been suggested that it was made at a later date, but these differences could probably better be attributed to the lesser wealth and status of the person buried there. Multiple burials known from other Kofun sites of the same general period also commonly involve three individuals, making it seem likely that the two retainers accompanying their superior at Koganezuka evidence a well-defined and widely shared pattern of funerary behavior rather than some vagary of individual sentiment or relationship.

Of particular interest at Koganezuka Kofun is the fact that the bronze mirror placed as a final offering outside the coffin of the principal personage is inscribed with a date that corresponds to A.D. 239 in the Christian calendar. This coincides closely with the date of an event described in the Chinese *Wei Chih*, or *Record of Wei*, where it is recounted that the Emperor of Wei, in the 12th month of the year 238, issued an edict for transmission to Princess Himiko, of the land of Wa (Japan), acknowledging his receipt of her emissaries and gifts, and naming, among many other items that he would send back with her envoys, a gift of 100 bronze mirrors. Himiko is said to have been ruler of the ancient Japanese country of Yamatai, which many (but not all) students of the subject identify with historic Yamato, the broad fertile land extending from Osaka Bay to the mountains east of Kyoto and Nara.

It seems possible that the mirrors from Koganezuka Kofun actually are some of those mentioned in the *Wei Chih*. Although only one has a dated inscription, all are typologically similar and of a style known from independent evidence to have been made on the continent during the period in question. It should also be noted, in connection with the archaeological identification of the principal personage at Koganezuka as female, that the *Wei Chih* account provides clear documentary evidence for the holding of high political station by women as well as by men in the Japan of this period. Whether or not Koganezuka Kofun is the resting place of Princess Himiko (the *Wei Chih* says she was buried in a tumulus of 100 paces) is an intriguing and probably insoluble romantic question, but the current opinion of most Japanese archaeologists is that the site dates too late in time (later fourth century) for that to have been the case.

Muro Miyayama Kofun is one of many burial mounds that cluster along the base of the hills at the southern edge of the Yamato Plain in the Katsuragi district, about 30 km south of the city of Nara (Akiyama and Aboshi 1959). The tumulus of Muro Miyayama is dated to a late subdivision of the Early Kofun period by its location at the juncture of hill and plain, and by the fact that its rear mound and frontal platform are of comparable height and width. The shape and composite form of its massive chestlike stone coffin, and the occurrence of *haniwa* figures in the shape of waterfowl and other forms, confirm this designation. A date in the first half of the fifth century is suggested.

The tumulus lies on the tip of a ridge overlooking the alluvial plain, the natural elevation giving it a dominating position over the lowlands that stretch away before it. It is of typical keyhole shape, 238 m long, with the rounded rear mound measuring 105 m in diameter and the rectangular frontal platform about 110 m across. The height of the rear mound is about 25 m, and that of the frontal platform about 22 m. A broad depression about 70 m across encircles the *kofun,* and a large pond for irrigation water now occupies one corner of the depression. The depression undoubtedly represents the borrow pit from which earth used in building the tumulus was obtained, and the irrigation pond probably is a remnant of a water-filled moat that once surrounded the monument.

Beneath the surface of the rear mound, just west of the longitudinal centerline of the *kofun,* was discovered a rectangular chamber of dry-laid masonry containing a stone coffin. The chamber, about 5.5 m long and 1.9 m wide, had walls about 1 m high. Five massive tabular stones had been laid across the tops of the walls to form the ceiling. The chamber's walls and roof had been coated from the outside with a heavy layer of clay up to 20 cm thick, apparently in an effort to prevent water from seeping in.

The coffin that lay within this burial chamber was made of six large slabs, fitted carefully together and held in position by their own massive weight. The side and end walls stood on edge to form a rectangle resting on a flat basal slab, and the arched, high-backed lid that locked them together overhung the walls slightly on all four sides. From either end of the two long slabs that formed the side walls of the coffin, a large, thick cylindrical knob protruded, and two such knobs also protruded from each end and side of the coffin's lid. These protrusions clearly would have been useful as purchases for the rope slings that must have been used to position the massive stones, and the care taken in the shaping of the knobs gives them an ornamental effect as well. The upper surface of the lid was further embellished by a series of eight rectangular panels cut into it, with broad low-relief balks separating the recessed panels.

As noted earlier, this burial complex lay immediately west of the longitudinal centerline of the *kofun*. It is evident that another once lay adjacent to it on the other side of the centerline, but was plundered and destroyed long ago. A long stone coffin lid with knobs at either end was found in disturbed soil in a shallow depression there, suggesting that the installation may have been similar to the one scientifically excavated. Traces of yet another chamber some distance away suggest that a third burial had also been made on the mound, but that was no doubt a later addition, whereas the paired chambers, aligned on either side of the long axis of the tumulus, clearly reflect an intention to make a double burial. A number of other Kofun sites of this period in the Yamato region have two or more chambers, which means that Muro Miyayama is typical of the period in this respect as well as others mentioned.

The grave opened by the archaeologists had also been previously plundered, as it turned out, though not with completely disastrous results. At some time prior to the archaeological excavations, one of six stone slabs that originally constituted the ceiling of the tomb had been removed, and the masonry walls were broken through in places. Artifacts and soil lay in a scattered and disturbed condition within the chamber, and a quantity of earth within the coffin itself showed that its lid had been pried open during these depredations. Despite the havoc thus wrought, however, and the probable removal of certain precious artifacts, many specimens of archaeological interest remained at the site.

Many fragments of iron armor and a dozen or so iron swords and other blades represent the usual military equipment of a Kofun burial. Along with the actual weapons were found 15 or so small stone imitations of metal spear or halberd points, made expressly for use as burial offerings. Only broken fragments of bronze mirrors were found in the excavation, but 10 or so Chinese mirrors of Han type, along with stone beads and other objects, had been found at a place on the frontal platform of the tumulus during an episode of forest clearance decades before.

A truly impressive number of *magatama* beads, over 600 in all, were recovered from the tomb chamber. They were made of soft, easily worked talc, and only roughly shaped. Clearly they were mass-produced to serve as burial offerings. Other items of stone were long, tubular beads, and short, barrel-shaped beads, as well as a few elaborately sculptured pendants.

The fired clay *haniwa* figures found at Muro Miyayama Kofun are of particular interest for their variety. The assemblage provides an excellent illustration of the character and use of *haniwa* during the early fifth century. Excavations showed that a series of house models and "umbrella" type cylindrical *haniwa* with elaborate lids had been placed from .5 to 1 m apart along lines forming three sides of a rectangle, immediately above the buried tomb. At the corners of the rectangle, oddly shaped but basically cylindrical *haniwa* were placed. Outside this alignment, and parallel to it, was a larger alignment of the same pattern. This was made up of *haniwa* representing shields, body armor, and quivers for arrows, interspersed among which were figures of the umbrella type. Since both alignments formed three sides of a rectangle, it seems likely that they once extended completely around the tombs, the now-missing figures perhaps having been destroyed during the later pilfering. South of this second series of figures was a short row of several more house models. North of the excavated tomb, on the opposite side of the *kofun*'s longitudinal centerline and adjacent to the depression where the previously destroyed burial chamber had been, was another row of *haniwa*. This corresponded in position to the second-order alignment of the excavated tomb, and the *haniwa* figures were also comparable—shields and armor—which suggests that similar arrangements of figures once enclosed both graves.

Udozuka Kofun is in the valley of a small tributary to the Yamato River, about 15 km west of Nara (Date *et al.* 1972). The area lies on the north side of a break in the hills that bound the western edge of the Nara Basin, through which the Yamato flows to debouch into Osaka Bay. The tumulus is built on a ridge tip that extends a short distance out onto the plain, the natural elevation helping to give the mound an imposing appearance when viewed from that direction, and in turn providing an impressive view out over the Nara Basin from its summit. Many other burial mounds occur in the immediate vicinity, all of them, like Udozuka itself, of the Late Kofun period.

The tumulus as a whole was about 60 m long, measuring from the inner side of the borrow ditch/moat that encircled it. Over half this length was taken up by the circular mound at the rear, which was 35 m in diameter. The frontal apron was about 25 m long, 30 m wide, and 3 m lower than the level of the rear mound. Test trenches made into the sides of the *kofun* showed that it had been shaped around a natural elevation by cutting and filling. The greatest actual height of the built-up mound above the natural hilltop was about 6 m, but its apparent height, as measured from a road along the visual base of the *kofun*, was about 12 m.

A large burial chamber, entered by a passageway leading in from the rear of the *kofun*, lay beneath the center of the rear mound. The passageway was 8.3 m long, 2.7 m wide, and 2 m high, with walls of massive, squarish stone slabs up to nearly 3 m across. It had presumably been roofed over by stone slabs, but none were present at the time of the investigation. Running the length of the passage floor was a trench about 20 cm wide and deep, with large stream cobbles laid along its bottom. This was evidently a drain, graded to eliminate water seeping into the tomb from above. The passage had been closed off by filling it from floor to ceiling along most of its length with large stones, which the archaeologists had to clear to gain access to the tomb beyond.

The entrance passage, once cleared, opened directly into a burial chamber of the same width, which measured 6 m from front to back and had a ceiling 4.3 m high. A series of massive stone slabs comprised the base of the chamber walls, and above them were two to three uneven courses of large boulders, only roughly shaped. Two gigantic stone slabs, laid across the tops of the walls to form the ceiling, completed the structure.

The base of a stone coffin was found near one wall at the inner end of the passageway, and within the high-ceilinged chamber were the remains of another. That the tomb had been pillaged and vandalized at some time in the past was shown by the fragmented condition of the two coffins. The remains were sufficient, however, to show that both coffins were of composite construction, with slab sides and ends that rested on grooved foundation stones. Fragments also showed that both had been equipped with lids having pairs of large cylindrical protuberances at both sides and ends. The coffin of the interior chamber was much the larger of the two, slightly under 3 m in length and 1.5 m in width. The one in the passageway, in contrast, was slightly less than 2 m long and 1 m wide. Its location and small size clearly indicate the subordinate status of its onetime occupant, who was perhaps a retainer of the principal personage of the tomb.

Artifacts were found around three sides of the principal coffin, in the space between it and the tomb walls. Whatever the previous plunderers may have taken, they left a good deal behind. Specimens also remained near the coffin in the entrance passageway, but they were few and badly broken up.

Horse trappings and other military equipment dominated the artifact assemblage from Udozuka. Equestrian gear included about 75 specimens of a dozen types, including such items as iron bridle bits and chains, saddle cinch loops and buckles, rivets with ornamental heads, and various decorative fastenings. Weaponry included iron halberds, several long and short swords of iron, the remains of two wooden bows, and a large sheaf of 138 iron arrowheads. The arrowheads, which were long, slender rods broadened and flattened at the end rather like the blade of a screwdriver, were apparently mounted in socketed arrowshafts, which no longer remained. From the kinds and numbers of specimens, it appears that one full warrior's kit is represented in the grave, although body armor and helmet are conspicuously absent.

Items of personal adornment were few, including only two rings, one of gold and one of bronze, and a large number of small glass beads. A single bronze mirror may also have been a personal possession of the deceased.

Ceramic offerings were numerous and varied. Short and long-necked jars, bowls, plates, small and large pedestaled bowls, covered dishes, and composite vessels consisting of a large bowl with a series of small covered dishes attached to its rim were represented by one to three specimens each. As with the equestrian and battle gear, it appears that a single complete set of offering vessels was provided the principal personage of the tomb. Pottery of identical type found near the retainer's coffin establishes the general contemporaneity of the two burials, but, perhaps because of the later disturbance, a complete set was not found there.

The shattered remains of several *haniwa* figures, including a house, a warrior, and a set of body armor, were found in the passage outside the main chamber. *Haniwa* fragments were also discovered at several places atop the tumulus, although no consistent pattern of distribution was determined.

Udozuka Kofun has been dated to about the middle of the sixth century. This assessment is based on an established seriation of ceramic vessel and *haniwa* types, on the scale of the tumulus itself, and on indices of the relative length and width of burial chambers and entrance corridors developed from evidence at a number of sites. Within this temporal framework it is inferred from the relative size of the mound, and the scale of the stone burial chamber, that the occupant must have been the overlord of a major regional clan. Of more than 20 burial mounds in the same valley, spanning a time from the end of the fifth century to the close of the Kofun period in the seventh century, Udozuka is the largest. The earliest written records state that the lord of a clan believed to have occupied this region around the middle of the sixth century was a chieftain of middle rank within the political structure of the Yamato state, whose rule ended sometime before the year A.D. 587. This is reasonably close to the archaeologically ascribed date for Udozuka Kofun, and it seems quite possible that Udozuka is the tomb of this personage.

Reuse of the site as a place of ritual centuries after the Kofun period

Figure 5.24 Iron horse-bridle of the Late Kofun period, from Negata Kofun, Shizuoka Prefecture, central Honshu. Width, ca. 17 cm. (Shown about one-half actual size.) (Kyoto University Museum.)

Figure 5.23 Imported open metal-work horse trappings of the Middle Kofun period, from

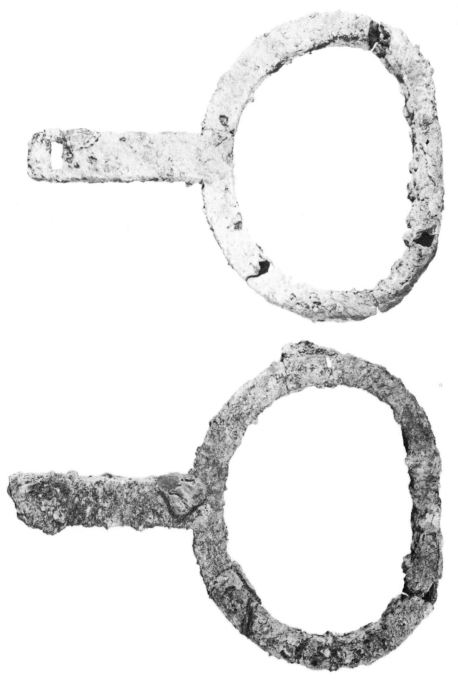

Figure 5.25 Iron stirrups of the Late Kofun period, from Shidani–Otsuka Kofun, city of Nagoya, Aichi Prefecture, south-central Honshu. Length of specimen at left, 24 cm. (Shown one-half actual size.) (Kyoto University Museum.)

Figure 5.26 Bronze bells and horse trappings of the Late Kofun period, from Shidani–Otsuka Kofun, city of Nagoya, Aichi Prefecture, south-central Honshu. Length of specimen at left, 24 cm. (Shown approximately one-quarter actual size.) (Kyoto University Museum.)

burials were made is indicated by evidence excavated at the inner end of the entrance passage to the tomb. Fragments of tile and porcelain of types historically dated to the twelfth century, and a thick lens of pure ash such as is derived from the burning of incense, were found there, suggesting use of the tunnel as a ceremonial grotto during medieval times. Quite likely this usage also dates the pillaging of the tomb, the excavations associated with that event having reestablished the existence of the sacred grotto after it had lain hidden for many centuries.

Shimanosho Ishibutai Kofun

Shimanosho Ishibutai Kofun is in the Asuka region at the southeastern corner of the Nara Basin, about 25 km south of the city of Nara (Hamada *et al.* 1937). It is one of the largest tombs of its type, and is believed by many students of the earliest native historical chronicles to be the resting place of an aristocrat of the seventh century, whose residence was at Shimanosho, and who died in the year A.D. 626. The tomb itself is of the megalithic type reported in the chronicles to have been in use during the earlier half of the seventh century.

In general plan and construction the stone-built burial chamber resembles those found within the keyhole-shaped tumuli of the later sixth century, having a long, narrow entrance passage leading into a somewhat wider, high-ceilinged burial chamber. The scale, however, is much larger and more massive. The Ishibutai dolmen at Shimanosho is 22 m in overall length, and stands 7 m from the base of its walls to the top of the huge rounded boulders that form its ceiling. The interior chamber is 8 m long and 3.5 m wide, with a ceiling 5 m above the floor. The 2-m-wide entrance passage is 12.5 m long, with a ceiling roughly 2 m high. Also, as in earlier tombs, a narrow drainage ditch filled with river cobbles ran from the back wall of the burial chamber to a point somewhat beyond the mouth of the entrance tunnel.

The stones of which the tomb was made are its most impressive feature, for their sheer size. The roof is made up of two great boulders, the larger of which was 5.4 m long, 3.8 m wide, and 2.7 m thick. This represents a volume of about 28 m³, and an estimated weight of 77 metric tons. The weight of its smaller companion stone is estimated at 64 metric tons. These stones were supported on walls made of a number of smaller, but still huge, boulders.

All the stones of the Ishibutai dolmen are of granite, from a source about 3 km away. Presumably the very large wooden sledges called *shura* were employed in the transportation of the boulders. *Shura* are described in the historic sources of a slightly later period, and actual specimens have been archaeologically discovered. The course from the source of the stones to the tomb site is mercifully downhill, but still the bringing of the great rocks must have required the labor of several hundred people, bullocks, and horses for weeks or months. The methods by which the rocks were raised into place can only be conjectured, but later techniques of megalithic building in Japan, and examples from other parts of the world, suggest that the stones were raised into position by dragging them up earthen ramps built for the purpose. Such ramps could have been raised progressively as the higher wall and ceiling stones were moved into place, thereafter serving as the base of the tumulus with which the stone chamber was covered after its completion, and which has since eroded entirely away.

Trenching outward from the edges of the stone dolmen revealed a large square earthen platform with sloping stone-paved walls, completely hidden by the earth eroded from the tumulus covering the stone chamber. At its base this platform measured 66 m square, and a second, smaller stage rested on the first. Atop the large, relatively low platform thus constructed, the stone tomb had been built and then covered by a mound that may have been either domed or rectangular.

Around the outside of the whole monument was a deep moat, no doubt the source of the earth used in building up the platform and burial mound. The moat, too, was square in plan, following the outline of the platform it enclosed. The cutting excavation was about 8 m wide, and around its outside edge was a built-up square bank, low, but slightly over 8 m in width. The sides of the moat and its surrounding bank were paved or riprapped with large cobbles, just as were the sides of the interior platform. The moat was not graded to a common level all around the platform, hence could only have been of the dry type.

The tomb was plundered long ago, perhaps 1000 years before the archaeologists got to it. No coffin remained, and the artifacts found in and about the burial chamber were a confused jumble of specimens ranging from Haji pottery of the Late Kofun period (seventh century) to bronze objects of the Nara and Heian periods (seventh–ninth centuries) and coins of the much later Tokugawa period (seventeenth-nineteenth centuries). The tomb may have been robbed as early as the ninth century, and was probably used thereafter as an occasional shelter and local shrine.

As the foregoing description shows, Ishibutai Kofun is very different from the burial tumuli of the preceding centuries. The stone burial chamber itself, though huge, is like those of the late sixth century, but the low square platform mound on which it rests departs radically from the shape and scope of the much larger and higher keyhole-shaped *kofun* that were its predecessors. The appearance of burial monuments in this new style, not only at Shimanosho but at a number of other places as well, coincides closely with the dawn of the historic age. Ishibutai Kofun, and others like it, were probably made within the memory of men still living at the time that scholars of the Yamato court were compiling the *Kojiki*, or *Record of Ancient Matters*, early in the eighth century.

Takamatsuzuka Kofun   Takamatsuzuka, a tomb in the village of Asuka not far from Shimanosho Ishibutai Kofun, is one of a group of mausolea dated to the latest part of the Kofun age. Nearby are tombs traditionally identified as those of the early emperor Temmu and the empress Jito. Takamatsuzuka was a small, round mound, 18 m in diameter and 5 m in height. The small rectangular burial chamber within was made of stone slabs, and had an entrance at one end. It was an aristocratic tomb, but clearly not that of a truly major personage.

The most significant features of this tomb, as well as of others first appearing in Japan during the sixth century—at first in Kyushu, later throughout much of the country—are the paintings found on the chamber walls. On the ceiling a stellar constellation is depicted. On the east wall, the sun and a blue dragon are centered, flanked by four men on one side, and four women on the other. On the west wall are the moon and a white tiger, again flanked by four men and four women. On the north wall a tortoise–snake spirit was represented. The figure presumably once present on the south wall is completely lost. The preserved figures portray three of the traditional Animals of the Four Quarters, which implies that the missing fourth figure would probably have been the red phoenix bird. The contents of the tomb had been plundered, leaving only a lacquered wooden coffin, some gilt and silver decorative plates, and a mirror of T'ang style.

The paintings at Takamatsuzuka are unique in their artistry and human representations, much more refined than the paintings found in the ornamented tombs of Kyushu and elsewhere. They closely resemble paintings known from Korean tombs, and the costumes of the women are clearly of Korean style. The tomb might well be that of a Korean associate of the early imperial court of the late seventh century, which was a time of intensive interaction between Japan and the continent.

Expansion of the Kofun Pattern and the Growth of the Japanese State

Details of *kofun* construction and contents could be multiplied almost endlessly, but the preceding examples suffice to show the main outlines of development in the form and furnishings of the major tombs of the Kinai region. In addition to the great, monumental tumuli of the heartland, lesser mounds of various types—rounded and square forms, among others—were constructed throughout the Kofun period (Kondo 1968). It was once thought that the various types were chronologically distinct, but much evidence now shows that a simple temporal explanation of this variability is not supportable. Data from several regions indicate that the differences are instead largely a reflection of sociopolitical relationships and economic subgroups that developed in the course of Kofun times.

The earliest Kofun sites known in Japan are those found in the old Yamato district, between Osaka, Nara, and Kyoto; this was clearly the center of Kofun development, where the grandest tumuli occurred and the densest concentrations existed (Suenaga 1961). The greatest *kofun* in all of Japan, that ascribed to the emperor Nintoku, lies near modern Osaka. With its length of 486 m, it is perhaps the largest earthen tomb structure in the world. Other tombs of lesser but still monumental size occur in the area. The largest *kofun* are traditionally identified as the graves of past Yamato emperors, and their excavation has been forbidden. Quite possibly they contain riches beyond anything known from the sites previously described. As for numbers of sites, an archaeological inventory of Nara Prefecture alone lists over 4500 burial mounds, and thousands more are known from surrounding areas.

In Yamato, impressively large tumuli were present from the very beginning of the Kofun period, showing that the distinctive keyhole-shaped form was from the outset closely identified with an established sociopolitical power able to marshal the labor of hundreds of people for extended periods of time. With a few notable exceptions the size of individual *kofun* tended to decrease later in the period, but at the same time there was a marked increase in the number of tumuli constructed. With this increase in numbers came the formation of groups of many relatively small *kofun* clustered around a few large, dominant ones, and the growth of a societal hierarchy of power and wealth is clearly attested in the contrasts of scale and richness of content that such groups afford. A societal structure of several apparent levels was well developed in the Yamato region before the close of the Early Kofun period.

The main economic base for these developments was unquestionably wet-rice agriculture. A substantial farming population had been well established in the region since Yayoi times, and it is a fundamental and crucial fact of Japanese geography and history that the Osaka–Nara–Kyoto area comprises by far the largest and most favored expanse of prime agricultural land in the entire country. Added to this are the transportational and economic advantages of its central location within easy reach of the Inland Sea, the Pacific Ocean, and the Japan Sea; its proximity to the seaboard and mountain routes into the Tokyo region; and its access to the products of mountainous central Honshu.

Not surprisingly, given these circumstances, Yamato became a region of great wealth, fostering not only agriculture but many specialized industries as well. Potters' villages, fishing villages, saltmaking sites, lapidary workshops, smithies, foundries, and other artisans' quarters uncovered by archaeologists indicate a flourishing and diversified economy. And the many large and small *kofun* to be found throughout the region show that an elite class of managers and high-level consumers flourished with it.

It has been suggested that the keyhole-shaped tumulus was specifically symbolic of a tie between the personage buried therein and the seat of Yamato power, and it is striking that in Early Kofun times, as keyhole-shaped tumuli spread across the country, they tended to appear first at points of importance for transportation and communication. In later times, after the country was secured, the tumuli were concentrated in the economically most important regions, and it is surely not mere coincidence that major *kofun* groups, including some very large keyhole-shaped tumuli, exist at places like Tsukushi (northern Kyushu), Kibi (Inland Sea region), Owari (central Honshu), and Kenu (western Tokyo region), which are named in the eighth century *Kojiki* and *Nihon Shoki* as major centers of the Yamato dominion. The fact that *kofun* groups of this kind appeared later in Kyushu and the Tokyo region than they did in Yamato is suggestive of a gradual spread of Yamato political and economic control outward into the hinterlands.

The earliest *kofun* in Kyushu are found in the north, in the rich coastal lands of Fukuoka and Oita prefectures, at spots well situated to serve as bases for marine transportation and commerce. Ishizukayama Kofun, Akatsuka Kofun, and Haraguchi Kofun, among the oldest of the keyhole-shaped tumuli in Kyushu, are dated by their architectural proportions, burial chamber type, and *haniwa*, mirrors, and other contents, to about the early fourth century. In archaeological terms, they correspond to tumuli that in the Yamato heartland are placed somewhat after the initial phases of the Early Kofun period.

By early in the fifth century, keyhole-shaped tumuli had expanded beyond their original coastal distribution, and appeared throughout Kyushu, from Kagoshima Prefecture in the south to the island of Tsushima in the Korea Strait on the north. In many cases these *kofun* appear in groups, a number of lesser mounds being associated with one or more larger ones. There is general agreement among most specialists that this spread was brought about by developments generated in the Yamato region, and that it probably reflects the absorption of Kyushu's local elites into the Yamato sociopolitical structure.

By about the middle of the fifth century, at Marukumayama Kofun, Yokotashimo Kofun, and other northern Kyushu sites, there appeared burial chambers that were entered via a side passage, making access to the tomb possible even after the original interment had been completed. At about the same time there began to appear large, sculptured stone figures of men and horses associated with the tumuli, incised and painted decoration on the inside walls of the burial chambers, new kinds of ornamental artifacts, and a new type of dark, wheel-made, high-fired pottery known as Sue ware. These elements were all new to Japan, and all clearly had Korean antecedents. Following their introduction into Kyushu, these traits spread rapidly throughout the Inland Sea and Yamato, and into the Tokyo region and beyond (Amakasu 1966; Oda 1966).

Throughout the Inland Sea region, just as in Kyushu, Early Kofun burial mounds of *zenpo-koen* form are most commonly found along the coast or on small islands near bays, where harbors might be established. The pattern is quite general, being recognized in the vicinity of Hiroshima, southern Okayama Prefecture, and Hyogo Prefecture on Honshu, as well as in Kagawa Prefecture on the island of Shikoku. The earliest keyhole-shaped tombs found in this region belong to the second and third phases of the Early Kofun period, and it is reasonable to infer, as many have done, that their appearance is evidence of the establishment of Yamato influence at key marine centers and shipping points along the Inland Sea.

By the latter half of the fourth century, the *kofun* of southern Okayama Prefecture were growing in scale, and by the fifth century there appeared tumuli of very large size. These larger *kofun* were in the interior, along major river valleys, where the best and most extensive agricultural lands were to be found. Soon after the appearance of the very large keyhole-shaped tumuli, lesser ones began to appear around them, in subsidiary groups that seem to reflect the presence of a lesser nobility surrounding the major figures of a region. Although often the lesser *kofun* were of *zenpo-koen* form, many were not, being simply round or square mounds.

The same pattern is evident in Kagawa Prefecture on Shikoku, where Chausuyama Kofun, the largest keyhole-shaped mound known there, is surrounded by 10 lesser tumuli. Other centers have been identified throughout southwestern Honshu, even on the Japan Sea side of the country, though there the centers tended to be smaller and farther between, as might be expected in such a remote region.

In the early sixth century the first side-passage tombs appeared in southwestern Honshu, and as in Kyushu metal headgear, gold earrings, and various horse trappings of Korean inspiration (if not Korean make) appeared at about the same time. Thus was the Korean influence previously noted as occurring at about this time in Kyushu reflected in the Inland Sea region as well.

In the Late Kofun period there appeared at many locations clusters of very small burial tumuli, usually round or square rather than of *zenpo-koen* form. A number of specialized industrial sites are dated to about the same time, and the conjunction suggests that increasing craft specialization and commerce may lie behind the development of such minor *kofun* groups. Increasing commercial activity might well have given rise to a petty aristocracy of merchant princes and bureaucrats who could afford the pomp of mound burial, on a small scale at least, but who were not entitled to use the distinctive keyhole-shaped *kofun* form with its connotations of Yamato power and allegiance (Amakasu 1966; Nishikawa *et al.* 1966).

That production of metal tools from the iron sands of southwestern Honshu was an important industry by about mid-Kofun times is suggested by the finding of pig iron and iron shards at Rokutsuzuka Kofun in Okayama Prefecture, and by analyses indicating that swords from another *kofun* in the same region were made of metal derived from red iron sands. It is believed that a number of regional centers in

Hyogo, Hiroshima, and Yamaguchi prefectures may actually have been engaged in iron production, inasmuch as blacksmiths' tools have been recovered in considerable numbers from Kofun sites there.

Industrial salt production is also indicated for certain locations in the Inland Sea region, based on the finding of sites, on small islands and along the coasts, which contain much coarse, porous pottery of a special type suitable for rapid evaporation of seawater. Some such sites have been found in the vicinity of side-passage tombs, suggesting that they date to the later parts of the Kofun period.

Ceramic kilns engaged in the mass production of wheel-made Sue ware are also known from several sites in southwestern Honshu. Wakasano in Hyogo Prefecture and Tozeiike in Okayama Prefecture are two well-known manufacturing sites of the Late Kofun period, and others are known from Hiroshima Prefecture as well. It is speculated that specialized potters' villages, such as have existed throughout historic times in Japan, may have originated at about this time. Wheel-made Sue ware is abundant in Late Kofun graves, and the large fired-clay coffins that appear during the closing phases of Late Kofun times were obviously the work of ceramic specialists.

The Kofun pattern also spread north and east from Yamato. On the coast of the Japan Sea north of Kyoto the earliest *kofun* are simple, round tumuli that perhaps indicate the existence of an independent local aristocracy, but by the end of the fourth century the *zenpo-koen* form had appeared, signaling the extension of Yamato influence into the area.

In this region several village sites contained lapidary tools and materials to indicate that curved and tubular beads, bracelets, and other ornaments were manufactured from local stone. The Katayamatsu site in Ishikawa Prefecture, for example, has yielded evidence of over 35 workshop areas, suggesting that it was an artisans' village specializing in the production of jewelry. It seems quite possible that the extension of Yamato power into the region may be related to the lapidary industry there, which produced items of great importance as status symbols to the increasingly numerous and powerful aristocratic class. The indented coasts of Ishikawa and Fukui prefectures around Wakase Bay also provided excellent points of departure for an over-water route to Korea via the Japan Sea, which would not have been exposed to potential interference from local chieftains in the way that the Inland Sea route was (Takahori and Yoshioka 1966).

In the great Kanto Plain, the site of modern Tokyo, the earliest *kofun* were relatively small and usually round rather than keyhole shaped. It is believed that they may reflect the emergence of local chieftains out of the preceding Yayoi culture, who had not yet been brought into the Yamato network. Significantly, the first *kofun* of *zenpo-koen* form are found at the western and southern edges of the Tokyo region, at gateways to the two natural routes leading through the central mountains and along the Pacific seaboard from the Yamato heartland.

The mountain road seems to have played a particularly important role in the expansion of Yamato influence into the Tokyo region, as is shown by the occurrence in *kofun* from Gumma Prefecture of Chinese bronze mirrors that are mates of specimens from the very important trove found at Otsukayama Kofun near Kyoto. It is even more interesting that the several *kofun* displaying either direct or indirect connections with Otsukayama are all small, suggesting that Yamato power began its expansion here by taking in the petty chieftains of the Tokyo region one by one.

Kofun tombs from along the Pacific shore southwest of Tokyo have also produced bronze mirrors that are mates of some from Kyoto's Otsukayama Kofun. The earliest tumuli to appear to this area were already of *zenpo-koen* form. This fact, their relative sparsity, their stepping-stone-like distribution, and their rich complements of burial goods, all suggest that they may have been directly established by Yamato forces.

In general, the artifactual content of the earliest tumuli from the Tokyo region indicates that the Yamato incursion began in the late fourth or early fifth century, about a half-century or more after the establishment of the Kofun pattern in the Osaka–Nara–Kyoto region.

It is characteristic of the Early Kofun period throughout the Tokyo region that really large *kofun* remained extremely few, whereas smaller ones were much more common. This suggests that the area was dominated by just a few major lords, in contrast to the Yamato region, where there seems to have been a much larger upper-level aristocracy. Furthermore, throughout the Kofun period the largest and richest sites were in the northwest, mainly in Gumma Prefecture, where the Yamato influence was first established. This area, astride a major route to the Osaka–Nara–Kyoto nexus, always exhibited close ties with it, as shown by the abundance of bronze mirrors and other grave goods of the latest styles there.

The wave of continental influence that swept through Kyushu, the Inland Sea, and Yamato was also felt in the Tokyo region. Metal goods of continental styles, particularly horse trappings and the various appurtenances of mounted warriors, are well attested in the tumuli of Late Kofun times. Side-passage tombs and Sue ware ceramics also appeared. These developments are dated to the end of the sixth century, approximately half a century later than their appearance farther south.

As elsewhere, there was a great proliferation of very small tumulus graves in Late Kofun times, and again the most plausible explanation seems to be that they reflect the emergence of a commercial class of some wealth. One notable craft specialization that emerged at about this time in the Tokyo region was a vigorous and creative tradition in the manufacture of *haniwa* figurines. This industry developed a large series of distinctive animal, human, and architectural forms, as well as figures depicting military equipment, tools, and other items. Other industries in ceramics, metals, stoneworking, and the like are implied by the archaeological evidence.

The basic pattern of Kofun burial ceremonialism persisted in the Tokyo region for quite some time after it had passed away in Yamato. The latest large keyhole-shaped tumuli of the Tokyo region may have been completed as much as a century after such forms ceased to be built farther south. Bronze bowls and other items, which in Yamato are associated with early historic Buddhist sites, are in the Tokyo region still to be found as Kofun burial offerings. Very large megalithic burial chambers, such as appeared at Shimanosho Ishibutai in Yamato after the *zenpo-koen* tumulus form had been abandoned there, are still found associated with keyhole-shaped tumuli in the Tokyo region (Amakasu and Kubo 1966).

Several large keyhole-shaped tumuli, and many smaller ones, are known from the vicinity of the city of Sendai in northeastern Honshu. Farther north, the evidence quickly becomes attenuated. Small, poorly furnished burial mounds have been found at various places throughout northeastern Honshu, but most of them are very late in time, probably corresponding to the fully historic Nara period farther south. The social changes affecting the rest of Japan were echoed in the north, but the area was clearly a remote and isolated frontier presided over by petty chieftains only distantly in touch with the center (Ujiie and Kato 1966).

In Hokkaido this was even more strongly the case. At Ebetsu and Eniwa near the modern city of Sapporo, some very small, low mound graves containing iron swords and pottery of Sue type give evidence of contact with developments to the south, but the level of social organization clearly did not approach that associated with the Kofun period elsewhere. Moreover, these graves postdate the Kofun period by centuries, apparently being contemporaneous with the late Nara or early Heian periods of Japanese history, thus roughly dating within a century or so of A.D. 1000 (Sakurai 1966).

Haniwa *and the Life of the*
Aristocracy

Virtually the entire archaeological record of the Kofun period pertains in some way to the life of the aristocracy, and the preceding discussion has already illustrated many aspects of it. As a resource of unusual richness bearing on the court life of the period, however, the fired-clay figures called *haniwa* merit a few additional notes.

Haniwa were made expressly as ceremonial objects of symbolic significance for use in funerary ritual associated with upper-class burials. In ancient China, beautifully lifelike fired-clay figures were associated with imperial burials, as in the case of the legendary emperor Ch'in Shih Huang Ti, part of whose vast tomb complex has yielded an entire army, consisting of thousands of realistic life-sized ceramic portrait models of soldiers and horses arrayed in marching formation (Topping and Yang 1978). In Kofun period Japan, the clay figures were not so magnificent or so numerous, and they were placed atop and around the edges of burial tumuli rather than in underground chambers, but there is little doubt that the Japanese custom was inspired by continental practices.

The earliest *haniwa* were simple fired-clay cylinders (the word means "clay ring"), perhaps representing jars and urns. These may have been symbolic storage containers, standing for offerings of food and wine. Later *haniwa* were much more expressive, reflecting in some detail the social roles, material culture, and architectural forms associated with the life of the upper class (Kondo and Harunari 1967).

A very famous set of *haniwa* figures from Chausuyama Kofun in Gumma Prefecture seem to reflect a grand ceremonial occasion, perhaps commemorative of an important event in the life of the personage whose burial tumulus they adorned. The series depicted an enthroned official, his female consort seated opposite him, presiding over a scene that included 12 warriors in armor, 12 functionaries wearing court dress and broad ceremonial swords, and 12 dancing women. Subsidiary figures included a row of horses attended by grooms, and a number of swans and roosters. Additional social roles are pictured by *haniwa* from other sites. Musicians are well represented, playing such instruments as the Japanese harp, or *koto,* the hand drum, and the mandolin-like *biwa.* Falconers, boar-keepers, deer-keepers, and farmers, the last identified as such by the hoes or sickles they carried, are also known.

Military attire and equipment are particularly well attested by *haniwa* representations. Warriors are shown in riveted helmets with cheekpieces and various ornamental crests, wearing heavy flared tunics and broad-legged trousers. Swords were invariably slung from a belt around the waist, and metal vests or cuirasses covered the upper bodies of some figures. War-horses carried high saddles and simple ringlike stirrups, and wore bridles and other trappings decorated by bells and a variety of ornamental fastenings.

Differences in the social rank of various status positions are clearly shown by the relative sizes of *haniwa* figures, by the degree of care with which they were executed, by the positioning of figures within groups, and by the degree of completeness of representations of various types. Important personages were shaped in full round, with detailed features, and lesser people such as court entertainers were shown as half-figures. Farmers were often represented by simple cylinders with only abbreviated facial features. That Kofun society was strongly class conscious, the *haniwa* that have come down to us leave no doubt.

Buildings were also frequently modeled. The most common architectural type was a large rectangular house of one story, with a high, steeply pitched gable roof and broad, deep side windows. No foundations are shown, and it appears that the structures represented may have possessed sunken floors—which indeed other archaeological evidence shows Kofun period houses to have had. Several known models depict two-story town houses or pavilions with bungalow-type roofs and even verandas, and one very famous model shows a fairly complex building consisting of a main central structure having four attached wings. From such *haniwa* it is evident that the buildings of the Kofun period were already cast in the general form that has persisted down to the present as the basis of traditional Japanese architecture (Tsuboi *et al.* 1977).

Hiraide: Village Life during the Kofun Period

The domestic village life of the Kofun period is known from only a few excavated sites, but several of these have proven extremely informative. Thus, even though details of regional variation and chronological change remain inadequately documented because of the smallness of the archaeological sample, we nevertheless have a good, concrete view of many aspects of day-to-day life among Kofun period villagers (Figures 5.27–5.34). Of the residential sites known, perhaps the most thoroughly studied and fully reported is the village of Hiraide, in the mountains of central Honshu's Nagano Prefecture, about 200 km northwest of Tokyo (Hiraide Iseki Chosa Kai 1955). In most general respects the view of farm life during the Kofun period that this site affords is duplicated by such other sites as yield records adequate for comparison (such as Nakada, in Tokyo's western suburbs), and Hiraide will serve well here as an exemplar of what is currently known.

A modern village clusters at the foot of a range of wooded hills, on the edge of the broad alluvial plain of the Narai River. Archaeological remains were found scattered over an area about 1 km long and .5 km wide, close to the modern settlement but slightly farther out on the river plain. The modern village and the archaeological site are both called Hiraide. Around Hiraide are many springs, including a very large one that is said never to have dried since ancient times, and from which the name of the locality is derived. The place has been a favored residential location for at least 5000 years, as shown by the occurrence there of Middle Jomon houses and Yayoi period pottery, found during the same investigations as exposed the later village that is of interest here.

The domestic life of the common people apparently changed little from Kofun times well into the historic Heian period. This is reflected at Hiraide, which paleomagnetic dates and comparative ceramic chronology indicate was occupied from roughly A.D. 450 to 1100. This span falls within what is often referred to by archaeologists as the Haji period, the name being derived from a particular kind of easily recognized domestic brownware pottery of Yayoi antecedents that was made throughout the Kofun, Nara, and Heian periods. There is some potential for archaeological confusion in subsuming three periods under yet a fourth term, but it is appropriate and convenient to speak of the Haji period when referring to the life of the common people, inasmuch as their cultural history was punctuated by a different rhythm than that affecting the aristocracies whose political and ceremonial behavior gave rise to the monuments and events that demarcate the Kofun, Nara, and Heian periods.

Nearly 50 houses of the Haji period were partly or wholly excavated at Hiraide, and more no doubt remain to be discovered. In a number of cases, houses had been built over the remains of previous structures, rendering some architectural details difficult to make out. However, about 30 house floors were well enough preserved to allow a clear understanding of the basic architectural patterns of the village. All the houses were semisubterranean, with floors dug approximately .5 m below the ground surface as it existed at the time of construction. Most were square or nearly so, but slightly elongate rectangular structures were also found. Most of the house pits measured between 5 and 6 m across, but units as small as 4.5 m, and as large as 8 m across were also found (Figure 5.27).

Most of the houses had four main roof-support pillars, deeply seated in large pits in the floor, and from the varying positions of these postholes and others encircling the house pits, the existence of several variant superstructure types is inferred. All houses are believed to have had pitched roofs with overhanging eaves, and a single entryway near one corner. One building was reconstructed on the basis of the exca-

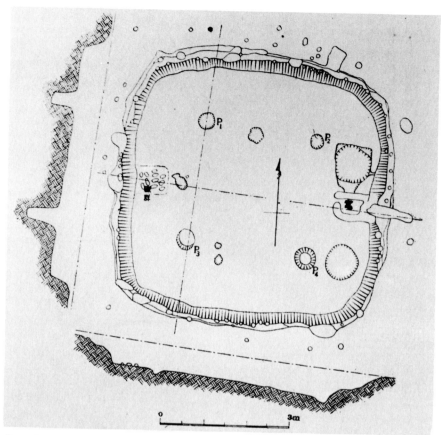

Figure 5.27 Plan and sections of house pit of Haji (Kofun) period House 3 at Hiraide, Nagano Prefecture, central Honshu. P_1, P_2, etc. indicate pits in which main roof support posts were footed. (From Hiraide Iseki Chosa Kai 1955:Figure 22.)

vation findings, informed by the further evidence of the many fired-clay *haniwa* house models recovered from burial sites of the Kofun period. From this reconstruction it is evident that the rural folk of this time lived in substantial, spacious dwellings not conspicuously different from the farmhouses of later historical periods (Figure 5.28).

Inside, a small stovelike feature, dome shaped with a round receptacle in the top for a pottery vessel, and having a flue leading out under the wall of the house, was almost invariably installed against one edge of the house pit. These are termed *kamado*, after the traditional ceramic device used for steaming rice up until recent times. The earlier specimens were made of clay; units built up of stone were more common in the later houses.

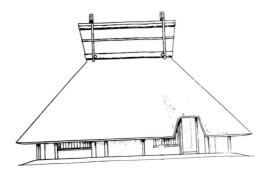

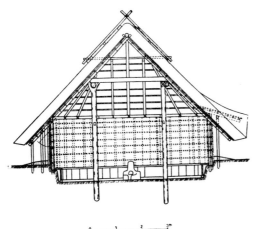

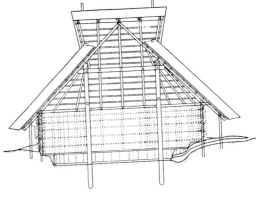

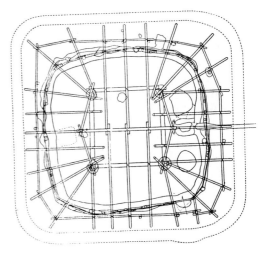

Figure 5.28 Reconstruction of House 3 at Hiraide, Nagano Prefecture, central Honshu. Based on evidence from excavations and clay *Haniwa* models of Kofun period houses. (From Hiraide Iseki Chosa Kai 1955:Figure 128.)

A

B

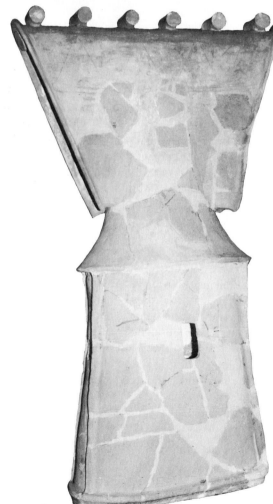

C

Figure 5.29 Clay *haniwa* house models of the Kofun period. A, Provenience unknown. Height, ca. 40 cm. B, Middle Kofun period Hashita Kofun, Tottori Prefecture, southern Honshu. Height, 29.7 cm. C, Late Kofun period, Myojinyama Kofun, Gumma Prefecture, central Honshu. Height, 99.8 cm. (Kyoto University Museum.)

Figure 5.30 Haji ware jar of the Middle Kofun period from the Karako site, Nara Prefecture, south-central Honshu. Height, 14.4 cm. (Shown approximately one-half actual size.) (Kyoto University Museum.)

In most houses the stovelike *kamado,* built against one wall, was the only structure expressly made for using fire. A few houses, however, had fireplaces rather than *kamado.* From this, and evidence from other sites as well, it appears that there occurred in early Haji times an important change in the use of fire within Japanese dwellings. Throughout Jomon and Yayoi times, a centrally located fireplace had been standard household furniture. Its central placement allowed the fireplace to function effectively in heating and illuminating the house, as well as in cooking. The *kamado* of the Haji period houses, however, were clearly specialized for cooking, especially the steaming of cereals, and neither their enclosed structure nor their placement at one side of the house against a wall suited them for the functions of heating and illumination. The shift from the use of central hearths to the use of the *kamado* manifestly took place during the time of the Haji period village at Hiraide, and the change suggests not only a shift in culinary prac-tices but also a different approach to the heating and illumination of the dwelling. Perhaps the unheated residences for which Japan is famous to this day reflect the history of the Haji period!

Three separate sets of deep postholes, systematically arranged in parallel rows to outline one small and two large rectangular patterns, were found near the eastern end of the Haji period settlement. It is believed that these pits held the bases of pillars supporting high-floored storage buildings. No domestic floor features or artifacts were found in association with them, and they conform in general to the

Figure 5.31 Haji ware jar of the Late Kofun period from Nishiyama Kofun 4, Kyoto Prefecture, south-central Honshu. Height, 33 cm. (Shown approximately one-half actual size.) (Kyoto University Museum.)

Figure 5.32 Pedestaled Haji ware jar with handle, of the Late Kofun period from Inamurayama Kofun, Shiga Prefecture, south-central Honshu. Height, 12 cm. (Kyoto University Museum.)

plan and dimensions of storage structures known from early historic times. The smallest building was about 4 m square, and the largest, only slightly bigger than its other companion, was about 7 m across. The intervals between postholes appear to have been measured in terms of the Japanese foot, or *shaku,* as it was defined in the Heian period. From this, and the fact that a house containing pottery of the Heian period was found nearby, these structures are attributed to that time. It is speculated that these storehouses, and the nearby residence, mark the precincts of the village headman. As local representative of the regional overlord, the headman might expectably have had the

Figure 5.33 Pedestaled Haji ware cup of the Late Kofun period from Shinmeiyama Kofun, Kyoto Prefecture, south-central Honshu. Height, 10.5 cm. (Kyoto University Museum.)

role of concentrating the profits of the villager's agricultural labors in such a place.

The agricultural output of the Haji farmers is directly attested by the finding of charred rice, barley, taro, and Japanese pepper in one of the houses. From another came millet, from another plum pits, and from yet another came rice and broad beans, as well as chestnuts, which were probably gathered in the woods around the settlement. Bones of horses, cows, and chickens were also recovered, from still other structures. The inventory of remains shows that both dry-field and wet-field farming were practiced by the ancient villagers, as they still are at modern Hiraide. Beans, which require much water and do well in heavy soil, may have been a fall-season crop planted in the paddies after the rice harvest. Horses, cows, and chickens could have provided fertilizer for the fields. In short, it appears that all the basic

Figure 5.34 Haji ware hearth and steamer of the Late Kofun period from Sanjo Kofun, Hyogo Prefecture, south-central Honshu. At right, assembled (shown one-half actual size); below, disassembled to show parts. Height, 23.5 cm. (Kyoto University Museum.)

products and practices of traditional Japanese agriculture as known from historic times were in use at ancient Hiraide.

Artifacts related to agricultural pursuits reflect cultivation, storage, and food preparation. A large U-shaped iron blade undoubtedly served as a cutting edge or "shoe" for a wooden hoe; such iron-shod tools are well known from later historic times. Iron reaping knives, or sickles, were also found. Large, deep jars and pots for storage, pots for cooking, and finely made bowls and dishes for serving were all well represented in the ceramic inventory. Pottery types included relatively low-fired brownish Haji ware, dark gray or black high-fired Sue ware, and a high-fired light-colored glazed ware.

Domestic chores are reflected by iron chisels, knives, and needles, and a whetstone for sharpening such implements. Stone spindle whorls complement the needle finds in suggesting the household manufacture and use of cloth. Iron projectile points suggest that hunting was still important in the household economy, though these specimens might also be taken to reflect involvement at the village level in the political strife of Kofun and early historic times.

Household ceremonialism, or at any rate the special serving of food as a form of expression, is attested by the very well made pedestaled vessels and covered dishes of Sue or glazed ware that were found in many houses. The offering of food and drink to household and local spirits, using special vessels for the purpose, is a well-known Shinto religious practice and continues to flourish in modern Japan. Other items of undoubted ceremonial importance are stone *magatama* beads, in both plain and elaborated forms. Their relative abundance in the Kofun burials of the time, and their status even now as symbols of the imperial household, make clear their association with high social status and religious symbolism.

That the Hiraide villagers must have been bound in some way to a higher political authority is a forgone conclusion, given the abundant evidence throughout southern and central Japan of the rise of a dominant ruling class during the Kofun period. Hiraide was in a remote rural area, but Kofun burial sites nevertheless occur in the region. Even though the village was undoubtedly part of a class-stratified society, however, there were no conspicuous differences in the wealth of its constituent households, and thus no evidence to suggest significant stratification within the village society itself. Nevertheless, it is plain that some degree of coordination and control was necessary to such a settlement, and the investigators suggest that the internal social structure of the village may have been comparable to that of historic Hiraide under the feudalism of later times.

During the Edo period (1600–1867), Hiraide was composed of a number of compact residential groups in turn composed of related families. These groups farmed adjacent lands and managed their own irrigation waters, which were channeled from a series of different springs found along the base of the hills behind the settlement. These groups were political as well as economic entities, which engaged not only in cooperative farming but also in petty factionalism and the formation of marriage alliances that would enhance the influence of individual groups within the village. The head of the strongest family within the most influential group was generally the local representative of the region's feudal lord, and this was a position that both validated and reinforced the intravillage preeminence of the group to which the headman belonged.

Beyond the Northern Frontier

In Hokkaido, a class-stratified society analogous to that known farther south did not develop during prehistoric times. Only some very small mound graves near Sapporo, containing iron swords and Sue pottery imported from Honshu, give evidence of tendencies toward the development of an aristocracy, and these tendencies clearly did not proceed very far. Other events to the south were, however, reflected in the basically egalitarian Satsumon culture, which flourished throughout Hokkaido coevally with the Haji, or Kofun–Nara–Heian, period on Honshu (Figures 5.35–5.37).

Some influential scholars fix the dates of Satsumon between about the eighth and thirteenth centuries A.D., but it may well have begun at least several hundred years earlier. Satsumon pottery bears unmistakable resemblance to the Haji ware of the Kofun and later periods on Honshu, and ^{14}C dates on two Satsumon houses in northeastern Hokkaido suggest a beginning date for the period as early as the fourth century. Some consider these dates extreme, but they are nevertheless within the established range for Haji pottery farther south.

The site of Sakaeura II, on the shore of the Okhotsk Sea in northeastern Hokkaido, affords an excellent example of Satsumon period architecture and material culture. From this very large and long-occupied site, on a long sand ridge lying between an old cutoff channel of the Tokoro River and the seashore, several Satsumon pithouses have been excavated. Two of these, virtually identical in form and content, illustrate the character of the Satsumon pattern (Komai 1963; Tokyo Daigaku Kokogaku Kenkyushitsu 1972).

House 1 was almost perfectly square, about 8 m across, and was dug down about .5 m beneath the level of the ancient land surface (Figure 5.35). A series of eight pits, which once held roof-support pillars, were placed equidistant from one another in the form of a square, set in about 1.5–2 m from the side walls of the house pit. Three unlined hearths lay in a row, slightly off the centerline of the floor. Near one corner of the east wall was found a small domed *kamado* structure made of clay, which had in its top a hole about 15 cm in diameter. Heavy fire-reddening showed that the unit had served as a stove, and directly behind it the edge of the pit had been cut back about 1 m to provide a sloping flue leading out under the wall of the house superstructure. Near the other corner of the east wall, a sloping ramp cut through the edge of the house pit apparently served as an entryway, and two large postholes found there are believed to have held pillars supporting some sort of shelter or porch built over the opening in the house wall. This house form—semisubterranean, large and square, with stoves and entryways built against the walls—was without a doubt inspired by the domestic architecture of the Kofun period, which it mimics completely.

Charcoal from the floor of House 1 returned a ^{14}C date of 1070 B.P., placing the house in the ninth or tenth centuries A.D. House 2, only slightly larger than House 1 and with the same interior features, was ^{14}C dated at 1610 B.P., or to the fourth century A.D. Both dates fall within the time range implied by the Haji-like Satsumon pottery from the site, and confirm the essential contemporaneity of this cultural manifestation with the Kofun, Nara, and Heian periods of the southern islands.

Sixteen complete or restorable pottery vessels from House 1, and several others from House 2, were of two basic shapes. Most numerous were deep vaselike pots, incurved at the base, with flat bottoms. These varied considerably in size, the largest being 44 cm tall, the smallest only 9 cm tall. Less common were pedestaled bowls, usually less than 10 cm tall, and up to 20 cm in diameter. Most of the ceramic specimens were decorated with bands of diagonal incised lines just below the rim; the lower portions of the vessels were plain or lightly striated. In form these vessels are very like Haji types known from Honshu, but they depart from the Haji pattern in details of decoration.

Artifacts of other kinds were not numerous. Four discoidal spindle whorls of fired clay were found in House 1, and a single specimen came from House 2. They were rather large and heavy, the biggest measuring 7 cm in diameter and over 1 cm in thickness. Two matched specimens were found together, prompting the excavators to note that the spinning technique practiced among the historic Ainu employed paired spindle whorls. Stone tools were very few. A stemmed scraper, two diamond-shaped projectile points with contracting stems, several nondescript scrapers, a small hand-held grinding stone and a larger grinding slab exhaust the lithic artifact inventory of the two excavated

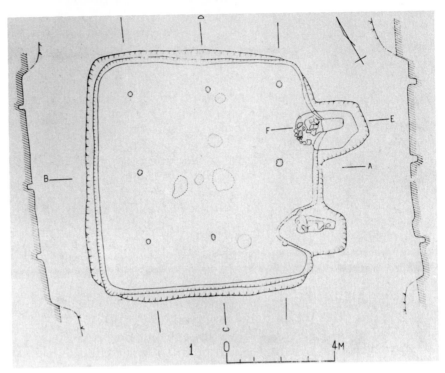

Figure 5.35 Plan and sections of Satsumon period house pit, Sakaeura II site, Hokkaido. Compare with Figure 5.27. (From Komai 1963:Figure 8.)

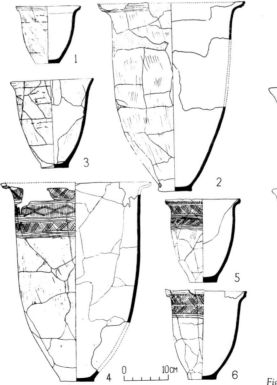

Figure 5.36 Satsumon period pots from the Sakaeura II site, Hokkaido. (From Komai 1963:Figure 19.)

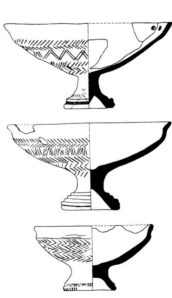

Figure 5.37 Pedestaled Satsumon period bowls from the Sakaeura I site, Hokkaido. Height of upper specimen, 10 cm. (From Komai 1963:Figure 5.)

structures. Stone tools are characteristically scarce in Satsumon sites, presumably because iron tools were by then in use and had replaced cutting implements of stone for most purposes. Iron has indeed been found in Satsumon sites, though usually in all but unidentifiable condition because of decomposition.

Cultivation of cereals apparently became widely established in Hokkaido during the Satsumon period, though no evidence of this was found at Sakaeura II. The characteristic stoves of Satsumon (as of Kofun) houses are believed to have functioned primarily in the boiling and steaming of grains, and at the Toyotomi site, millet, green beans, and a metal plowshare were found in association with Satsumon pottery. Additional evidence of cereal cultivation comes from the Nishitsukigaoka site, in extreme northeastern Hokkaido, where a quantity of charred millet was found on the floor of a burned Satsumon house (Yawata 1966).

The Sakaeura II site, and others along Hokkaido's northern seacoasts, also yielded evidence of a distinctively non-Japanese culture of northern maritime type. This is the Okhotsk culture, named for the fact that it occurs along the shores of the Okhotsk Sea in Hokkaido and Sakhalin, and in the Kurile Islands, which lead like stepping-stones northward from Hokkaido toward the peninsula of Kamchatka (Figures 5.38–5.45).

Sites of the Satsumon and Okhotsk cultures co-occur all along the northern seaboard of Hokkaido, and in some sites around the mouth of the Tokoro River houses of both cultures are found together. The general contemporaneity of the two cultures is established by the occurrence of both Satsumon and Okhotsk pottery on the same house floors at sites such as Sakaeura II, Rausu, and Omambetsu, and by a parallel series of overlapping ^{14}C dates (Komai 1963, 1964; Oba and Ohyi 1973; Tokyo Daigaku Kokogaku Kenkyushitsu 1972; Yawata 1966).

One of the best preserved and most fully reported representatives of the Okhotsk culture is the site of Tokoro Chashi, located several kilometers from Sakaeura II, on a high point near the mouth of the Tokoro River (Komai 1964). The word *chashi* means "fortress" in the Ainu language, and fortification ditches that were cut across the site after its abandonment as a dwelling place by Okhotsk people confirm that it served that function in later times. Two large rectangulate pithouses excavated at this site produced an abundance of Okhotsk pottery and other specimens. A ^{14}C date of 990 B.P. (tenth century A.D.) on charcoal from House 1 established the approximate age of the Okhotsk culture occupation there.

Initial excavations in the depression marking House 1 yielded some

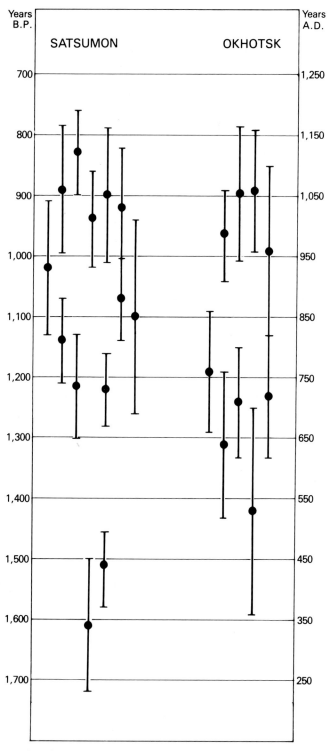

Figure 5.38 Carbon-14 dates for Satsumon and Okhotsk pithouses in northeastern Hokkaido. (Data from Tokyo Daigaku Kokugaku Kenkyushitsu 1972:489–490.)

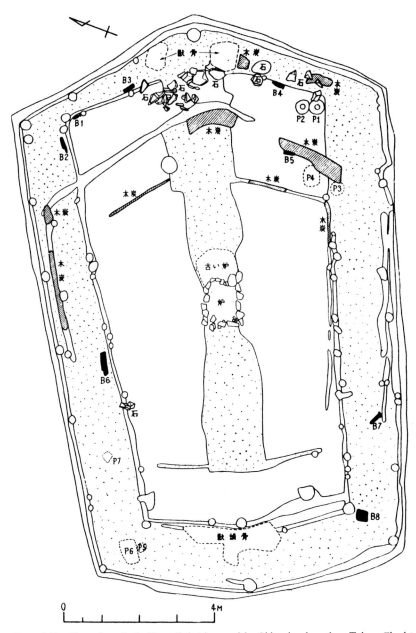

Figure 5.39 Floor plan of a double-walled pithouse of the Okhotsk culture from Tokoro Chashi, Hokkaido. The plan of a later house, smaller but of identical type, is superimposed inside the original structure. (From Komai 1964:Figure 14.)

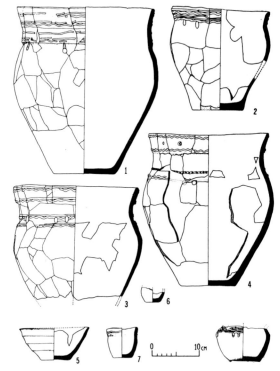

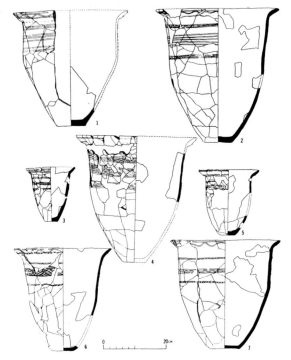

Figure 5.40   Okhotsk pottery from Tokoro Chashi, Hokkaido. (From Komai 1964:Figure 63.)

Figure 5.41   Transitional Okhotsk–Satsumon pots of the Late Okhotsk period from the Tobinitai site, Hokkaido. These vessels are decorated in typically Okhotsk style, but are of typical Satsumon shapes. (From Komai 1964:Figure 102.)

timbers and a wooden bowl in an advanced stage of decomposition, the rusted remains of iron hooks or needles, iron blades, and the sherds of iron kettles. Beneath these remains, which are attributed to the historic Ainu, lay a stratum of dark soil, 30–40 cm thick, containing few artifacts. Immediately below this was a layer of burned earth and charcoal, rich in Okhotski pottery and other specimens, which rested upon the floor of the house. The floor was reddened over large areas, indicating that the building had been destroyed by fire.

Clearing of the floor revealed the outlines of a large structure 15 m long and 9 m wide (Figure 5.39). It was essentially rectangular, but significantly broader at one end than the other, and had V-shaped end walls that imparted a somewhat hexagonal form. Around the outside edge of the floor ran a shallow trench about 10–20 cm wide, in or immediately adjacent to which postholes occurred at frequent intervals. It appears from this evidence that the house had vertical walls, which were footed in the trench and lashed to pillars set in the postholes. An alignment of large postholes down the central axis of the

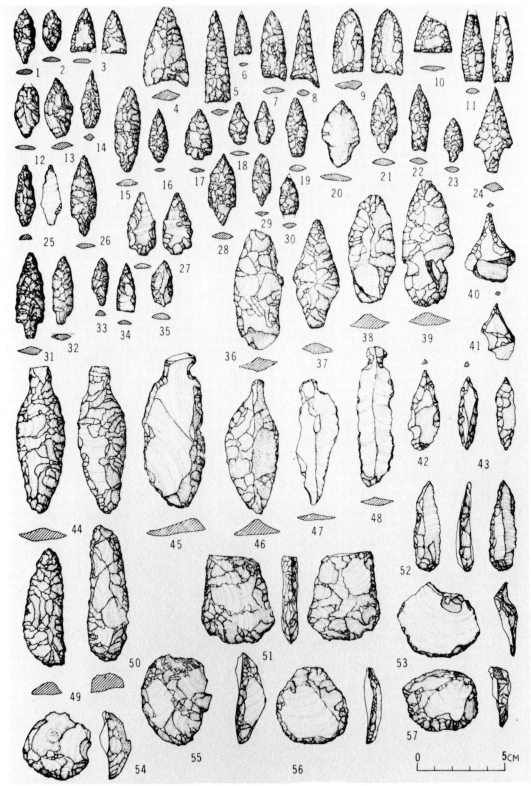

Figure 5.42 Flaked stone points, gravers, and scrapers of the Okhotsk culture from Tokoro Chashi, Hokkaido. (From Komai 1964:Figure 52.)

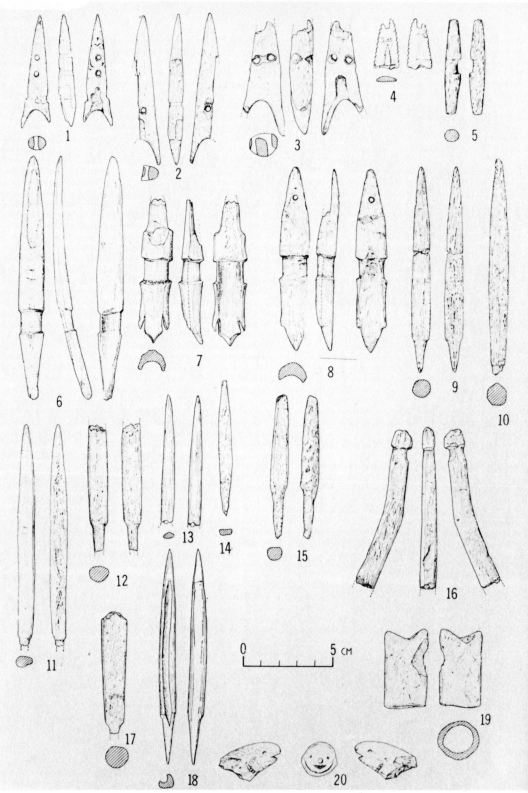

Figure 5.43 Bone harpoon and fish-spear parts of the Okhotsk culture from Tokoro Chashi, Hokkaido. (From Komai 1964:Figure 39.)

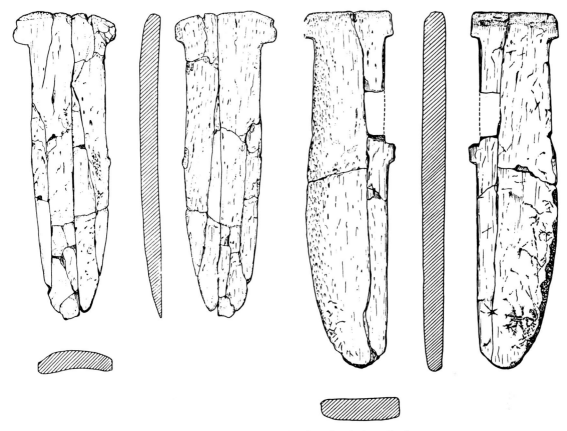

Figure 5.44 Bone adzehead (left) and knife (right) of the Okhotsk culture from Tokoro Chashi. Length of specimen at left, 30 cm. (From Komai 1964:Figure 35.)

structure could have supported a ridgepole, and it seems likely that the building had a gabled roof.

Inside the house was a second set of walls, also outlined by trenches that contained postholes at regular intervals. These outlined a room conforming to the plan of the outer structure. The inner room had a smooth, clay-paved floor with a fireplace at the center. The space between the walls of this inner room and outer walls of the house comprised a corridor about 1.5 m wide, which ran all the way around the building. It is easy to appreciate the advantages of this unique form of double-walled construction for a northern people, for it would have provided both insulation for the occupants of the inner room and protected storage space for their gear in the corridor outside.

Inside House 1 were also found the traces of a later structure that had been built in the same place. The later structure was smaller, but of the same elongate hexagonal plan as the first. It too was delineated

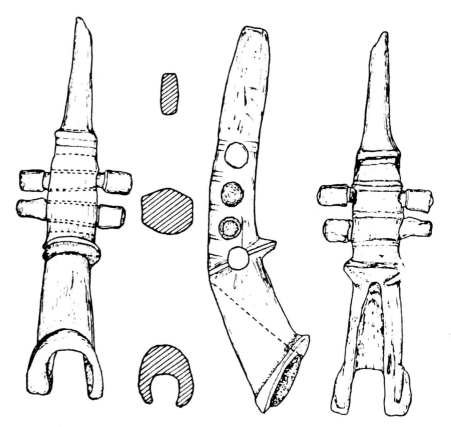

Figure 5.45   Bone tuning head for a stringed musical instrument of the Okhotsk culture, from Tokoro Chashi. (From Komai 1964:Figure 60.)

by wall trenches and associated postholes, and it too exhibited the same double-walled construction. A centrally located stone-lined fireplace about 1 m in diameter occupied the center of the inner room, partially overlying a filled-in fire pit that had served the original structure.

House 2, a few meters away, was smaller than House 1, but otherwise like it in plan and technique of construction. House 2 was about 10 m long and 8 m wide, with a central room and encircling outer passage. Beneath the plastered floor of House 2, and beyond its outer edge, were encountered many postholes and other remains relating to a prior occupation. These traces were not investigated in detail, but sherds of cylindrical cord-marked vessels indicated that Middle Jomon people had lived on the same spot in earlier times.

In the outer passageways at the eastern ends of both House 1 and

House 2, heaps of bear skulls and other bones were found. They were placed on one or both sides of what was apparently the exit. Such heaps of bones, dominated by bear skulls and deer antlers, have been found in similar positions in most of the Okhotsk houses known from the Tokoro region. They have been found elsewhere as well, as at the Mayoro site in Abashiri, and the Bentenjima site near Nemuro, and they are clearly a major feature of Okhotsk household ceremonialism.

The Okhotsk pottery recovered from the two houses was markedly different from the Jomon and Satsumon wares of the region. The predominant form was a large, widemouthed pot, the walls of which belled out slightly just below the rim, then tapered back inward and downward to end in a broad, flat bottom. Smaller pots of similar shape equipped with pouring spouts also occurred but were less common. Most vessels were embellished around the rims with parallel bands of spaghetti-like appliqué decoration, the lower parts of the pot being left plain or lightly polished. On some vessels, incised parallel lines or cord impressions were also used as decorative elements.

Projectile points included lanceolate and diamond-shaped forms, as well as triangular specimens having broad stems tapering inward toward the base. Both large and small items occurred in each of these general shapes, suggesting that both arrowpoints and spearpoints (or possibly knives) are represented. Stemmed scrapers, side- and end-scrapers made on large, broad flakes, drill and graver bits fashioned at the corners of angular flakes, flaked stone axeheads, and polished stone celts of both large and small sizes are all tools that might have served in manufacturing other artifacts of wood, bone, and antler, and, in some cases, leather. A few lithic specimens were made on long end-struck blades, although short, broad flakes were most commonly used.

Tools of ground or polished stone, in addition to the celts already mentioned, included perforated stone disks, presumably spindle whorls; large, irregular stones perforated near one edge, possibly net weights; and irregular stones with elongate grooves worn into their surfaces, possibly celt sharpeners or whetstones. Flat stones having from two or three to six or eight small, circular depressions ground into their surfaces, and rounded stones roughly of a size to have fitted these depressions, were also found. The use of these roughly matched objects is obscure, and it cannot be readily decided whether they formed functional sets of some kind, whether the rounded stones may have simply been tools used in grinding out the circular depressions, or whether the association of the two kinds of specimens is meaningful at all.

The specimens of bone and antler recovered from Tokoro Chashi seem clearly related to the killing and processing of the very kinds of large game that provided the raw material used in their manufacture. Socketed harpoon heads were no doubt used for taking marine mammals such as the sea lion or dolphin so charmingly represented by a small carving on a piece of ivory. Some of the harpoon heads were perforated for line attachments, and some were transversely grooved and perforated near the tip, as if they had once been armed with an iron point set in the groove and riveted in place. One triangular iron point, perforated near its base, was obviously such an armature. Heavy, flat, bone specimens, shaped by grinding, were sharpened either along one edge to serve as knives, or at the point, possibly to serve as heads for chopping adzes used in stripping blubber from sea mammals.

Sharpened bone points, and gracefully curved specimens having knobs against which to secure lashings at one end, were probably parts of composite fish-spears and/or leisters. Other long-bone specimens shaped by carving, and grooved at one end to provide purchase for the attachment of a line, were probably parts of large composite fishhooks such as those still made by native fishing peoples of the North Pacific region. The lower ends of these specimens were curved outward, and had a slightly angled flat surface at the end of the curved portion, against which a protruding pin of metal or bone could be lashed to make the device a V-shaped hook.

The art of carving, common among the North Pacific peoples of the historic period, is also attested. Carved animal representations include the head of a sea lion or dolphin mentioned above, a very nice full-round carving of a bear, made from the penis bone of a brown bear, and a curious-looking animal head that could make one think of a bear, a snake, or a frog by turns. A masterfully made object is a bone tuning head for a four-stringed musical instrument. The base is socketed to fit onto a neck or shaft, and the head has two small bone tuning pegs still in position, with perforations for two more now lost.

Metal objects were few. An iron harpoon point armature has already been mentioned, and beyond this there were found only several badly decomposed bronze or iron knife blades. These had narrow tangs at one end for hafting, and a socketed piece of bone found in the excavations was evidently a handle for such a knife. A few other metal specimens were recovered from the excavations, but they belonged to the later Ainu occupation.

A large recollection of bones, impressive in both quantity and variety, was recovered from the excavations at Tokoro Chashi. Most abundant were the remains of sea mammals, predominantly sea lion, seals of various kinds, and small whales. Bear was the most important land animal, apparently taken in large numbers. Interestingly, most of the bears were apparently fully grown males. The remains of the small raccoon-dog (*Nyctereutes*) were also particularly abundant. Other mammals included rodents, as well as rabbit, fox, wolf, dog, and deer. Birds identified included duck, snipe, heron, crow, kite, and hawk. Fish were represented by, among other species, halibut, bream, tuna, mullet, sea bass, dog salmon, and dace. Shellfish of several species were also identified. A predominantly marine economy is indicated, although special stress was also laid on the taking of bear, a creature of the inland woods and mountains more than of the coast.

The antecedents of the Ainu, who dominated the island of Hokkaido in historic times until their relatively recent submergence by Japanese moving in from Honshu, have long been the subject of academic debate. One important view, long held by major scholars, perceives the Ainu as a remnant of an ancient Jomon population, crowded into the far north by developments in the southern islands. Other authors have suggested, on the contrary, that the Ainu may have entered Hokkaido in relatively recent times, from the north. The archaeological evidence of the Satsumon and Okhotsk cultures bears directly on this problem, and in the opinion of the present writers strongly indicates that the Ainu were indeed ancient and original inhabitants of Japan's northernmost island.

The Ainu

The nature of the relationship obtaining between the Satsumon and Okhotsk cultures has long been one of the major questions of Hokkaido archaeology. It was once considered by some prominent researchers that the Okhotsk culture had succeeded the Satsumon on the northern coasts of Hokkaido, but majority opinion now favors the view that the two cultures coexisted there for many centuries. Continuing excavations and surveys by teams from Tokyo University and other institutions since the early 1960s have produced an abundance of evidence firmly supporting the latter view (Komai 1963, 1964; Oba and Ohyi 1973; Tokyo Daigaku Kokogaku Kenkyushitsu 1972; Yawata 1966).

Beyond a coastal zone of co-occurrence, both cultures had separate distributions. Satsumon pottery is found throughout Hokkaido, whereas Okhotsk ware is limited to its northern coasts, occurring principally along the shore of the Okhotsk Sea, and to some extent along the northern reaches of the Japan Sea and Pacific sides of the island. Farther north, Okhotsk or Okhotsk-like pottery is known from Sakhalin, the Kurile Islands, and elsewhere in the Soviet northeast, places where Satsumon ware does not appear at all. The evidence thus shows with rare clarity that old established occupants of Hokkaido, and newcomers who crossed the sea from the north, coexisted for hundreds of years along the northern shores of Japan's northernmost island.

The degree to which the two peoples maintained the distinctiveness of their respective cultures through several centuries of close association is remarkable. Both Satsumon and Okhotsk pottery evolved stylistically during the time that their makers were living side by side, but there was for long a striking lack of convergence between the two traditions. The same is true in the case of architecture, both communities maintaining distinctive house types until the very end of their long period of coexistence.

Clearly both societies deliberately sought to maintain their separate identities. They were successful in doing so until the final phase of Okhotsk culture, when signs of change appeared just before the Otkhotsk pattern vanished entirely. House 12 at Sakaeura II contained pottery and other artifacts of late Okhotsk type, but the structure itself was completely different from the traditional Okhotsk house it overlaid. This final Okhotsk dwelling was a smallish, square unit with a central fire pit and a series of roof-support posts along the walls. Though it was not a typical Satsumon building, it resembled that type much more closely than it did the typical elongate Okhotsk house with its distinctive double-wall construction. The usual cache of bear skulls and other bones so characteristic of traditional Okhotsk houses was also missing from the structure.

Late Okhotsk pottery too shows signs of assimilation toward the later Satsumon types. This is most clear in some specimens of the so-called Tobinitai group, which bear the spaghetti-like appliqué decoration of traditional late Okhotsk pottery, but are of typical Satsumon shapes.

According to available ^{14}C dates, the Okhotsk culture no longer existed in Hokkaido after about the eleventh century. Satsumon pottery is believed on comparative grounds to have persisted until about the thirteenth century. Satsumon houses are extremely numerous in the region around the mouth of the Tokoro River, and it is thought that a major increase in the Satsumon population coincided with the disappearance of the Okhotsk culture. Whether an increasingly numerous Satsumon folk drove out the Okhotsk people, or grew by absorbing them, is debated. In the absence of conclusive evidence the debate will surely continue, but it is here hypothesized that the main body of Okhotsk people, coming under increasing pressure from their Satsumon neighbors, simply withdrew northward to lands that were still Okhotsk territory in Sakhalin and elsewhere. A few families or communities would inevitably have stayed behind for one reason or another, and would ultimately have lost their identities in the Satsumon population, as in the case of House 12 at Sakaeura II.

This limited sort of absorption seems to be attested by the archaeological facts. But it does not seem at all realistic to postulate the sudden complete absorption of the entire Okhotsk population, in view of the previous resolute maintenance by both Okhotsk and Satsumon peoples of their cultural identity during several centuries of coresidence. Only during the final phase of Okhotsk occupation is there significant evidence of Okhotsk acculturation to the Satsumon pottery style, and this can be most easily understood as the behavior of a dwindling remnant no longer large and solidary enough to maintain its own traditions.

There are good grounds for identifying the Satsumon people as Ainu. A history of the T'ang dynasty of China (A.D. 618–907) mentioned a people in Hokkaido who have been identified as the Ainu, and the early Japanese accounts of clashes with northern barbarians during the Heian and Kamakura periods describe a people who are unmistakably the Ainu. These notices all fall during the Satsumon period, and establish beyond any reasonable doubt the ethnic identity of the Satsumon people.

Identification of the Okhotsk people with a historically known ethnic group is difficult. The Okhotsk people were gone from Hokkaido by perhaps the end of the eleventh century. Their culture is attested on Sakhalin until somewhat later, but by the sixteenth or seventeenth century, the historic Ainu had assumed possession of former Okhotsk territory in Sakhalin and the Kurile Islands. In historic times the end of Sakhalin nearest the continent was occupied by the Gilyak, and farther north around the shores of the Okhotsk Sea were the Koryak and Kamchadal. These people, maritime hunter-fishers in the northern tradition, seem most likely to be the sought-for descendants of the Okhotsk people, but archaeological evidence for those regions is as yet insufficient to engender full agreement on this interpretation.

The impetus behind the colonization of Hokkaido's northern coasts by the Okhotsk people is obscure, and must be sought in the archaeology of the Soviet northeast. But the force that stimulated the Ainu expansion that ultimately drove back the Okhotsk people and later spread the Ainu over much formerly Okhotsk territory is easier to identify. The agricultural way of life introduced into Japan from the south fostered a well-attested northward-spreading growth of the human population. By the end of the Kofun period, societies energized by the horticultural economy were pushing into far northern Honshu and Hokkaido, and when written records finally appear in the cultural centers of the south, they tell of conflicts with northern barbarians brought on by this expansion.

At the same time that the Ainu were coming under external pressure from the south, they were probably building up an internal expansive pressure as well. As noted previously, archaeological sites of the Satsumon period are more abundant than those of any other age, attesting a growth of the Ainu population that was no doubt helped along by the spread of cereal cultivation introduced from the south. It can readily be imagined that under such conditions the Okhotsk people, persistently alien, less numerous, and hence relatively easy to expel, might be driven out. As the pressure from behind and within continued, some of the Ainu themselves apparently yielded to it, for many manifestly did eventually follow the course of their erstwhile Okhotsk neighbors outward and northward over the sea, as their historical presence on Sakhalin and in the Kurile Islands attests.

Conclusion   During the four centuries of the Kofun period, between about A.D. 300 and 700, sociopolitical organization in Japan evolved in power and pervasiveness from the small local and regional chiefdoms of Yayoi times into the great Yamato empire, which unified all of civilized Japan under one ruling house.

The Early Kofun period, between the early fourth and late fifth centuries, was a time of major expansion of Yamato political domination, as districts increasingly distant from the Osaka–Nara–Kyoto heartland were brought into the network of ceremonial, exchange, and alliance relationships that are archaeologically attested by the Kofun cultural pattern. The distinctive keyhole shape of the classical Kofun burial tumuli themselves seems to have been symbolic of some sort of connection with the Yamato power, perhaps in the same way as sumptuary rules of the historic period governed the kinds of dress, housing, and symbols of rank appropriate to given status levels within the Yamato hierarchy. Chinese bronze mirrors, and later mirrors of similar type made in Japan, were widely exchanged among the nobility, doubtless as ceremonial gifts in token of alliance or common cause between and among powerful lords.

During Late Kofun times, after about the beginning of the sixth century, the Japanese state achieved a level of organization and power that allowed it to undertake military adventures in Korea, and these are attested in both Japanese and Korean traditional histories. Archaeologically, the intensified continental intercourse of these times is attested by the appearance in Japan of side-passage chamber tombs and the engraving and painting of tomb walls, by a great increase in the incidence of horse trappings and other items related to mounted cavalry warfare, and by the widespread establishment of the Sue ware ceramic industry and other craft specializations. All these cultural elements were present in Korea, and a combination of evidence from archaeological and historical sources suggests that this was a time when many artisans and specialists, probably whole guilds or corporations of them, were brought into Japan to serve the needs and increasingly continental tastes of the ever more rich and powerful elite stratum of Japanese society.

The establishment of this auxiliary class seems to have led to the formation of a kind of petty aristocracy. Clusters of small burial mounds appeared in most main centers during Late Kofun times, suggesting the rise of a significant new social segment enjoying a reasonable prosperity, a group emulating to the extent it could the conceits of the upper stratum. This petty aristocracy was most probably composed of the heads of corporate groups of artisans and traders, and the minor bureaucratic officials of the imperial state.

The early chronicles record that in the middle of the seventh century the emperor Kotoku forbade the construction of massive tombs because of the excessive cost involved, and with the cessation of such construction, the Kofun period as archaeologically defined came to an end. The process of expansion and consolidation of Yamato control, and the deliberate and earnest absorption of continental knowledge and culture, continued unabated, but archaeological treatment of these developments can be brought to a close at this point, where written history adequately takes up the narrative.

The common people, on the fruits of whose agricultural and other labors the growing Japanese state depended, lived a life quite apart from that of the upper classes, and in many ways not much different from that of Yayoi times. The substantial rectangular houses in which they lived were made with semisubterranean floors, as had been the Japanese tradition since the Jomon period, though they also had distinctive characteristics of their own. A few new crops expanded the inventory of cultigens known for Kofun times, but the basic wet-rice economy remained as established in the Yayoi period.

Metal sickles replaced stone *ishibocho* reaping knives, wooden hoes and spades were probably more often shod with iron tips, and iron cutting tools replaced stone implements almost completely. This increased use of iron was the culmination of a trend begun early in the Yayoi period. The Haji ceramic ware that constituted the basic utility pottery of the time was also clearly in the Yayoi tradition, being all but indistinguishable from Yayoi pottery to any but the specialist's eye.

Probably the most important new element in rural farm life during Kofun times was the appearance of large community storage facilities such as were found at Hiraide. These surely bespeak the systematic, organized, extracommunity taxation of the countryman's labors that must have been necessary to support the military campaigns, public works projects, commerce, and aristocratic display of the ruling elite.

Beyond the northern frontiers, in farthest Honshu and especially in Hokkaido, the influence of the burgeoning new Japanese civilization was expressed only faintly. The Satsumon people, who at the last emerged into written history as the Ainu, took up the cultivation of millet and other cereals, but never approached the societal complexity of the south. The people of the Okhotsk culture, aliens from the extreme north beyond the Okhotsk Sea, seem never to have been culturally touched by the developments of the Japanese heartland, though the pressures that caused them finally to return northward may be ultimately traceable to the expanding civilization of the south.

6 : *Summary*

The self-containment of Japan as an island country, coupled with its long and well-researched prehistory, make it a fascinating example of cultural evolution; its smallness makes it a manageable universe of study. Its relative isolation, far enough yet not too far off the eastern coast of Asia, has allowed it to develop in its own terms as a discrete cultural system in touch with, but not dominated by, events taking place on the continent.

The present-day Japanese speak a tongue anciently related to Korean, Manchu, Mongolian, Turkish, and the other Altaic languages of central and northeastern Asia. Linguistic evidence suggests that it has been thousands of years since Japanese and its nearest relatives, Korean and Manchu, diverged from a common ancestral language—at least five or six millennia, and perhaps twice that. The Ainu language, until quite recently spoken in northern Japan, is so divergent that linguists have not been able to definitely relate it to any existing speech community. It has apparently persisted in isolation for so long that related languages have either become extinct or diverged so far that connections are no longer determinable. Ainu does, however, share a few linguistic features with Japanese, which could be the result either of borrowing based on long association or of the mutual descent of both languages from an extremely remote common ancestor, far back in time. These considerations suggest that the linguistic and cultural ancestors of both Japanese and Ainu are of ultimately north-central Asiatic origin, that they have occupied the Japanese islands for many thousands of years, and that the archaeological record from at least Jomon times onward, and perhaps even from Late Paleolithic times, pertains to the direct ancestors of the modern inhabitants.

Pronounced regional differences in dialect, which remained strong in Japan up until recent times and persist in attenuated form even in the modern electronic era of instantaneous nationwide communication, are evidence of long-maintained subcultural differences within the country. Written records show that people of the Yamato court in Nara were well aware of such differences in the eighth century A.D., and zonal distributions of distinctive pottery and stone tool types show that analogous regional subdivisions may be traced back through the Yayoi, Jomon, and Late Paleolithic periods as well.

These deeply rooted divisions of course reflect geographical factors to a significant extent, but the fact that cultural boundaries changed somewhat over time suggests that they were not controlled by geography alone. Borders were apparently affected also by the internal social dynamics of various local groups, and the millennial continuities of artifact style shown by the archaeological record to have existed within such borders suggest that highly persistent local folk traditions were fostered and maintained by both environmental and cultural factors.

Though Japan is now an island country, it was for much or most of the Pleistocene attached to the Asian continent, and no doubt its initial peopling dates to that period. Fossils of the arboreal species *Liquidambar* and *Metasequoia,* and bones of early Southeast Asian elephants, have been found at various localities in Japan. These indicate a southerly connection with the continent during the Early and Middle Pleistocene. Fossil remains of cool-temperature conifers, and of Naumann's elephant, indicate a more northerly continental connection during the same general period. Bones of the later Giant deer, horse, bison, and mammoth show that northerly connections existed in Late Pleistocene times as well.

Given the geographical circumstances, it is quite possible that Japan may have been early occupied by a counterpart of the human population known from Choukoutien, China, which is conventionally dated to about 400,000 years ago. The lithic assemblages from such sites as Sozudai, in Kyushu, and Hoshino, north of Tokyo, have been said to resemble the industry from Choukoutien, and it has been suggested that a culture incorporating a very crude lithic industry persisted in Japan from around 400,000 years ago down to about 35,000 years ago. These specimens lack, however, clearly perceptible hallmarks of human workmanship such as striking platforms, bulbs of percussion, ripple marks, and striations, and for this reason are believed by most leading archaeologists not to be artifacts at all.

The site of Gongenyama has produced some clearly man-made specimens resembling Lower Paleolithic Euro-African Acheulian handaxes, but their age is unclear. They are believed to have come from a stratum dated between 35,000 and 50,000 B.P., but this assignment is postulated on the basis of recollections by the discoverer long after the original finding of the artifacts, and so is open to question. In any event it is likely that these tools, which typologically resemble Euro-African specimens of an age comparable to or greater than that attributed to the Choukoutienian occupation, are not nearly so old as it is.

In short, although it is possible that the earliest occupation of Japan might go back 400,000 years or even more, the finds from Sozudai, Hoshino, Gongenyama, and other such sites are not sufficient to establish this possibility as fact.

The earliest well-controlled evidence so far available for human occupation in Japan comes from a series of sites in the Tokyo region, which are buried in the Tachikawa Loam or its local time-stratigraphic equivalents. These are deep volcanic ash layers dating to the latest stage of the Pleistocene. The Tachikawa Loam accumulated between about 29,000 and 11,000 B.P., according to ^{14}C dates from several localities. Black bands, representing old soils that formed during intervals between major ash falls, provide markers of stratigraphic succession within the loam, and the finding of artifacts above and below these old soils establishes that people producing lithic industries were present essentially throughout this period.

The lowest levels of Nakazanya, Nishinodai, Heidaizaka, and San-rizuka contain pebble choppers and simple cutting and scraping tools made on short, broad flakes, which are placed roughly in the interval 25,000–30,000 B.P. by the ^{14}C and obsidian hydration dating techniques. These might, with some trepidation, be characterized as broadly Mousterian-like assemblages.

Industries characterized by large end-struck blades and bladelike flakes struck from prepared cores began to appear in the Tachikawa sequence sometime before 20,000 B.P. These assemblages are clearly akin to those of the classical Eurasian Advanced Paleolithic known from northern Europe to Lake Baikal and beyond, though they also include the variant side-blow Setouchi technique that seems to be a more localized development. Many sites throughout the country give evidence of such industries, most prominent among them being Iwajuku, north of Tokyo, where in the year 1949 the existence of undeniable artifacts in a clearly Pleistocene stratum was first unequivocally established for Japan.

Actual living floors have been uncovered in some instances. At the Nogawa site in Tokyo, a series of occupation floors were studied in detail, revealing the existence of apparent workshop, food-processing, cooking, and general-purpose activity areas.

A very interesting progression evident in the stratigraphic sequences from Nogawa, Takei, Tsukimino, and other sites is a development leading from edge-retouched knives made on blades, to uniface points, to biface points, as the marginal flaking used to shape a blade into a knife was progressively extended to cover the entire surface of the worked specimen. Such an evolution, suggested by Sugihara (1956) on primarily typological grounds, seems to fit the stratigraphic data as well.

Microblades, and the boat-shaped mircocores they were struck from, became widespread in Japan between about 13,000 and 14,000 years ago. It is fascinating to note that their appearance was foreshadowed by a tendency toward reduction in the size of blades in immediately preceding assemblages, as clearly illustrated at Hyakkadai in Kyushu. There does not, however, so far appear to have been a completely continuous intergradation of size between the "macro-" and microblade industries.

Bifacially flaked projectile points, which had appeared previously in the context of large-blade industries, continued to occur in association with microlithic industries at sites such as Yasumiba, Etchuyama, Shirataki–Hattoridai, and many others. Large blades (nonmicroblades) often persisted as well. As strikingly illustrated by Hokkaido's Yubetsu-type microcores, biface and microlithic techniques even came to be combined in a single manufacturing technology. By this technique, microcores were fashioned from leaf-shaped bifaces by peeling off large, longitudinal flakes, essentially splitting the biface, to create a striking platform for the progressive removal of many tiny blades from the remaining half of the original piece.

A fascinating continuum of apparently developmental relationships between prepared-core-and-blade technology, biface technology, and microblade technology is thus well documented by both typological and stratigraphic evidence in the Japanese case. The integration of this perception with an equally compelling perception of undeniable typological relationships between the Japanese artifacts and types widespread in Northeast Asia and beyond requires that the evolutionary process be conceived as one that involved both autochthonous development, and diffusion, going on more or less simultaneously throughout Eurasia.

Biogeographers have long been aware of a high degree of continuity and similarity in flora and fauna throughout the circumpolar zone of Eurasia, and even North America. All across this vast zone, toolmakers were faced with providing implements for the taking and processing of food, and the working of wood, fiber, bone, antler, and hide, derived from identical plant and animal species. Under these circumstances, similar innovations might arise among many groups. Furthermore, given that many of the toolmakers could only have been wide-ranging hunter–gatherers whose annual round of movements inevitably and regularly brought them into contact with neighboring groups, it is completely expectable that when a particularly effective innovation in manufacturing technique or functional tool type appeared, its mechanical value would be quickly recognized by others obliged to cope with similar problems. It might thus be communicated within the interval of a few decades or centuries throughout the area where such problems existed.

Regional differentiation in early Japanese culture, beginning after about 20,000 years ago, is indicated by minor variations in tool types. Within the class of large retouched blades characterized as knives are a number of types, which vary from one another according to small differences in the amount and position of secondary marginal flaking. Microcores also exhibit regional variation, shown most plainly by the restriction of the distinctive Yubetsu-type microcore to the northern regions, but expressed in other nuances of formal variation as well. These variations add up to a clear distinction between the lithic industries of northeastern and southwestern Japan, with a zone of interdigitation lying across central Honshu.

The cultural division roughly coincides with the modern boundary between Japan's north temperate and warm southern forest zones. The relative lack of sharpness of the coincidence between cultural and biotic distributions no doubt owes something to climatically induced fluctuations of the biotic boundary itself over the past 20,000 years. It is one of the striking facts of Japanese culture history that this cultural divide, established so long ago, persisted thereafter down through all subsequent archaeological periods, to become ethnologically and linguistically attested in the folk life and dialect geography of modern times.

Exchange relationships extending over considerable distances appear to have been established as early as 20,000 years ago in the Tokyo region. Obsidians from the Shinshu area in the central mountains west of Tokyo, the Hakone region near the base of Mount Fuji, and the island of Kozujima in the Pacific Ocean south of Tokyo Bay have been found in Paleolithic sites as far as 150 km distant from their geological sources. The finding of Kozujima obsidian on Honshu in sites dated between 15,000 and 20,000 B.P. also implies the use of watercraft by Japan's Paleolithic occupants, since Kozujima, about 50 km offshore, rises out of water sufficiently deep that it would have remained an island during even the lowest sea level stage of terminal Pleistocene times.

The Jomon tradition, which dominated the Japanese islands from about 12,500 B.P. down to about 2500 B.P., grew out of the Late Paleolithic. Dates for the earliest pottery suggest that ceramics, probably introduced from the continent via Korea, spread from southern Kyushu to northern Hokkaido between about 12,500 and 8500 B.P. The stone tool industry associated with the earliest pottery in Kyushu was microlithic, clearly akin to the microlithic industries that had become established throughout Japan in the preceding Late Paleolithic period. The nonmicrolithic stone tool industry that was later to become characteristic of the mature Jomon tradition emerged only after the initial appearance of pottery, apparently the result of developments within Japan itself. These cultural changes coincide broadly with the interval of major climatic change at the end of the Pleistocene, and obviously reflect some aspects of the readaptation of Japan's Ice Age occupants to environmental conditions more like those of the present.

The site of Natsushima, in Tokyo Bay, shows that this readaptation was fully mature by 9500 B.P., and the finds made at Torihama, north of Kyoto, could extend the date back even earlier. From at least the time of Natsushima onward, Jomon sites give clear evidence of a prosperous and stable hunting–gathering economy based on Japan's rich forests and heavily indented coastlines. Small but long-occupied villages of substantial semisubterranean pithouses are known from at least the middle of Initial Jomon times, their very existence documenting a high degree of sedentism based on the resources of woodland and littoral.

The abundance and range of natural food resources available to the Jomon people, especially along the coasts and in the central and northern regions covered by mixed forests, would be difficult to overestimate. The thousands of bays, inlets, and estuaries of the rugged Japanese coastline provide optimum habitat for dozens of species of fish and mollusks, as well as for sea mammals, sea turtles, and many edible plant and animal life forms of the intertidal zone. Although there might be seasonal constraints on the availability of certain species, the littoral is a reliable source of food the year around.

The terrestrial ecosystem in premodern times was equally productive, and even more readily exploitable. Acorns, walnuts, chestnuts, and certain roots, available in huge quantities in the fall of the year, are especially suited by their own evolutionary adaptation for overwinter preservation. People had only to gather them and protect them from competing species that also sought them as food. Trout, dace, and other fish; deer, bear, boar, and many smaller mammals; and pheasant, grouse, dove, and other birds, were all available the year around in the streams and woods. In winter, when the availability of plant foods tapered off, proportionately more time might be given to hunting. In spring and summer there would be greens, shoots, bulbs, medicinal flowers, ferns, fungi, fruits, and seeds in abundance, all of which could be obtained dependably year after year in the same gathering localities. Insects and their larvae, turtles, snakes, and snails were also available, ubiquitous and easily obtained, to embellish what must have been a predominantly vegetarian diet.

By the beginning of Middle Jomon times, around 5000 B.P., a high point of cultural development was reached. Around Tokyo Bay, where marine and terrestrial ecosystems conjoined in a particularly favorable setting, many small but apparently thriving villages were established on estuaries, inlets, and wooded points overlooking the water. Fish-hooks and fish-spear points of antler and bone, net floats of pumice stone, notched sinkers made on pebbles or sherds of pottery, and the remains of dugout canoes and paddles are evidence of marine ex-ploitation. Flaked stone arrowpoints and scrapers, rough stone hoe-heads or digging-stick tips, and grinding stones indicate the processing of land animals and plants. Bones, shell remains, seed coats and the like directly indicate some of the species taken.

Villages, consisting of clusters of pithouses ranged about an open central area, give evidence of residential stability. At Kasori, pottery types of different ages show that occupation of the site continued throughout the Middle and Late Jomon periods, and the house pits excavated there overlap and crosscut one another in a way that indi-cates building and rebuilding, time after time, of the same kinds of dwellings on essentially the same spots. Many other sites give similar evidence.

In mountainous central Honshu, sites such as Togariishi, Idojiri, and Fudodo also give evidence of a considerable population, growing in both size and social elaboration. These villages too were stable, occupied apparently over many decades and more probably over sev-eral centuries. The site of Yosukeone, for example, appears to have been a daughter village of Togariishi, established after nearby To-gariishi had been in existence for quite some time. Similar indications of a growing and fissioning population are also known from the region around Idojiri and elsewhere.

A cult of female figurines and phallic altars flourished at Togariishi–Yosukeone, and is known from many other regions as well. At Togariishi, caches of clay figurines, invariably broken, were found beneath house floors, and other dwellings featured low, slab-paved altars along one wall, upon which phallic stones were erected. The open center of the village cluster at Togariishi was dominated by a large pointed boulder, toward which a flagstone path led, and beneath which was found buried a large ceramic offering vessel.

A great hall erected at the site of Fudodo, 17 m long and 8 m wide, is an expression of a major cooperative effort. This building, surrounded by smaller, typical dwelling structures, probably had a public character as a focal point of community activity. Nearby Mizukami-dani also had outsized structures associated with more typical Jomon dwellings, though they were not as large as the major building at Fudodo.

The stability and comfort obviously enjoyed by the Jomon people, as well as their centralized villages and increasingly elaborate ceremonial patterns, have led some archaelogists to the conclusion that the Japanese of this period must have been already practicing some form of agriculture. No plant remains identified as actual domesticates have been found, but it is suggested that native root-bearing plants may have been cultivated, as part of a slash-and-burn system. Periodic firing stimulates the growth of grass and other understory plants, and trees licked by fire are said to produce bumper crops of nuts after such an event. It seems obvious that the Jomon people must have had great knowledge of the food resources of their environment, and quite possible that the cumulative effect of human actions on the biotic communities from which the people harvested might well have been leading them in the direction of domestication.

The Jomon case poses very clearly the question of the processes by which foraging might become cultivation, and what is now known supports suggestions based on archaeological and ethnological experience in other parts of the world, that the two food-gathering regimes blend almost imperceptibly under certain circumstances.

When cultivation does become unambiguously attested in the archaeological record, however, with the appearance of rice and other cereals in deposits dated to the very end of the Jomon age, the cultigens are clearly of nonindigenous, imported species. Whatever the eventual answer to the question of whether or not the earlier Jomon people were actually cultivators, it is nevertheless evident that with its long-established village pattern and relatively dense population, the whole Jomon way of life prefigured the later Yayoi farming culture in a manner that undeniably must have fostered the Japanese adoption of the alien grains.

The village of Itatsuke, in northern Kyushu, is the type site for earliest Yayoi culture. Here, dating to about 2300 B.P., were found charred grains of Japanese rice (*Oryza japonica*), ground stone reaping knives, water-control ditches, paddy fields, and indications of weaving and the use of metal tools. These are the major diagnostics of Yayoi culture, which began appearing individually and sporadically in Late and Final Jomon sites, but were first found together as a characteristically Yayoi complex at Itatsuke. The pottery assemblage of Itatsuke is transitional from Jomon to Yayoi; the Final Jomon Yusu type and the Early Yayoi Itatsuke type, both of which are common at the site, are very similar to one another in both form and decoration.

The diagnostic elements by which Yayoi culture is archaeologically recognized are indisputably of continental inspiration, and many have seen in this fact evidence of a massive migration of new people into Japan from the outside. Two important considerations, however, make it seem far more likely that the new elements are not indicative of a population replacement, but rather were spread primarily among an indigenous Jomon population. First and most compelling is the evidence that the new culture traits did not all arrive in Japan at the same time, as would have been the case had the Yayoi complex been the baggage of a wave of old-established immigrant rice farmers from the continent. Second, the observed typological intergradation and gradual temporal transition between Jomon and Yayoi ceramic types suggest change over time in the habits of indigenous Japanese potters, rather than an overwhelming influx of new potters with new ways of doing things.

During Early Yayoi times, villages based on rice farming sprang up all over Kyushu and along both sides of the Inland Sea as far northeast as the Osaka–Nara–Kyoto region and slightly beyond. North of Nagoya, the initial agricultural expansion halted, and only in the Middle Yayoi period was the northward spread resumed. It appears from this that the new economy was taken up quickly throughout the part of Japan covered by semitropical broad-leaved evergreen forest, but was less fully successful in the cool-temperate mixed forests of central and northern Honshu. Yayoi culture, as such, never became established in the farthest north, in Hokkaido. There, the poorly understood Epi-Jomon complex continued what was essentially a Jomon way of life well into the time of the Yayoi age.

When the Yayoi pattern did spread into central and northern Honshu, it retained a decidedly Jomon-like cast. This is expressed especially in the pottery, which exhibits a number of shapes obviously inspired by contemporary Yayoi traditions farther south, but is decorated by cord-marking and imprssing in the older Jomon tradition. Furthermore, Yayoi sites decrease significantly in size and numbers toward the north. The differences noted between the Yayoi complexes of southwestern and northeastern Japan no doubt are reflective of the fact that the underlying Jomon way of life had always prospered and flourished most fully in the rich forests of the northeast, whereas classical Yayoi, conversely, was weakest there, and flourished most richly in southwestern Japan, with its warmer climate and longer growing season. Under such circumstances it is not surprising that some aspects of Jomon traditional behavior were especially persistent in the north.

In important respects the coming of the Yayoi age did not alter the domestic life of the Japanese. Sturdy single-family semisubterranean dwellings very little different from those of Jomon times continued in use. Villages remained stable and sedentary, occupied over generations and even centuries, as before. Pottery vessels for carrying, storage, cooking, and eating were made as before, though in a new style and increasing variety. Many technological traditions were carried over. The nature of the working day, however, changed significantly.

The cultivation of rice, wheat, millet, melons, and other crops of the Yayoi complex, which initially merely added to the variety, interest, and security of the established woodland–littoral food economy, came eventually to dominate the activities of the Japanese villagers. Stone projectile points, knives, and scrapers; canoes, fish-spears, fish-hooks, and sinkers; and milling stones and digging-stick tips were the tools most used in Jomon times. The same types continued to be made during the Yayoi age, but as cultivation increased in importance, the broad-ranging hunting and gathering activities that these artifacts represent occupied a smaller and smaller proportion of the villagers' time. Wooden hoes, rakes, picks, spades, paddy field clogs, mortars, and pestles, a tool kit for the cultivation and processing of rice and other plants, all these were added to the inventory of domestic equipment during the Yayoi age. Activities involving their manufacture and use came ever more to fill the working day and keep the workers close to home.

Sociopolitical organization began, in Yayoi times, to take on a form more closely centralized around powerful individuals than had apparently been the case during the Jomon age. From the early Yayoi period onward, distinctions of social status are evident in burial patterns. Bronze mirrors, metal blades, and glass beads imported from the continent set off the graves of an increasingly wealthy elite from those of the common folk. Special burial plots for the representatives of certain groups, known from Early Yayoi times, had by Middle Yayoi times begun to grow into small tumuli that foreshadowed the monumental burial mounds of the following Kofun period's kings and warlords. The Uriyudo site provides the most striking example. Yayoi society obviously existed under circumstances that fostered an ever greater accumulation of wealth and power in the hands of a few, in a way that the conditions of existence of the Jomon age never did. The political, economic, and military developments of the following Kofun period evolved directly out of the milieu established during Yayoi times.

The extraction of wealth from a working population, a necessity for the support of a privileged upper class in the extravagant manner that is referred to as "civilized," cannot proceed far without an ability on the part of the upper stratum to enforce its special demands. Essential to this is that the way of life of the working population be such that the populace can be controlled by an economical amount of force when necessary. The Late Jomon people's cultivation of alien cereals, at first taken up casually, sporadically, and on a small scale for the relatively minor benefits it added to the older forest economy, led the way by Yayoi times into a pattern of social existence that could be regulated by a few in a way not previously possible.

The florescence of Early Yayoi agriculture was probably due in considerable part to the persuasion—later, the demands—of local leaders, successors to the village headmen of the Jomon age, who recognized the possibilities of the embryonic new cereal cultivation for providing increased economic input into the public affairs they traditionally guided. As such affairs grew in magnitude and expense, their organization and conduct would have increasingly necessitated an intensification of production, which would in turn have provided greater and greater opportunity for personal advantage and profit to the managers. Once a sufficient coterie of beneficiaries and supporters of such leaders had accumulated, the power to enforce ever greater production would have been achieved. A growing investment in the preparation of land for cultivation, as well as natural limitations on the availability of land suitable for farming, gradually brought the mass of people into a more and more circumscribed situation, one in which they could not readily avoid increasingly insistent and coercive taxation. By the end of Yayoi times the basic institutions of political–economic control needed to support the superstructure of civilization and the state were firmly in place and growing rapidly in strength.

Bronze spears and halberds, iron swords, and other weapons and symbols of war were attested early in the Yayoi period. By Middle Yayoi times, many villages were encircled by moats or situated in otherwise defensible locations. The Otsuka site, in Yokohama, seems to have been a fortified village, situated on a hilltop and ringed by a dry moat and earthwork. There is, in short, ample evidence that by the end of the Yayoi period many local groups had already begun to come under more than occasional serious military pressure, probably from neighbors who coveted their lands and other forms of wealth. The following Kofun period saw the consolidation of the competitive, squabbling local chiefdoms of Yayoi times into the wealthy and powerful political network that emerged into the time of written history as the imperial Yamato state.

The Kofun period, dated between roughly A.D. 300 and 700, is set off from the Yayoi most obtrusively, and most importantly, by the great burial mounds for which it is named. Interred in these tumuli are personages who manifestly were able to command the labor of hundreds of people over periods of months or years. At Koganezuka Kofun, one of the earliest of such sepulchers, was buried a principal personage accompanied by ceremonial and ornamental artifacts. This interment was flanked by two others, obviously of warriors, who were heavily equipped with iron body armor, shields, swords, spears, arrowheads, and other military trappings. The evidence of hundreds of *kofun* burials containing similar gear leaves no doubt at all that the ruling elite's control over Kofun period society was fully supported by a capability for coercion, which had been growing since at least Middle Yayoi times.

The oldest Kofun burial mounds known occur in the Osaka–Nara–Kyoto region, the heartland of what was to become Japan's early Yamato state. The distinctive keyhole shape of these earthworks, with a trapezoidal platform at the front end and a round mound at the rear, is believed to be the symbolic property of the central Yamato authority. Outside the Yamato heartland such structures first appeared perhaps a half-century to a century later than the earliest of the Yamato tumuli, and they appeared primarily in the vicinity of strategic geographical locations from which transport and communication could be controlled. Secondarily, and somewhat later, they began to appear in the richer agricultural regions of the country. Before the end of the Early Kofun period, such burial mounds had been established from Kyushu in the southwest to Tokyo in the northeast, with the largest and most numerous specimens centered in the Osaka–Nara–Kyoto region.

Everywhere the basic pattern and content of the sepulchers was the same, everywhere the graves were dominated by weapons of war, and everywhere there occurred, as apparent tokens of gift-giving or alliance relationships among the ruling elites, exotic Chinese bronze mirrors. Troves containing sets of identical mirrors made from the same models indicate that these Chinese products were imported from the continent in wholesale lots. Specimens found at Otsukayama Kofun, near Kyoto, were mates of other mirrors found as far away as Kyushu and Tokyo, suggesting that powerful lords obtained quantities of them expressly for the purpose of establishing formal exchange relationships with other chieftains. The practice must have been effective, for in later times it was continued using imitations of the Chinese specimens, which were made in Japan by craftsmen in the service of certain lords.

These data suggest that the extension of Yamato hegemony, which culminated in the earliest Japanese state, operated by a process of incorporating local chiefdoms already established in Yayoi times, and giving the chieftains themselves places within the Yamato hierarchy. In part the process might have been advanced by realities of mutual advantage, and in part it was no doubt furthered by war or the threat of war. The almost incredibly elaborate system of ranks and titles dispensed by the historic Yamato court at Nara may well have been a latter-day elaboration of measures earlier adopted to give potentially troublesome members of formerly autonomous local elites a personal stake in the imperial system.

As the early Japanese state grew in power, it embarked on military adventures in the adjacent Korean peninsula. The traditional histories give some account of these operations, and though there is disagreement among scholars about dates and details, the basic facts of Japanese incursions into Korea and the bringing of Korean artisans and specialists back into Japan (whether willingly or otherwise is disputed), are well documented historically and archaeologically.

By about the middle of the fifth century, a number of elements of clearly Korean antecedents began to appear in Japan as burial furniture in Kofun graves. First in Kyushu, then in southern and central Honshu as far northeast as the Tokyo region, side-passage tomb chambers began to supersede the older type of tomb entered from the top. Many of these chambers had painted interior walls, and both the architectural and art forms were closely related to forms known from Korea. Metal headgear, gold earrings, and such trappings of equestrian warriors as bridle bits and chains, saddle cinch loops and buckles, and ornamental rivets and leather fastenings became common in the graves of later Kofun times. Wheel-made ceramics of a hard, dark, high-fired fabric known as Sue ware came into widespread use among the aristocracy. Sets of such pottery, comprising a variety of both serving dishes and offering vessels, became standard furniture in Kofun graves, and occasional specimens have also turned up in rural village sites of the common people.

The influx of continental elements that is attested archaeologically after the mid-fifth century would seem to mark the first serious beginnings of the Japanese aristocracy's energetic and fully conscious emulation of the Chinese arts of civilization that so dazzlingly culminated in the highly Sinicized art, literature, architecture, society, and government of the historic Nara and Heian periods. The increasing craft specialization demonstrated archaeologically for later Kofun times, and the development of an extensive petty aristocracy that is indicated by the proliferation of small burial tumuli, were a part of this process; the importation of Korean scribes, potters, metalworkers, and other artisans is well documented in the early historic accounts.

It has been suggested that the wave of continental influence that entered Japan during mid-Kofun times came about, not as just described, but rather as the result of an invasion of equestrian warriors from somewhere in central Asia. These would have been conquerors who, like the army of Genghis Khan in thirteenth-century China, dominated the country for a time, only to be ultimately absorbed into it with a complete loss of their former identity. This thesis has been argued by many scholars, but is not pursued here because it depends without warrant on unknown tribesmen emerging from an unknown land for unknown reasons, and then, having conquered Japan (and Korea on the way), melting into the scene so thoroughly that no document or tradition of their war of conquest was left behind. It is, in short, an implausible theory, which only raises more questions than it bids to resolve.

The political, military, and increasingly artistic preoccupations of the burgeoning Japanese aristocracy rested, at bottom, on a rural wet-rice economy that continued essentially as established during the Yayoi period. Rice, wheat, millet, barley, beans, melons, peppers, and taro were cultivated as major staples, as they were during the Yayoi period and as they are today. Horses, cows, pigs, and chickens were typical livestock. There were of course some changes in the life of the country folk, at least in part reflective of the increased continental intercourse that was taking place. The countrymen's houses of Kofun and later times were squarish in ground plan, with vertical walls and gabled roofs, quite different in appearance from typical Yayoi structures and probably influenced by continental prototypes. Iron tools became more common, and the Sue pottery so prominent in upper-class burials appeared as luxury ware in some households. In such ways the prosperity of the times, generated by the activities and demands of the aristocracy, was reflected (however faintly) in the lives of the common people.

Beyond the northern frontier, in the upper reaches of Honshu and especially in Hokkaido, the ancestors of the historic Ainu took up the cultivation of millet and other cold-tolerant crops, and built houses after the pattern of the Kofun period peasantry. They were not effectively incorporated into the Japanese state, however, and their society apparently remained at a level of complexity more or less comparable to that of Jomon or Early Yayoi times. The Okhotsk people, an alien maritime group that occupied the northern shores of Hokkaido during much of the Kofun period, returned to the far north in later centuries, their departure perhaps stimulated by growing expansionist tendencies on the part of their Ainu neighbors, who were themselves increasingly affected by the march of Japanese civilization to the south.

References

Aikens, C. Melvin
1981 The last 10,000 years in Japan and eastern North America: Parallels in environment, economic adaptation, growth of societal complexity, and the adoption of agriculture. In *The affluent foragers: Pacific Coasts east and west,* edited by Shuzo Koyama and David Hurst Thomas. Osaka: Senri Ethnological Studies, National Museum of Ethnology. (In press.)

Akiyama, Hideo, and Yoshinori Aboshi
1959 *Yamato muro no ohaka.* Nara-ken shi-iseki meisho kinenbutsu chosa hokoku, Vol. 18. Nara: Nara-ken Kyoiku Iinkai.

Amakasu, Ken
1966 Josetsu: Kofun bunka no chiikiteki gaikan. In *Nihon no kokogaku, IV: Kofun jidai (Jo)*, edited by Yoshiro Kondo and Choji Fujisawa. Tokyo: Kawade Shobo Shinsha. Pp. 102–113.

Amakasu, Ken, and Tetsuzo Kubo
1966 Kanto. In *Nihon no kokogaku, IV: Kofun jidai (Jo)*, edited by Yoshiro Kondo and Choji Fujisawa. Tokyo: Kawade Shobo Shinsha. Pp. 428–498.

Aso, Masaru, and Hiroyuki Shiraishi
1975 Sempukuji doketsu no dai rokuji chosa. *Kokogaku Jyaneru* 116:5–11.

———
1976 Hyakkadai iseki. In *Nihon no kyusekki bunka 3, iseki to ibutsu*, edited by Masaru Aso *et al.* Tokyo: Yuzankaku. Pp. 191–213.

Bleed, Peter
1977 Early flakes from Sozudai, Japan: Are they man-made? *Science* 197:1357–1359.

Bunkazai Hogo Iinkai
1953 *Oyu-machi kanjo resseki* [The stone remains of Oyu]. Maizo Bunkazai Hakkutsu Chosa Hokoku, Vol. 2. Tokyo. (English title and summary.)

Chang, K. C.
1977 *The archaeology of ancient China,* 3rd ed. New Haven, Conn.: Yale University Press.

Date, Muneyasu, *et al.*
1972   *Udozuka kofun.* Nara-ken Shi-iseki Meisho Tennen Kinenbutsu Chosa Hokoku, Vol. 27. Nara: Nara-ken Kyoiku Iinkai.

Esaka, Teruya (Editor)
1972   Shinpojiyamu: Jomon jidai no kokogaku. Tokyo: Gakuseisha.

Esaka, Teruya, and Sakae Nishida
1967   Aichi-ken Kamikuroiwa iwakage. In *Nihon no doketsu iseki,* edited by Nihon Kokogaku Kyokai Doketsu Iseki Chosa Tokubetsu Iinkai. Tokyo: Heibonsha. Pp. 224–236.

Fujimori, Eiichi (Editor)
1965   *Idojiri. Nagano-ken Fujimi-cho ni okeru chu-ki Jomon iseki-gun no kenkyu* [Idojiri. A Middle Jomon culture from the southern foothills of Yatsugatake]. Tokyo: Chuo Koron Bijutsu Shuppan. (English title and abstract.)

Fukuoka-ken Kyoiku Iinkai
1975   *Ihara Mikumo iseki hakkutsu chosa hokoku, Showa 49 nendo.* No. 52. Fukuoka: Fukuoka Kyoiku Iinkai.
1976   *Ihara Mikumo iseki hakkutsu chosa hokoku, Showa 50 nendo.* No. 53. Fukuoka: Fukuoka Kyoiku Iinkai.

Gardner, Charles S.
1938   *Chinese traditional historiography.* Cambridge: Harvard University Press.

Groot, Gerard J., and Yoshihiko Sinoto
1952   *The shell mound of Ubayama.* Nipponica First Series, Archaeologica Nipponica, Vol. II. Ichikawa: Archaeological Institute of Japan. (Published in English and Japanese.)

Hamada, Kosaku, *et al.*
1937   *Yamato Shimanosho ishibutai no kyoseki kofun* [Megalithic tomb Ishibutai at Shimanosho in the province of Yamato]. Kyoto Teikoku Daigaku Bungakubu Kokogaku Kenkyu Hokoku, Vol. 14. Kyoto. (English title and summary.)

Haraguchi, Shozo
1977   *Kokogaku kara mita genshi, kodai no Takatsuki.* Takatsuki-shi shi, pp. 115–130. Takatsuki: Takatsuki-shi Yakusho.

Hattori, Shiro
1959   *Nihongo no keito.* Tokyo: Iwanami Shoten.

Hayashi, Kensaku
1968   The Fukui microblade technology and its relationships in Northeast Asia and North America. *Arctic Anthropology* 5(1):128–190.

Higuchi, Kiyoyuki (Editor)
1977   *Yayoi to Yamataikoku.* Genshi Nihon no Saihakken 2. Tokyo: Gakken.

Higuchi, Takayasu (Editor)
1974   *Tairiku bunka to seidoki.* Kodaishi Hakkutsu 5. Tokyo: Kodansha.

Hiraide Iseki Chosa Kai (Editor)
1955   *Hiraide: Nagano-ken Soga-mura kodai shuraku-iseki no sokai kenkyu* [Hiraide: Synthetic study on the remains of ancient villages at Sogamura in Nagano Prefecture]. Tokyo: Asahi Shinbunsha. (English Title and Summary.)

Hymes, D. H.
1960   Lexicostatistics so far. *Current Anthropology* 1(1):3–44.

Imamura, Yutaka
1968   Toa ni okeru Nihonjin. In *Nihon minzoku to nampo bunka* [The Japanese and cultures of the southern areas], edited by Kanazeki Takeo Hakase Koki Kinen Iinkai. Tokyo: Heibonsha. Pp. 3–18. (English in title only.)

Ito, Genzo
1966   Tohoku. In *Nihon no kokogaku III: Yayoi jidai,* edited by Seiichi Wajima. Toyko: Kawade Shobo Shinsha. Pp. 204–220.

Kagawa, Mitsuo
1965   Kyushu tonanbu. In *Nihon no kokogaku, II: Jomon jidai,* edited by Yoshimasa Kamaki. Tokyo: Kawade Shobo Shinsha. Pp. 268–284.

Kamaki, Yoshimasa
1965   Jomon bunka no gaikan. In *Nihon no kokogaku, II: Jomon jidai,* edited by Yoshimasa Kamaki. Tokyo: Kawade Shobo Shinsha. Pp. 2–28.

Kamaki, Yoshimasa
1974   *Kyusekki jidai ron. Nihon rekishi 1: Genshi oyobi kodai.* Tokyo: Iwanami Koza. Pp. 35–74.

Kamaki, Yoshimasa, and Chosuke Serizawa
1965   *Nagasaki-ken Fukui iwakage [The rockshelter of Fukui, Nagasaki Prefecture]. Kokogaku Syukan, Memoirs of the Tokyo Archaeological Society 3*(1):1–14. (English in title only.)
1967   Nagasaki-ken Fukui doketsu. In *Nihon no doketsu iseki,* edited by Nihon Kokogaku Kyokai Doketsu Iseki Chosa Tokubetsu Iinkai. Tokyo: Heibonsha. Pp. 256–265.

Kanazeki, Takeo, *et al.*
1961   Yamaguchi-ken Doigahama iseki. In *Nihon noko bunka no seisei,* edited by Nihon Kokogaku Kyokai. Tokyo: Tokyodo Shuppan. Pp. 223–261.

Kanzawa, Yuichi
1966   Kanto. In *Nihon no kokogaku III: Yayoi jidai,* edited by Seiichi Wajima. Tokyo: Kawade Shobo Shinsha. Pp. 185–203.

Kato, Minoru
1975   Etchuyama iseki. In *Nihon no kyusekki bunka, 2, iseki to ibutsu,* edited by Masaru Aso *et al.* Tokyo: Yuzankaku. Pp. 112–137.

Kidder, J. Edward
1966   *Japan before Buddhism,* rev. ed. New York: Praeger.

Kidder, J. Edward, *et al.*
1970   Preceramic chronology of Kanto: ICU Loc. 28c. *Jinruigaku Zasshi 78*(2):140–156.

Kidder, J. Edward, and Teruya Esaka
1968   *Prehistoric Japanese arts: Jomon pottery.* Tokyo: Kodansha International.

Kidder, J. Edward, and Shizuo Oda
1975   Nakazanya site. *ICU Archaeology Research Center, International Christian University, Occasional Papers 1.*

Kobayashi, Tatsuo, *et al.*
1971   Nogawa sendoki jidai iseki no kenkyu [A study of the preceramic site, Nogawa]. *Dai Yonki Kenkyu 10*(4):231–270. (English title and summary.)

Kobayashi, Yukio
1961   *Kofun jidai no kenkyu.* Tokyo: Aoki Shoten.
1976   *Kofun bunka ronko.* Tokyo: Heibonsha.

Kohama, Mototsugu
1968   Nihonjin to Ainu. In *Nihon minzoku to nampo bunka* [The Japanese and cultures of the southern areas], edited by Kanazeki Takeo Hakase Koki Kinen Iinkai. Tokyo: Heibonsha. Pp. 19–39. (English in title only.)

Komai, Kazuchika (Editor)
1963   *Ohotsuku Kai engan, Shiretoko Hanto no iseki* [The archaeological sites on the Okhotsk Sea coast and the Shiretoko Peninsula in Hokkaido]. Tokyo: Tokyo Daigaku Bungakubu. (English title and abstract.)

1964   *Ohotsuku Kai engan, Shiretoko Hanto no iseki: Tokoro, Utoro, Rausu no iseki* [The archaeological sites on the Okhotsk Sea coast and the Shiretoko Peninsula in Hokkaido], Vol. II. Tokyo: Tokyo Daigaku Bungakubu. (English title and abstract.)

Kondo, Yoshiro

1968   Zenpo-koen fun no seiritsu to hensen. *Kokogaku Kenkyu 15*(1):24–32.

Kondo, Yoshiro, and Hideji Harunari

1967   Haniwa no kigen. *Kokogaku Kenkyu 13*(3):13–35.

Kotani, Yoshinobu

1969   Upper Pleistocene and Holocene environmental conditions in Japan. *Arctic Anthropology 5*(2);133–158.

Kyushu Bunka Sogo Kenkyujo (Editor)

1958   *Ankokuji* [Ankokuji: An archaeological survey of an ancient farming settlement at Ankokuji, Oita Prefecture, Japan]. Tokyo: Mainichi Shinbunsha. (English title and summary.)

Lewin, Bruno

1976   Japanese and Korean: The problems and history of a linguistic comparison. *Journal of Japanese Studies 2*(2):389–412.

Makabe, Tadahiko, and Hiroshi Shiomi

1965   San'in, Chugoku sanchi. In *Nihon no kokogaku II: Jomon jidai*, edited by Yoshimasa Kamaki. Tokyo: Kawade Shobo Shinsha. Pp. 211–229.

Maringer, J.

1956a   A core and flake industry of Palaeolithic type from central Japan. *Artibus Asiae 29*(2):111–125.

1956b   Einige faustkeilartige gerate von Gongenyama (Japan) und die frage des Japanischen Palaolithikums. *Anthropos 51*:175–193.

1957   Some stone tools of Early Hoabinhian type from central Japan. *Man 57*:1–3.

Martin, Samuel E.

1966   Lexical evidence relating Korean to Japanese. *Language 42*(2):185–251.

1975   Problems in establishing the prehistoric relationships of Korean and Japanese. *Proceedings of the International Symposium Commemorating the Thirtieth Anniversary of Korean Liberation.* Seoul: National Academy of Sciences, Republic of Korea. Pp. 149–172.

Matsumoto, Nobuhiro, *et al.*

1952   *Kamo iseki: Chiba-ken Kamo hitorikibune shutsudo iseki no kenkyu* [Kamo: A study of the Neolithic site and a Neolithic dugout canoe discovered in Kamo, Chiba Prefecture, Japan]. Kokogaku, Minzokugaku Sokan, Vol. 1. Archaeological and Ethnological Series, No. 3. Tokyo: Mita Shigakukai, Keiogijuku Daigaku. (English title and summary.)

Miller, Roy Andrew

1967   *The Japanese language.* Chicago: University of Chicago Press.

1971   Japanese and the other Altaic languages. Chicago: University of Chicago Press.

1974   Review of *Nihongo no kigen*, by Shichiro Murayama and Taryo Obayashi. *Monumenta Nipponica 29*(1):93–102.

1976   The relevance of historical linguistics for Japanese studies. *Journal of Japanese Studies 2*(2):335–388.

Minato, Masao, *et al.*

1965   *The geological development of the Japanese islands.* Tokyo: Tsukiji Shokan.

Miyazaka, Eiichi

1957   *Togariishi.* Tokyo: Nagano-ken Suwa-gun Chino-cho Kyoiku Iinkai.

Mizuno, Seiichi, *et al.*
1960 *Nihon I.* Sekai bunka-shi taikei, Vol. 20. Tokyo: Kadogawa Shoten.

Mori, Teijiro, and Takashi Okazaki
1961 Fukuoka-ken Itatsuke iseki. In *Nihon noko bunka no seisei* [The origin and growth of farming community in Japan], edited by the Japan Archaeologists' Association. Tokyo: Tokyodo Shuppan. (English title and summary.)

Morikawa, Masakazu
1976 Fukui-ken Torihama kaizuka no chosa. *Kokogaku Jyaneru 119*:19–22.

Morlan, Richard E.
1967 The preceramic period of Hokkaido: An outline: *Arctic Anthropology 4*(1): 164–220.

Morlan, Valda J.
1971 The preceramic period of Japan: Honshu, Shikoku, and Kyushu. *Arctic Anthropology 8*(1):136–170.

Murayama, Shichiro
1976 The Malayo-Polynesian component in the Japanese language. *Journal of Japanese Studies 2*(2):413–436.

Murayama, Shichiro, and Taryo Obayashi
1973 *Nihongo no kigen.* Tokyo: Kobundo.

Nakagawa, Hisao
1965 Sozudai kyusekki hoganso no soigakuteki yosatsu [A preliminary report on the stratigraphic horizon of the Paleolithic implements from the Sozudai site, Hiji-machi, Oita Prefecture, Kyushu, Japan]. *Nihon Bunka Kenkyusho Kenkyu Hokoku 1*:121–141. (English title and abstract.)

Nakamura, Kozaburo
1960 *Kosegasawa Dokutsu* [Kosegasawa Cave]. Nagaoka Shiritsu Kagaku Hakubutsukan Kenkyu Chosa Hokoku, Vol. 3. (English title and abstract.)

Nihon Kokogaku Kyokai Kenkyukai
1949 *Toro.* Tokyo: Mainichi Shinbunsha. (English summary.)
1954 *Toro.* Tokyo: Mainichi Shinbunsha. (English summary.)

Nishikawa, Hiroshi, *et al.*
1966 Setouchi. In *Nihon no kokogaku, IV: Kofun jidai (Jo)*, edited by Yoshiro Kondo and Choji Fujisawa. Tokyo: Kawade Shobo Shinsha. Pp. 175–224.

Oba, Toshio, and Haruo Ohyi (Editors)
1973 *Ohotsuku bunka no kenkyu 1: Onkoromanai kaizuka* [Studies on Okhotsk culture, Vol. 1: The Onkoromanai shell Mound]. Tokyo: Tokyo Daigaku Shuppan-kai. (English title and summary.)

Oda, Fujio
1966 Kyushu. In *Nihon no kokogaku IV: Kofun jidai (Jo)*, edited by Yoshiro Kondo and Choji Fujisawa. Tokyo: Kawade Shobo Shinsha. Pp. 114–174.

Oda, S., and C. T. Keally
1975 Japanese preceramic cultural chronology. *ICU Archaeology Research Center, International Christian University, Occasional Papers 2*.

Ohno, Susumu
1970 *The origin of the Japanese language.* Tokyo: Kokusai Bunka Shinkokai.

Okada, Shigehiro
1965 Kinki. In *Nihon no kokogaku II: Jomon jidai*, edited by Yoshimasa Kamaki. Tokyo: Kawade Shobo Shinsha. Pp. 193–210.

Okamoto, Isamu, and Mitsunori Tozawa
1965 Kanto. In *Nihon no kokogaku II: Jomon jidai*, edited by Yoshimasa Kamaki. Tokyo: Kawade Shobo Shinsha. Pp. 97–132.

Otomasu, Shigetaka
1965   Kyushu seihokubu. In *Nihon no kokogaku II: Jomon jidai,* edited by Yoshimasa Kamaki. Tokyo: Kawade Shobo Shinsha. Pp. 250–267.

Otsuka, Hatsushige
1966   Kofun no hensen. In *Nihon no kokogaku IV: Kofun jidai (Jo),* edited by Yoshiro Kondo and Choji Fujisawa. Tokyo: Kawade Shobo Shinsha. Pp. 39–101.

Otsuka, Hatsushige, (Editor)
1973   *Shinpojiyamu: Yayoi jidai no kokogaku.* Tokyo: Gakuseisha.

Pearson, Richard J.
1969   *The archaeology of the Ryukyu Islands: A regional chronology from 3000 B.C. to the historic period.* Honolulu: University of Hawaii Press.

Poppe, Nicholaus N.
1950   Review of G. J. Ramstedt, *Studies in Korean etymology. Harvard Journal of Asiatic Studies 13*:568–581.

1960   *Vergleichende grammatik der Altaischen sprachen,* Teil I, *Vergleichende lautlehre.* Porta Linguarum Orientalium, n.s. IV. Wiesbaden: Otto Harrassowitz.

Ramstedt, G. J.
1949   Studies in Korean etymology. *Memoires de la Societe Finno-ougrienne 95.*

Rea, John A.
1958   Concerning the validity of lexicostatistics. *International Journal of American Linguistics 24*(2):145–155.

Sakurai, Kiyohiko
1966   Hokkaido. In *Nihon no kokogaku IV: Kofun Jidai (Jo),* edited by Yoshiro Kondo and Choji Fujisawa. Tokyo: Kawade Shobo Shinsha. Pp. 538–550.

Serizawa, Chosuke
1959   Niigata-ken Araya iseki ni okeru saisekijin bunka to Araya-gata chokokuto ni tsuite [A new microblade industry discovered at the Araya site, and the Araya-type graver]. *Dai Yonki Kenkyu 1*(5):174–181. (English title and abstract.)

1965   Oita-ken Sozudai ni okeru zen-ki kyusekki no kenkyu [A lower Paleolithic industry from the Sozudai site, Oita Prefecture, Japan]. *Nihon Bunka Kenkyusho Kenkyu Hokoku No. 1*:1–119. (English title and abstract.)

1967   Nihon ni okeru kyusekki no soiteki shutsudorei to C-14 nendai. *Nihon Bunka Kenkyusho Kenkyu Hokoku, No. 3.*

1968   *Tochigi-shi Hoshino iseki, dai-niji hakkutsu chosa hokoku.* Tochigi: Tochigi-shi Kyoiku Iinkai.

Serizawa, Chosuke (Editor)
1974   *Kodaishi hakkutsu, 1: Saiko no kariudojintachi.* Tokyo: Kodansha.

Shimizu, Junzo (Editor)
1959   Kamegaoka iseki: Aomori-ken Kamegaoka teishitsuchi iseki no kenkyu [Kamegaoka: A study of the Kamegaoka Neolithic site, Aomori Prefecture, Japan]. Kokogaku, Minzokugaku Sokan, Vol. 3. Archaeological and Ethnological Series, No. 5. Tokyo: Mita Shigakukai, Keiogijuku Daigaku. (English title and summary.)

Suenaga, Masao
1961   Nihon no Kofun [Aerial observations on ancient tombs of Japan]. Osaka: Asahi Shinbunsha. (English title and summary.)

Suenaga, Masao, *et al.*
1954   Izumi Koganezuka kofun [Kogane-Zuka: Ancient tomb at Shinoda in Japan]. Kyoto: Nihon Kokogaku Kyokai, Shugeisha. (English title and summary.)

Sugihara, Sosuke
1956   Gumma-ken Iwajuku hakken no sekki bunka [The Stone Age remains found at

Iwajuku, Gumma Prefecture, Japan]. Tokyo: Meiji Daigaku Bungakubu Ken-kyu Hokoku, Kokogaku, Vol. 1. (English title and summary.)

1973   Nagano-ken Uenodaira no sentoki sekki bunka [Point tool culture of Uenodaira, Nagano Prefecture, Japan]. Tokyo: Meiji Daigaku Bungakubu Kenkyu Hokoku, Kokogaku, Vol. 3. (English title and summary.)

1974   *Nihon sendoki jidai no kenkyu.* Tokyo: Kodansha.

Sugihara, Sosuke (Editor)
1977   *Kasori Kita Kaizuka.* Tokyo: Chuo Koron Bijutsu Shuppan.

Sugihara, Sosuke, and Shinichi Ono
1965   Shizuoka-ken Yasumiba iseki ni okeru saisekki bunka [Microlithic culture of Yasumiba sites, Shizuoka Prefecture]. *Kokogaku Syukan, Memoirs of the Tokyo Archaeological Society* 3(2):1–33. (English in title only.)

Sugihara, Sosuke, and Chosuke Serizawa
1957   Kanagawa-ken Natsushima ni okeru Jomon bunka shoto no kaizuka [Shell mounds of the earliest Jomon culture at Natsushima, Kanagawa Prefecture, Japan]. Tokyo: Meiji Daigaku Bungakubu Kenkyu Hokoku, Kokogaku, Vol. 2. (English title and summary.)

Sugihara, Sosuke, and Mitsunori Tozawa
1975   Hokkaido Shirataki–Hattoridai ni okeru saisekki bunka [Microlithic culture of Shirataki–Hattoridai, Hokkaido, Japan]. Tokyo: Meiji Daigaku Bungakubu Kenkyu Hokoku, Kokogaku, Vol. 5. (English title and summary.)

Suzuki, Masao
1974   Chronology of prehistoric human activity in Kanto, Japan, Part II: Time–space analysis of obsidian transportation. *Journal of the Faculty of Science, The University of Tokyo, Section V,* 4(4):395–469.

Suzuki, Yasuhiko
1977   Jomon doki shutsugen no yoso. *Dorumen* 15:81–104.

Takahori, Katsuki, and Yasunobu Yoshioka
1966   Hokuriku. In *Nihon no kokogaku IV: Kofun jidai (Jo)*, edited by Yoshiro Kondo and Choji Fujisawa. Tokyo: Kawade Shobo Shinsha. Pp. 319–352.

Takatsuki-shi-Shi Hensan Iinkai
1973   *Takatsuki-shi-shi dai roku-ken koko-hen.* Takatsuki: Takatsuki-shi Yakusho.

Takatsuki-shi Kyoiku Iinkai
1977   *Ama-iseki hakkutsu chosa hokokusho, 9 chiku no chosa.* Takatsuki: Takatsuki-shi Bunkazai Chosa Hokokusho, Vol. 10.

Takeda, Munehisa (Editor)
1968   *Kasori kaizuka I* Tokyo: Chuo Koron Bijutsu Shuppan.

Takiguchi, Hiroshi (Editor)
1977   *Kasori kaizuka IV.* Tokyo: Chuo Koron Bijutsu Shuppan.

Tokyo Daigaku Kokogaku Kenkyushitsu (Editor)
1972   *Tokoro: Hokkaido Saromako engan, Tokoro kawashimo ryuiki ni okeru iseki chosa* [Tokoro: The report of the archaeological investigations in the Lower Tokoro River and Lake Saroma regions, northeastern Hokkaido]. Tokyo: Tokyo Daigaku Bungakubu. 3 vols. (English title and summary.)

Topping, Audrey, and Hsien-Min Yang
1978   The first emperor's army: China's incredible find. *National Geographic Magazine* 153(4):440–459.

Toyama-Ken Kyoiku Iinkai
1974a   *Toyama-ken Asahi-cho Fudodo iseki, dai ichiji hakkutsu chosa gaiho.* Toyama: Toyama-ken Kyoiku Iinkai.

1974b *Toyama-ken Kosugi-cho Mizukamidani iseki kinkyu hakkutsu chosa gaiyo.* Toyama: Toyama-ken Kyoiku Iinkai.

Tsuboi, Kiyotari
1971 Jomon bunka ron. In *Nihon no rekishi: Genshi oyobi kodai, 1.* Tokyo: Iwanami Koza. Pp. 109–138.

Tsuboi, Kiyotari, and Akira Machida (Editors)
1977 Hekiga, sekizobutsu. *Nihon genshi bijutsu taikei 6* [Archaeological treasures of Japan: Mural paintings, stone structures.] Tokyo: Kodansha. (English title, captions, summary).

Tsuboi, Kiyotari, and Tatsuo Kobayashi (Editors)
1977 *Jomon doki. Nihon genshi bijutsu taikei 1* [Archaeological treasures of Japan: Jomon pottery. Tokyo: Kodansha. (English title, captions, summary.)

Tsuboi, Kiyotari, Mitsukazu Nagamine, and Masayoshi Mizuno
1977 *Dogu, haniwa. Nihon genshi bijutsu taikei 3* [Archaeological treasures of Japan: Clay figurines, haniwa]. Tokyo: Kodansha. (English title, captions, summary.)

Tsude, Hiroshi
1979 Mura to mura to no koryu. In *Nihon bunka no rekishi 1: senshi, genshi,* edited by Takayasu Higuchi. Tokyo: Shogakukan. Pp. 153–230.

Tsuji, Hideko
1973 Hokkaido Kamishihoro-Shimagi iseki no chosa hokoku [A report on the site of preceramic culture at Shimagi, Kamishihoro, Hokkaido]. *Sekki Jidai* 10:39–71. (English title and abstract.)

Tsunoda, Ryusaku, and L. Carrington Goodrich
1951 *Japan in the Chinese dynastic histories.* Perkins Asiatic Monographs No. 2. South Pasadena, Calif.: P. D. and Ione Perkins.

Ujiie, Kazunori, and Takashi Kato
1966 *Tohoku. In Nihon no kokogaku IV: Kofun jidai (Jo),* edited by Yoshiro Kondo and Choji Fujisawa. Tokyo: Kawade Shobo Shinsha. Pp. 499–528.

Umehara, Seuji
1964 *Tsubai Otsukayama kofun. Kyoto-fu Bunkazai Chosa Hokoku,* Vol. 23. Kyoto: Kyoto-fu Kyoiku Iinkai.

Uriyudo Iseki Chosa Kai
1971 *Uriyudo iseki,* Vol. I. Osaka: Uriyudo Iseki Chosa Kai.
1973 *Uriyudo iseki,* Vol. II. Osaka: Uriyudo Iseki Chosa Kai.

Watanabe, Naotsune (Editor)
1977 *Shinpojiyamu: Kyusekki jidai no kokogaku.* Tokyo: Gakuseisha.

Yasui, Ryozo
1969 *Kasajima iseki.* Wakayama: *Kasajima Iseki Hakkutsu Chosa Hokokusho Kankokai.*

Yawata, Ichiro (Editor)
1966 Hokkaido Nemuro no senshi iseki [Prehistoric sites in Nemuro, Hokkaido]. Tokyo: Tokyo Kyoiku Daigaku Bungakubu Kenkyu Hokoku, Vol. 1. (English title and summary.)

Yawata, Ichiro and Mitsuo Kagawa
1955 *Sozudai.* Oita-ken Bunkazai Chosa Hokoku, Vol. 3.

Yoshioka, Kunji
1974 Vegetation map of Japan. In *The flora and vegetation of Japan,* edited by M. Numata. Tokyo: Kodansha Limited; Amsterdam: Elsevier. P. 295.

Yoshizaki, Masakazu
1961 Shirataki iseki to Hokkaido no mudoki bunka. *Minzokugaku Kenkyu* 26(1):13–23.

Yoshizaki, Masakazu (Editor)
1973   *Tachikaru-Shunai iseki 1972.* Engaru: Hokkaido Engaru-machi Kyoiku Iinkai.
Yoshizaki, Masakazu
1974   *Shukubai-Sankakuyama chiten.* Chitose: Chitose-shi Kyoiku Iinkai.
Young, John
1958   The location of Yamatai: A case study in Japanese historiography, 720–945. *The Johns Hopkins University Studies in Historical and Political Science,* Series 75(2).
Yubetsu–Ichikawa Chosa Dan
1973   *Yubetsu–Ichikawa iseki.* Yubetsu: Yubetsu-cho Kyoiku Iinkai. (English summary.)
Zaidan Hojin Kodaigaku Kyokai
1963   *Nyu. Oita-ken Nyu iseki hakkutsu chosa hokoku* [Stations de Nyu. Les Fouilles des Stations Primordiales sur le Plateau de Nyu a la Prefecture d'Oita, Cote Est de Kyushu]. Kyoto: Zaidan Hojin Kodaigaku Kyokai. (French title and summary.)

Index

STUDIES IN ARCHAEOLOGY

Consulting Editor: Stuart Struever

Department of Anthropology
Northwestern University
Evanston, Illinois

Thomas F. King, Patricia Parker Hickman, and Gary Berg. **Anthropology in Historic Preservation: Caring for Culture's Clutter**

Richard E. Blanton. **Monte Albán: Settlement Patterns at the Ancient Zapotec Capital**

R. E. Taylor and Clement W. Meighan. **Chronologies in New World Archaeology**

Bruce D. Smith. **Prehistoric Patterns of Human Behavior: A Case Study in the Mississippi Valley**

Barbara L. Stark and Barbara Voorhies (Eds.). **Prehistoric Coastal Adaptations: The Economy and Ecology of Maritime Middle America**

Charles L. Redman, Mary Jane Berman, Edward V. Curtin, William T. Langhorne, Nina M. Versaggi, and Jeffery C. Wanser (Eds.). **Social Archeology: Beyond Subsistence and Dating**

Bruce D. Smith (Ed.). **Mississippian Settlement Patterns**

Lewis R. Binford. **Nunamiut Ethnoarchaeology**

J. Barto Arnold III and Robert Weddle. **The Nautical Archeology of Padre Island: The Spanish Shipwrecks of 1554**

Sarunas Milisauskas. **European Prehistory**

Brian Hayden (Ed.). **Lithic Use-Wear Analysis**

William T. Sanders, Jeffrey R. Parsons, and Robert S. Santley. **The Basin of Mexico: Ecological Processes in the Evolution of a Civilization**

David L. Clarke. **Analytical Archaeologist: Collected Papers of David L. Clarke. Edited and Introduced by His Colleagues**

Arthur E. Spiess. **Reindeer and Caribou Hunters: An Archaeological Study**

Elizabeth S. Wing and Antoinette B. Brown. **Paleonutrition: Method and Theory in Prehistoric Foodways.**

John W. Rick. **Prehistoric Hunters of the High Andes**

Timothy K. Earle and Andrew L. Christenson (Eds.). **Modeling Change in Prehistoric Economics**

Thomas F. Lynch (Ed.). **Guitarrero Cave: Early Man in the Andes**

Fred Wendorf and Romuald Schild. **Prehistory of the Eastern Sahara**

Henri Laville, Jean-Philippe Rigaud, and James Sackett. **Rock Shelters of the Perigord: Stratigraphy and Archaeological Succession**

Duane C. Anderson and Holmes A. Semken, Jr. (Eds.). **The Cherokee Excavations: Holocene Ecology and Human Adaptations in Northwestern Iowa**

Anna Curtenius Roosevelt. **Parmana: Prehistoric Maize and Manioc Subsistence along the Amazon and Orinoco**

Fekri A. Hassan. **Demographic Archaeology**

G. Barker. **Landscape and Society: Prehistoric Central Italy**

Lewis R. Binford. **Bones: Ancient Men and Modern Myths**

Richard A. Gould and Michael B. Schiffer (Eds.). **Modern Material Culture: The Archaeology of Us**

Muriel Porter Weaver. **The Aztecs, Maya, and Their Predecessors: Archaeology of Mesoamerica, 2nd edition**

Arthur S. Keene. **Prehistoric Foraging in a Temperate Forest: A Linear Programming Model**

Ross H. Cordy. **A Study of Prehistoric Social Change: The Development of Complex Societies in the Hawaiian Islands**

C. Melvin Aikens and Takayasu Higuchi. **Prehistory of Japan**

Kent V. Flannery (Ed.). **Maya Subsistence: Studies in Memory of Dennis E. Puleston**

Dean R. Snow (Ed.). **Foundations of Northeast Archaeology**

in preparation

Charles S. Spencer. **The Cuicatlán Cañada and the Rise of Monte Albán**

Steadman Upham. **Polities and Power: An Economic and Political History of the Western Pueblo**

Vincas P. Steponaitis. **Ceramics, Chronology, and Community Patterns: An Archaeological Study at Moundville**

Michael J. O'Brien, Robert E. Warren, & Dennis E. Lewarch (Eds.). **The Cannon Reservoir Human Ecology Project: An Archaeological Study of Cultural Adaptations in the Southern Prairie Peninsula**